Th

CHRIS

DOCTRINE

of the

CHURCH, FAITH,

and the

CONSUMMATION

DOGMATICS: Vol. III

Books by

EMIL BRUNNER

Published by The Westminster Press

The Christian Doctrine of the Church, Faith, and the Consummation, Dogmatics: Vol. III
(*Die christliche Lehre von der Kirche, vom Glauben, und von der Vollendung*)

I Believe in the Living God
(*Ich glaube an den lebendigen Gott*)

The Letter to the Romans
(*Der Römerbrief*)

Faith, Hope, and Love

The Great Invitation, and Other Sermons
(*Fraümunster-Predigten*)

Eternal Hope
(*Das Ewige als Zukunft und Gegenwart*)

The Misunderstanding of the Church
(*Das Missverständnis der Kirche*)

The Christian Doctrine of Creation and Redemption, Dogmatics: Vol. II
(*Die christliche Lehre von Schöpfung und Erlösung*)

The Scandal of Christianity

The Christian Doctrine of God, Dogmatics: Vol. I
(*Die christliche Lehre von Gott*)

Man in Revolt
(*Der Mensch im Widerspruch*)

The Mediator
(*Der Mittler*)

The Divine Imperative
(*Das Gebot und die Ordnungen*)

Revelation and Reason
(*Offenbarung und Vernunft*)

The Divine-Human Encounter
(*Wahrheit als Begegnung*)

EMIL BRUNNER

The CHRISTIAN DOCTRINE *of the* CHURCH, FAITH, *and the* CONSUMMATION

DOGMATICS: VOL. III

Translated by
DAVID CAIRNS
in collaboration with
T. H. L. PARKER

Philadelphia
THE WESTMINSTER PRESS

The book originally appeared as *Die christliche Lehre von der Kirche, vom Glauben, und von der Vollendung,* Zwingli-Verlag, Zürich and Stuttgart, 1960.

Library of Congress Catalog Card No. 50–6821

TYPESET IN GREAT BRITAIN
PRINTED IN THE UNITED STATES OF AMERICA

CONTENTS

PART 3

GOD'S SELF-COMMUNICATION AS HIS SELF-REPRESENTATION THROUGH THE HOLY SPIRIT

Section I: Ekklesia and Church

Section II: The New Life In Christ

PART 4

THE CONSUMMATION IN ETERNITY OF THE DIVINE SELF-COMMUNICATION

PREFACE

In the year 1946 the first volume of my *Dogmatics* appeared under the title of *Die christliche Lehre von Gott.*[1] Its intention was to sum up in three or four parts my work in the field of Biblical Theology. In 1950 followed the second volume, *Die christliche Lehre von Schöpfung und Erlösung.*[2] Since then no less than ten years have passed. I therefore owe my readers an explanation of the reasons for the delay in the appearance of this present and final volume, *Die christliche Lehre von der Kirche, vom Glauben, und von der Vollendung* (The Christian Doctrine of the Church, Faith, and the Consummation). As these reasons are partly of a practical and partly of a personal nature, it will be understood if I indulge in a rather longer introduction than usual.

The Protestant theology of the last decades received its decisive stimulus from the rediscovery of the message of the Reformers, which was in turn due in no small measure to the rediscovery of the great Danish writer Sören Kierkegaard. Whereas the preceding epoch had been dominated by the questions of the philosophy and history of religion, this change restored to its central position the question of the nature of faith.

The quest of the Biblical doctrine of faith was pursued, in fact, in two clearly distinct camps, which yet remained in constant communication with each other. In the one camp the problem of faith was taken up in close dependence on the traditional church creeds. Here above all others it was Karl Barth who, by having recourse to the exegesis and dogmatics of the classical Fathers of theology, undertook to restore the "true doctrine" to the Church in new formulations. In the other camp, of which Rudolf Bultmann must be called the guiding spirit, attention was directed, not to the "object of faith", to doctrine, but to the act of faith itself. In this group, faith's understanding of its own nature, and in consequence the fundamental questions of interpretation, have become the cardinal problem.

If I am to indicate my own standpoint between these two

[1] E.T. *The Christian Doctrine of God,* Lutterworth Press, London, 1949; Westminster Press, Philadelphia

[2] E.T. *The Christian Doctrine of Creation and Redemption,* Lutterworth Press, London, 1952; Westminster Press, Philadelphia

theological camps, then I must say that it is represented by what I described as early as 1937 in my discussion with objectivism and subjectivism in my book *Wahrheit als Begegnung*[1] as the guiding norm of all theological doctrine. It was natural and necessary that this teaching should be developed principally in this concluding volume of my *Dogmatics*. It gave me quite a new insight into the unique character of the fundamental phenomenon of the Biblical message, the unity of truth and fellowship.

As a preliminary study for the first part of this volume on the Church there appeared in 1951 my *Das Missverständnis der Kirche*.[2] The reception of this book showed how hard it is to make a critical examination of the customary conception of the Church. In this preliminary work it became clear to me how the situation of the Church as time goes on makes such an examination a more and more urgent necessity.

There was a second point where it seemed to me that the theme of this volume required additional preparatory work. The World Conference of Evanston 1954 had the Christian Hope as its theme. As a participant in the preparatory theological studies, I became aware that the problems of eschatology required a clarification which would free them from traditional ideas and place them in direct relation to the centre of the Biblical faith. My book *Das Ewige als Zukunft und Gegenwart* (1953)[3] originated from my efforts to fulfil this task.

Both books have been assimilated into the present volume in an abbreviated form, their material having been reconsidered and reshaped. Since both for the problem of the Church and for that of the Christian Hope the understanding of faith is fundamental, it is comprehensible why the question of faith became the central theme of this work. The nature of faith is not to be understood by starting from the creed of the Church, but by starting with the Biblical witness. The chief concern of this concluding volume is to vindicate the Biblical concept of faith in contrast to that supplied by the tradition of the creed. From this beginning there followed quite of itself the new understanding of the Ekklesia as fundamentally different from everything covered by the concept "Church", and of the Christian Hope as fundamentally superior to all mythological and

[1] E.T. *The Divine-Human Encounter*, Westminster Press, Philadelphia, 1943; S.C.M. Press, London, 1944

[2] E.T. *The Misunderstanding of the Church*, Lutterworth Press, London, 1952; Westminster Press, Philadelphia

[3] E.T. *Eternal Hope*, Lutterworth Press, London, 1954; Westminster Press, Philadelphia

apocalyptic ideas; a superiority which results from this Hope's sole dependence on Jesus Christ as this is expressed, for example, in the Pauline witness in Romans 8: 38–39, which consequently became the guiding motif of this section.

The fulfilment of my promise to complete the last volume of my *Dogmatics* had to be postponed as a result of an invitation which came to me in 1953 to collaborate in the setting up of the International Christian University in Tokyo, and there, as tutor in "Problems of Christianity", to undertake a missionary activity in academic and intellectual circles. I felt a deep personal compulsion to obey this call, since a first visit to Japan in the year 1949 had shown me what great historical significance a Christian Japan would have for the world of today. For this reason it was a fascinating task to help in the schooling of a new generation of academically trained Christian laymen.

It was not till after my return home in the year 1955 that I was able to resume work on my *Dogmatics*. The years had not indeed passed for me without leaving any trace. A medical veto on the continuance of work at my accustomed tempo, and my own self-imposed obligation to fulfil at last my promise to my readers, brought me into a difficult situation. How much more difficult my work was made by a slight stroke which prevented the use of my right hand, can be easily gathered. This impediment was made the more troublesome by the fact that hitherto I had been accustomed to develop my thoughts in writing. To use the help of dictation in creative work was at first a very strange experience for me. I have so much the greater cause for gratitude that in Frau Dr. iur. H. Guanella-Zietzschmann, a faithful hearer of most of my lectures and sermons, and a friend of our household of many years' standing, I found a fellow-worker whose admirable gifts of intuitive understanding and unprecedented appetite for work made possible the writing of the manuscript. I should like also at this point to thank very heartily my dear former scholar, Fräulein Pfr. G. Epprecht, who at great expense of time together with Frau Dr. Guanella prepared the manuscript for the printer and corrected the proofs. What in these last years and indeed in the whole time of my theological work the quiet support and company of my dear wife has meant, I should mention merely for the benefit of those readers who do not know us personally.

This book is dedicated to Christoph Blumhardt. It was he, the prophetic witness to Jesus, who in the days of my youth by direct personal contact and, later, through men like Kutter and Ragaz, rooted me deep in the life-giving power of the Holy

Spirit. I have always loved and honoured him as one of those in whom the divine light shone forth, and in gratitude I regard my theological work as the harvest of his sowing.

Finally I should like to thank the English translators and to express my appreciation of their superb work, which so completely belies the Italian saying: "Any translation is a falsification".

EMIL BRUNNER

The
CHRISTIAN DOCTRINE
of the
CHURCH, FAITH,
and the
CONSUMMATION
DOGMATICS: Vol. III

PART 3

GOD'S SELF-COMMUNICATION AS HIS SELF-REPRESENTATION THROUGH THE HOLY SPIRIT

Section I

EKKLESIA AND CHURCH

INTRODUCTION

THE revelation of God in the Bible is a history. In the Old Testament God manifests Himself to His people through acts, and at the same time as He thus manifests Himself He creates His people for Himself. God communicates Himself to His people in the double sense that He manifests to them the mystery of His nature, and that He causes His people to share in His life. "I will be your God, and ye shall be my people." The message of the Prophets culminates in the promise of a new, final self-communication of God, a Messianic age, a Messianic reign, when God's being will be a perfect "God with us". Yet at the same time there appears another, enigmatic figure of the Last Times, the "Servant of God"[1] who takes upon himself the sin and guilt of his people and lets himself be broken by it. But that the Messiah might be identical with the Suffering Servant of God—this insight was not achieved by the Old Testament.

The New Testament is the glad tidings that this Messiah has appeared, that with Him the Messianic Age has drawn near, and that He as the Crucified is at the same time the Servant of God. Further, it is the witness to an act of God in history and to a new life which it initiates. This act of God which the New Testament proclaims is the coming of Jesus, the Christ, His reconciling Passion on the Cross and His Resurrection. Thus the witness of the New Testament is at the same time a witness to Jesus the Christ and to the new life of the people of God, the Ekklesia, the Messianic life in fellowship with God through the Holy Spirit.

This Christ was the theme of the second volume of our work. This last volume deals with His people and the new life, life in fellowship with God in the Holy Spirit and its consummation. How God chooses and creates a people for Himself, and is present in His people; this is its first theme, the doctrine of the Ekklesia.

[1] The form of the *Ebed Yahweh* in the 53rd Chapter of Isaiah has indeed been interpreted in many ways. But unless we keep Jesus Christ in view, none is really satisfactory. Here the "Christological interpretation of the Old Testament" becomes a hermeneutic necessity

CHAPTER I

CHURCH AND HOLY SPIRIT

(1) THE HISTORICAL REPRESENTATION[1] OF THE PAST SELF-COMMUNICATION OF GOD, THE CHURCH

WE have just described the revelation of God in Jesus Christ as a historical event, as something which happened, at that time and at that place, for all men. Faith is first and foremost a relationship to this *factum perfectum*, to God's saving act in the past. "The Word *became* flesh", "God so *loved* the world, that He *gave* His only begotten Son", "When the fullness of the time *was come*, God *sent forth* His Son."

But how is it possible to know about this event which happened nineteen hundred years ago? How is it possible to participate in it? Past events come to us through historical transmission, by *paradosis* or *traditio*. But where we are dealing with the event which is God's self-communication, it cannot be a question of historical tradition in the generally acknowledged sense as historical information or tradition. The saving event cannot be historically transmitted in the same manner as common world events. The special manner in which the present is bound together with the past saving event, the bridge that spans the temporal abyss of nineteen hundred years, is the proclamation of the Church or the proclaiming Church. This is the character of transmission which is peculiar to this "fact".

The Church is in the first place merely the instrument, the bearer, of the proclamation. Everything that serves this proclamation is Church, and it is this function and nothing else which makes the Church the Church: a "proclaiming existence" as the historical continuum of the revelation. We must indeed bear in mind that this proclamation cannot be confined to words. This was why we said "proclaiming *existence*". It is not a mere matter of uttering words, but of passing on the life in which God has communicated Himself. Thus, before we define

[1] *Translator's Note:* Here and in other passages in this book, this term is used in a special sense to be defined here. This is a fuller and richer sense than is normally given to the word "representation". The German word *Vergegenwärtigung* or *Selbst-vergegenwärtigung* which it translates has retained, in a way that the English term has not, the original rich significance of its components. Hence "representation" in this translation contains the twofold thought of "making present": (1) making contemporary in contrast with what is past, and (2) making personally present in contrast with what is absent

the concept of the Church more exactly, we must regard as Church every form of historical life which has its origin in Jesus Christ and in which God's self-communication is continuously active. Not only as the bearer of the Word of Christ is the Church the "bridge", the continuum we spoke of, but also as the bearer of His Spirit and life, as He communicated Himself to His earliest Ekklesia. It is thus not only the instrument, the bearer of the Word of Christ, but at the same time the place of His self-representation and the instrument whereby this self-representation is transmitted.

This Church has indeed from its very beginning laid down a norm for this proclamation and this process of self-perpetuation, by setting up the Biblical "canon" as a criterion for proclamation and norm for all tradition. By so doing it has held fast to the unique event as such. The proclamation of the Apostles as a compact unity in contrast to all later proclamation, the spirit and life of the Ekklesia of primitive times in contrast to all later Church life, is meant to be the criterion according to which all future proclamation is to be shaped, and according to which all the future life of the Church is to be regulated. One can indeed say that even the canon, the Bible, is a form of Church tradition, since it was the Church that created it and set it up as a norm, so that the "scripture principle" would be included in the principle of tradition and founded on it. But it is just as correct to say that the Word of Christ and the Apostles created the Church and its tradition, and that only that tradition and proclamation, only that preaching existence of the Church which corresponds to this Word, is genuine Church tradition and genuine Church existence.

We have not yet come to the place for dealing with this question in the thorough manner that is requisite.[1] But the thought of this contrast of tradition and scripture which, without lessening the fundamental significance of tradition, was there from the very beginning and whose basis is the uniqueness of the event of revelation, should remind us at the very beginning of our doctrine of the Church that we have to do with a critical concept of tradition. On the other hand, the question of differentiating between what belongs to the Church in a narrower and direct sense and a wider and more indirect sense need not concern us further at this early stage. The Roman soldiers who carried their faith in Christ into the northern and eastern lands of Europe and there diffused it, in part without

[1] See below, Ch. 3

any "Church" support, rather in the manner of a contagion than in that of explicit mission, may yet be considered as instruments of the Church and bearers of its mission. In this sense the Church is everywhere present where men are apprehended and moved by Christ and infect others with this enthusiasm. In a later connection we shall have to deal expressly with this non-churchly form of the Church. We repeat: the Church is every form of historical life which has its origin in Jesus Christ and acknowledges in Him its foundation and supreme norm.

This reference to the tradition of the Church as the continuum which binds the unique historic event to the present at any particular time is, however, not the only thing that is necessary in order to answer the question, "How can the revelation of that time become revelation for us men of today?" The tradition of the Church is the *historical* mediation. But there must also be mediation of another, namely intra-personal, character in order to make the revelation of that time revelation for us today. "We must now see", begins the third book of Calvin's *Institutes*,

> in what way we become possessed of the blessings which God has bestowed on his only-begotten Son. . . . And the first thing to be attended to is that, so long as we are without Christ and separated from him, nothing which he suffered and did for the salvation of the human race is of the least benefit to us. To communicate to us the blessings, which he received from the Father, he must become ours and dwell in us. Accordingly, he is called our Head, and the first-born among many brethren, while, on the other hand, we are said to be ingrafted into him, and clothed with him, all which he possesses being, as I have said, nothing to us until we become one with him [*in unum coalescimus*]. And although it is true that we obtain this by faith, yet since we see that all do not indiscriminately embrace the offer of Christ which is made by the gospel, the very nature of the case teaches us to ascend higher, and inquire into the secret efficacy of the Spirit, to which it is owing that we enjoy Christ and all his blessings.[1]

A merely historical Christ and a merely historical knowledge of Him would be in fact a pitiful affair. Faith is a personal and immediate relationship to God. We must therefore ask: How is it possible that what then happened in Jesus Christ becomes present to us? How can we "become contemporaries with Christ" (Kierkegaard)? The answer to this question is the theme of the next section.

[1] Calvin, *Institutes* III, I, I (quoted from Beveridge's translation)

(2) GOD'S SELF-REPRESENTATION IN US THROUGH THE HOLY SPIRIT[1]

(*a*) The revelation of God in Jesus Christ is a historical event, and faith is therefore in the first place a relationship to this event which happened at that place and time. It is dependent on this perfect tense, the reconciliation of the world in the Cross of Jesus Christ is the content of faith in Christ.

This historical element in the Christian faith is the stumbling-block both for the rationalistic and for the mystical man. These seek for the timeless eternal, the *nunc aeternum*; they wish for immediacy in their relation to God, an immediacy not dependent on anything historical. They regard the attachment of Christian faith to a past event as an imperfection, as a primitive mythological embarrassment which ought to be transcended, the confusion of the historical occasion (Jesus) with the eternal ground (the Christ principle), and over and above this a source of the uncertainty which infects everything historical. But the fact that they find this an offence is the sign that decisive issues are at stake. It is, in fact, no accident that man on his part seeks a relationship to God which shall be pure immediacy, and wishes to free himself from dependence on the historical. The historical element in faith points to the sore spot in human existence, to the gap which separates it from immediacy. The man who evades the historical Mediator does this because he neither will nor can see the brokenness of his own existence. The counterpart of unhistorical religion, religion without a Mediator, is the failure to recognize the radical character of the guilt of sin. It is an attempt to create a relationship with God which takes no account of the fact of guilt. "Philosophical faith" (Jaspers) and the mysticism of all nations and all ages speak also of redemption or reconciliation. But this redemption and reconciliation are not the removal of the *guilt* of sin, not the restoration of a broken fellowship, but the knowledge or experience of timeless unity, of an immediacy of relationship with God, which ignores what separates man from God.

The perfect tense of the saving fact of Christ corresponds exactly to the perfect tense of the damning fact: the Fall, the breach of the original fellowship with God. Were there no Fall, there would be no need of a historical revelation. In an unbroken order of Creation man would be permitted and able to

[1] Cf. my book *Vom Werk des Heiligen Geistes* (On the Work of the Holy Spirit), 1935, in which faith is for the first time portrayed under the aspect of past, present and future

have immediate intercourse with God, without the historical Mediator of reconciliation. The perfect tense of saving history is a cancellation of the breach, of the brokenness of fellowship with God. The saving event in Jesus Christ has the character of a *recapitulatio*; it is an event that reverses, that restores, that creates anew. The re-establishment of fellowship with God through the historical Mediator is at the same time the acknowledgment that previously fellowship with God was broken and destroyed. As the liquid in two communicating pipes always stands at an equal height, so the witness to the historical Mediator corresponds to the acknowledgment of the guilt of sin, and conversely, the evasion of the historical fact implies always the evasion of the guilt of sin. This twofold perfect tense is therefore the fundamental structure of the Christian faith.

(*b*) But this perfect tense does not cover everything that needs to be said. The belief that true religion, true fellowship with God, must be something contemporary, is certainly not wrong but on the contrary wholly true. Without prejudice to the relationship of faith to the past, it is always at the same time presence: it belongs to the present and is direct, immediate relationship to God. This also is a part of the central witness of the New Testament. The series of utterances referring to the accomplished act of reconciliation is paralleled by another series, expressing pure contemporaneity. "Nevertheless I live; yet not I, but Christ liveth in me" (Gal. 2: 20). "Abide in me, and I in you" (John 15: 4). "Know ye not your own selves, how that Jesus Christ is in you?" (2 Cor. 13: 5). "That Christ may dwell in your hearts by faith" (Eph. 3: 17). "Christ in you, the hope of glory" (Col. 1: 27). "God is love; and he that dwelleth in love dwelleth in God, and God in him" (1 John 4: 16). Life in fellowship with God is *presence*. Faith is no mere memory of a past event, but life and activity in the presence of Him who creates anew and is Himself present in His gifts. To the question: "How can the perfect tense of saving history become the present experience of salvation and fellowship with God?" the scripture, and with it the Church, answers by referring to the Holy Spirit and His work in the hearts of the faithful and in the Christian community.

Have we therefore now the task of teaching about the Holy Spirit just because scripture does so? Such a biblicist procedure does not conform to the rule which we found as a criterion for our theological work and have followed hitherto. Further, a mere reproduction of Biblical statements about the Holy Spirit and His work is not possible, if only for the reason that these are not so unanimous and clear as they would have to be to serve such a purpose. In so doing we would have almost entirely to exclude the Old Testament at the outset, for while it speaks much of the Holy Spirit, it only seldom and indistinctly does so in connection with the theme of the representation of the historical revelation. In it the Spirit of God is principally characterized as the creative power of God, as the breath of life in the creature, or again as what causes special, exceptional phenomena and astonishing demonstrations of power, and is immanent in them. Finally the Spirit inspires the revelatory language of the Prophets, but it is not His work to make men's hearts accessible to the prophetic Word. The word from St. John's Gospel is specially true of the Old Testament: "For the Holy Ghost was not yet given" (John 7: 39).

But even the utterances of the New Testament about the Holy Spirit are not of such a kind that we could summarize them in a "Doctrine of the Holy Spirit". A glance at the Concordance shows us that this most central concept does not occur at all in the sense indicated by us in many of the New Testament writings—as for example, in Matthew and Mark, in the Epistle to the Hebrews and the Epistle of James and the Pastoral Epistles. A more exact comparison of the statements indicates that very diverse views of the nature and working of the Holy Spirit are to be found, which could only with violence be brought to one common denominator. A doctrine of the Holy Spirit built up on biblicist principles always rests therefore on a more or less unconscious self-deception, namely that one should attempt subsequently to support an already determined doctrine by Bible passages chosen more or less at random. An unprejudiced investigation of the New Testament shows that there is no one "Biblical doctrine of the Holy Spirit". Quite apart from our objection to it in principle, the biblicist method turns out to be impossible.

On the other hand there is in certain quarters (Bultmann) a tendency to conceive of the concept "Holy Spirit" as one of the "mythical" elements in the New Testament, and therefore to exclude it as a concept unintelligible, and not only superfluous but also useless, for our theological thinking. We cannot evade this objection by simply appealing to the theology of the Reformers or the Confessions of Faith. Our task is rather to show why and how far, when we talk of the new life based on faith, we *must* speak of the Holy Spirit.

(*c*) Let us start from the objectively given fact of the revelation of God in Jesus Christ, from the historic perfect tense and the witness borne to it by the apostolic Word: "The Word became flesh"; "Jesus Christ crucified for us and risen". We assert as a fact of experience that this witness of scripture is believed by some, but not by others. This strange fact reminds us that it is anything but a matter of course that the Word of Christ should find credence. When we remember what we have learnt the nature of the natural man, the sinner, to be,[1] the question is inevitable: How can he, the sinful man, come to believe the Word of Jesus Christ? How can he who is entangled in his egocentricity and pride of intellect—and that means his sinfulness—allow this Word to be said to him as the Word of truth, as the Word of God? Can he then do anything but react to it by rejecting this gospel as "foolishness and a stumbling-block"? (1 Cor. 1: 23.) Can then sinful, autonomous man do anything, in face of this assault upon his autonomy, but resist it and assert his autonomy by making the counter-attack: "This message is senseless, contrary to all reason, and the judgment on me implied in it is unjust, an affront, which for the sake of my human dignity I cannot tolerate"? How can we expect that proud man should renounce this self-defence, when precisely self-defence and self-assertion are the sign of his condition as sinful man?

There are here only two possibilities: Either we believe that sinful man can himself achieve the penitence necessary for faith, this conversion and self-surrender. If so, then his sin cannot be so bad as we have hitherto claimed. Or else something from outside of him must penetrate within him to transform his unreadiness into readiness, his self-assertion and resistance into self-surrender and acceptance. In the first case, theological thought is involved in a self-contradiction. We believe man capable of acknowledging himself as a sinner, and at the same time we believe him able to achieve this knowledge himself, by which he would prove that he is not so bad a sinner after all.

The objection could be made: "This is a quibble, for it is precisely the operation of the Word which brings about this conversion in man." We do not need the intervention of yet a third power. The Word itself is powerful enough to bring a man from impenitence to penitence, to change his self-assertion and resistance to self-surrender and acceptance. It is not I that open my heart to the Word, it is the Word itself that opens my heart for itself. But now we see that the Word by no means does this in every case. Some continue to resist; they do not believe.

[1] See my *Dogmatics* II, Ch. 3, "Man as Sinner"

Others give up their resistance; they accept the Word. Whence this difference? Are there then two kinds of men, some who are open for the Word, and others from whom it rebounds; one kind accordingly, who are repentant and obedient to the Word, the other kind unrepentant and closed to the Word? The decisive act, the change from sinful imperviousness to believing openness, would thus have its origin in man himself.

But it is precisely this which both the witness of the scripture and the experience of faith denies. At this decisive point faith makes the confession *sola gratia*—"by grace alone"—acknowledging itself to be the pure gift of God. Yet once more an act of God is put in the place of unaided human activity, and this act of God is called the work of the Holy Spirit. God, in so far as He intervenes in the heart of man, in so far as He bears effectual witness to Himself in the spirit of man, is *the Holy Spirit,* and that which then takes place within the human heart is *the working* of the Holy Spirit. Talk of the Holy Spirit is thus not a residuum of ancient mythical conceptions of an animistic or dynamistic kind, but an expression of the experience of faith itself, and the necessary consequence in theological reflection of the knowledge of sin and the bestowal of grace.

(*d*) We can and must clarify the same point from another side. Revelation and faith—this is our principal article of belief which determines all else—are personal encounter. The step forward from the Old Testament to the New consists in this, that the Word of God is no longer "mere word", but a Person, the Word of God incarnate in Jesus. It was He, Jesus Himself, in whom the first disciples recognized God present in speech and action (Matt. 16: 16). Their witness was to this personal presence of God, this Immanu-el (God with us); this was their message. But we later believers would be dependent again upon a mere word about Him, our faith would not really be encounter, if we were merely confronted with the word, the witness *about* Him. Indeed, this would really have happened to the Apostles themselves after the death of Christ. Earlier "while He still lived" they had God's Word as Person, but now, since His death, they would have had it only as a memory of Him, their faith would no longer be encounter, no longer real fellowship with Him. But the witness of the Apostles is not to this effect. Even after His death, nay, now all the more, they stand in personal fellowship with Him and their prayer and their faith has altogether the character of personal encounter. He is "in their midst" as the Risen One, who bears witness to Himself in them through His Spirit.

It is especially the Gospel of John which emphasizes this unity of the Person of Jesus with the experience of the Holy Spirit. The representative of Jesus, in whom the presence of Jesus is continued, is the Paraclete, the Holy Spirit. Nowhere is the personal character of the Holy Spirit and, at the same time, His oneness with the Christ of history so clearly attested as in John. We understand how in an early stage of reflection the statement could be made: "The Lord *is* the Spirit" (2 Cor. 3: 17). The experience of the living presence of God and of His power was identical with the presence of the Risen One. It was, however, wholly based upon the saving act of Jesus Christ, in the gift which had been bestowed upon the disciples in His Person. Everything that was implicit in this new presence of God, and everything which took shape therefrom, they called the operation of the Holy Spirit.

When we say "Holy Spirit" we mean that mode of God's being by which He is present within us, and operates in our spirit and heart. His first and decisive activity is this, that He makes Christ present to us, who stands over against us as a fact of the past in the Word, in the witness to Jesus as the Christ (John 14–16). Only when we do not merely confront the Word of the past, but this Word as a Word present, and operative in us today, is it true that faith is personal encounter. Thus we understand also why it was only in the New Testament, and not in the Old, that the Holy Spirit could be spoken of in this pregnant sense. The Holy Spirit in the New Testament sense is the presence of God which bears witness to, and makes effectual, the historical Christ as a living personal presence. The operation of the Holy Spirit is necessary for the Word about Christ to become the Word of Christ for us, and for the Word of Christ to become the Word of God.

(*e*) But now there arises from the opposite side the question whether in this manner the human subject is not short-circuited, and man does not become the mere stage on which the divine action is set. This objection must not be lightly thrust on one side. Faith is indeed a *bestowal* of God, but it is certainly not an act of God in the sense that it is God who believes within us. To say this would be to contradict both the witness of the Apostles and that of the experience of faith. Faith is without question an act of man, just as surely as it is on the other hand a bestowal of God, a work of the Holy Spirit.

We face here a mysterious paradoxical fact, which can never be altogether and wholly elucidated, which Calvin describes as the secret operation of the Holy Spirit (*arcana operatio spiritus sancti*). All attempts to estimate the respective shares of the divine subject and the human in faith and in the new life of the Christian are idle and instead of serving to clarify have done injustice now to this side and now to the other. But one thing at least we can do to illuminate the issue: we can recall what we saw earlier[1] about the nature of human personality and realize from this that the mystery of the unity of divine grace and human freedom lies at the very heart of human nature.

In contrast with all other beings known to us, man has his being in the Word of God as a responsible agent. He is the one called by God. Man's being is always being in decision. He is always answering God's call, even when he denies God. There is only one thing he cannot do: not answer. He can indeed—and this is the "impossible possibility" (Karl Barth)—answer in the contrary sense to that to which he is called. That he does this, makes him a sinner, and with this perverted use of freedom the deepest contradiction invades his nature, through which he does not indeed lose but perverts the humanity of his being. But the Word of revelation calls him back to his origin, back to his true being, and thus to true freedom. To be moved by God is his true life. *Deo servire libertas* (Augustine). As the man set free from sin by the Son he is "free indeed" (John 8: 36). His independence is not a freedom alongside of or over against God, but in God; it is the freedom to recognize himself as one created by God in love and to treat himself as one moved by God's will. His freedom is not independence, but dependence upon God.

Thus when through the operation of the Holy Spirit man's heart is opened for the Word of God, what happens is not something that short-circuits man as a free subject, that estranges him from himself, but something on the contrary that alone makes him really free and truly active. The reason for this is that it frees him from a life in contradiction to a life in the truth, and heals and integrates his will and makes it genuinely his own, a will which when sinful was never truly *his* will, but lay under the domination of an alien power. To be led by the Spirit of God is not to be possessed. On the contrary, it is to be liberated from possession, from the alien domination of evil. Man only becomes himself through the operation of the Holy Spirit.

Our natural thought does not understand this, for we think in terms of the isolated "independent" self, and therefore conceive of being "in God" or "through God" as an encroachment

[1] Cf. my *Dogmatics* II, Ch. 3, "Man and Creation"

upon our freedom. Here is the deepest reason for our rejection of the message *sola gratia*. We start from the apparently obvious presupposition that a self is something existing in isolation, and that dependence upon God is equivalent to a diminution of our freedom. But this conception of the self turns out to be destructive of the self; for the absolute, unlimited freedom leads in the last resort to the denial of God and of responsibility, and thus also to denial of all meaning to existence, to pure nihilism.[1] Freedom in God is true freedom, because, being founded in the self-bestowing love of God, it understands this same self-bestowing love as the source and meaning of existence. It is only through being loved that we become capable of loving, and only in loving is there true freedom. To be apprehended by the love of God and to be truly free are one and the same thing. To let oneself be apprehended by the self-bestowing love of God in Christ is the outpouring of the Holy Spirit. "Because the love of God is shed abroad in our hearts" (Rom. 5: 5). To be made open to receive this love is the event of man's liberation from the strain and the feebleness of the self turned in upon itself, the release of the heart turned in upon itself (*cor incurvatum in se*)—and therefore the liberation to true selfhood. To be led or apprehended by the Holy Spirit does in fact mean the annihilation of one freedom, namely the false, imagined freedom of the independent self. Therefore from the standpoint of the independent self this must appear as the completest bondage, as the crippling of its independent activity, until this standpoint is surrendered in the event of belief, which is a gift of God and an act of the man who accepts it.

(*f*) Now we have gained access to the New Testament witness on the operation of the Holy Spirit, and have found at the same time a critical standard by which to distinguish essentials from non-essentials in the variety of the witnesses. We made it our point of departure that the truth in Christ, which as an objective-historical fact outside us stands over against us, lays hold on us inwardly and so breaks the resistance in us. This is not done by the written or heard Word alone, for this too is something external, that stands over against us. Something must be added to the "Word", or rather in the Word of Christ

[1] The assertion, first made by Fichte, of the absolute freedom of man is identical with the denial of God the Creator. It lies at the root both of the philosophy of Nietzsche ("Were there gods who could bear not to be a god?") and of the philosophy of his antipodes Karl Marx ("Man is free only when he owes his existence to himself"). But it comes to its culmination in the nihilistic philosophy of J.-P. Sartre, whose aggressive atheism leads inevitably to the denial of all norms

He Himself must speak to us. What the old writers called the internal testimony of the Holy Spirit (*testimonium spiritus sancti internum*) is just this; that Christ bears witness to Himself in us through His Word. According to the Gospel of John the first and most important task of the Paraclete, who is to represent Jesus in the world after His death, is to bear witness to Him, the crucified and risen, the historical Jesus, as the Christ. Only now does the perfect become a present, and not a present *something*, but the present *Lord*, who speaks to me as His own (Gal. 4: 6; Rom. 8: 16).

(*g*) But the operation of the Holy Spirit is not confined to bearing witness to us of Christ. Rather is He borne witness to by the Apostles as creative power, that produces new life, new will, new feelings, new spiritual, psychological, and even physical powers. For this reason the operation of the Holy Spirit cannot in the last resort be conceptually grasped. It transcends all that can be said, it is in its depth and fullness something "that cannot be uttered" (Rom. 8: 26). Just as natural life escapes all definition, so much more does life "in the Spirit". The concept which in the apostolic witness most frequently refers to this paralogical side of His operation is that of *dynamis*. Paul does not appear with "persuasive words of wisdom" but "in demonstration of the Spirit and power". Thus also the new, wonderful, and to us, indeed, in some ways strange "powers" which are astir in the community, are referred to His operation (1 Cor. 12: 6). The power of the Spirit who is given to the community with the Word of Christ reaches deep into the unconscious, even into the organic and physical realm, and we should beware of the attempt to judge the miracles of the Holy Spirit with the yard-stick of our "enlightened" rationalism. But there is one thing to which the scriptural evidence itself gives us the right, namely to say that the decisive expression of this new life in the spirit is *agape*—self-bestowing love.

It is indeed understandable, though not therefore warrantable, that in theological reflection, in the *doctrine* of the Holy Spirit, the relationship of Spirit and knowledge, of Spirit and doctrine should have always stood in the foreground; so much so, that that "paralogical", no longer conceptually formulable, purely dynamic element in the operation of the Holy Spirit has for the most part had less than justice done to it, and held a much less important place than in the New Testament witness to the Holy Spirit (*pneuma hagion*). This is indeed one of the principal roots of the theological intellectualism from which most of the Churches—at least the Churches of the West—suffer. Theological teaching itself cannot do very much to remedy this defect; for the correct doctrine, that the operation of the Holy Spirit is not exhausted by (correct) doctrine, is of little help in gaining the fullness of the gifts of the Spirit. But it can at least remove hindrances which have been placed in the way of the operation of the Spirit by a false theologism. It is an important and liberating insight that new knowledge is not the only fruit of the Spirit, and ways are thereby opened for Church practice which have often been barred by a too narrow doctrine. Knowledge of Christ is the first, decisive fruit of the Spirit. "No man can say that Jesus is Lord, but by the Holy Ghost" (1 Cor. 12: 3). With this sentence Paul laid the foundation of the correct theology of the Holy Spirit. But this word must be understood in its general context, in which the theme is the manifold gifts of the Spirit (1 Cor. 12–14). The miracle of Pentecost, and all that is included under the concept of the *charismata*—the gifts of the Spirit—must not be soft-pedalled from motives of theological Puritanism.

Or was perhaps this paralogical-dynamic element only a phenomenon accompanying the *first* outpouring of the Holy Spirit? An objection to such a theological restriction of the understanding of the Spirit in post-Reformation theology was justifiably made by Johann Christoph Blumhardt on the grounds of his own tremendous experience of the power of the Holy Spirit, but, in his modest way, less in the form of a protest than in that of a tireless intercession for a new outpouring of the Holy Spirit so much lacking in the Church. And we, who today must see with distress that a revival of doctrine has not as yet brought with it the bestowal of the powers and gifts of the Spirit which we find recorded as a reality in the primitive Christian community, shall we not have every reason to associate ourselves with Blumhardt in this prayer?

(*h*) As we can see after this systematic discussion about the relation of historical revelation and Holy Spirit, the Church can deviate from the right path in two directions—by one-sided emphasis on mediacy or immediacy. The Holy Spirit *is* immediacy, pure presence, pure personal fellowship, but He is immediacy on the basis of the revelation in the historical Mediator—and thus on the basis of mediacy. It is precisely this unity of the present and the historical which is the distinctive mark of faith in Christ in contrast to all mysticism and "philosophical faith". Where only one of the two is emphasized, the nature of faith is altered, and it degenerates either into mysticism without a Mediator or into mere orthodoxy and correct churchmanship. When people speak of Christian mysticism,[1] such a thing may be found in Paul. But precisely in Paul it is clear that we have not to do with an immediacy without a Mediator. For the "mystical" statement "I live, yet not I, but Christ liveth in me" continues by emphasizing faith in the Mediator; "and the life which I now live in the flesh, I live by faith in the Son of God, who loved me, and gave himself for me" (Gal. 2: 20).[2]

The paradoxical unity of mystical immediacy and historical faith in the Mediator, which is the essence of Christian faith, finds here its incomparable expression. "Christian mysticism" is one with historical faith in the Mediator.

(*i*) Now that we have thus learnt the relationship of faith to the past and to the present, a further indication must be given of the relationship of the Holy Spirit to the third dimension of time, the future, although this must later be the theme of the third part of this work. According to the New Testament witness the Holy Spirit is the pledge (*arrabōn*), the certainty of hope in that which is to come, the coming consummation, and the Ekklesia, which through Him is formed as the Body of Christ, is at the same time the Messianic community of those who await the coming of the Lord in glory. As faith has its foundation in the revelation of God and redemption which has happened, so hope reaches forward to what is going to happen. Therefore the exegetes are right in saying that the Holy Spirit in the New Testament is an eschatological entity. One cannot be a believer without sharing in the final hope. Just as a wanderer by night is suddenly illuminated by the searchlight which picks him out, so the Ekklesia of the faithful is the community illuminated by the light of Him who is to come. Their openness for this future is what gives believers their freedom, their joy, and their confidence in victory.

Only in these three temporal dimensions[3] is the existence of

[1] Albert Schweitzer (*The Mysticism of Paul the Apostle*) distinguishes himself very favourably from most of the advocates of this thesis, by very exactly defining what he means by mysticism. But he has not seen that in Paul this mysticism is wholly identical with faith in Christ crucified for us, which is most evident from the passages cited above

[2] The same is true of the later passage in Galatians: "But when the fulness of the time was come, God sent forth his Son . . . that we might receive the adoption of sons" (Gal. 4: 4, 5). For this statement too has the paradoxical continuation: "And because ye are sons, God hath sent forth the Spirit of his Son into your hearts, crying, Abba Father" (Gal. 4: 6)

[3] This relation of the three temporal dimensions to faith, love and hope has been worked out in my Earl Lectures *Faith, Hope and Love*, 1956 (Westminster Press, Philadelphia; Lutterworth Press, London)

the man who is "in Christ" complete, and apprehended with the full knowledge of its paradoxical and mysterious character. Does the Christian live in the past? Yes, through faith in Him who *has come*, and *has* redeemed him. Does he live in the present? Yes, wholly and utterly. For to be in the love of Christ, to live in it, is to live in the presence of Christ, and to be oneself a person living in the present. Does he live in the future? Yes, through hope in Him who will fulfil all things in His Coming. Christian existence, being in Christ, is the only possible and only real unity of past, present, and future, and thus is the beginning of eternal life.

For this reason everything that we say about the new being, the new life in Christ, stands under the eschatological reserve.[1] It *is* a new life. But it is so in such a fashion that it is at the same time a being in the future, a certain, joyful hope of fulfilment. We have been "born again unto a living hope" (1 Peter 1: 3). This eschatological reserve is the sign before the bracket, which determines everything that stands within the bracket. All the entities of faith are at the same time eschatological entities. The character of "not yet" belongs to the essence of faith, and therefore also to the essence of the Ekklesia. We are redeemed, we "are delivered from the power of darkness and translated into the Kingdom of his dear Son" (Col. 1: 13), but "we wait for the adoption, to wit, the redemption of our body" (Rom. 8: 23). We hope for what we do not see, for "we live by faith, not by sight" (2 Cor. 5: 7). But He who thus makes the past present for us and directs us towards the future is the Holy Spirit. He is the element in which the Ekklesia lives its life, which makes the Christ of the past its present Lord, and which makes the Ekklesia the fellowship of those that wait for Him.

[1] Cf. also what is said under the heading "Sanctification", pp. 290 ff.

CHAPTER 2

THE GROUND AND NATURE OF THE EKKLESIA

(1) THE PROBLEM

SHOULD the doctrine of the operation of the Holy Spirit begin with the doctrine of the Church? Reformed Tradition speaks against this order. In Calvin's *Institutes* the Doctrine of the Church is handled in the last, Fourth Book, and, as we have already said, this arrangement has governed the whole teaching tradition of the Reformed Church.[1] But this means that the doctrine of the Church comes after the doctrines of faith, of repentance, of justification and of the Christian life. Faith, the new life in Christ, is thus dealt with before the Church and considered independently of it, and this is actually what happens in the Third Book of the *Institutes*. The only justification for this arrangement is that Calvin regards the Church as an external support of faith (*externum subsidium fidei*).[2] Accordingly for him it is not essentially bound up with faith but is only a support, though certainly a necessary one, and explicitly an *external* support of faith. Between faith and the Church there is no inner necessary relation but only an accidental, subsidiary one, in which faith is essentially regarded as something individual, the fellowship of faith being added to it as something which does not belong to its nature. That is to say that although Calvin in practical matters was in the highest degree a Churchman and a founder of churches, he makes an individualistic separation of faith from the Church. Believers indeed require the Church, but they are believers even apart from it. That is also the customary conception of reformed Protestantism.

In diametrical opposition to this stands the Catholic conception; not only the Roman Catholic conception but also that of the Greek Orthodox Church and the Anglicans and the Old Catholics, who all of them brand this individualism as a fundamental heresy, since for all of them—even though in very

[1] Calvin, *Institutes* IV. In H. Heppe's *Dogmatik der evangelisch reformierten Theologie*, 1861, which is a synopsis of the Reformed Dogmatic Systems, the chapter on the Church is the twenty-seventh, the second last of twenty-eight chapters

[2] *Institutes* IV, 1, 1. The justification of the necessity of such external helps (*externa subsidia*) is as follows: "But as our ignorance and sloth (I may add, the vanity of our mind) makes necessary such external helps. . . ."

different ways—Church and faith form an essential unity; faith without Church is unthinkable.

There is indeed also in Calvin a concept of the Church of which it can be said that he correlates faith and the Church as essentially belonging together, namely the invisible Church (*ecclesia invisibilis*). But this is defined as the number of the elect (*numerus electorum*), and so not as a fellowship but as an aggregate, a number of such as already, even without the Church, are elect. The objection could be raised that the *electio* was such from the beginning as to have regard for the Ekklesia and the Kingdom of God, and thus from the beginning not individualistic. But that does not in the least alter the fact that Calvin describes faith without any reference to the fellowship. Faith is thus comprehensible for him without his thinking of fellowship with men. The *fellowship* of faith is added to faith as another, secondary thing. This shows itself in the very fact that he was able to equate the concept of the *ecclesia invisibilis* with the *numerus electorum*, which has no reference to fellowship. Even this concept of the *ecclesia invisibilis* does not neutralize the individualistic concept of faith, i.e. the accidental concomitance of faith and Church. Thus, in spite of what is said about *ecclesia invisibilis*, we must describe the Calvinistic understanding of faith as an individualistic one, and therefore admit the justice of the reproach levelled against it by the Catholics.

For, when we ask what the New Testament witness about the Ekklesia says, there can be no doubt as to the answer: Ekklesia and faith belong essentially together. The idea that the Ekklesia is an *externum subsidium fidei* (an outward support to faith) is not to be found in it and is essentially alien to it. One is a believer only in virtue of being in the Ekklesia, a member of the Body of Christ, and never on any other terms. The Ekklesia is the form of life in which faith itself necessarily finds expression, and not a mere subsidiary help. And so the Catholics are right and the Reformed Church is wrong? Certainly not; it would be true rather to say that both of them are in the right and in the wrong at the same time, because both of them understand the Church as a thing—that is, as an institution,[1] while this never happens in the New Testament. There, as we shall

[1] When Calvin calls the Church an *externum subsidium fidei* he is thinking of organizations like the Churches of Geneva, Strasbourg, the Electorate of Saxony and Zürich, i.e. corporations with a definite organization of a legal kind, chiefly recognized by State law, not as private corporations. He has continually in mind the national Church which is established by the State as the only recognized Church, while he regarded the condition of Churches under the Cross, to which the State did not extend this monopoly, as a troublesome misfortune for them

immediately show in more detail, the Ekklesia is never conceived of as institution; but exclusively as a fellowship of persons, as the common life based in fellowship with Jesus Christ as a fellowship of the Spirit (*koinōnia pneumatos*) and a fellowship of Christ (*koinōnia Christou*). To be in Christ through faith and to be in this fellowship are one and the same thing. The fellowship is not an addition of secondary importance or even an *externum subsidium*. It is rather the conjoint fellowship which has its ground in Christ, fellowship with one another on the basis of fellowship with God. Precisely this is the new life which is founded on Christ, life in the fellowship in love (*agape*) instead of a life by oneself in isolation.

One can say in a word, God has given us His Son that we may have fellowship with Him, and through Him with men. For the sin from which He redeems us is in fact nothing other than the destruction, the loss, of fellowship with God, which brings in its train destruction of fellowship with men. This togetherness of fellowship with God and fellowship with man, of faith and love, is already implicit in Jesus' double commandment "Thou shalt love the Lord thy God with all thy heart . . . and thy neighbour as thyself." It is manifest also in Paul's statements in Romans and Galatians where the shedding abroad of the love of God in our hearts is called the first consequence of faith (Rom. 5: 5), the first fruit of the Spirit (Gal. 5: 22) and the criterion of true faith (Gal. 5: 6). Fellowship is nothing other than the existence with each other whose ground is God's existence with us, and conversely sin is nothing other than existence apart from Him and apart from each other. God's self-communication is the communication of His life, His love, and love is the will to communicate oneself. For this purpose Christ is given to us, that we may live in God's love and draw our life from it. A life of broken fellowship, without God and without our neighbour—this isolation is darkness and death. Reconciliation means that this isolation is brought to an end by God's self-communication.

The Ekklesia is this new humanity which is reconciled with God by God, and in which, therefore, each has fellowship with his brother. It is the community of those who have been reconciled and draw their life from the reconciliation. It is nothing other than men in fellowship, in fellowship with God and in fellowship with each other. For this reason the idea that it is an *externum subsidium fidei* is wholly impossible. It is always the *people* of God in history, the "true Israel". As such it is named Ekklesia and, further, not *ecclesia invisibilis*. For this

Augustinian conception does not correspond to the nature of the Ekklesia as a real togetherness, as the brotherhood of the reconciled. We must admit that we mortals cannot finally and certainly determine whether the brotherhood is the genuine one which is based on God's reconciliation, and thus on faith. The line of demarcation that distinguishes the true brotherhood from a sham brotherhood is invisible, but the brotherhood itself is just as visible as was the bodily existence of Jesus Christ. The New Testament Ekklesia is the true, visible brotherhood of the reconciled, even if there may have been in it some who only seemed to belong to it.

This spiritual brotherhood, which was yet visible in the world and recognizable to some extent even by unbelievers through its manifestations, through the love of its members for one another, is the Ekklesia of the New Testament. But this is something different from the Church. For what we call Church is not a brotherhood but an institution; not the Body of Christ, but a corporation in the juristic sense of the word. For this reason, if we wish to follow the New Testament, we cannot simply translate Ekklesia by the word "Church", and we have the right to say only of the Ekklesia and not of the Church that it is essentially bound up with faith in Christ. Jesus Christ wills to have a people—a people, but certainly not an institution. A people *has* institutions, but it never understands itself as an institution. And if this is true of any people, it is especially true of the people of Israel. It was not like the majority of peoples of our times, a national State. As a people it never understood itself in terms of its organization as a State, but in the light of its relation to God, and this is far more true of the "true Israel"—the Ekklesia.

Thus the two questions which we asked at the beginning of the chapter—"Is the Ekklesia an essential and necessary implication of faith?" "Why may we not translate 'Ekklesia' by 'Church'?"—must be answered from the same standpoint: namely in the light of the essential character of faith in Christ. Jesus Christ is the revealed will of God for fellowship. He wills to have a people, and not merely individual believers. As the Risen One He is the Lord, the Head of this people. He wills to have, not an institution but a fellowship in which God alone, God and His love, rules.

(2) THE BASIS OF THE EKKLESIA

There are three classical definitions of the Church, each of which contains an answer to the question about the basis of the

Church. The Church is the Company of the Elect, the Body of Christ, the Communion of Saints (*coetus electorum, corpus Christi, communio sanctorum*). These three definitions of the Church may serve as indications of the aspects under which we must think of the Ekklesia from the standpoint of faith in Christ.

(*a*) *Coetus electorum* (the Company of the Elect)

The basis of the Ekklesia lies in the *eternal election*. We refer back to what was earlier said on the subject of election.[1] As there we asked: "What is said to us in Jesus Christ about our election?"—so now we ask: "What is said to us in Jesus Christ about the nature of the Ekklesia?"

This question compels us to advance to the transcendent ground in the election. The fellowship of the Ekklesia with Christ and the fellowship of Christians with one another has its basis in the eternal loving will of God. In Christ, God's plan for the world and humanity is revealed (Rom. 8: 28; Eph. 1: 9–11). There *is* a fellowship of Christians because God has willed from eternity that it should be so, because He did not create men as isolated individuals intelligible in themselves and living in their own strength, but as beings to whom He wills to give His own life, binding them to one another by this gift. That is His decree in Creation. But this is shown to us in Christ as at the same time His decree of salvation. Men have indeed come into conflict with the divine destiny, their unity with the Creator; and in consequence also their bond with one another has been torn asunder. In fact men do not live in God and in God's strength, and they do not live in love. In order to cancel out this corruption and heal this rift, God has sent us the "Saviour". God's plan of Creation has become the plan of Redemption. In Christ we know God's love as love in spite of us, as the love which gives and communicates itself to man who has become a sinner. God wills to be our God in spite of us; the separation is not on His side; we must know this, and for this reason He sends us His Son. But not only must we *know* it, but what God wills must *come into being*. God's will revealed in Christ is a creative will. In Christ not only is something given us to know, but a new fact is created, a new humanity established, and this new humanity is the Ekklesia.

When the Ekklesia reflects on its foundation, it understands itself as the people of God whose origin lies in God's eternal will.

[1] Cf. *Dogmatics* I, Ch. 22, "God's Eternal Decrees and Election"

In no other way can it—as the brotherhood of Christians—understand its existence and nature, especially since (as the world must see it) it is by no means yet this new humanity, but only a little flock in the midst of a world in which the love of God counts for nothing. Its claim to be the new, the redeemed humanity, must therefore appear to the world as a grotesque piece of self-conceit. The Ekklesia must indeed concede the point, not only on account of its smallness but also on account of its own imperfection, that this claim to be the new humanity sounds incredible. And yet it knows that such it *is*. It knows because it understands itself, not in terms of its visible appearance, but in terms of its (invisible) eternal ground. It knows itself as a chosen people of God; in itself, the little flock of Christ's redeemed, it recognizes the vanguard of the Kingdom of God, of the new humanity united with God and in God.

(*b*) *Corpus Christi* (the Body of Christ)

This, its transcendent origin, is known by the fellowship through the *historical* Christ, Jesus. Not in mystical visions, not in speculative thoughts, but in the history of Jesus Christ is this eternal will of God made known to it. Its members did not first learn to know their election as pre-temporal, eternal and transcendent, but in the historical fact that One came among them, the fishers by the Galilean lake, and called them out (*ek-klesia*) and chose them to be His disciples and apostles. It was not they who united themselves to form a people of Christ, but this same Lord who united them. "Ye have not chosen me, but I have chosen you" (John 15: 16). His "Follow me" was the beginning of their corporate existence over against the world, first as a band of disciples, and later as a community bearing witness to Christ, the Risen One. On the last evening they spent together He spoke the great word of the "New Covenant". By referring to His broken body and His blood to be shed He established them as the new Israel, the people of the New Covenant, and their membership rooted in Him was historically established in the making of this Covenant. After His death on the Cross and after His Resurrection it was the experience of the Holy Spirit which caused the disciple-fellowship to think of itself as "the body of Christ". For, as during His earthly life He was its Lord and Head, so was He now also invisibly but really "the Head and we the members."

What the Apostle says in 1 Corinthians 12 of the living organism which the Holy Spirit creates for Himself, which He rules by assigning to each member his spiritual gift (*charisma*) and thereby his service, is a living experience and reality for everyone in the Ekklesia. Paul does not teach this in order that the Christians should believe it, but he expresses it as an experience of the faith of all. They know that it is so! They *are* the one Body whose Head is Christ, and whose members they all are. So, as before Good Friday their visible companionship with the Lord and with the other disciples was a reality in which they did not need to believe, but which they experienced as a visible fact as members of the disciple band, so now also they experienced as an indubitable reality this togetherness which bound them together in one Ekklesia where the place of the visible Lord had been taken by the invisible Lord present in His representative, the Paraclete.

True, this is an experience of faith; that is, something which possesses reality only for those who through faith are in Christ. But that one has to *believe* in the Ekklesia was an idea that never would have entered their heads. And there is not even a single word to indicate this in the New Testament. "So we, being many, *are* one body in Christ, and every one members one of another" (Rom. 12: 5). And when the Apostle tells them of other congregations in other towns and lands and transmits their greetings, they acknowledge the same reality in these other *ekklesiai*: the unity of the Body of Christ created by the invisible Lord. Through the reports of the Apostle, which at the same time were a paean of praise to God for "the great things that God had done with them" (Acts 15: 4), they experienced the bond of kinship between the individual house-congregations and local congregations in Macedonia, Achaia, Asia, and so forth. Thus for them the unity of the Ekklesia was no tenet of faith, but a living experience, just like the nature of their own brotherhood. In their faith in Christ and in the experience of the Holy Spirit the social character of the Ekklesia was implicit. Through their faith they had sure knowledge about the ground of their fellowship, and about its reality, through the daily experience of their bond of union. Visible and invisible Ekklesia were just as little to be severed as the love of Christ in the strength of which they lived, and the love with which they loved their brethren.

(c) *Communio sanctorum* (the Communion of Saints)

The third definition, *sanctorum communio*, refers to the ground of the Ekklesia in the faith of individual Christians. When the circle of the disciples grew, when—as at Pentecost—hosts of new members were "added", it became clear to them that the

Ekklesia has its ground in the faith of the individual members. The election, the transcendent ground, becomes immanent in the individual's experience of faith, just as, conversely, it is faith which acknowledges the eternal election as its ultimate and highest origin. The Holy Spirit, who apprehends and creates anew the individual when the Word of Christ is heard, makes the eternal decree of God a present experience. The living Christ builds His body for Himself by taking possession of the hearts of men and "adds them" as saints called (*Klētoi hagioi*) to the community of disciples. The Ekklesia is the community of the *sancti*, of those who have been called out of the world and into the service of Christ. It is the community of believers.

Fellowship with Him, who has bound each one to Himself through the word of reconciliation, is what now also binds the members to each other. Faith is in itself—fellowship. By believing we became capable of fellowship and willing for it, companionable, because faith is the reception of the love of God. The God who communicates Himself creates through His Spirit men who wish to communicate and should communicate the thing that they have received. Sin consists in the fact that the self is closed to God and man, but faith signifies that a man becomes open for God and for his brother, that he is willing to be open and to communicate himself. God reveals Himself as the One who wishes to be with us, and therefore faith is the will and readiness to be with, to be with our fellow-humans, communicative life. It is therefore in the nature of the case impossible that as a believer one should be or wish to remain a solitary, one who lives for himself. It is just this living for oneself, this existence of a "Monad without windows", which is abolished by faith. Faith is "communicating existence".[1] Therefore, it leads of necessity through *communicatio* to *communio*.

And yet we must never lose sight of the other fact: that just as faith leads *to* fellowship, so also it always comes *out of* fellowship. For a man has always received his life in Christ through faith from a Christian community that was there before him. Every believer has been "added". The Ekklesia is always prior to the individual believers; they have become believers through being drawn into it. Every believer has received his

[1] It was only after the writing of this part that Hendrik Kraemer's book *The Communication of the Christian Faith* came to my knowledge. (Westminster Press, Philadelphia; Lutterworth Press, London, 1957.) Its ideas are very similar to my own. I find Kraemer's distinction between communication-of and communication-with an extraordinarily felicitous one, which exactly corresponds to the intention of the New Testament

faith through the communication of others. He is thus already in a fellowship when he becomes a believer.

The formula of the Apostles' Creed, "sanctorum communio", seems to leave the question open whether *sanctorum* is the genitive of *sancti* (saints) or *sancta* (holy things). But in fact the Ekklesia is the *communio* of the *sancti*, for *sancta*, the holy things of the sacraments, create no fellowship but only a common participation. The interpretation of *communio sanctorum* in the neuter sense is the source of a spiritual collectivism, which confuses the nature of fellowship with the nature of participation in a thing. The thought of a *sanctum* in which individuals participate has no place in the New Testament. For "that" in which the individuals participate is precisely not a thing, but a Person —the Christ. *Participatio* in something creates a collective; fellowship with the Christ creates fellowship with one another.

Each of the three definitions of the Ekklesia shows us a special aspect of its basis: the transcendent (*electio*), the historical-objective (*corpus Christi*) and the spiritual-subjective (*sanctorum communio*). Each of them taken by itself would necessarily lead to a one-sided conception; either to an abstract spiritual intellectualism (the number of the predestined, *numerus praedestinatorum*), or to a sacramental hierarchism (the Body of Christ, *corpus Christi*), or to an emotional and pietistic individualism (the communion of the faithful, *communio fidelium*). Only in their unity do they reproduce the reality of the Ekklesia. It is at once *coetus electorum*, *corpus Christi* and *communio sanctorum*.

(3) THE PROBLEM OF THE INVISIBLE AND VISIBLE EKKLESIA

These three definitions with their basis comprehend at the same time the nature of the Ekklesia in its spiritual theological aspect, i.e. that element in it which is visible only to faith but invisible to the natural eye. About the nature of the Church of faith, about its nature as visible only to the eye of faith, the teachers of our Church since the Reformation have always been quite clear, and there have been no differences in their conception. These differences began only when man reflected on the fact that the Church of faith is always at the same time a visible, empirical entity. But at this point most of them became the victims of a misunderstanding, which, although understandable in the light of tradition, was none the less disastrous. This misunderstanding attached in the first place to the word "Church". The New Testament "*ekklesía*" (Greek) had been translated for almost fifteen hundred years by "*ecclésia*" (Latin) and thus understood to refer to the Church as it had developed in the West. And even though they wished to reform this Roman Church and restore the original New Testament one, yet they were quite sure that it was the Reformation of the *Church* that was in question, that the New Testament Ekklesia was the normative form of the *Church*.

The visible form of the Church, they believed, is something similar to what has existed for fourteen hundred years as Church, a structure of a social kind with this or that type of order, a structure constituted by a determinate order or system of Church law, and whose chief characteristic and function is to be a serviceable instrument for the proclamation of the Word of God and the administration of the Sacraments. The social structure was thus—as we would say today—an organization serving a purpose, or as we have already heard from Calvin an *externum subsidium fidei*, and, as such, an institution which is to be constituted and regulated by laws. And an attempt was made to close the gap between this Church and the Ekklesia of the New Testament by using the distinction which Augustine had already made available, between *ecclesia invisibilis* (as defining that entity which we have described in our three definitions given above), and the *ecclesia visibilis*, by which Augustine had understood the Catholic universal World Church of his day, which it was necessary to reform.

Augustine had arrived at this distinction through his study of Paul on the one side, and on the other side through his perception of what had happened since Constantine and Theodosius. In his time Church membership was already, by a decree of the Emperor Theodosius, a statutory obligation, as indeed a full half-century earlier through Constantine's action the Church had become the acknowledged, and later the privileged, national church. His study of Paul had taught him something of the Pauline idea of the Ekklesia which referred to something wholly different from the all-inclusive Church. The connection between these two so completely disparate entities lay in the concept "*ecclesia*" which applied to them both.

Both Zwingli and Calvin took over this fundamental concept. And it was their intention to reform this same visible Church. And keeping in mind what they understood to be the New Testament Church, they could do this only by understanding the "visible Church" as an institution which served the purpose of proclaiming the Word of God or of pure doctrine, and which for this reason, as Calvin says, is an external support of faith.

This double concept of the Church[1] is wholly foreign to the New Testament. There is in it only the one Ekklesia, which is at the same time spiritual and invisible (intelligible to faith alone) and corporeal (recognizable and visible to all). No Apostle would ever have agreed that this visible entity, the Ekklesia, was only a support of faith, let alone an external support. For the disciples it was wholly impossible to distinguish between visible and invisible Ekklesia. They too were indeed well aware that among the faithful there might be individuals who did not really belong to Christ. But this consideration had no influence upon their concept of the Ekklesia. For them the Ekklesia which belongs to Christ through faith was at the same time the Ekklesia which everyone could see.

In other words, the social form of the Ekklesia was a necessary consequence of their faith. For since God had communicated Himself to them in Christ, it followed that they must communicate themselves to each other. From the knowledge of reconciliation, the fellowship which we have with Christ, there followed immediately the "fellowship which we have among ourselves". The *agape*, the love of God which was communicated to them through Christ, was now living and present in them and united them to one another. This means that the social character of the Ekklesia resulted from its spiritual character as an association of men through the Holy Spirit, through the love of Christ. And that itself was the structural law of this social entity. There was no other law, nor was there need for any. The Ekklesia was a spiritual brotherhood, free from law. The spiritual and bodily character of this brotherhood is a consequence of the spiritual and bodily character, the God-manhood, of Jesus Christ.

This structural law of the Ekklesia is, however, something totally different from the structural law of the Institutional Church. The fundamental difference between these two entities —spiritual brotherhood on the one side, institution for the administration of supernatural Sacraments and the promulgation of revealed doctrine on the other—could be perceived by a good sociologist at the first glance, even if, for the rest, he did not more exactly know or understand the deeper foundation of this spiritual togetherness. Sociology distinguishes between fellowship and association (F. Tönnies). It speaks of "authentic fellowship" and understands thereby a fellowship in which the presence of the persons with each other, or the bond of union

[1] Cf. Seeberg, *Lehrbuch der Dogmengeschichte* II[3], p. 472

which joins them together, determines as such the character of this social grouping. True, the Ekklesia cannot be *wholly* "defined in sociological terms". In this sense we must modify K. L. Schmidt's thesis.[1] But by a sociologist who is at the same time a believer in Christ it can be understood very well in its peculiar character as a fellowship—a character different from that of all other societies. The brotherhood can *have* laws and institutions but it can never regard these as belonging to its *essence*. But, above all, it can never *understand itself as an institution*. And precisely that is the essential thing. The Ekklesia's understanding of its own nature is not that of an institution. The nature of the Christian brotherhood is basically different from the nature of an institution, which is called the Church, and is indeed incompatible with it.

The social character of the Ekklesia is determined by its spiritual character, by its faith in Christ in the sense of *pistis*. And what we have just said about it as an entity constituted by faith determines also its character as a social entity. The Ekklesia is the people of God. Even the Israel of the Old Covenant did not understand itself as a State, as an institution, but as the creation of the Covenant of God. And this non-institutional character is much more evident still in the Ekklesia of the New Testament whose life-element is the Holy Spirit. Sociologically the Ekklesia would have to be defined as a fellowship in the most authentic sense, in distinction from an association. But in the last resort the social character of the Ekklesia can be understood only in the light of Christ. It has characteristics which the sociologist cannot understand as compatible with each other, but which in his experience exclude each other. *Either* a society is a fellowship of persons, a brotherhood, *or* it is an association held together by a universal idea. Either the one or the other, but not both together. But the unity of these two apparently mutually exclusive characters is the paradox of the Ekklesia.

Nearly a hundred years ago, the jurist Rudolf Sohm saw something of the *quid pro quo* of the visible Church. As a jurist, however, he paid too little attention to the social character of the Ekklesia as such but only drew attention to the incompatibility of the legal element with the Ekklesia.[2]

[1] *Theologisches Wörterbuch zum Neuen Testament* (*ThWb*), III, p. 515 (*Theological Dictionary of the N.T.*) Article "Ekklesia".

[2] Between the first and second volumes of Sohm's *Kirchenrecht* there is a very profound difference, which for the most part has passed unnoticed. Sohm I, which first appeared in 1892, has in general a conception of the New Testament Ekklesia which in many ways anticipates the results of later and

Fifty years later Ernst Troeltsch, who was familiar with the sociological approach, but who, as an idealist theologian, had but little insight into the spiritual nature of the Ekklesia, quite simply reckoned the New Testament Ekklesia as belonging to the "sect-type of the Church"—a judgment in which there was doubtless some truth, but at the same time a great deal of error. The social character of the Ekklesia can be understood only in terms of its faith in Christ, but from that standpoint it must be conceived of as brotherhood in Christ. But it still continues to be a sociological paradox.

But Zwingli and Calvin from the start regarded the Ekklesia of the New Testament in the perspective of the institution known to Church history and therefore did not notice at all its specific social character. Luther alone saw intuitively something of this. He always had an aversion to the word "Church" but it was not given to him to distinguish clearly between Church and Ekklesia. He too stood under the influence of Augustine, and he on his part spoke of the Church in two senses: of the true Church, which is known only in faith, and of the institution of the Church, which is constituted by laws. And the reason for this is that even in his thought, which had penetrated so deeply to the heart of the New Testament teaching on faith in Christ, the connection between faith and love did not stand so clearly in the centre as it does in the New Testament. And further, he was still strongly dominated by the Constantinian and Theodosian idea of the Church.

In the more recent discussion on the Church, especially in the New Testament studies, there is another prejudice which stands in the way—a prejudice which is to be found as early as

contemporary scholarship. He describes the Ekklesia as a spiritual and social reality, ruled by the Word of Christ and the Holy Spirit, which has not yet developed an institutional character. His picture agrees with that drawn by H. v. Campenhausen in his work *Kirchliches Amt und geistliche Vollmacht in den ersten drei Jahrhunderten*, 1953 (Church Office and Spiritual Authority in the First Three Centuries), a view similar to my own, which may also be regarded as the result of scientific Biblical criticism. In this first volume of Sohm there is as yet no mention whatever of the concept of the *ecclesia invisibilis*. The second volume on the other hand, published posthumously in 1922, is wholly dominated by this concept, which was probably suggested to him by the Lutheran Dogmatics of his time.

Since critics have made no distinction between Sohm I and Sohm II, Sohm has been "refuted" and discredited by arguments which applied to the second volume, but not to the first. These one-sided verdicts reflect the uncertainty of the Protestant Doctrine of the Church, i.e. the discrepancy between the requirements of contemporary New Testament scholarship, and Dogmatics, which was not ready to take the former seriously. We must also indeed take into account the fact, which we noted above, that Sohm did not raise the question of the social structure of the Ekklesia at all, since he was not a sociologist and did not possess this concept in Calvin: the belief that we must interpret the Ekklesia in the light of the significance given to *kahal* in the Septuagint, the assembly of the people of God, or in the light of the significance given in secular Greek to Ekklesia as a popular assembly. Then the meaning of the word Ekklesia is always that of the *assembly* for the worship of God. But the New Testament gives us no grounds for this conclusion. It has filled both the Old Testament concept and the secular Greek concept of Ekklesia with entirely new Christological content. It is not the assembly that the Apostles mean—that above all Paul means when he speaks of the Ekklesia—but the *klesis*, the election and the call of God in Christ. The assembly plays in the New Testament a wholly subordinate rôle, and only in 1 Corinthians 14 does Paul picture it in some detail and there, above all, from the standpoint that everyone must make his own contribution and everyone have his turn. What belongs to divine service, to Sunday, the "cultic", the sacred element, falls entirely into the background compared with the vocation of mission to the world and loving service to men.

We could summarize the content of the Pauline writings in the one phrase "Sacrifice of the Body, as Christ has sacrificed Himself." He says this himself. The technical term for the cultus, *latreia*, occurs only once in the New Testament and even there it has not a cultic significance but an ethical existential meaning "that ye present your bodies a living sacrifice, holy, acceptable unto God, which is your reasonable service" (Rom. 12: 1). So also the mention of divine service on Sundays falls into the background compared with "everyday matters", our daily service of our brother. And we shall show later that thus the sacrament, in the sense of a saving ordinance which the Church administers, becomes questionable.

Divine worship has indeed its place in the life of the Ekklesia brotherhood. Ekklesia is founded by God's Word in Christ and the believing, worshipping answer of man. But the Ekklesia becomes visible, not as a cult-fellowship, but as a brotherhood proclaiming Christ and living in mutual love. Paul presupposes that "the word of God dwelleth richly among you", that the Christians "pray without ceasing". Therefore the sociological description of the Ekklesia as "authentic fellowship" used above is the right one, because fellowship differs from association precisely in that it has its goal in itself and is not there to serve a further end. It is an end in itself, willed by God, even though this is only absolutely true of the Ekklesia in its consummation, in the Kingdom of God.

Even though the Ekklesia may have appeared to the unbelievers of its time as one of the many *thiasoi* or cultic unions—the apostolic instruction about the Ekklesia goes in the contrary direction: the permeation of everyday life with the Spirit of Jesus Christ. The Ekklesia is a thoroughly uncultic, unsacred, spiritual brotherhood, which lives in trusting obedience to its Lord Christ and in the love to the brethren which He bestows, and knows itself as the Body of Christ through the Holy Spirit which dwells in it. The whole of life is a service of God and this service of God is at the same time brotherly service to one's fellow men.

(4) THE SOCIAL REALITY OF THE EKKLESIA

This sociological character of the Ekklesia corresponds exactly to its theological nature. The self-communication of God in the Cross of Christ through the Word of grace becomes by means of the secret operation of the Spirit (*arcana operatio spiritus*) the self-communicating love of the brethren. God, the Creator of all life, has no need of self-bestowing love. To Him are due thanksgiving, praise and the humble worship of man. But *agape*, which He Himself is, and which He pours into men's hearts through faith in Jesus Christ, is by Him directed through man towards those who stand in need of it. For *agape*, in contrast with *eros*, as the Greek philosophers understand it, reaches ever downwards and not upwards, towards emptiness and not towards fullness (Nygren). The believer who is moved by *agape* wills to put not only the Word of grace, but everything that he has received, at the disposal of those for whom, just as much as for him, Christ sacrificed Himself on the Cross.

The universally understandable and most immediately credible expression of this self-giving love is that primitive Christian community of goods of which it is said "and all that believed were together, and had all things common; and sold their possessions and goods, and parted them to all men, as every man had need" (Acts 2: 44, 45). "Neither said any of them that ought of the things which he possessed was his own; but they had all things common" (Acts 4: 32).

This kind of self-giving brotherly love was, however, exaggerated and therefore unrealistic. It was too direct a translation of *agape*. It anticipated the Last Things and paid no heed to "the form of this world". Thus it led to the impoverishment of the Jerusalem community and from that time onwards was not to be found either in Jerusalem or in any of the other communities. But in respect of its motive it is not only characteristic of the Ekklesia but an ideal for it. That is the ideal—even if it is not practicable. That is the spirit of the Ekklesia brotherhood.[1]

Paul made clear to his congregations the nature of their fellowship, the nature of the Ekklesia, by means of a figure which he did not himself invent but which was already a common parable of fellowship in the ancient world: the figure of the body (1 Cor. 12: 12). Here, however, this figure of the body is filled with a wholly new content, because this body which suffers and simultaneously rejoices along with its members is at the same time the Body of Christ. For this reason the collections which he took for "the poor in Jerusalem" were for Paul not only a concern of charity, but a concern filled with the deepest knowledge of Christ and genuine faith in Him. This act *of love* he understood at the same time as an act *of faith* in the sense that in it the grace of Christ was repeated and came alive. "For ye know the grace of our Lord Jesus Christ, that, though he was rich, yet for your sakes he became poor, that ye through his poverty might be rich" (2 Cor. 8: 9). So in the Ekklesia, in its social reality, the self-communication of God is recognizable as the principle of its life.

We have said already that the Ekklesia is a sociological paradox, because it is on the one hand a quite intimate fellowship, on the other a world-embracing new humanity. It had no local limits, it was not "one community". The brethren in Corinth or Thessalonica obviously participate with the greatest interest in the lot of the brethren in Jerusalem or Asia. They take cognizance of Paul's news about these distant people as one receives news about a son or brother living abroad. The Ekklesia is an ecumenical family, that is, a family spread over the whole world and in principle encompassing the whole round earth.

This is the fact which shows the bankruptcy of that sociological either-or: *either* personal concrete fellowship *or* an association without that character of fellowship, held together by a universal idea. The social character of the Ekklesia is world-embracing, genuine brotherhood. Why is this so? Because

[1] We may describe the Primitive Christian Communism as a communism of love, naïve because of the absence of all system—as the story of Ananias and Sapphira shows—but above all naïve because it applied only to consumption and not to production. It is therefore clear that it could not be of long duration. Also the impoverishment of the Jerusalem community, which was the cause of the Pauline collections, may well have had its cause in this socially and economically impossible form of life

the same Jesus Christ is present in living power in all, this Jesus Christ who represents in His person the new humanity, the same Christ who in His act of salvation recapitulates the whole history of humanity. In truth, it is right to say that the Ekklesia can only be understood through Christ and in Him. Ecclesiology is Christology. But once more we must emphasize that everything relates, not to an "invisible Church", but to the concrete visible brotherhood which calls itself *ekklesia tou Christou*. Thus to pay attention to the social character of the Ekklesia is a most urgent requirement for Christian theology. It is *today* especially urgent and necessary because only so, always at the same time reflecting on faith, can we: *first*, grasp the concomitance of faith in Christ and the Ekklesia; *secondly*, perceive and grasp the difference between Ekklesia and Church; *thirdly*, because thus and only thus can we recognize the peril of our time, which consists in the fact that humanity today is seeking fellowship in vain—without Christ; and only thus can we learn to know what steps in this search are leading nearer to Christian fellowship.

From all this we can see the clamant need of a Christian sociology as a branch of theology. The lack of such a discipline, the one-sided concern with the intellectual side of the Christian message, has had tragic repercussions and right up to the present shows its urgency in the fact that most Protestant theologians are so misled as to believe that the institution of the Church is the necessary visible form of the Ekklesia, and that the Catholic Church for its part makes the identity of Ekklesia and Church its dogma and thereby hinders ecumenical understanding. Were it acknowledged that the Ekklesia of the New Testament is not an institution, but that rather its social form as a world-embracing brotherhood is a necessary consequence of faith in Christ, while on the other hand each of the institutions that we call Church does justice to only one partial aspect of the Ekklesia of the New Testament, a very great step would have been taken towards the theological understanding of the Ekklesia as well as of the gospel in general. Yet we cannot make this thesis completely clear until in the second part of this work we have learnt the misunderstanding and the true nature of faith.

The Ekklesia of the New Testament is not only a project of faith implicit in faith in Christ, but this Ekklesia about which Paul gives us Christological and Pneumatological teaching is at the same time a social reality which impressed the men of that time, and which was especially disquieting to the Jews and roused them to contradiction, since, on the one hand, it was so like what they knew in their synagogue, and, on the other, was based on the "absurd" faith in the crucified and risen Jesus, as the Christ. They were able indeed ever and again to note that these Christians not only lived a life void of offence, but that in the Christian fellowship a "Spirit" unknown to them was at work. One of the pagans, a scoffer (Lucian) was the author of the striking saying "See how they love one another!" and thereby expressed, with an accuracy which can only make us wonder, the characteristic which distinguished the Ekklesia from all *thiasoi*. It was indeed also this spirit of love which ever and again drew Jews and pagans to the Ekklesia, this same love which was proclaimed in the apostolic preaching as the great gift of God in Jesus Christ.

CHAPTER 3

THE PRIMITIVE CHRISTIAN EKKLESIA AND THE PAULINE IDEA OF THE EKKLESIA

THE objection which necessarily thrusts itself upon us as a result of the picture drawn in the preceding pages is this: this Ekklesia never existed, it is an ideal picture. Granted that this picture is one-sided and does not take into account the human weakness, the all-too-human element, which was there even in primitive Christian times. The question is only whether the author is to be blamed for this idealization, or whether it is what Paul in fact *teaches* about the Ekklesia. The Christian communities of Corinth, Philippi, Colosse, etc., which Paul knows intimately, are doubtless not ideal fraternal fellowships. And yet Paul's teaching on the Ekklesia is the same as ours. Is then his concept of the Ekklesia a Platonic idea, an ideal of which the reality comes far short? No, the Pauline teaching about the Church is not a Platonic idea, but a concept of faith which has its basis in the encounter with the historical Christ, and therefore has a wholly different dialectic from that of idea and experience.

The case here is the same as that of the Pauline concepts of love, the new man, and faith, which all arise within the same fundamental context of the revelation in Christ. For example, the love which Paul describes in 1 Corinthians 13—is this an ideal or reality? It is in the first instance something which Paul has experienced in the Ekklesia and has recognized as a necessary consequence of faith in Christ. This love is a reality, a new life in the Ekklesia. But this love is nowhere completely and unchallengeably dominant in the Ekklesia. The new life is at war with the old. Faith in Christ has continually to defend itself and to assert itself against sin. For all that, just as surely as faith is a reality in the Ekklesia, so surely love and brotherhood are also a reality. When Paul teaches, he teaches the implications of faith in Christ. But since faith itself is always only coming into being, so also the Ekklesia is always only coming into being, not only in its outward expansion but in its spiritual and physical being. Yet a distinction is to be made between the Pauline form of the Ekklesia and its other primitive Christians forms.

(1) THE DIFFERENT FORMS AND CONCEPTIONS OF THE EKKLESIA IN PRIMITIVE CHRISTIANITY

The first point to note is that, in spite of the different tendencies in primitive Christianity, the Ekklesia was always conscious of its unity, even its identity in the different types of congregation and was also able to protect this identity against all divisive tendencies. In particular Paul was never in any doubt that the Ekklesia owed its existence to the mother community of Jerusalem. He acknowledged "the twelve" as original Apostles, as those who by their witness to the Resurrection had founded the Ekklesia. Even the sharpest contention with them[1] could not impair this fundamental conviction and attitude. Even though we may not be able to square the Lucan narrative with its account of the Apostolic Council, which glosses over the actual conflict, with the older and authentic account of Paul, and therefore are unable to give full credence to the picture of the Ekklesia as represented in Acts, yet it remains true that the original Apostles and Paul were reconciled, and at the end gave each other the right hand of fellowship. For faith in the Lord Christ as the living Lord of the Ekklesia was common to them all; and common also was the faith that with Him the new age of salvation had dawned and the new way of salvation had been opened; and common, lastly, was their expectation of fulfilment in His Parousia. Further we must make clear to ourselves that the original Apostles as non-theologians were hardly so sharply conscious of the differences as was Paul the Apostle-theologian. He, however, not only saw the differences clearly, but expressed the general significance of Christ and faith with such clarity as none before him or since has been able to do.

The Christian community of Jerusalem was not the only pre-Pauline Christian community. We know of others in Palestine, in Syria, and even in Rome. But we know but little of their faith and their communal life. The description of Luke in the Acts, as we have said, does not bear a close resemblance to the facts, since we must take into account the eirenic tendency of his reporting which would tend to smooth over differences. Yet Luke seems to rely upon very old and reliable sources. Certain fundamental characteristics which distinguished these Jewish-Christian communities from the Pauline Gentile-Christian

[1] Cf. on this point the Epistle to the Galatians, especially chapters 1 and 2, in which the two conflicting conceptions (of pre-Pauline Jewish Christianity, and the new views of Paul) are reflected, and are much more clearly recognizable than in the harmonizing account of Acts

communities are, however, evident, and correspond to what we would have naturally expected. The primitive Christian community in Jerusalem was in the days of its first beginnings as yet hardly aware of its newness and its difference from the synagogue. It is therefore understandable that it assimilated itself in a naïve and unquestioning manner to its model, the synagogue, and took over from it its presbyterial organization. True, this happened only to a limited degree because the presence of Peter and some other members of "the twelve" made the leadership of the community from the outset by these "pillars"[1] seem natural. Later James, the brother of the Lord, who was one of those that had seen the Risen Lord, came into prominence as the leading authority.

The Christian community in Jerusalem had, however, a position of special privilege even among the Jewish Christian communities, a position which Paul himself acknowledged in some measure. Jerusalem was the mother-community, the parent-cell of all the later communities, and from this drew certain conclusions as to its rights; for example, the right of a certain not exactly defined supervision and the right to request, on the ground of its own position of exceptional spiritual privilege, a kind of tribute from other communities in the form of collections for the poor in Jerusalem. From the manner in which Paul at the "Apostolic Council" had to fight for the independence of his Christian communities it is clear that two different concepts[2] of the Church were here in conflict, a theocratic-authoritarian concept and a spiritual one which in principle excluded all legal obligation. It cannot be said that the Pauline conception on that occasion entirely won the day. The original Apostles did indeed make three concessions to Paul: that as an Apostle he had equal rights with them, that his preaching of a gospel free from the law came from Christ, and that his congregations were congregations of Jesus Christ. And yet the continuance of the conflict after this event shows that the Jewish Christian Apostles had not properly understood his doctrine of Christ and his conception of the Ekklesia; that, in fact, the treaty of peace had not been able to overcome the contradiction completely.

[1] This expression, as is well known, comes from Paul's polemic in the Epistle to the Galatians against the Jewish-Christian conception: "James and Cephas and John, who seemed to be pillars" (Gal. 2: 9)

[2] Karl Holl's essay *Der Kirchenbegriff des Paulus in seinem Verhältnis zu dem der Urgemeinde* (Ges. Aufs. II, pp. 44–67) is still one of the most illuminating contributions to this subject, although some of its details may have been outdated by more recent research

On his side Paul acknowledged the minimal demands of the original Apostles, that a tribute to "the poor" or "the saints" of Jerusalem should be paid. His Epistles, especially his Second Epistle to the Corinthians, show how conscientiously he fulfilled his "agreed undertaking", as does the fact that he endangered his life in order to bring the collections in person. The unity of the Ekklesia was saved, but the theological foundations of this unity were not deeply enough laid. And so the conflict was constantly breaking out afresh, until at last the authoritarian legalistic canonical conception triumphed over the Pauline one. In fact, it even came about that writings expressing this conception were produced[1] under the pseudonym of Paul and accepted into the canon of the New Testament.

(2) THE PAULINE DOCTRINE OF THE EKKLESIA AND THE PAULINE COMMUNITIES AS ITS EMBODIMENT

Paul was the first writer, and the only writer in the New Testament, to develop a doctrine of his own about the Church which is explicit and therefore intelligible to us.[2] This doctrine is very closely linked with his teaching about the work of Christ and about faith. "Ecclesiology is Christology and Christology Ecclesiology."[3] But this is like what happened later to Luther in his conflict with the Roman Church; Paul was not conscious from the beginning of the special character of his conception of the Ekklesia, but he was conscious of "his gospel" and its conflict with "the other gospel" (Gal. 1: 8) by which he means the interpretation of Jewish Christianity.

The Ekklesia is for Paul the implicit consequence of faith in Christ and as such the necessary consequence of his concept of faith and his conception of Christ. The Ekklesia is the Body of Christ. This expression is of course on the one hand an inadequate figure of speech, for a body does not have persons

[1] The question whether the Pastoral Epistles came from the hand of Paul, or whether they must be regarded as pseudonymous writings of the second century, which indeed contain many genuine Pauline fragments but must as a whole be regarded as spurious, has been decided by critical scholarship, which has given its verdict in favour of the second alternative. In the light of Paul's idea of the Ekklesia we can only confirm this conclusion. The man who teaches about the Ekklesia as Paul does in the Epistles to the Romans, to the Corinthians, to the Galatians and the Philippians, cannot at the same time have taught as the Pastoral Epistles do. The reasons for this assertion of the spurious character of these Epistles are however not only ecclesiological, but also of a formal and biographical nature. Cf. on this point Eduard Schweizer, *Gemeinde und Gemeindeordnung im Neuen Testament*, 1959, pp. 67–79

[2] Cf. Adolf Schlatter, *Die Kirche des Matthäus*, 1930

[3] K. L. Schmidt, *ThWb* III, p. 515

as its members. But, on the other hand, the expression is certainly more than a mere figure.[1] It might actually be said that we can only truly understand the physical organism in the light of the Ekklesia. Thus the Ekklesia would be the *authentic* organism or body, because only in its light can we understand how something invisible makes the visible parts into a unity, and how it is possible to say, "the whole has precedence over the parts".[2] It is Christ the Kyrios, the living and present Lord, who binds believers together. He does this through His Spirit. It is the Spirit who creates faith. "No man can say that Jesus is the Lord, but by the Holy Ghost" (1 Cor. 12: 3). To be sure, the converse also holds, for the other proposition is also true that as a consequence of justifying faith "the Spirit is poured into our hearts" (Rom. 5: 5). In any case, Spirit and faith form an indissoluble unity. But faith comes into being through the witness about Jesus Christ, through the Word of "reconciliation", through the Word of the Cross. Faith is nothing but trust in Jesus Christ, in whom a new way of salvation "apart from the law" (Rom. 3: 21) is opened up. But as Christ is always proclaimed as the Lord, so faith is always at the same time obedience. Paul loves the play upon words which lies in "*hypakoē pisteōs*" (the obedience of faith). We must translate it by some such term as "hearing from below".

But what has faith or the Spirit to do with the Ekklesia? Through faith we receive the love of God as our new life. We ourselves become loving. God's self-communication in the Cross of Christ causes the man who receives it to become on his side one who communicates himself, one whose heart has been opened for the other man, one who gives himself to him. The Holy Spirit binds us, not merely to God, but to man. Paul did not think this through in detail. He finds the Ekklesia in existence as something which results from the *kerygma* and from the reception of the Holy Spirit, and he recognizes *agape* as the necessary "fruit of the Spirit."

Like faith, the Ekklesia comes into being as a result of the

[1] We must mention here the beautiful book by the Anglican writer L. S. Thornton, *The Common Life in the Body of Christ*, which is not so much a work of scholarship in the narrower sense as a theological meditation. Cf. also J. Robert Nelson's good and complete survey of the investigation and discussion of the concept of the Church, *The Realm of Redemption*, Ch. 3

[2] This thought seems to contradict what contemporary biology teaches about the nature of the organism, and also what Aristotle said long ago about the organism in *De Anima*. Of course, organism can be understood without Christology. What I have said above is merely intended to indicate that the concept of organism is most clearly distinguished from a mechanism, where the thing, or rather the Person who integrates the individual with the whole, and the manner in which He does so, is known

proclamation of the gospel. But it is equally true to say that both of them come into being as a result of repentance and obedience. Therefore *Baptism* as the outward sign of repentance is an integral part of the rise of the Ekklesia. Ekklesia happens, takes shape by necessity, where the Word of salvation in Christ is received in trust and obedience. Baptism as an act in contrast to this inner event has no *independent* significance. It merely marks on the one side the serious character and the reality of this inner event which demands to be made public, to be confessed, and on the other side it manifests the acknowledgment of its authenticity on the part of the already existing community or on the part of the man who has proclaimed Christ. Beyond this it is clear that Paul did not reflect more exactly about the origin of Ekklesia and the relationship of the obedience of faith or repentance to Baptism. There can be no question of his having ascribed any independent significance to the *act* of Baptism. Baptism is a seal which on both sides, on the part of the believer and on that of the preacher, is imprinted as "witness" of the inner event.[1]

Here is the link between the Ekklesia in the spiritual sense and in the social sense. In the act of Baptism there happens visibly what already has happened invisibly through the Word and faith. Inner membership of the Body of Christ becomes visible in this sign. There is no question of Paul thinking that this sign itself effects something which had not previously been effected by the Word. Baptism is not itself a factor in salvation except in so far as it is the making visible of an invisible event, the visible reception and entry into the community, and thus belongs to this inner event and constitutes its consummation. The baptized person says, "I now belong to Christ and wish also to confess my faith before the whole world." The preacher says, "Through your confession you show that you really belong to Christ." In this two-sided act of visible proclamation of an inner reality, the work that has already been achieved by the Word and the Spirit of Christ comes to its completion.

Since Baptism is not thought of as an agent of independent significance, any sacramental interpretation of it becomes impossible. But on the other hand it is clear that a purely interior loyalty to Christ must be considered as a loyalty which has not matured to its full reality. The visibility of the Ekklesia is surely one of its essential marks. If we belong to Christ, then we belong to the Ekklesia, just as necessarily as the reality of

[1] Cf. on this point the appendix on Baptism which follows this chapter

faith depends on its expressing itself effectually in love. The criterion of the effectuality is identical with the reality of the event. If we forsake other loyalties we must enter into the Ekklesia, the realm where men belong to Christ. Reception into the Ekklesia is the necessary final act of proclamation, which proves its effectiveness. In this sense Word, Spirit, faith, love, Baptism and Ekklesia form an indivisible unity.

From this the conclusion follows that in the nature of things the Ekklesia is both an invisible spiritual reality and a visible social reality. The Body of Christ is at once something which can be apprehended only by faith and something which is visible even to the unbeliever as a social fact. But this social visible entity is not an institution of the nature of the Church. Rather is its social character determined by its spiritual character as a brotherhood or fellowship of love. This does not mean that it has no determined order. Every "social reality" has a definite form and therefore also a definite order. The remarkable and unique thing about the order of the Ekklesia according to Pauline doctrine and in the Pauline communities, is that this order is a spiritual and therefore not a legal one. Paul expressly says that the one Spirit gives to each member *his* position and *his* function. Since Christ the Lord rules, there are no rulers. There are indeed persons to whom an official duty has been allocated, the *episcopoi* who are mentioned only on one single occasion by Paul. But this differentiation of the gifts of grace (*charismata*) does not create any differences in jurisdiction or rank. Paul knows nothing of Presbyterian or Episcopal Order. It was also an error to translate the word *diakoniai*, the "ministries", by "offices". The Spirit does not create "offices" but "ministries". Although we must not force the figure of the Body (of Christ) and must not claim "organic structure" for the congregation, the biological concept of "function" is more apposite than the legal concept of "office". Faith in Christ gives rise to a fellowship in which men share their life, Ekklesia, but not to an institution, a Church.

Just as it is certain that Paul's conception of faith is different from that of Jewish Christianity, so it is certain that his conception of the Ekklesia is different from that of the Jewish Christianity which had taken over its Presbyterian order from the synagogue. The difference does not lie where Sohm thinks it does.[1] His opinion is that Paul understands the Church as an invisible entity. It lies rather in the fact that the brotherhood

[1] Cf. on this point what has been said on pp. 30-31, n. 2, about Sohm I and Sohm II

corresponds, as a correlate, to the fellowship with Christ, and thus is not merely an object of faith but an object which, although in the last resort it can be understood only by faith, yet at the same time can be perceived by everyone. Granted that the empirical community of Corinth or Philippi is not without further qualification the Ekklesia of which Paul teaches in 1 Corinthians 12 any more than the faith of the Christian dock-labourers in Corinth corresponds to what Paul teaches in the letter to the Romans about faith. But the picture which the conscientious and critical Church historian von Campenhausen[1] draws of the Pauline community corresponds throughout to Pauline teaching. The basic thought is that of the Body of Christ, and "the Spirit is regarded as the organic principle of the Christian community. There is no need then for any determined Church order with its regulations, its commands and prohibitions. Nor do we find in Paul regulations of this kind laid down either for the individual congregation or for the Church in general" (p. 62).

"In principle there is no leading caste in the community and even the men of the Spirit do not constitute for Paul a spiritual aristocracy" (p. 68). "The community is not regarded in Paul as a hierarchical, graduated, stratified organization however constituted, but as a homogeneous and living cosmos of free spiritual gifts, which serve and supplement each other, but whose bearers can never exalt themselves over against each other or harden themselves against each other" (p. 69).

"Here there is really almost nothing to be seen of rigid regulations or customs which would govern the meetings" (p. 69). "In Corinth there is neither in practice nor in theory room for an office like that of the Presbyterate or the later monarchical Episcopate" (p. 71). "We must not picture things as if a community without a rigid order were in Paul's mind still incomplete and only provisionally organized and had yet to await a fully detailed constitution" (p. 74).

"The most striking trait of the Pauline picture of the community is the complete absence of a legal organization, the thoroughgoing exclusion of every formal authority within the individual community" (pp. 75–76). This is "all the more striking, since at that time at least in the Jewish Christian communities there was in all probability already a definite patriarchal office, the presbyters" (p. 76).

"Further, his conception of the ordering of the community as

[1] H. v. Campenhausen, *Kirchliches Amt und geistliche Vollmacht in den ersten drei Jahrhunderten*, 1953. The page numbers in brackets refer to this book.

a free fellowship which unfolds itself in the living interplay of spiritual gifts and ministries without official authority, did not at once disappear even after his death" (p. 76). As late as the first Epistle of Peter "the Church is regarded as a brotherhood". It is the elect race, the kingly priesthood, and the holy people (p. 80).

Thus, if we ask whether the Ekklesia of which Paul teaches is an ideal or a reality, the answer must be: it is both; it is what is true and real "in Jesus Christ" and thus "in faith". It is the real fellowship of real men, which Paul ever and again saw coming into being as a result of his *kerygma* about Christ. Thus he teaches what on the one hand he understands only "in Christ", and what on the other hand he has experienced as empirical matter of fact and experiences time and time again. The Ekklesia in Corinth or Philippi *is* the Ekklesia which he means when he speaks of the Body of Christ as a work of the Holy Spirit, as a fellowship of the Spirit whose ordering is determined only by the Holy Spirit inasmuch as the Spirit allots to each his special gift and corresponding to it his special service. There is not in addition a further "organization", for the Body of Christ organizes itself. It is just for this reason that it is called the *Body* of Christ. Above all there are no legal regulations which—as is the essence of law—might be considered to have a formal validity, so that because "it has been so laid down" things must henceforward take the course which "has been laid down". On the contrary, that is by the nature of things excluded in the Ekklesia, and so, as we saw, was in fact absent. Although the brotherhood is composed of quite ordinary men, it is not ordered by the will and the law of men, but simply and solely by the Spirit (*pneuma*), His gifts of grace (*charismata*) and His ministries (*diakoniai*).

This may seem fantastic to us. We cannot repress the question: Did this charismatic order actually work? Was there not perpetual strife, or at the least uncertainty and the awkward question—what was to happen now? But this strange, this even wonderful charismatic ordering by the invisible Lord alone, did work. Precisely that is the miracle of the Ekklesia, which certainly Paul and the other Christians themselves regarded with ever renewed astonishment as a miracle. Even the worldwide scope of the Ekklesia was not able—and that is a second miracle—to call the charismatic leadership and order in question. The brotherhood in the house-community of Colosse knew itself as the same Body of Christ as it recognized in those other distant communities of Macedonia and Achaea.

When it called itself Ekklesia it did not mean to say that it was one *community*, but that it was one manifestation of the same Body of Christ which also manifested itself in Corinth, Philippi and Galatia.

The Church historian, with his eye on the later world-wide development of the Ekklesia, must indeed name this first stage, and the idea of the Ekklesia formed in it and for it, fantastic or "utopian". "Inasmuch as all compulsion, all permanent power of command is expressly excluded, the picture of the fellowship that results, understood in the sense of a human social organization, is utopian." "But the Church"—we would say the Ekklesia—"is for Paul not a human, natural entity, but an absolutely wonderful superhuman phenomenon."[1] In this judgment of the historian, "utopian", there lies this truth: that the Ekklesia of Paul was something *unique*. Anxiety about its continuance in the future could not arise in the mind of Paul, since he reckoned with the speedy return of the Lord and thus did not wish to build something that would last for hundreds or even thousands of years. But even if the historian, with an eye on the actual history of Christianity, calls Paul's idea of the Ekklesia "utopian", yet *we* shall not hesitate to acknowledge it as the necessary outcome of Paul's understanding of the gospel of Jesus Christ, and therefore as the necessary norm for all time of the believing fellowship of Christians, who are conscious that they have their foundation in Jesus Christ alone.

What united the Ekklesia or Church of primitive Christianity was not this Pauline understanding of faith and of Christ, but solely the common faith in Jesus Christ Himself. But as opinions in primitive Christianity diverged to some extent even in the interpretation of this faith, so of course also there was divergence in the conceptions of the Church or Ekklesia and its form. Jewish Christianity—here the New Testament scholars and Church historians are at one—never really understood Paul's doctrine of justification; much less did it appropriate it. And when we look at the history of primitive Christianity we must call the Pauline theology also a *unique* phenomenon. The Church which rose out of the Ekklesia as early as the second century had already not only not understood it, but forgotten it. The "Church of Matthew" (Schlatter), which leaned towards Judaism and the corresponding view of the Church, was more akin to it, and also proved itself to be practically more useful. The Pauline formulations are still

[1] H. v. Campenhausen, *op. cit.*, p. 69

Himself far more clearly than in the oracle of the lot which, according to Luke, the Apostles organized at the very start of the history of the Ekklesia, and by which Matthias was chosen as twelfth Apostle as substitute for the rejected Judas.

This implies a negative answer to the question whether an order of rank was implied in the sequence which Paul, in 1 Corinthians 15: 5–8, sets forth as a chronological one. No, there is definitely no order of rank in the sense of greater or lesser degrees of authority. This was established beyond any doubt after the great discussion in the "Apostolic Council" (Gal. 2: 1 ff.), and was a result of this discussion in the course of which the truly spiritual and Apostolic authority of Paul had won the victory over the existing tendency to a certain hierarchical order. The Holy Spirit had spoken, the equal authority of the Apostolate of Paul with that of Peter, James and John was acknowledged on all sides. But this means that there is in the Ekklesia no other authority than Jesus Christ Himself. It was not Paul that had won the victory, but Christ.

Therefore even the Apostle himself has no other authority in the Ekklesia than that of the primary witness to Christ and of the Holy Spirit. Where there is real Ekklesia in the heathen world, which has come into being without the activity of an Apostle, it recognizes the identity of what Paul brings to it with what it has already received from some other witness to Christ (Rom. 15: 14ff). The more mature a Christian community it is, the less is the Apostle an authority for it, the more he is simply a brother in Christ. Only where it is essential to assert the primitive witness to Christ in its purity over against false doctrine does Paul stand forth as an original witness and make use of his apostolic authority, in order to call back the Ekklesia to the truth in Christ (cf. Gal. 1 and 2). But in so doing he no more asserts his *personal* authority than he acknowledges the *personal* authority of other Apostles. Neither he, nor another Apostle, is able to do anything against the truth, but only for the truth (2 Cor. 13: 8). He, the Apostle, challenges the community "to judge for itself."

This gives us answers to two further important questions:

1. Is the authority of the Apostle transferable? and
2. What happens to the authority of the Apostles when they have all died?

The first question is to be answered with a simple "No." If there is anything which is in the absolute sense untransferable, it is having been present there oneself, the position as first link of the historical chain, the character of an eye-witness in the sense common to history and sacred history. It was just this which had formed the sole basis of the privileged position of the Apostle. Henceforward only one authority can still be valid, namely, loyalty to the tradition of the primitive apostolic witness.

The idea which is current among us, and has its sources in the Pastoral Epistles, that Paul invested a younger co-worker who was not an eye-witness with a quasi-apostolic authority, is just as impossible on the basis of a genuine Pauline interpretation of the Apostolate, as would have been at that time the acknowledgment at the Apostolic Council of gradations in apostolic authority. And the so-called transmission of Apostolic authority to an *episcopos* was even more clearly an impossibility where faith was understood as Paul understood it. For the *episcopoi* were those to whom was given the function of organization, and not that of preaching the Word. What the Pastoral Epistles seek to make credible to us stands in clear contradiction to what Paul teaches about Christ and the Ekklesia.[1]

This of course makes the second question even more urgent. What happens when the eye-witnesses die out? To this question we can expect absolutely no answer from Paul. He did not raise this question, since he looked for the speedy appearing of the Lord and the accompanying Consummation. An earlier answer which we gave[2] is correct, but requires amplification: "Since the death of the Apostles the Apostolate has validity only in one form: as the norm of the original tradition fixed in writing, the norm of the original witness, the New Testament."

The original witness crystallized in the New Testament canon is, in Pauline thinking, not a fully valid substitute, for no letter (*gramma*) can replace the spirit (*pneuma*). But an Apostle without *pneuma* is not an Apostle. The sentence should therefore be formulated thus: "The authority in the Church is the witness to Christ in agreement with the apostolic witness, as we possess it in the New Testament, so far as it is borne in the power of the Holy Spirit. The witness must always be an uttered word, behind which stands the person of the witness as a man apprehended by Christ.[3] This distinguishes the Ekklesia from the synagogue; bare scripture is not the authority, but scripture as it is witnessed to by the Holy Spirit and

[1] See above, pp. 40 ff.

[2] *Das Missverständnis der Kirche*, p. 39. (E.T. *The Misunderstanding of the Church*)

[3] See below, Ch. 13, §2: "The Rôle of Witness in the Rise of *Pistis*"

interpreted by Him. The source from which the Ekklesia draws is a double one, the Christ-tradition which has the original tradition of the apostolic witness as its norm, and the Holy Spirit which bears witness to Christ.

The New Testament canon is the vessel created by the Christian fellowship, in which the original tradition is collected, protected and, at the same time, distinguished from later tradition as regulating norm (*norma normans*) from the regulated *norma normata*. If the Church added to this its canon, the canon of the Old Testament,[1] it did so because it was vitally aware that God's self-communication did not begin with the history of Jesus of Nazareth, but went far back to the origins of the people of Israel. In this literary form is reflected the historical nature of revelation. God is One who comes. His self-communication has a historical beginning and a historical end. The Bible is the document of His historical revelation. But the Church allowed itself to be too much influenced in its interpretation of the canon by the example of the synagogue from which it took over, though not always in the strict sense, the conception of the verbal inspiration of scripture, and also the concept of a canon determined legally by a Church synod. In the history of the New Testament canon two things stand out; on the one hand the unquestioning way in which certain central parts of the apostolic tradition were reckoned from the beginning as belonging to the canon, and on the other, the long uncertainty of the Church's judgment in relation to the "boundaries" of the canon.

The expression in the Epistle of the Ephesians "built up on the foundation of Apostles and *prophets*" emphasizes, however, the other truth that the canon alone is not the foundation of the Church, but only in combination with the spirit-filled, oral exposition. In the Ekklesia, because and so long as the Apostles were still alive, there was no New Testament canon. The canon is clearly the successor of the apostolic authority. But it is not so as the letter, but as the norm of the living oral witness to Christ which originates from the Holy Spirit. Yet both had their unique and sole foundation in the truth of Christ, which is also absolutely authoritative for the Apostle. Christ alone is the authority in the Ekklesia as the Head of the Body. The existence of a personal apostolic authority had its sole foundation in the historical contingence of the event of revelation. And this

[1] Historically this expression is incorrect. The Ekklesia regarded the Old Testament as its Bible from the beginning, and only later, after the death of the Apostles, added the New Testament to it

moment could without loss and danger be transferred to the New Testament canon.

The element of leadership in the community on the other hand, authority in the sense of government, was not an apostolic function at all but a function transferred to the living Ekklesia by the Spirit, who gives to each member his *charisma*. It had no specific relation to the *charisma* of preaching and therefore remained completely without emphasis within the Pauline Ekklesia. Only Paul knew—and even he probably did not see it so clearly as we see it in retrospect—that a concept of the Ekklesia incompatible with that of Jewish Christianity was implicit in his understanding of faith, a concept wholly and solely founded on his knowledge of Christ, a concept which must ever and again come into head-on conflict with the Jewish Christian one.

History, however, left Paul behind, and forgot both his theological knowledge of Christ and of faith and also his idea of the Ekklesia. At the same time as the new non-Pauline concept of faith[1] took its rise, so did the legalistic conception of the Church, which misunderstood the nature of the Ekklesia and made of it a legal entity, a sacramental institution. Here, however, the motive power in the historical development was not so much the organization of the Jewish synagogue but something quite different, which did not stem from the world of Jewish faith, but from Hellenism. It was not primarily a juristic transformation but the sacralization or sacramentalization of the understanding of Christ which was the ground of the transformation of the Ekklesia into the Church.

[1] See below, Ch. 13, pp. 181 ff.

APPENDIX

ON THE DOCTRINE OF BAPTISM

Baptism is the sign, common to all the Christian Churches, of membership of the Church. The doctrine of Baptism, on the other hand, like the doctrine of the sacraments in general, is, as everyone acquainted with the history of dogma knows, like a jungle in which one can only find one's way if one is led by a fundamental conception. For us this fundamental conception is the Pauline concept of the Ekklesia. It is, however, not possible in the space here at our disposal to establish or refute the individual doctrines in the *pro* and *contra* of their arguments, or even to give an adequate account of them. But on the basis of this religious concept of the Ekklesia it is possible to understand and assess their basic motifs, even those of the Catholic Church. More in this short survey we cannot do.

Paul is the only Apostle in whom anything like a doctrine of Baptism is visible, and in his writings, as in those of the other New Testament witnesses to Christ, the correlation between faith in Christ, repentance, Baptism, and the Christian fellowship, is a *datum* which in the first instance is accepted as such, and which is not the subject of further reflection. As Paul develops this material (Rom. 6: 1 ff.), it is above all a doctrine about the repentance which is necessarily bound up with faith, about dying with Christ. "Know ye not that so many of us as were baptized into Jesus Christ were baptized into His death?" This dying was also sensibly and symbolically represented by the visible act of submersion. This does not mean, however, that Baptism was thought of merely as this dying with Christ. For the passage we have cited continues thus: "Therefore we are buried with him by baptism into death, that like as Christ was raised up from the dead by the glory of the Father, even so we also should walk in newness of life." Baptism is the point of transition from the death of the old man to new being and life in Christ. Thus the act of Baptism as such was simply regarded as one with the inner event, so that it might appear that without the *act* of Baptism this inner event would not take place.

But the whole of the rest of Paul's religious and Christian witness is against this interpretation, as is the fact that he speaks of baptizing with a certain casualness, when he says he thanks God that he baptized no one in the congregation at Corinth except Crispus and Gaius, and, as it comes to his mind afterwards, also Stephanas and his household. "For Christ did not send me to baptize, but to preach the Gospel" (1 Cor. 1: 14–17). And indeed he says this at the very point where with the greatest precision he avers that he laid the foundation of this same community. The man who speaks thus cannot possibly regard the act of Baptism as something fundamental. Since Paul has not expressed himself further about the relation of the act of Baptism to the inner event of repentance and faith we mentioned, we must assume that this external act had for him no central essential fundamental significance. We tried above (p. 42) to fill the gap which Pauline teaching leaves at this point, by an interpretation which, although it is hypothetical, yet in some degree makes intelligible what for Paul the unexpressed connection between faith or penitence, Ekklesia and act of Baptism, may have been.

There is not only no trace of evidence that Paul conceived of Baptism as a sacrament, but that belief contradicts the clear correlation of Christ's Word and Act with faith. Either we take this personalism seriously—then there remains no place for sacramental thinking, or else one lays hold of certain expressions of Paul which suggest sacramental conceptions. But then in view of his doctrine of the fundmental significance of the Word and faith alone, one must regard these as untranscended fragments of a type of Hellenistic thinking which is really alien to him, which confuse his clear teaching, rising from an unintelligible background very much as we shall find happening in the case of Luther. Above all it is impossible to harmonize Paul's teaching about faith and in particular his explicit teaching about Baptism with the thought of Infant Baptism. This does not mean that there was in fact no Infant Baptism in the primitive Church, or even in the Pauline Church, but it does mean that it played no part in his doctrine of Baptism.

The Catholic doctrine of Baptism on the other hand is unambiguously sacramental; salvation is imparted in an event which makes no personal claim on the man, which works automatically and mechanically, *ex opere operato*. Within such a conception it remains a matter of indifference whether it is an infant who is baptized or a man capable of answering the Word in faith. Catholic doctrine is familiar indeed even with uterine baptism in which by the mediation of the priest a foetus, which certainly is incapable of any personal act, receives salvation, the Spirit of God. Neither the Word in the sense of the intelligible communication of the grace of God in Jesus Christ, nor faith in the sense of the human answer to the divine Word is constitutive in this doctrine, although we must certainly assume that the references to Christ and His grace are intended to find expression in it. Catholic Baptismal doctrine which, of course, finds nothing objectionable in Infant Baptism is not only easily compatible with the Catholic conception of the Church, but is actually demanded by it. Through Baptism a human being becomes a member of the visible institution of the Church, or, better, he participates in its blessing of salvation.

Such a communication of salvation is absolutely incompatible with the concept of the Ekklesia as we have developed it. What in Catholic baptismal doctrine is understood by grace has nothing to do with what we find witnessed to in the New Testament as grace. It presupposes a conception of the working of the Holy Spirit which we must describe as magical. To this magically working Spirit there corresponds the fact on the human side that no faith is necessary for Baptism, but that Baptism is effective as an act of the saving institution, the Church. If we can find similar thoughts even in Lutherans, this has little significance, in comparison with the radical transformation which Luther's conception of faith brought with it. Their self-contradictory doctrine was obviously only created in order to give theological justification and legitimacy to Infant Baptism, which they were determined at all costs to retain, whatever their grounds for so doing may have been.

Luther's new knowledge of the personal character of faith as trust in the grace offered in Jesus Christ was bound to crack this whole sacramental structure. We become members of the Body of Christ through faith in the Word of God's grace, which is offered to us in the message of God's reconciliation in the Cross of Jesus. On the basis of his new understanding of faith this became clear to Luther: "no sacrament without faith" (*nullum sacramentum sine fide*). The connection with the concept of the sacrament was suggested by Augustine's conception of the sacrament as a "visible word" (*verbum visibile*). In this sense it was very possible to connect the thought of the sacrament with the Pauline conception of faith. But how was Infant Baptism—which was at that time, so to speak, the only form of Baptism to be found in the Church—to be united with this conception? Luther was determined to keep Infant Baptism at all costs. Both *sola fide* and Infant Baptism were to be retained. In the dilemma into which Luther thus fell nothing availed except the absurd assertion that in fact the infant had faith; an assertion that was made more extreme in post-Reformation theology by the pedantic claim that the infant in fact had real faith in the threefold sense of knowledge, assent and trust (*notitia*, *assensus* and *fiducia*).

The Reformers Zwingli and Calvin, who were disinclined to accept such an absurdity, saw themselves compelled to seek another theological foundation. For them also Infant Baptism was the only form of Baptism. In order to justify it they had recourse to another series of concepts which in themselves were thoroughly Biblical but none of which by itself alone was adequate to give a real foundation for Baptism as a sacrament. One thought was that of the Covenant which, reaching out beyond the single individual, had the power to include even the infant as a member of a believing household. Closely akin to this thought was that of the grace which is prevenient to faith. A third, of a more biblicist character, was that even in the Old Testament there was a sign of the Covenant which included the individual Israelite in the people of God. And to conclude—and this also was biblicism pure and simple—the appeal was made to the fact that the Lord Himself commanded to baptize and that in the well-known scene of Matthew 19: 13 ff. He promised the Kingdom of God to children.

We will not attempt to depreciate these thoughts. But there is one thing they cannot do, either individually or taken together; they cannot give a basis for Baptism, that is, for Infant Baptism, as a sacrament. While Calvin held to the latter with passionate conviction, Zwingli was the only man to reject the idea of the sacrament altogether as heathen. And yet he too, as we see above all from the struggle with the Anabaptists, advocated tenaciously the necessity of Infant Baptism. Why? One cannot avoid the impression that it was motives quite other than theological which made him fight so stubbornly for this rite which was practised over the whole breadth of Christendom. It was the thought that without Infant Baptism the whole structure of the Church might be torn assunder. A Church other than a national Church—and that indeed a Theodosian Church, a Church supported by compulsory Baptism—Zwingli could not conceive of as a Visible Church. The discussions with the Anabaptists were unsuccessful in convincing them, not only because they were "stubborn and obtuse", as they were accused of being, but because Zwingli's arguments *are* not convincing. His real reasons, however, of which he was only faintly aware, he could not give to them. "You come too soon with your idea, historical development has not progressed far enough, we must not endanger the Reformation of the Church by a threatening ecclesiastical anarchism." That would have been in fact the only conclusive argument after the concept of the sacrament had been surrendered.

What is the theological status of the concepts which have been adduced in defence of the argument? The thought of the Covenant is certainly a central concept of the Bible. But as Zwingli takes it over from the Old Testament, it presupposes an identity of the Ekklesia with the people of God of the Old Covenant which did not take into account the newness of what had happened through Jesus Christ. For this is the new thing in the Ekklesia in contrast with Israel, that one does not enter the people of God by being born but by being born again, i.e. through faith. The sign of circumcision had nothing to do with faith; it was applied, so to speak, *ex opere operato*. Also the thought that the fellowship or the "house" believes for the infant did indeed correspond to a concept of solidarity like that of the Old Testament, but not to Paul's concept of faith which equates being baptized with dying with Christ.

What are we now to say to Baptism from the standpoint of faith as Paul understands it? What is true of the Lord's Supper is true of Baptism. It is a mysterious rite which stems from the history of Jesus, a rite bound up with saving history, through which the Ekklesia reminds itself of what has happened in Jesus and at the same time knows itself to be built up by the Spirit of God present in the Ekklesia. This is what even the Catholic sacrament of Baptism at bottom means and intends. It is, above all, this which was striving for expression in the so widely ranging thoughts of the Reformers about Baptism, and about the sacrament as such in general—without ever really finding it. Because the Church was institution and not Ekklesia, these baptismal doctrines had to be, in one way or another, unsatisfying, unconvincing and contradictory.

In this oldest primitive Christian rite, taken already for granted in the Ekklesia and by it traced back to a command of Jesus to baptize, the feeling is concealed that in all the working of the Holy Spirit through the divine Word a mystery is to be guarded that cannot be expressed in any doctrine, the secret working of the Holy Spirit (the *arcana spiritus operatio*), which as such transcends all theological understanding and must be "left *in situ*" by us simply as a mystery. Baptism in particular is the event which points to the grace and the prevenience of Him Who is the foundation of the Church. In this sense even Infant Baptism could be acknowledged and rightly administered, as the sign that points to Him, His grace which precedes all preaching and all faith. Especially in the true Ekklesia, parents who believed in Christ must have placed their children who as yet did not understand a single word under the hand of blessing of Him who is "the Father of every family in heaven and on earth" (Eph. 3: 15), in the certainty that as to believers, so also to their children, His grace and His loving Fatherhood is assured in Jesus Christ, with the prayer to fulfil this promise. They also wished that His name should be joined with the name of this child of theirs and that it should thereby be placed under His power and His protection.

Directly implicit in the nature of the Ekklesia is the knowledge that no man can say when God's Spirit began to work in him. Even in the case of those who are as yet incapable of faith, the intention of the Spirit is towards fellowship, that fellowship which in faith is known and realized as a fellowship with the Father through the Son in the Holy Spirit, and at the same time as a fellowship with men.

CHAPTER 4

THE DEVELOPMENT OF THE EKKLESIA INTO THE CHURCH

ALTHOUGH our theme is not Church history, but the Christian doctrine of the Church, a chapter of a historical character is necessary to answer the question, "How did the Ekklesia of primitive Christianity turn into the Church?"

We Protestants cannot avoid putting this question, because it is at once clear to us that here a disastrous misdevelopment has taken place. The Church which is the end-product of this development—the Roman Catholic Church—is certainly not identical with what we know as the Ekklesia of the New Testament, but something fundamentally different. How did this mighty, imposing but also strange structure, the Catholic Church, grow out of the Ekklesia? For us this historical question is at the same time a theological and personal question because the Churches of the Reformation also share in this development, and because the word "Church" which we also use inescapably fetters us to the Roman Catholic misunderstanding.

Light is best thrown on the problem by our contrasting on the one hand the point of origin of this history, and on the other its end-result: the New Testament Ekklesia on the one side as it understood itself in the writings of Paul; and the Roman Catholic Church on the other side as it understands itself in the authoritative definitions of the Codex of Canon Law of 1917. How did the one come to develop out of the other? how from the brotherhood governed only by the Holy Spirit, in which there was no element of legality, did there arise that Church which juristically directs in a Codex of Canon Law the whole life of the Church and depicts itself as an authoritarian structure like a totalitarian State, whose name is the Roman Church and whose spiritual nature is declared to be inseparable from the institution with its ecclesiastical law, and is indeed declared by dogma to be indistinguishable from it?

By small, almost unnoticeable, steps, not by a violent revolution, the one grew out of the other. If continuous process is regarded as the decisive characteristic of development, then the Roman Papal Church has gradually developed out of the

Ekklesia, and this development can then be easily conceived of as an "evolution", an unfolding of essential characteristics present in the original seed. In this light Catholic thought regards it[1] and therefore is not perturbed by the obvious difference between the primitive Christian Ekklesia and the Roman Catholic Church.

True, the oak is different from the acorn, but everyone acknowledges that what is implicit in the acorn has become explicit in the oak. The view taken by Protestantism is quite different. It also sees the gradual process, but it sees in every one of the almost imperceptible steps a continual alienation from the original, and condemns therefore the whole "development" as a progressive deformation, as an ever-increasing self-misunderstanding of the Ekklesia. The *causal* concept of "development" is indifferent to this opposition; both processes can equally well be called development. But the *teleological* concept of development places us before an alternative. The train runs either in the wrong direction, or in the right, in both cases continuously. Looking at the end-result Protestantism can admit no question; the totalitarian authoritarian structure, the Roman Catholic Church, is, from the standpoint of the New Testament, an incredible misunderstanding, and the "development" which has taken this course is a tragical misdevelopment, the history of an aberration, where every step forwards is in reality a step away from the truth. We say this not with polemical intent, but solely in the interests of clarity. It is in this way that the "development" must be regarded, where the Ekklesia of Paul is the norm.

To some it appears limitless presumption to look back on history in such a critical manner. They hold with Hegel that "all that is real is rational." God has made it so, or at least has allowed it to become so, therefore it must be right. We are not authorized to sit in judgment over history. This "historical tolerance" overlooks the fact—as indeed does all radical tolerance—that it is in the last resort self-stultifying. If everything historical, just because it was and has come into being, is

[1] I am well aware that in addition to this legalistic self-understanding of the Roman Church there is also another quite different self-understanding in terms of faith or mysticism, which found expression in violent protests against this conception of mine when I expounded it earlier in *The Misunderstanding of the Church*. Cf. O. Bauhofer in "Schweizer Rundschau", 1953, pp. 407 ff. To this I must reply that the self-understanding formulated in *Corpus Iuris Canonici* is that expressed by the highest authorities and acknowledged as possessing more or less the status of Dogma. It will become clear in the sixth chapter that I am very well acquainted with the non legally-conditioned elements in the Catholic Church and assign to them a high positive value

accepted without criticism, then we end up in pure self-contradiction. Then we must at the same time approve the Catholic Church *and* Protestantism, at the same time approve of the *ancien régime* and the French Revolution, at the same time approve of Christian faith *and* nihilism, at the same time say "yes" *and* "no" to everything. The Christian belief in Providence is necessary in its place, but as a fundamental concept of the philosophy of history it is disastrous, just as is Hegel's own belief in Providence, to which he appeals in his *Philosophy of History*.

But now—what were the decisive steps which turned the Ekklesia into the Roman Catholic Church? Above all, where does the first deviation in the wrong direction occur, and whence comes the constant *direction* of this evolution?

Our thesis is as follows: the origin of the Roman Catholic Church, hardly yet recognizable as such, lies in two factors which reciprocally influenced each other: the sacramental view of salvation and the assertion of formal legal authority. At the same time we must concede that both were implicit in seminal form in a certain tendency in primitive Christianity, but they do not belong to the essence of faith in Christ, and were there in contradiction to the Ekklesia, thus without any right to be there.[1]

(1) THE SACRAMENTAL UNDERSTANDING OF SALVATION

The real point of departure, the crystallization-point of the deviation, is the fact that the Lord's Supper was no longer

[1] In O. Karrer's book already referred to (p. 47 above), the learned Catholic author expounds a sympathetic, ecumenically eirenical thesis. "It is a moral presupposition to respect their *bona fides*" (p. 19). But on the other hand I find in his discussion of my book *The Misunderstanding of the Church* that both his representation of my ideas and also his counter-arguments are tinged by a fundamental attitude of smiling irony, which certainly does not help him to fulfil his intention of serious appreciation and discussion. E.g. "How blind we are, not to have read this out of Paul till now" (p. 51). It was precisely thus that men objected to Luther in his day. As a matter of fact, Karrer's argument consists in the assertion of the fact that besides Paul's there was also a quite different conception of apostolic authority and Church order, and thus that the Protestant principle of scripture cannot be carried through. In fact this is the case if the principle of scripture is understood in the orthodox fundamentalist sense, that is, in the sense of formal authority. Karrer says ironically "Should we not rather say instead of 'scripture alone'—'the Professor alone'?" (p. 54). I understand that it is hard for Catholics to follow my thoughts, for whenever authority is mentioned they at once think of formal authority. Thus they cannot see in the manner in which I seek to understand Paul and his concept of the Ekklesia anything but professorial arrogance and subjectivism. Perhaps in the second part of this book the actual criterion of my decisions will be rather more clearly and better protected from the reproach of subjectivism. But it always remains improbable that a genuine Catholic will ever allow himself to be persuaded by a genuine Protestant

understood in its original significance but in a sense foreign to personal faith and the Ekklesia, namely a sacramental sense, and thereby became an authentic means of salvation. Originally, that is, in Paul's view and in the Pauline Ekklesia, the Lord's Supper was an act of fellowship which the faithful continually repeated according to the Lord's command, in order to build themselves up as a fellowship in Christ and with Him; above all, to strengthen their hope in the coming of the Lord Jesus in His glory in the Parousia.

According to the oldest tradition (1 Cor. 11: 23 ff.) Jesus founded this meal as a rite on the night before His death, by His action and words giving His disciples to understand that in His (imminent) death on the Cross God would take the decisive action for the establishment of the New Covenant, the Messianic Age of salvation, in so far as this act and word of God should be laid hold of in faith. He underlined the nature of this act and word by not only speaking, but also accompanying His words with a symbolic action: the breaking of the bread and the giving of the cup, and thus drew His disciples into this action as its recipients. So on that night not only was the rite, the meal, instituted, but—in anticipation of what was about to happen on the following day—the New Covenant itself. That first Lord's Supper was thus the founding of the Ekklesia as the fellowship of those who were bound to God and to each other by the death of Jesus.

When the fellowship of the faithful after His death repeated this act of institution by His command, they received assurance that the death of Jesus was their life, namely the new life in the presence of the Lord, and also the foundation of their faith, as their union through the bond of love. But at the same time also that which had happened, the death of Jesus, became the certainty of His return, the anticipation of the perfect communion feast in the Kingdom of God to which Jesus had made a prophetic allusion on that evening. Thus the Supper in a wonderful manner united the faith, the love, and the hope of the first Christians, and served to establish anew their bond of brotherhood, after its previous establishment by the preaching of the Apostles. It is the already existing Ekklesia which repeats the first Lord's Supper.

The later interest in the material elements of bread and wine is missing both in the New Testament accounts and in the Pauline teaching. There is no word of a sacramental magic happening, of a "miracle" either in the account of the first Lord's Supper or in Paul—who is indeed the only person who gives instruction about the Lord's Supper (1 Cor. 10: 16, 17). How could there be the thought of any such thing, seeing that in the first celebration of the Supper the broken body and the shed blood were still present, unbroken and unshed in the bodily presence of Jesus? It is to this that 1 Corinthians 10 refers.

Thus the Lord's Supper is understood by Paul as the repetition of events that happened for the first time on that evening before the crucifixion—"Do this in remembrance of me"—and it is now, after the Resurrection of Jesus, at the same time the feast of fellowship with the Risen Lord, and thus the continually repeated re-establishment of the fellowship of believers. What has happened, what is happening in the present and what will happen, are woven together in one through the common action of the brothers in Christ in a unique and at the same time symbolic and real manner, through a rite of common action, of mutual giving and receiving from one another; a rite, however, which was not invented or created by the fellowship, but was instituted by the Lord Himself in that evening hour within the story of the passion of Jesus, and thus is a part of the saving event and itself a part of that same saving history and history of the Passion.

Is the Lord's Supper celebrated by the Pauline community symbolic? Yes, certainly, for it is the same as that first Supper where Jesus was still Himself bodily present, and where consequently there could as yet be no talk of a transubstantiation of "elements" in a miraculous sense. With bread and wine Jesus *said* something, He underlined what He was saying in His words, and oriental man had no difficulty in understanding such sign-language. Are we to understand the Last Supper realistically? Certainly, for what Jesus said will happen in massive reality on the next day, and this historical event is for faith the act and word of God, and thus for faith the reality of His Word of reconciliation on which everything depends. Is the Last Supper a miracle? Yes, certainly, for what greater miracle could there be than the institution of God's covenant with sinners? But it is not a miracle in the sense that something happens to the bread and wine so that this "magical" event deserves special attention. It is the great miracle of the grace of God, but not the prodigy of the transubstantiation of the elements.

That this interpretation of ours is on the right lines is shown specially by the manner of Paul's teaching, in 1 Corinthians 10, about the Lord's Supper. "The bread that we break, is it not the communion of the Body of Christ? Because it is one bread, we, who are many, are one body." The "Body of Christ" has here a double sense. First the historical: the Body is the Body of Christ broken then and there. But it is at the same time the "Body of Christ" in the sense in which Paul always speaks of it at other times: the Body of Christ is the Ekklesia. The Lord's Supper is the feast at which the Ekklesia is instituted. This is again made specially clear by what Paul censures as unworthy eating and drinking (1 Cor. 11: 27). What he censures is that a number of Corinthians should eat and drink without having any regard for the others. Thus, through the disturbance of the fellowship of the Ekklesia it happens that "the Body of Christ is despised" and this feast is treated like an ordinary meal.

This last fact draws our attention to a further significant characteristic of the celebration of the Supper, to the emphatically non-cultic, one might almost say everyday character of the celebration of the Supper. In its simple form it is closely akin to the Jewish *Chabura*, the customary daily supper in a pious Jewish family, in which bread was broken and the "cup of thanksgiving" was passed round. By this simplicity of an everyday supper it is distinguished from the cult-rites of the mystery religions. As it was in the earliest times daily celebrated in the houses of the faithful, it was the hallowing of everyday living. For this reason Paul censures some for doing this unworthily: "For in eating every one taketh before other his own supper, and one is hungry, and another is drunken" (1 Cor. 11: 21). Hence the question—"What? have ye not houses for (mere) eating and drinking in? or do you despise the Ekklesia of God and shame them that have not?" (1 Cor. 11: 22). If the Lord's Supper had not been something scarcely different from hallowed everyday practice, such disorderliness would not have arisen.

We must not close this discussion without conceding that the sacramental tradition of many centuries makes it hard for us to grasp the unsacramental thought of the Apostle, and all the more because the language of Paul himself suggests certain echoes of sacramental thought which may have come from his Hellenistic environment and interwoven themselves with his completely non-sacramental, personal thinking, as we have seen was far more decidedly the case in Martin Luther's rediscovery of the personal concept of faith and of the Ekklesia.

This primitive Christian Lord's Supper, reported by the three synoptic evangelists and Paul, and made the subject of instruction by Paul alone, is fundamentally different from what was later called the Sacrament of the altar or the Mystery of the Eucharist. The very fact that, apart from the synoptic accounts, this rite is mentioned only twice in the New Testament, 1 Corinthians 10: 16, 17, and 1 Corinthians 11: 20–29, tells against the sacramental conception. If it were a Sacrament, that is, the bestowal of salvation, then it would necessarily be clearly taught as the decisive thing, and would be made the central theme of the preaching. But not only the word, but even the concept "Sacrament" is unknown to the New Testament. The Lord's Supper is never brought together with Baptism under one co-ordinating concept. An unprejudiced reader of the New Testament would never think that this meal was the decisive thing, and yet it would have to be, if it were a Sacrament. Nowhere does the reader get the impression that this rite as Sacrament stood beside the Word and was of equal importance with it, as is suggested by the formula of Lutheranism, "Word and Sacrament". A Sacrament is something sacred—and it is precisely this character which is lacking in the Lord's Supper of the Ekklesia. And conversely we find in the Ekklesia brotherhood nothing of a distinction between a bestower and a recipient, between priests and laity. Paul never says that in the Lord's Supper which the Ekklesia celebrates, someone, and in fact always the same person, took over the rôle of Jesus and thereby was lifted into prominence above the rest of the crowd. As late as the first letter of Peter, it is only because there are as yet no special persons who hold the rank of priests and exercise the priestly right of administering the Sacrament that the Ekklesia can be called "a priestly people". The Sacrament belongs just as much to the institution of the Church as the fellowship-meal belongs to the Ekklesia.

But when the Lord's Supper is conceived of as Sacrament, there takes place a fundamental sociological change in the structure of the Ekklesia.

(*a*) The Ekklesia, the brotherhood or fellowship with one another which is rooted in fellowship with Christ, turns into an "association for profit". This is concerned with the dispensing and reception of a means of salvation which is administered by a person who is qualified for the task and legally appointed to it, a priest. Christ is present in a thing, concealed in the elements. The various "participants", even though this thing is a *supernaturally* material thing, are not immediately and personally bound together with one another, but only mediately by the reception of the same sacramental grace.

(*b*) As a result of this misunderstanding of the Lord's Supper as a Sacrament, the Supper itself gains a dominating significance and becomes incomparably more important than any spoken word. Anyone who conceives the Lord's Supper thus, namely as a Sacrament, can have no doubt that as the real thing, as the means of salvation, it is of incomparable importance. The Supper, understood as Sacrament, is now placed without competitor in the centre; everything else is only of secondary importance, subordinate to it. The Ekklesia becomes, above all, this—a sacred institution, a holy priesthood, which dispenses the means of salvation; while the relation of the recipient to this institution, the "Holy Church", remains undefined and has so remained until the present day.

(*c*) A further result is that the act of administration, the delivery of the means of salvation, is contrasted with the act of reception as superior to it. In the Ekklesia it is known that the community is a brotherhood which together celebrates the Supper. No special accent falls on the administering, not a word is said of a differentiation between the one who administers and the one who receives. But if what is distributed is itself the means of salvation, it is inevitable that differentiation should enter in; the priest as the one who administers, the community as the recipient. The Ekklesia becomes the Church of the priests who, as mediators of the means of salvation, stand over against the laymen. How far the receiving laymen belong to the Church has now become questionable. So the Church is, in the first instance, the institution whose means of salvation the priests administer.

(*d*) This differentiation would necessarily receive a quite particular emphasis after the Sacrament began to be considered as a sacrifice. Everywhere in the field of religion the principal function of the priest is the offering of sacrifice. It is this which really makes him a priest, a holy person. With this conception the Old Testament sacrificial cultus penetrated the Church, a cultus which according to the Epistle to the Hebrews had once for all been abolished by Christ. There is once more a holy place, the altar, and with it a barrier between those who administer holy things, the clergy, and the "profane" people.[1] There is once more the division between that which is sacred and holy and that which has a workaday profane character. The Church is essentially *the* holy thing and it is so in the form of the priest and the altar. And the thing that was really novel in the New Testament—its transcendence of the opposition

[1] *Profanum* (profane) is that which is to be found before the temple. It is the exact correlate of *sacrum* (sacred)

between the profane and the holy, since, firstly, the brothers in Christ are all holy in the sense of being "called to be saints" by God, and since, secondly, the whole of everyday life was sanctified as "service of God" (*latreia*) because on the ground of Christ's self-dedication it was a "sacrifice well pleasing to God" (Rom. 12: 1)—has been annulled by the return to the division between a sacred and a profane sphere. The priest, the altar, the space round the altar, are holy; the everyday world of the layman is profane. Thus the structure of the Ekklesia has suffered a total change through this new understanding of the Lord's Supper as the Sacrament of the altar. The brotherhood in Christ has turned into the sacramental priestly Church.

(2) THE INSTITUTIONAL UNDERSTANDING OF THE CHURCH

From this change in the understanding of salvation arises a second: a changed understanding of the order of the Ekklesia. In the Pauline Ekklesia the order was, as we saw, of a spiritual-charismatic kind. The Holy Spirit gives order to the community by "distributing" to each person a special gift (*charisma*) and with this the different ministries (*diakoniai*) which, as services rendered, are fundamentally of *equal value* because they are equally necessary for the "Body" (1 Cor. 12: 15–25). There are indeed in every community some persons who are described as "leaders", in relation to whom subordination in respect of certain functions is expected. But this function of order is itself only one among others, and, at that, one which is little emphasized. But, above all, this charisma creates no rank, no power of command, no *right* to obedience. There is no other obedience than that which results from the acknowledgment of the one Lord who through His Spirit allocates to each his service.

But now there intrudes into this spiritual organism a quite different kind of order, the authority of rank, the formal authority of jurisdiction or power of command. The First Epistle of Clement makes it clear that, once they have been appointed by the Apostles, the leaders have the *right*, the jurisdiction of leadership in the community, and that this right must be obeyed, just because it has been decreed. The "leaders" are now distinguished over against the brethren as men with special jurisdiction. They stand *over* them in virtue of their office. The quite casual, unemphatic mention of the leaders (*hegoumenoi*) has now become an actual principle of organization. In apostolic times, even where the community was regulated according to the presbyteral principle of the synagogue, this element of order was a very subordinate aspect of the whole compared with the corporate life of the Ekklesia, and above all in comparison with the salvation it possessed in Christ and in the Holy Spirit. Further, this order was not a purely presbyteral one, but contained also a patriarchal, monarchical element. But because the community, as the "Apostolic Council" shows, allowed itself to be persuaded by the views represented by Paul, that Christ alone was the decisive authority, it was possible in spite of this fundamental difference for both sides to acknowledge the unity of the Jewish Christian and the Gentile Christian Church. But in proportion as the bishop came into prominence, things changed.

For now the first, sacramental, element is linked with this second, institutional, one. The Lord's Supper, which has become a Sacrament, and through this transformation has become the true centre of the Church, imparts now a dominating position to the person who as priest administers this Sacrament, a spiritual and legal authority. The priestly *episcopos* or bishop, as we find him in the letters of Ignatius, is the central point around whom the Church is built. *He* holds it together, he ever and again constitutes it through the Sacrament which he dispenses. Through the predominant position which he takes up, the fellowship has been transformed from a spiritual brotherhood into a group of laymen who are sanctified only by his repeated administration of the Sacrament. The Word entirely cedes priority to the Sacrament. The conjunction of the Sacrament as the essentially holy thing with the priest's office makes the latter, and with it the legal organization of the Church, into a sacred, holy Church law. This consciousness of office as having a sacred and legal character finds expression in the sentence: "Follow all of you the bishop as Jesus Christ followed the Father, and follow the presbytery as you would the Apostles."[1] And also, "But where the Shepherd is, there follow ye like sheep."[2] And also, "For all who are God's and Jesus Christ's are with the bishop."[3] "Only that Eucharist may count as the true one which takes place *under the bishop's authority*."[4] "But where the bishop shows himself, there let the community also be, just as where Jesus Christ is, there also the universal Church is."[5]

Now here not only have we sacred Church law, but the Christian community already understands itself as an *essentially*

[1] Ignatius to the Smyrnaeans, 8, 1 [2] Ignatius to the Philadelphians, 2, 1
[3] *Ibid.*, 3, 1 [4] Ignatius to the Smyrnaeans, 8, 1 [5] *Ibid.*, 8, 2

legal, ecclesiastical entity, as the institution of holy Church law. Now the Church is present, and, what is more, in the form of a sacred priestly and sacred legal institution. This self-understanding of the Church as an "It", as a holy and divine object which stands above the faith of individual Christians—this is the decisive step of deviation from the New Testament Ekklesia, not only in its Pauline but also in its Jewish Christian form.

Now for the first time the local Christian community appears as an entity. Of course the Church of Paul consisted of local communities. But the principle that in one place, in one town, there *must* be only one Church, appears only with the monarchical bishop. Again it is above all Ignatius in whom this change in the understanding of the Church becomes visible. *One* bishop, *one* community. In Paul the conception was that the one indivisible Ekklesia manifests itself in individual communities, whether they be house communities or town communities. Therefore it is no matter for concern that in the same place, Colosse, there are different communities and it would never have entered the Apostle's mind to make an effort to unite them. *This* concern only came into being with the monarchical bishop.

In this connection it is very significant that the passage from Deuteronomy should be adduced to establish this principle, a passage whose chief drift is known to be: There is only one place where God is truly honoured, namely Jerusalem. There is a fundamental difference between the saying, "Where two or three are gathered together in my name, there am I in the midst of them", and the legally constituted Church, which exists only where the bishop is present. What was earlier left to the free direction of the Spirit is now regulated by Church law, and —what is nearly the same thing—rationally regulated. The community has only status as the one community in the one place. The principle: in one place (for example, in one town) only one community, only one Church, comes into evidence at the same time with the monarchical episcopate, and necessarily so. The unity of the local community and the monarchical episcopate come into being at the same time as two sides of one and the same process. It is the rational juristic spirit of Rome which takes the place of the *pneuma hagion*—the Holy Spirit.

It is therefore also significant that the First Epistle of Clement, in which for the first time the legal authority of ecclesiastical office over the local community is emphasized, was written in Rome. By means of its letter the community in Rome exhorts the community in Corinth to restore discipline by acknowledging the *legal*, appointed officials. But it took centuries before this supremacy of the Roman bishop, which was logically implicit in the notion of rational order, was acknowledged, and the Bishop of Rome became the master of the whole Church. It is not the rise of the Papacy which is to be wondered at, but the fact that it was delayed so long. For once the formal right of the holder of office, the government by jurisdiction, considered as something at once spiritual and legal, had taken the place of the charismatic spiritual order of the Ekklesia, and the priest-bishop who administered the means of salvation had taken the place of the brotherhood that celebrated the Lord's Supper, the Roman Catholic Church was in principle present. What happened in the next centuries is the natural consequence of this first deviation from the original Ekklesia. The Sacrament of the altar and (holy) Church law created the Roman Church.

(3) THE NEW UNDERSTANDING OF TRADITION

A specially important step in the development into the Roman Catholic Church was the coupling of office and tradition. Before this, in the Ekklesia, *paradosis* (tradition) meant the true transmission of that which had been received from Christ. This had in fact to be demonstrated, as Paul demonstrated it to the Apostles. But now we are told the *office* (of the bishop) guarantees tradition. How little this was really the case, the experience of the Church in the matter of heretical bishops proved in no uncertain manner. But, for all that, it adhered to this linking of tradition and office, and even exaggerated it by holding since the time of Cyprian that the Holy Spirit was bound to the office. Since Irenaeus the first principle holds good, the guarantors of the trustworthiness of tradition are the bishops; since Cyprian the second principle holds good—the Holy Spirit is bound up with the office, guaranteed by the office, and therefore *that* Church *cannot* err, which is episcopally organized and guaranteed by the continuity of transmission of office. From now on there is a central interest in unbroken lists of bishops as a proof of the unbroken tradition.

Reference must be made to a further fact which is important for the understanding of the Roman Catholic Church: the development of theology and dogma. Theology has indeed other sources than this institutional one within the Church.[1] But now

[1] See *Dogmatics* I, appendix 3 to Ch. 11: "The Threefold Root of Dogmatics in the History of Theology"

it is held that belief in the theological sense is necessary, and that faith comes into being through the teaching Church putting forward certain theological propositions to be believed—*ad credendum.* This *credendum* was then defined in its principal tenets in the law of faith (*lex fidei*), and in dogma, and determined by Church law. Everyone *has* to believe this and this, otherwise he is a heretic and (since the time of Theodosius) punished by the State. Thus the witness to Christ effected by the Spirit is transformed into a theology which takes into account only the doctrinal element, the "content" of the witness, and which gives to this the clearest and most perfect conceptual form. And this transformation influences and is influenced reciprocally by the development of the Church as an institution, as we shall see in greater detail in Section Two. Especially true is this of dogma as something which is to be believed (*credendum*).

The common denominator of this development and of the development of the Church as an institution is the tendency to materialize the gift of the Holy Spirit and to place it at human disposal. Prophetic witness effected by the Spirit is not at man's disposal, it can neither be taught nor learnt; but theological doctrine can both be taught and learnt. Through theology the Church has control over doctrine, as through its orders it has control over tradition. Orthodoxy can be guaranteed but faith in the sense of New Testament *pistis* cannot. The means whereby the faith is taught is the catechism. From now onwards dogma is the faith whose content the Church—once for all—has determined, and now declares also to be obligatory for belief. What has once become dogma is by definition fixed once for all and therefore subject neither to criticism nor to further development. The rise of Church theology and of dogma thus gave a powerful impetus to the Church as an institution.

(4) THE PERFECTING OF THE HOLY CHURCH INSTITUTION

A further very significant step in the development of the Ekklesia into a holy Church institution is the transition from the persecuted "confessing Church" to the popular Church of Constantine. Now nothing is needed for Church membership but Infant Baptism followed by instruction in the catechism. The Church is now a national Church, and after some decades becomes an obligatory or compulsory Church, to which everyone *must* belong. Of this Church we must say not only "outside the Church no salvation" (*extra ecclesiam nulla salus*), but "outside this Church there is no possibility of existence"—within the Roman Empire. This state of affairs lasted practically to the French Revolution, even in the Churches of the Reformation, which took up the same ground as the national Church of Constantine and the compulsory Church of Theodosius.

Although these two factors do not apply to the Catholic Church alone, inasmuch as even the Reformation changed nothing in this situation, yet they did have a powerful influence in institutionalizing the Church. It was now clear and certain for everyone to see: the Church is this holy institution to which it is almost impossible not to belong. Anyone who opposed this development became either a schismatic or a heretic. By his anti-Donatist writings which culminated in the famous and notorious "compel them to come in!" (*cogite intrare!*), Augustine, the greatest theologian of ancient times, contributed not a little to the development of the compulsory Church, while on the other hand by his anti-Pelagian writings he supplied an important corrective, which was to become significant in the Reformation. As already stated, he had a great influence on the formation of the Reformed conception of the Church, the distinction between *ecclesia visibilis* and *ecclesia invisibilis* which was determined by the thought of election—understood as predestination—of the number of the elect (*numerus electorum*).

The view represented by Rudolf Sohm, in his second volume on Church law,—that the authentic Roman Papal Church came into being only as the result of a revolutionary change in the concept of Church law which occurred at the turn of the eleventh century through the penetration of Roman Law into the Roman Curia, is indeed right in itself; but he rated its significance far too highly. For it is merely a final consequence of the idea of sacred Church law; it only proves that at that time the canonical conception of law received a sharper juristic precision. This juristic innovation, and the doctrine of the Pope as the lord of the whole Church, was only the frankly worded formulation of a fact of long standing. The juristic formation of Church law and its clear formulation of the Bishop of Rome's claim to dominion over the whole Church led on its part to the division of the Church into an Eastern Church free from Rome and a Western Roman Church, and this state of affairs has, speaking generally, lasted till the present day.

On the other hand, it is no accident that just at that moment also the doctrine of the supremacy of the Pope over the Emperor, that is, over the civil power, was formulated by Thomas Aquinas and solemnly declared by Boniface VIII as a dogma which must be believed by every Catholic on the penalty of forfeiting eternal blessedness.[1] With this the latent totalitarianism of the Church institution, the Papal Church, became evident—what the future added were only still more extreme formulations of this monarchical institutionalism. The Decrees of Trent affirmed as dogma the equal authority of tradition and scripture, the Vatican Decrees affirmed as dogma the superiority of the Papal authority over that of episcopal synods, and culminated in the assertion that the Pope alone was supreme expositor of tradition and scripture and therefore, *ex sese non autem ex consensu Ecclesiae,*[2] could create and proclaim dogma. Thus at last the supersession of the apostolic concept of tradition by the institutional concept became complete. What tradition is, and what the scripture teaches, can be declared in the last instance only by the highest official of the Church, the *vicarius Christi.*

The *Codex Iuris Canonici* of 1917 which places the whole life of the Church and Christians, their faith as well as their morals, under the Roman legal system is the completion of the process which began so quietly in the First Epistle of Clement, and, in language still so reminiscent of the New Testament, in the letters of Ignatius: the apotheosis of the Church as an institution of sacred Church law, one might also say the juridification of the Ekklesia by office and institution. When we Protestants are reproached by Roman Catholics on the score of our subjectivism we can with full justification make a counter-charge. The Pope is the only person who is authoritatively inspired by the Holy Spirit; everything in this tremendous structure of the institution of sacred Church law depends on his inspiration, his *ex cathedra* infallible spoken word.

[1] Bull *Unam Sanctam*—Mirbt. p. 210, Denzinger p. 205
[2] "On his own authority and not by consent of the Church"—Vaticanum, Denzinger p. 490

CHAPTER 5

DELAYING FACTORS IN THE DEVELOPMENT OF THE EKKLESIA INTO THE CHURCH, AND ATTEMPTS TO RESTORE THE EKKLESIA

As we have said, the astonishing thing is not so much that the Roman Papal Church developed from these first beginnings of the transformation from the Ekklesia into the priestly Church, but that this development of the seed into the tree took so long. There must clearly have been powerful delaying forces working against this logic of consistent systematic development, forces which alone could make intelligible the slowness of the process of development from the First Epistle of Clement (*c.* 100) and the Ignatian Epistles (*c.* 120) to the *Codex Iuris Canonici* (1917). The Ekklesia of primitive Christianity was such a tremendous reality that it did not fall a victim to the process of estrangement without the greatest resistance. Where faith as the New Testament understands it and the life created by Christ Himself was maintained, this development into the sacramental Church regulated by ecclesiastical law could make only very restricted progress.

I

It is not possible here to follow up these delaying factors in detail. Both the sacramental and sacerdotal developments met at every stage of their advance with a more or less violent resistance. In saying this we are by no means of the opinion that these varying forms were, each in its turn, pure expressions of New Testament faith. For these manifestations of resistance on their side contributed to the stream of the general development. And yet we may say that there was something of the original spirit of the Ekklesia at work in the Montanist movement, which endeavoured to vindicate the Spirit as over against Church order; in Novatianism, which protested against the relaxation of the moral requirements of the Church; in Donatism, which did not wish to give up its right to judge even the priest, who administered the gift of Christ, by the "fruits of the Spirit". The monastic and anchorite movement must indeed be primarily explained as an expression of the ascetic mood of late antiquity. And yet this movement is at the same time a protest of serious Christians against an all too cheap sacramental

Christianity, just as the Cluniac and Cistercian monastic reforms have their deepest roots in the ethics of the New Testament. But the original Franciscan movement is nothing less than the incursion of the brotherhood-spirit of the Ekklesia into the mediaeval world, a movement which was continued in the lay-brotherhoods of late mediaeval times.

While all these movements strive only for reforms within the Catholic-priestly, sacramental Church, with the Waldensians begins the succession of those who repudiated the Roman Church itself and endeavoured to build afresh by returning to the primitive Christian, priestless Church. As we have already remarked, the break of the Eastern Church with the Church of Rome was the immediate consequence of the juristically established Papacy. In its opposition to papal Rome the Eastern Church has consciously remembered its old Catholic foundations, has preserved and to a limited extent enlarged them.

II

Like an earthquake from the deepest depths, the Reformation convulsed to its foundations the mediaeval world of the sacerdotal Church. These depths from which it broke forth were nothing other than the resurgence of primitive Christian faith—to be more precise, of Pauline and Johannine faith. From the knowledge of this faith there resulted inevitably a horrified realization of the antithesis between Ekklesia and the institution of the Papal Church. In virtue of his own tremendous experience of faith and his intuitive grasp of the New Testament message of faith, Martin Luther was not only the first but the greatest of the Reformers. He realized that the true Church, the Ekklesia, was based wholly on the Word and Spirit of God, and not on the Sacrament. He realized that faith is not the obedient acceptance of a doctrine but encounter with Christ present in His Word and Spirit. He realized that the fellowship in Christ—which even he calls "Church", although he had a deep mistrust of this word[1]—is a fellowship of faith and the love which flows therefrom, and thus that law has no place in the Ekklesia. He realized that the holy Church law is the total ruin of the Church, and illustrated this by burning the books of Church law; one of the first manifestations of the spirit of the Reformers.

Like his conception of faith, his understanding of the Church is also through and through personalistic; the Church is the community of the faithful, those who through Christ are

[1] See The Great Catechism, *De ecclesia* 4

"called to be saints" (*klētoi hagioi*). For this reason, because the fellowship is holy and spiritual in all its members, the distinction in the Church between those who are clergy and those who are not disappears. They are all, as is said clearly already in the First Epistle of Peter, "a priestly people" and the true Church is nothing other than this believing, priestly people.

But even Luther inherited the Catholic past, which had lasted more than a thousand years, and could not see how the fellowship in Christ could be anything else than Church. So he set himself to the task of creating a Church which should be free from the evils of the Roman Catholic Church system. What he really intended, what appeared to him as the ideal form of the Christian fellowship, he has expressed in his *Deutsche Messe*—a writing which has been found distressing by the Lutheran Church and Theology and more or less absolutely ignored.[1]

In it Luther speaks of three kinds of divine worship which provisionally shall continue to exist alongside each other. The first is the Latin Mass, the second is the "German Mass and divine worship". "These two kinds then we must let alone, and allow it to happen that they are held publicly in the Churches before all the people among whom there are many who do not yet believe or are Christians, but the more part stand and gape if they see something new, just as if among the Turks or heathens we were to hold a divine service in an open place or field. For here there is not yet any ordered and certain assembly in which one could govern the Christians according to the gospel, but there is a public incitement to faith and to Christianity"—in our language this would be called mission or evangelization. But

> the third kind, which should have (the) true nature of evangelical order, would not have to happen so publicly in the open among all kinds of folk, but those who earnestly wish to be Christians and confess the gospel with hand and mouth would have to register their names and assemble themselves somewhere in a house alone for prayer; for reading (of the Scriptures), for Baptism and to receive the Sacrament and to practise other Christian works. . . . In brief: if one had the people and persons who earnestly desired to be Christians, the order and manner would soon be contrived. But *I cannot and do not wish yet* to set up or to organize such a congregation or assembly. For I have not yet people and persons

[1] Usually this is justified on the grounds that only later did Luther realize the danger of forming sects. But in truth there is here a confusion between Sect and Free Church. In the days of the Theodosian compulsory Church, to which even the Churches of the Reformation belonged, all founding of Free Churches would have been regarded as sectarian

for this, and also I do not see many who ask for such a thing. But if it comes that I must do it and am compelled, so that I cannot with good conscience leave it undone, then I shall gladly do my part in it, and give the best help that I can.[1]

The Church which, instead of this, Luther set up is for him a second-best, which he provisionally holds to be necessary and which he justifies by two reflections: first, by the purpose that through this Church, the "visible Church"—through its preaching and its (two) Sacraments—faith may be created in those who are not yet Christians, especially the young. Secondly, that in every place where there is true preaching and true administration of Sacraments the certain inference may be drawn that a true congregation will be present.[2] Thus, in principle, he realized that the inheritance of the compulsory and popular Church of Constantine and Theodosius was something to be got rid of, and in "the third manner" regarded the simplest brotherly fellowship as something worth striving for. In this he came very near to the Ekklesia of the New Testament.[3]

III

The Reformation of Zwingli and Calvin took other paths because neither of these two Reformers appreciated so deeply and fundamentally the opposition between Ekklesia and the institutional Church. This means that neither Zwingli nor Calvin thought of faith in such personalistic terms as Luther. Although at first the New Testament Ekklesia in the form of the *Kilchhöri* was in his mind, Zwingli took over the inheritance of the national compulsory Church when he persuaded the Council of Zürich to carry through the Reformation, that is, the compulsory purification of the Church from Popery by State action.

[1] Luther's Works, *W.A.* XIX, pp. 74–75

[2] Seeberg, *Dogmengeschichte* IV 14, p. 358: "Thus the preaching of the gospel, according to Isaiah 55: 11, is always the sure token of the presence of a congregation of believers"

[3] Only in very recent times, when the Churches of the Reformation in the lands of the New World take the form of Free Churches and are fully recognized as Churches even by the Reformation Churches of Europe, has Martin Luther's *Deutsche Messe* again become a live issue. And yet even a theologian of the stature of Friedrich Gogarten in his book *Die Verkündigung Jesu Christi*, 1948 (The Preaching of Jesus Christ) makes the following assertion: "Luther knows too well that every such attempt contradicts the nature of the Church as the Church of Christ" (p. 385). Thus he, too, confuses the national Church with the Ekklesia and says: "Luther's unshakable grasp of the 'visible' Church, in which believers and unbelievers live together unseparated, actually serves the purity of the invisible Church whose nature is that no other than Jesus Christ has power in it and that no human law holds sway in it. And all that Luther says about order and law in the visible Church has the one purpose that the freedom of the Word of God in it should be assured" (p. 385). Thus according to Gogarten there would be no free Word of God in the Free Churches

By making the distinction of the *ecclesia invisibilis* from the *ecclesia visibilis* he was able with a good conscience to look on this Reformed Church of his, the National Church of Zürich, as the necessary visible form of the Invisible Church.

On the other hand Calvin, who in his thought about the Church was also influenced by Augustine, created a Church which without the help of the State gave itself independent form and which—a unique historical phenomenon—was at the same time a Confessing Church and a compulsory one, since every citizen in the town of Geneva was compelled to confess his faith in the form prescribed by Calvin. This Church was reckoned to be the true Visible Church.[1] He believed that in it he saw a reincarnation of the Ekklesia of primitive Christianity, since, by a very forced exegesis of the New Testament, he believed he was able to identify his Church order with that of the Apostles. But however violent this identification and however high-handed the manner in which he set to work realizing it, this was the form of the Church of the Reformation which proved itself strong enough to stay the assaults of the Counter-Reformation.

In succeeding times many attempts were made to restore the New Testament Ekklesia in a freer form. The multiplicity of the Churches, the so-called Sects which arose, especially in Reformed territories, is best understood by regarding them as so many attempts to solve a problem whose insolubility they did not recognize, namely the problem of forming a *Church* to express the new understanding of New Testament faith, and after the model of the New Testament Ekklesia. This task was insoluble because the Ekklesia of the New Testament is not a Church at all, not even a Free Church.

These attempts began with the first congregation of the Anabaptists, which was born of the spirit of the Reformation.[2] When the Reformers, Luther as well as Zwingli and Calvin, opposed the Anabaptist movement as "enthusiasm" or "the spirit of faction", we can today, in historical retrospect, understand their entanglement in the old tradition of the compulsory Church, and their consequent misunderstanding of the intention

[1] This concept comes in fact from Melanchthon, but is also implicit in Calvin's discussion in the *Institutes*

[2] In his work *Brüder in Christo*, 1955, F. Blanke has proved that the first congregation of Anabaptists in Zollikon near Zürich was based entirely on the faith of the Reformers, and by no means claimed to be the pure congregation—consisting of none but saints—of Jesus Christ. Here also there is missing any indication of anarchist and pacifist ideas. On the other hand, the concept of brotherhood is made central

of the Baptists, and at the same time the historical inevitability of this position which they adopted. When they called the attempts of the Anabaptists "Sectarianism", they took over a concept of the Roman Catholic Church which inevitably characterized every Christian form of fellowship outside the Roman Catholic Church as a sect. They understood the New Testament concept of the necessary unity of the Church to mean that there might be only one Church in one place.[1] That the Reformers thereby condemned their own Church was concealed from them by the fact that they claimed that *their* Church, the Reformed Church, was not a new foundation, but rather the true Catholic Church "reformed according to the Word of God", and the Roman Papal Church, on the other hand, a sect. They refused, however, to allow the Anabaptists on their part to make use of this concept.

The main reproach which the Anabaptists on their side levelled at the Zwinglian or Lutheran Church was that they adopted the principle of the popular and compulsory Church of Constantine and Theodosius,[2] the principle, namely, that everyone living in a certain territory must belong to this one Church, and in virtue of Infant Baptism really could belong to it. Against this the Anabaptists asserted rightly that neither this automatic membership—which finds expression in Infant Baptism—nor compulsion was a character of the New Testament Ekklesia. They were thus the first protagonists of Free Church principles.

This was the first and most important thing that distinguished them from the Church of the Reformers. The second thing was their emphasis on the decision of faith as the mark of the true fellowship of faith. In this also, from the standpoint of the New Testament, they may have been right, and in saying this we leave open the question whether the unconditional rejection of Infant Baptism must necessarily follow from this. On a third point also they were doubtless able to appeal to the New Testament, namely in their emphasis on the fundamental principle that, on the basis of the universal priesthood of all believers, the true fellowship of faith must have the character of a brotherhood and not that of a Church institution. On the other hand, the latest researches[3] have shown that the first

[1] See what was said above on p. 68 about Ignatius

[2] Indicative of this outlook is the fact that the Rescript of Justinian, which gives clear and authoritative expression to the principle of the Theodosian compulsory Church, is prefixed to such a sound expression of the Reformed Faith as the Second Helvetic Confession

[3] See above, note 2 on p. 77

community of Baptists did not think of itself at all in perfectionist terms as possessing perfect holiness, and that it did not in pacifist enthusiasm repudiate the State. The reproach of "enthusiasm" levelled by all the Reformers, that is, the reproach of subjectivism and illusionism, is at all events not justified in regard to the beginnings of the Anabaptist movement. Rather do the sources give the picture of a sober faith in Christ based entirely on the teaching of the New Testament as sole authority, a faith wholly in agreement with the Reformers' understanding of the faith.

On the other hand, there is point in the criticism of this biblicist lay-movement which Luther brought against his scholar Karlstadt, and which prevented him at first from following up his thoughts expressed in the *Deutsche Messe*; the criticism that the time for these things had simply not come, since their practical application could only have brought in its train a new legalism. It was clearly similar reflections which led Zwingli high-handedly to repress and in part to persecute the Anabaptists, a procedure which he justified by frankly most unconvincing arguments from the Bible. At that time it was in fact perhaps too risky to undertake at the same time the Reformation of the Church and the dissolution of the thousand-year-old connection by which Constantine and Theodosius had linked Church and State.

The Baptist Movement had to pay the price of being premature: it was thrust down into obscurity or into revolutionary opposition, where indeed in part it deteriorated dangerously. But its seed came to full blossom in the Free Churches of the New World, where also the Churches of the Reformation (Lutheran, Calvinist-Presbyterian, Zwinglian-Reformed) were forced to adjust themselves (and it was the saving of them) to the State principle of the separation of State and Church, and to organize themselves as Free Churches.

IV

The Free Churches of England and America are in part descendants of the Anabaptist Movement, in part "colonies" of European Churches which were, however, compelled by the State to stand upon their own feet. This holds good of Lutherans and Episcopalians just as much as of Baptists and Methodists. It is just this independence of the State which has created the new type. But this freedom from the State, this fact that they are all Churches which rest upon voluntary membership, is only one of their characteristics, and indeed that one from which they have developed the rest.

Through this fact of voluntary membership on the one hand, and on the other the fact of the plurality of different Churches existing in the same area alongside of each other, the Churches were placed under the principle of mutual competition. They could not simply continue the forms and structures which had been taken over, but were forced to adjust themselves to the new conditions or, to put it better, they were forced to give themselves the forms which suited their inner nature under the new conditions. The law of competition has had a beneficial effect in that it has compelled the Churches to exert themselves. Only by remaining vital could they exist at all.

Multiplicity must not be regarded merely as an evil, as we easily do regard it in the age of Ecumenism, and above all because our perspectives are European and our motives doctrinaire. Much of the great vitality of the American Churches is doubtless explicable as a result of the pressure of this necessity of mutual competition. It would certainly be a misfortune if there were only *one* Church in the U.S.A. But even in this case the urge of the voluntary principle would continue to be effective. By it the Church was forced to make clear to its members and to impress upon them that they were responsible for their Church, and to make them take the thought of self-sacrifice as a matter of course. How effectual this training in self-sacrifice was can be seen from the fact that these Churches not only meet all their own financial needs but, in addition, collect vast sums for home and foreign missions. Only those who have seen this on the spot can have any idea how tremendous is the achievement of these American Free Churches. There are actually congregations which contribute to missions and Christian service, that is to social work of the most various kinds, several times as much as they require for their own upkeep. And this is not the result of the givings of individual rich contributors who are easily able to afford it, as the European sometimes lulls himself into believing. It is rather the simple man's sacrifice for the Church which forms by far the greatest part of these contributions which are at the Church's disposal.

And this has one further very significant consequence. The Church member, from whom so much is expected, will have something to say too about the spending of this money. And so by necessity there arises in the Church a right on the part of lay people, men and women, to make themselves heard; to which right again there corresponds a spiritual duty of joining in the Church's work. All American Churches are—even if not in the same degree and sense—laymen's Churches. And this fact in its turn has an influence on the Church; the lay element manifests itself not only in the deep-rooted connection between Church and people but also in the necessary realism of its preaching and pastoral care. It is unthinkable that in these Churches, for long periods, preaching should be "over people's heads", and that preaching should have such a one-sidedly dominant position as is the case in the Churches of the Reformation in Europe.

From this co-operation of ministers and laymen there naturally results fellowship. This may at first be limited to certain active laymen, but the mere fact that they are laymen, and that these lay people are women as well as men, leads to an enlargement of the circle of Church members who are active in fellowship for the Church. Thus it comes about that in the Free Churches, to quite a different degree from our national Churches, the element of fellowship or brotherhood comes into its own. Even if this fellowship is not in the strict sense "fellowship in the faith of Jesus Christ" it is yet a fellowship which can take on this character and will ever and again do so in proportion as the spiritual vitality of the Church is maintained.

The greatest danger for this Church of voluntarism consists in the temptation to water down, for popularity's sake, to a bourgeois morality the challenge of the gospel and the claims of God. When this happens, the true substance of the Ekklesia, the message of the reconciliation of sinners, is lost. Central concepts of the Bible, like sin and grace, lose their New Testament sense, and the purpose for which the Church believes itself to exist approximates to a "natural religion" and ethic, and preaching becomes only too intelligible and pedestrian. On the other side the decisive rôle of the lay element can easily have the result that the interpretation of the Bible suffers from a repudiation of all critical Biblical scholarship and the Church tends to identify God's Word with the letter of scripture.

But here also the truth of the saying *Abusus non tollit usum*[1] holds good. The discovery and vindication of the universal priesthood within the American Churches is primarily a great gain, and only secondarily a danger. That it also had a decisive influence in the formation of American democracy and in the shaping of American life has long been acknowledged. When

[1] The abuse of a thing does not imply its uselessness

from the perspective of the Free Churches we see the Constantinian and Theodosian inheritance of the Churches of the Reformation in Europe, we recognize what a real curse it has been. We shall have more to say about this later.[1] From the standpoint of the New Testament the Free Church is unundoubtedly a more successful attempt to restore the primitive Christian Ekklesia than are the European institutional Churches.

V

Alongside the Churches of the Reformation and the Free Churches—earlier described as sects—there is, however, yet a third form: the Brotherhoods. Here after the success of the Reformation, that is, under the presuppositions of the Reformers' conception of faith, an attempt was made to realize a fellowship in Christ in harmony with the idea of the Ekklesia. Here the divergence from the Church as institution is particularly great.

A Brotherhood is a life-fellowship in Christ in which the element of divine worship is much more firmly anchored in everyday life than is the case in our "Sunday Churches". What happens on Sunday in divine worship passes over without clearcut boundaries into the workaday life of the Brotherhood. These Brotherhoods also stand on the foundation which the Apostle laid (1 Cor. 3): Bible reading, prayer and meditation are interwoven with the everyday existence of the fellowship. In this emphasis on the life-fellowship the Brotherhood comes particularly close to the New Testament Ekklesia. Some among them are distinguished from the mediaeval monastic movement by their inclusion of marriage and family within the Brotherhood. Others have erected the ascetic motif into a principle, in order to be wholly dedicated to their service to the world. These non-Catholic Brotherhoods are organized as "communist" corporations, in which this communism of love is distinguished from that of the primitive Christian community in Jerusalem by the fact that it is organized not only on the side of consumption but also on that of production. This introduces of necessity a certain legalistic motif, which can, however, be very much moderated in proportion as faith and love are active. From an economic point of view this form of "utopian communism" (Marx) has stood the test as little as other, worldly forms, and these Brotherhoods have therefore mostly remained mere ephemeral apparitions. The Brotherhood of

[1] See on this Ch. 7, "The Crisis of the Church in Europe"

farmers and craftsmen of the "Herrnhut Brothers" has alone been able to survive for centuries until the present day.[1]

It is highly significant that especially in our day the idea of the Christian Brotherhood is again rousing great interest, after the Church of the Reformation had suppressed this, like all attempts to form Free Churches, as sectarianism. Brotherhoods on a non-Roman Catholic basis are a thoroughly legitimate and significant attempt at the creation of Ekklesia, and give expression to a special and specially important aspect of it.[2]

VI

Each of the three attempts to restore the Ekklesia of primitive Christianity on the basis of the Reformers' understanding of faith, the national Churches, the Free Churches, and the Brotherhoods, gives bodily expression to a different element of the same Ekklesia. The national Churches of the Reformation, the Lutheran as well as the Reformed, proposed to reform the existing Church by the preaching of true Biblical faith. But by their identifying the Word of God too closely with the Word of Scripture, they forfeited the possibility of preserving in its fully self-critical sense the element of *semper reformanda* ("ever-continuing reformation"), which they had inscribed on their banner. Through their emphasis upon clerical office they had at first a great advantage over against the Free Churches and Brotherhoods, the advantage of continuity and stability. Historically speaking, we can very well see the necessity of this "conservative" Church Reformation, but with an eye on the present we must acknowledge its problems, which in the age of religious freedom have brought the national Church into the situation of the crisis of the Church.

On the wide view, the chief significance of the Brotherhoods is that they have been models and examples whose significance has been to remind Christendom that the Ekklesia of primitive times was a brotherly life-fellowship. Especially at the present time, when the hunger for true fellowship is great and the challenge to realize in practice the idea of the Ekklesia is confronting us ever more urgently, they are in a special degree significant as a reminder and a signpost.

[1] An exception is provided by the Japanese Omi Brotherhood, which, on an industrial basis, represents a Christian love-communism which also seems to be economically viable. (See the fascinating book by Wm. Merrell Vories, *The Omi Brotherhood in Nippon*, 5th edn., 1940, 1st edn., 1934)

[2] I am thinking, for example, of the Iona Community founded by MacLeod in Scotland, the Brotherhood of Taizé (France), the Sisterhoods of Grandchamp and Gelterkinden (Switzerland), and the Anglican monasteries in England

The Free Churches, which were formerly called Sects but which are now acknowledged even in the national Churches as "Churches" of equal status—as indeed they are today the numerically strongest form of Protestantism—stand in the middle between the national Churches and the Brotherhoods. The bigger and older they grow, the more they approximate in their social form to the national Church type, but they are able more easily to throw off the fundamental disease of institutionalism than the latter. This is because in them, through the elements of voluntary membership and of competition with other Free Churches, this danger is very much relegated to the background. The more the Church is conscious of this danger, the more it regulates itself by the Ekklesia-idea of faith in Christ. That is to say, the more spiritual life it has, the less it can fall a prey to institutionalism, and the freer it is to create its own social form.

Thus from this historical retrospect the conclusion forces itself upon us that none of the present forms, neither the national Church, nor the Free Church, nor the Brotherhoods can lay claim to be the Ekklesia of primitive Christianity. What we said above[1] is confirmed; *the Ekklesia of the New Testament is something unique*. But as an idea which is implicit in faith in Christ, it is the norm for all social expressions of Christian faith, which everyone must know and acknowledge who understands faith as the Apostles and Paul in particular understood it. For him the principle holds: Ecclesiology is Christology. For him it is thus a cardinal principle that the true "Body of Christ" can exist only in a fellowship in which that faith is dominant which shows itself effectual in love. For the Body of Christ is present only where faith in Christ and love of Christ are effectual.

But faith in Christ must manifest itself primarily in humility and self-denial. This holds true for every Church. The Word of Jesus, "Whosoever would keep his life will lose it, and he who loses it for my sake will find it," must in such fashion become the norm of the Church that it never loses sight of the maxim *ecclesia reformata semper reformanda* ("a Church reformed and ever willing to be reformed") and understands ever more clearly that it is there for the world's sake.

[1] See Ch. 3, especially p. 46

CHAPTER 6

THE CHURCH AS INSTRUMENT AND SHELL OF THE EKKLESIA

THE result of our previous investigation has confirmed the thesis that none of the Churches which have come into being in the course of the centuries is the Ekklesia of the New Testament. The transformation of the Ekklesia into the Roman Catholic Church has made it into something fundamentally different—the institution of holy Church law, in which, at least in theory, everything is determined by this hierarchical system of Church law, co-ordinated with it and subordinated to it. But even the Churches of the Reformation, which came into being as a result of the rediscovery of what the New Testament calls the Ekklesia and which made the attempt to restore this Ekklesia, did not attain their goal. They do indeed call themselves "Reformed" Churches. But by calling themselves Churches they have assimilated into their nature the character of an institution and have to that extent lost the character of brotherhood in Christ.

But that is not all that is to be said on this theme. For, in spite of this, all these Churches have believed in Jesus Christ as their Lord, the man in whom God was wholly present for man's sake, and who was wholly at God's service, and they have all confessed their faith in Him. And therefore something of His Spirit has lived and worked in them. We must now speak of this second theme, of this working of His Spirit even in the institutions, showing how these Churches in spite of their institutional character served as the instrument and shell of the Ekklesia, the instrument—the *organon*—through which the Word of Christ maintained its vitality in the world; as the framework in which something of the brotherhood in Christ was able to take shape. This positive aspect must be underlined in what follows.

I

We begin, as is natural, with the *Ecclesia Catholica Romana*. Our Reformed, Biblical New Testament faith will have to vindicate itself precisely by the fact that we do justice to this Church which confronts us in so strange a manner, and regard it, in spite of all profound differences, as a Church of brothers in Christ. For true though our picture of gradual estrangement and slow development of the Ekklesia into the Papal Church may be, true though it may be that this Church officially understands itself as an Institution of holy Church law, thereby making the Institution the object of faith as an article of dogma —yet it is just as true that this is not for the pious Catholic the heart of the matter. It is not indeed permitted for him to regard this legal institutional element as inessential to faith, but it is not the foundation of his faith. For him too the decisive thing is that he recognizes in Jesus Christ his Saviour and Redeemer and knows himself to be loved by Him; for him also love is of necessity bound up with faith. It is of this life in the Spirit of Christ preserved in the Roman Catholic Church that we must first of all speak.

The first thing that even we Protestants have to acknowledge is the fact that this *Ecclesia Romana* for centuries was the only channel which mediated the Biblical gospel to mankind. Consequently—at least in the West—we stand all of us on the shoulders of the Catholic Church. True, the assertion is incorrect that the Church from the beginning was this Catholic Church. But it is true that in fact it alone through many centuries was guardian of this tradition.

It was also this Catholic Church which preserved the Bible for the whole of Christendom in later days, which translated it, and made known its content through its preaching, its teaching, its liturgy and not least by its creative art, to the peoples of the West. Luther became the Reformer when he as yet hardly knew the Bible in any other form than that of the Vulgate version. This achievement of tradition is one which we cannot sufficiently admire, and for which we cannot be too grateful. But we owe to it not only the Bible but also the mighty treasure which we call the Corpus of the Church Fathers, those interpreters of the message of salvation from whom the Reformers too draw richly and some of whom at least they gladly acknowledge as their fathers in the faith. That this agreement between the doctrine of the Reformers and that of the Church Fathers was a very far-reaching one can be seen at once from the fact that the idea of the *consensus quinque-saecularis* (the consent of five centuries)—which was in substance taught by Calvin and Bullinger but was first formulated by the Lutheran Calixt as an ecumenical basis and received with enthusiasm by a Leibniz—found much approval among Protestants and Catholics. Here, however, we must emphasize that the reason why we can so largely identify ourselves with the doctrine of the Church Fathers is because it has not yet developed into the teaching of the later

Church, which is in the authentic sense the Roman Church.

We may further acknowledge with deep gratitude to the *Ecclesia Romana* that it was this Church which preserved this great and precious treasure in safety throughout the upheavals of migration movements, the onslaughts of Islam and the Mongol invasions of the Middle Ages. Indeed, to tell the honest truth, we must go a step further and say that without its stern hierarchical structure, resembling a totalitarian State, it would not have been able to perform this service for mankind. Even as convinced Protestants we must in historical retrospect acknowledge that Protestantism with its divisions and its lack of dominating leadership would not have been capable of such an achievement in world history.

And yet, as we have said above, even for a pious Catholic the hierarchical system with its Church law is not the decisive thing. It is the shell but not the kernel of the Roman Catholic Church. Within this hard legalistic shell there is the living kernel of spiritual life, there is a splendid liturgical treasure, which Protestantism has lost; there is fellowship of brothers and sisters closer to what is visible in the New Testament as *ekklesia* and *diakonia* than is the average life of a Protestant congregation. There is a *vita meditativa* and *contemplativa*, there is spiritual discipline, which altogether reminds us of New Testament days. There is, on the other side, an expansion of Christian thought into political, social and cultural fields, which is only too lacking amongst us Protestants. In brief, there is genuine fruit of the gospel in rich abundance, which it would be narrow Protestant confessionalism not to acknowledge.

Especially significant is a phenomenon of the most recent times. After the legalistic totalitarian emphasis on the Church system had reached its peak there began within the same Church an unmistakable process of assimilation of elements of the Reformation; there is in our time a marked return to the Bible which by-passes the Scholastics, there is an adoption of many forms of Church life which have grown up within Protestantism, there is, above all, an approximation to the Reformed understanding of the gospel which ever and again causes us astonishment. There is a widespread willingness for ecumenical conversations and even for ecumenical co-operation which would have been unthinkable fifty years ago. When we see all these facts, we are impelled to thankful astonishment at the wonderful ways of divine Providence which has preserved for us through two thousand years of history the apostolic message of salvation in Jesus Christ.

II

This appreciation is specially applicable to the Greek Orthodox Church. It has to a large extent remained in the condition which the old Catholic Church had reached before the development of specifically *Roman* Catholicism. For this reason the first reaction of a Protestant, when, as continually happens in the Ecumenical Movement, he first makes contact with this ancient Catholic Church, is a feeling of brotherly sympathy, and only subsequently perhaps one of surprise at some of its characteristics. He feels himself enriched and attracted by the wealth of the treasures handed down from the early days of the Church. He sees in this Church a Catholicism which looks back on a continuous history without massive irruptions of foreign elements, a history full of gallantry in the repulsion of external enemies, especially of Islam and the Turks. There are many elements of primitive Christianity which have hardly anything to correspond to them in the history of the Western Church—as, for example, the triumphant Easter Mass with its culminating point "Christ is risen, He is risen indeed", the monastic brotherhoods and the unique phenomenon of the *Stareze*, the hermit pastor—which fill us when we learn of them with pure delight and admiration.

We cannot indeed avoid noticing the almost complete absence of a will to change the world and the danger of an almost exclusively otherworldly eschatological orientation, but we must let ourselves remember at the same time the contrary danger of all Western Christendom, and consider whether perhaps this non-activistic Christianity may not have more profoundly transformed the peoples of the European East than the ethical pragmatism of the West.

III

Similar things would have to be said about the Anglican and Old Catholic Communions. They arose from the endeavour to maintain the Catholic tradition but to purify it at the same time on the basis of the insights regained at the Reformation. Thus they have a profound significance in the ecumenical conversation, because their historical and doctrinal characteristics qualify them to act as bridges between the Catholic and Protestant Churches.

IV

We must in the same way supplement our previous study in relation to the Protestant Churches. The Reformation was born from the realization that the Church system of the Roman

Catholic Church did not correspond to the Ekklesia of the New Testament, and that in its understanding of faith a contradiction of the original faith in Christ becomes evident; a contradiction which in the course of the centuries has become ever more radical. Even today there can be no retreat from this fundamental insight of Luther's. On the contrary, the progress of Biblical criticism has not only confirmed this insight, but has also essentially clarified it. The gulf cannot be bridged between the Catholic Church's sacramental understanding of salvation and the personalist understanding of faith as found in the New Testament and Luther. And he gave true expression to the idea of the Ekklesia which he had won from this source, when as a first great manifestation of the Reformation he burnt the canonical books of Church law. Here indeed he hit the centre of the target.

But now we have seen how Luther's intuitive grasp of New Testament faith and the Ekklesia found only partial expression in his Reformation of the Church, since this Reformation was impeded partly by mediaeval sacramental rudiments in Luther's own spirit, partly by the historical circumstances, and by the necessary consideration of what was historically possible. Yet the description of this aspect lies behind us, and we may turn to the positive aspect in reference also to the Protestant attempts to give shape to the Ekklesia. These imperfect attempts to give shape to the fellowship of faith of believers in Christ also became the instrument and shell of the true Ekklesia, and as such performed a service just as invaluable as that which we acknowledged just now in the case of the Catholic Churches. We shall limit ourselves here in essentials to the creative achievements of the European national Churches, since otherwise we would hardly be able to avoid the danger of repetition. The Protestant national Churches also have done this tremendous service to the Ekklesia through the centuries. The first word then that we have to say as we look back at history is without doubt a word of deepest gratitude to our Reformed and Lutheran fathers in the faith. By the *ecclesia reformata* the message of Christ was delivered in purer form than in the centuries which preceded the Reformation, even though, through anxiety about "pure doctrine", less than justice was done to the proclamation of the message of love.[1]

[1] Luther certainly said wonderful things about the love which flows from faith, and certainly the Protestant Churches can look back on a magnificent record of works of love. No one can read Uhlhorn's 3-volume history *Die Christliche Liebestätigkeit* (Christian Works of Love) without being moved by the love shown in the various forms of the Church

And yet this preaching has borne rich fruit in faith, in love and in hope, as can be learnt from the documents of history, above all from our treasury of hymns, from the biographies and autobiographies of Christians of the last centuries, and from the convincing confessions of their own experiences of faith given by members of the Christian Church of today. Above all, this *ecclesia reformata* as a tremendous ethical dynamic has moulded the character of the Protestant peoples and influenced the whole of life, the development of culture, the political and legal institutions and the social pattern, in the very highest degree. The picture that the Lutheran Elert has drawn in his book on the Morphology of Lutheranism could be paralleled by another volume on the Morphology of the Reformed Church. Max Weber's Essays on the Sociology of Religion[1] represent a striking, if one-sided, preface to such an attempt.

Such a picture would indeed have to include the negative traits as well as the positive ones, namely those which are conditioned by the institutionalism of the Churches of the Reformation, and further by their confusion between orthodoxy and true faith. From such traits stems that lack of social understanding and interest which has often been noted, as well as a great amount of intolerance and unbrotherliness. But all this that is negative cannot call in question the mighty positive achievement: the loyal service in the proclamation of the message of Christ. The most important fruit of this service can indeed never be scientifically or statistically estimated; the vital Christian faith itself and its life-changing power. Only He "who knows the hearts" knows this. But, on the other hand, we can assess what has become visible as "fruit of the Spirit", the influence of the Church on the shaping of society in family, school and State. The Church of the Reformation more than any other factor has given the Protestant lands that character which distinguishes them from the rest of the world. At this point it is especially necessary to remember what we said about the "colonies" of the Churches of the Reformation.[2] We owe it above all to these Churches and Free Churches of the Reformation that there is in this part of the world personal freedom, social sense of responsibility, free criticism of the *status quo*, critical scholarship, even Biblical criticism, free science and an

[1] Reference is here of course made to both Max Weber's Essays, *Die protestantische Ethik und der Geist des Kapitalismus* (E.T. *The Protestant Ethic and the Spirit of Capitalism*, London, 1930) and *Die Protestantischen Sekten und der Geist des Kapitalismus* (The Protestant Sects and the Spirit of Capitalism), *Gesammelte Aufsätze zur Religionssoziologie*, I, pp. 17–236

[2] See above, Ch. 5, pp. 79–82

understanding of the dignity of the person and also a sense of the dignity of service, though this has been more vigorously protected in the territories of the Catholic Church.

To this we must add a further consideration which is of fundamental significance. All the Churches of the Reformation have been conscious from the first that the "Church of the Reformation" (*ecclesia reformata*) as a human institution is always "in need of reform" (*semper reformanda*). But there can be no doubt that it was especially in the Reformed Church, i.e. that branch of the Protestant Church which stems from Zwingli's and Calvin's Reformation, that this consciousness of the "*semper reformanda*" was active. True, the Reformed Churches of the European Continent are structures just as conservative, just as tenacious of old custom as the Lutheran Churches. But this principle came to its full effectiveness above all in the Free Churches of the New World (particularly in the U.S.A.), which are descendants of the Zürich and Geneva Reformation in such a manner that, thanks to this principle, the Church was able to accommodate itself to new conditions of existence and to a new political and social system.

The Protestant national Churches have one and all made far too sparing a use of this *semper reformanda* and have fallen a prey to a Lutheran or Reformed traditionalism and confessionalism.[1] The Lutheran Church especially has prided itself on remaining always the same. In so doing it has appealed to the fact that the witness of God's revelation in the Old and New Testaments is the same for all ages. But, like the Reformed Churches also, it has falsely interpreted this genuine insight to imply that there is here to be found a revealed *doctrine*, which it had itself deposited in Confessional writings with a more or less canonical validity.

By so doing it has evoked the conflict between scholarly Biblical research and Church doctrine, it has altered the nature of faith itself and begotten a false theologism, that is, an over-valuation of theological doctrine, and thus profoundly obscured the character of the Ekklesia as a fellowship. By not noticing that the words "*semper reformanda*" apply just as much to the Confessional writings of the Church as to its institutions, it has played its part in creating the situation which today oppresses us as the crisis of the Church.

It was precisely the churchly character of the national

[1] The Lutheran and Reformed World Alliances are certainly an instrument for fostering the ecumenical spirit. Are they not at the same time instruments of a new hardening of Confessionalism and a too confident "We are the people who possess the truth"?

Churches of the Reformation which was the reason why the Church so long closed its eyes to the social problem of modern times, so that thus the distinction between Church and world became an actual separation. As time went on, people who were living in a social world environment which had been revolutionized by the machine knew less and less what to make of a Church which in its preaching and in its own structure was so much cut off from this reality. The rigidity of the Lutheran Church, conscious of its possession of the truth, which so long rejected every accommodation to the new social conditions, has now resulted in the appearance of an acute Church crisis.

We owe it above all to the unswerving progress of Biblical criticism, its endeavour to understand rightly the Biblical witness concerning revelation and faith, that the Church is beginning again to take the "*semper reformanda*" in earnest. It is true that this cry rang out quite soon after the Reformation. Men like Spener, Gottfried Arnold and later Zinzendorf had already some considerable perception of the non-identity of the *ecclesia reformata* with the Ekklesia of the New Testament. But so long as Church teaching obscured this insight with the distinction between the invisible and the visible Church, a thoroughgoing continuation of the work of the Reformation was not to be thought of; for the true cause of the non-identity could not even be recognized. None of the manifold Reforms attempted since the nineteenth century went to the root of things, because the depths of the problem had not been perceived. It was not until the dynamic revival of theology in our days, in conjunction with that of the Reformers themselves, that the urgent need for a new study of the nature of the Church became clear. The Church of the Reformation has less excuse than any other for thinking of itself as something definitive, and it must ever and again allow itself to be called in question in the light of the Pauline idea of the Ekklesia. This will to self-criticism proves that the inheritance of the Reformers is living in the Church, and in the exercise of such criticism it does its greatest service to the Christian world.

CHAPTER 7

THE CRISIS OF THE CHURCH IN EUROPE

BY "the crisis of the Church" we describe the fact that since the French Revolution, that is, since the removal of Church compulsion, the peoples of Europe have been involved in a process of progressive estrangement from the Church. We must first examine in somewhat more detail the manifestations of this fact, and then discover the reason for them.

(I) THE MANIFESTATIONS OF THE CRISIS

Since in the course of the eighteenth century compulsory Baptism and Church membership had been abolished, and freedom of faith and conscience introduced as a political principle, a quickly progressive alienation of certain classes of the populace from the Church became noticeable. In the eighteenth century these were the educated and intellectual circles; since the middle of the nineteenth century the industrial workers; in most recent times it has been more and more that portion of the populace which hitherto was reckoned most decidedly loyal to the Church: the peasantry and the lower middle class. The great (today half-empty) churches of our towns, partly dating from the Middle Ages, are symptoms of this alienation from the Church. It is all the more obvious and shocking because the building of new churches does not by a long way keep pace with the increase of populations.

The picture in the Free Churches is only a little different from that in the national Churches. They have certainly often been able to catch a part of those who were leaving the Church, but in general only that part which is recruited from the lower middle class. The attractive power of certain Free Churches, as, for example, English Methodism, which was able to win a large percentage of the English industrial working class, turned out to be a very significant but transitory phenomenon.

It is indeed a feature of modern times that certain movements which have not a rigidly Church character, as for example the Y.M.C.A., the movement of popular Christianity among the people in Denmark associated with the name of Grundtvig, or the *Innere Mission* called into life in Germany by I. H. Wichern, have been able to attract many people who otherwise would have been lost to the Church. But the general picture of the situation of the Church was not essentially altered by this. For the success of these movements spent itself in proportion as their dynamic character was lost and they became "churchy".

This manifest estrangement of the world from the Church did not have to be reckoned as evil, but could actually be reckoned as gain in so far as the earlier attachment to the Church was to a large extent a façade which for the most part rested upon the then obligatory nature of Church membership, the *compulsion* of the Church. The visible shrinking of the membership of the Church was thus nothing but the natural consequence of the discontinuance of this compulsion. It therefore revealed simply the fictitious character of the Church loyalty of the earlier time, and created a far more honest situation, in which a minority of Christians confront a majority of the un-Christian world who do not belong to the Church. And we must add a second point. Not all those who do not belong to the Church are on that account to be regarded as un-Christian or unbelieving. Even at the beginning of the Reformation era there were individual Christians who stood outside the Church, Christian individualists who appealed to the doctrine of the Invisible Church and who for this reason repudiated all Church organizations as contradictions of the true Church of Christ, and in contrast with them represented a Church-free Christianity. Today the number of these churchless Christians is considerably greater because churchlessness is no longer the exception but the rule.

This individualistic Christianity must indeed from the standpoint of the New Testament Ekklesia be judged as an abnormal phenomenon, since life in the fellowship of believers is an integral part of the life of faith; but we would do wrong to judge it as simply un-Christian. After we have recognized the problem of the Church as an institution, it is no longer possible to claim that membership of a *Church* is imperative for the Christian. After all, even the Reformers did not dare to assert that membership of the *ecclesia visibilis* was a necessary condition of being a Christian.[1] As a matter of fact we find in every

[1] Among the Reformers it is Calvin who regards membership of the *ecclesia visibilis* if not altogether then at least almost as a *conditio sine qua non* of salvation. He says under the heading "Concerning the Visible Church": "Except in its bosom no remission of sins nor any salvation is to be hoped for", *Inst.* IV, 1, 4. He justifies this as follows, saying that "God . . . chooses not to bring them to manhood in any other way than by the education of the Church", *ibid.* 1, 5. He can only regard unwillingness to belong to the Visible Church as godless arrogance, which is unwilling that God's Word should be

century since the Reformation Christians remarkable for the quality of their faith and love who were more or less decisively opposed to the Church.

The Church and its theology have never been able properly to account for this fact. It has satisfied itself by referring to the necessary connection between Christian faith and visible fellowship, taking it without further question that the visible fellowship was the Church. Thus to this very day it has not become conscious of the full gravity of the estrangement of the world from the Church, and still less was it capable of recognizing the cause of the crisis. Even the knowledge that the end of the era of Constantine had come and that consequently the Church had to reorganize itself for missionary work has penetrated only very slowly, since the fact that even up to the present most Europeans have been baptized, deceived it as to the true state of affairs.

After Theodosius there was no longer any missionary work in "Christian" Europe, for since that time every inhabitant of the Roman Empire was by State obligation a baptized Christian. It was for this reason that the phrase "Home Missions" (*die Innere Mission*), which came into currency through Grundtvig and Wichern, had the effect of an alarm signal. But even then the Church still tried to regard the situation as harmless, by understanding "Home Missions"—contrary to Wichern's intentions—as a mere work of charity, as covering all sorts of philanthropic and social service, which had now become necessary in this complex modern world and required special methods of expression. So long as by far the greater majority of people were still baptized, they belonged to the Church and therefore ought not to become objects of evangelization. It was above all the Lutheran doctrine of Baptismal grace which allowed the Church to adhere to its Constantinian Church concept and prevented it from seeing the real situation of the Church. It was still believed that the millions of those who, though baptized, were yet severed from all Church life in other respects could be regarded as members of the Church, and that in preaching also one could presuppose this fictional Church membership, and appeal to them on this ground. Only as gradually an authentic atheism of the masses came into existence, taking hold of ever wider circles of the population, did

spoken to it by a man. This last sentiment comes very near to Luther's thought and yet has a quite different intention. For Luther nowhere identified any Church order with the primitive Christian Ekklesia, while this is just what Calvin did people begin to realize that here we had before us not indeed a new heathenism but something far more alarming, namely a post-Christian estrangement from the Church and from faith.

Modern atheism, which so easily fell a prey to the systematic godless Marxist ideology, has a "Christian" element in it only to this extent, that it cannot be conceived in its radical nature except in relation to Christianity. This means, however, that it makes the task of evangelization more difficult, for the post-Christian atheist has passed through Christianity and said "No" to it, and thus is much less accessible to the preaching of the gospel than the pre-Christian heathen or atheist. The problem is thus no longer one of ignorance of the Church but of conscious opposition to it, of nihilistic anti-Christianity.

This whole view of the circumstances is supported by a highly significant fact of a positive character, namely that in the same epoch in which the Churches of Europe have been overtaken by the crisis, the Churches of the United States show an entirely contrary picture. There, instead of the European exodus from the Church, a strong increase of Church membership is to be noted. While the European Churches have lost more and more ground, there a really astonishing increase of Church interest and sympathy on the part of the populace are noticeable. This phenomenon itself, as we saw above, is not to be judged wholly favourably but has, on the contrary, brought its own tremendous problems. None the less, it is of significance for the illustration of our thesis. Partly from interior reasons, partly by the action of the State, the Churches in America have been protected from becoming "Churches" in the same manner and degree as the Churches of Europe. The tradition of Constantine and Theodosius was radically swept away, so that voluntary Church membership alone remains. Thus while the Church in America has surrendered precisely what it was judged necessary in Europe to retain and has remained vital by so doing, the Churches of Europe, by clinging to historical tradition, have to a large extent lost their popular character and influence upon the life of the people. The crisis of the Church is a specifically European phenomenon.

(2) THE CAUSES OF THE CRISIS

The crisis of the Church in Europe is a fact which is much more clearly perceived by non-theologians and Christians who are not Church people than by the theologians. What has been the cause of this? The cause lies—as the example of the American Church shows—not where it is generally believed to lie, in the intellectual situation created by modern science or the rationalistic Enlightenment. For if these two factors were necessarily going to lead to the ruin of the Church anywhere, it would certainly have happened in America. For nowhere, with the exception of the lands dominated by Communism, is so naïve a faith in science dominant as in America, and nowhere has the influence of the Enlightenment been so deep and so bound up with the national history as in the U.S.A. And in spite of this the phenomenon of the Church's crisis, in the sense we have just described, does not exist there. Consequently the cause must lie somewhere else. The Church in Europe would have had every reason for seeking this cause in itself, and not in an external factor. The fact is that the Church itself is responsible for the loss of confidence from which it suffers today, and this loss is the result of the gulf which separates the Church as such from the Ekklesia of primitive Christianity. We see this difference in the following four points.

(*a*) *The Self-understanding of the Church as a gathering for Divine Worship*

It is part of the sickness of our Church that it still understands itself only as a gathering for divine worship on Sunday morning, while in the Ekklesia of primitive Christianity it was taken for granted that the daily fellowship of life was lived under the Word of God. "Let the Word of God dwell richly among you" (Col. 3: 16). The gathering to hear the Word of God and for common praise and worship of its Lord played a significant and necessary rôle, but the Ekklesia did not understand itself as a cultic fellowship. It is Ekklesia also outside this gathering for divine worship, in mutual self-communication and service. Worship of God is indeed a necessary and centrally important manifestation of its nature as the Ekklesia, but the Ekklesia is protected from the danger of becoming a mere Sunday Church by the fact that divine worship is the formative influence of daily life and penetrates every workaday concern. This is why mutual service and life together in the Lord is so important to the Apostle and is so often emphasized by him. A true brotherhood of Christ would have, even today, to begin and end every day with a gathering for worship of God, and manifest thereby that the people of God live upon God's Word and daily build up their life upon it. The Ekklesia is the fulfilment of the command to love God and man.

(*b*) *The Sacrament as Dispensation of Salvation*

The sacramental concept was unknown to the New Testament witnesses to Christ. There was indeed Baptism and the Lord's Supper, but neither the one nor the other as Sacrament, that is, as a means of communicating salvation. With the Sacrament the emphasis on the sacred as contrasted with the profane penetrates once more from the world of the religions into the Ekklesia. At this point above all even the Reformation failed to penetrate through mediaevalism to the sources of the New Testament faith.

The fact that here the stream of the movement of the Reformation divided and lost its impetus has not been without significant consequence. In no other point does the theology of the Reformers become so confused and self-contradictory as in the doctrine of the Sacraments, finding expression in a certain sacramentalism which has lasted to the present day, for example in the understanding of the Lord's Supper in the Anglican and Lutheran Churches. Above all, the retention by the Reformers of the Catholic practice of Infant Baptism, which was based really, though never avowedly, on the desire to retain the national Church, made it clear that the new understanding of faith was incompatible with the Church as an institution, and brought both concepts under the suspicion of ambiguity and muddled thinking. Men of today, at least, have no time for a Church which on the one side indiscriminately baptizes every child and declares it to be a member of the Body of Christ, and on the other side preaches justification by faith alone.

As the Word of God must encounter man in the everyday concern of his life for him to understand it, so nothing will serve to give him a new appreciation of Baptism and the Lord's Supper but a new understanding of them. There must be no thought of a quasi-material gift of salvation, but Baptism and the Lord's Supper must bring us in faith into the presence of the living risen Lord, who here according to His promise imparts Himself to us in a special way and bestows upon us His grace. What we need is not a Church of the Sacrament but a genuine personal event of faith in Baptism and the Lord's Supper, which renews and builds up the Christian brotherhood upon the deepest foundations of union with Jesus Christ.

(*c*) *The Transformation of Service into Office*

Institutionalism is manifest most obviously in the clerical office. Although it was precisely at this point that Luther attacked the structure of the mediaeval Church by preaching the priesthood of all believers and therefore not recognizing an official priesthood, neither he nor any other of the Reformers took this universal priesthood seriously in practice.

Even in the Protestant Church the clerical office—whether under the name of *ministerium* (the ministry) or *sacerdotium* (the priesthood)—continued in being as something constitutive for the existence of the Church. That the New Testament has no knowledge of such an office we have shown above.[1] The ministries (*diakoniai*) of the Ekklesia are wholly misunderstood when the word is translated as "offices". But it is just this official character of the Church which has become particularly suspect and offensive to the man of today. He is sensitive to the contradiction between the two concepts "spiritual" and "official", and quite outstandingly so when this office appears to be bound up with official positions in the State. "If we must have Church and office, then we would actually rather have the Catholic Church and the Catholic priesthood."

On the other side ministerial office is the thing that most hinders the creation of true fellowship or brotherhood. It is this official character of the Church above all which is the reason why the element of brotherly fellowship is so much lacking in the institutional Church. What is done for the Church and through the Church is done by the official churchman, the priest, the minister. What is there left for "the laymen" to do? So the fellowship is always in danger of falling under the tutelage of the "official clergy". We must win through to a conception of the office of the clergy as service, which can be so exercised that the whole congregation is drawn in to share responsibility and share in the work according to its gifts and powers.

(*d*) *The Preaching Church*

Since the Reformation the sermon, that is, the exposition of the words of Scripture by a theological specialist who is called the minister of the divine Word (*verbi divini minister*), has been without doubt the centre, the authentic heart of the Church. This was for centuries uncontested and apparently constituted no problem. But it is precisely here that today the crisis of the Church is most evident—as a crisis of preaching. Even the powerful movements for the renewal of theology,[2]

[1] p. 66

[2] Among the figures who have decisively contributed to the renewal of theology, Karl Barth is pre-eminent. Movements akin to the Dialectical Theology took shape before his time in Sweden under Einar Billing. Nor should

for the new understanding of the Biblical message, have up to date made no decisive difference at this point. These movements have indeed contributed much to the revitalization of the Church's preaching, but they have not succeeded in bridging the gulf which yawns between contemporary man and every kind of Church preaching. What is the use of the best, most conscientious and, at the same time, in the best sense Christological preaching, when this no longer gets a hearing, when even the best evangelization can teach only those who are on the edge of the Church, not those who are really estranged from it?

We start our inquiry from the human side and ask why people have so little interest in the preaching of the Church and so little understanding of it. There are indeed, even today, a considerable number of people who have entirely the same relation to a vital sermon as in earlier times. But more and more this is true only of those who already wish to belong to the Church, that is, for that continually decreasing number of whom we have just spoken. When we ask why the others write off preaching, even of the most vital kind, as uninteresting and even unintelligible, the answer is "Preaching doesn't say a thing to me." Thus they wish to express the fact that this procedure which we call "preaching" has, so far as they can see, no relevance to their existence. Because it does not "get home" where their interests lie, they are also unable to understand it.

It is true that the preaching of evangelists, revivalists, which has a quite different structure from the preaching in a church service, has a better chance of reaching the man who no longer goes to church. But because the very phenomenon of preaching as such is strange and even from the outset uncongenial to the contemporary independent-minded and therefore critical man, there is little hope even in this quarter.[1] Modern man wishes us to give reasons for what we say to him; he wishes to bring forward his own objections and can be

the German revival of interest in a new interpretation of Luther, initiated chiefly by the great Church historian Karl Holl, be neglected. The representative of this movement, who still carries on a lively discussion with Barth, Bultmann and other representatives of the Dialectical Theology, is Paul Althaus

[1] The great exception of our time is Billy Graham, the successful mass evangelist. His personal integrity and dedication to the cause of Christ is obviously more impressive than one would have expected from his fundamentalist faith. His significance should not indeed be rated too high, but must by no means be ridiculed. This limitation, however, is ever and again visible in his case: even he reaches principally those who are to be found on the edge of the Church, but not those who are genuinely outside it, and to this extent provides confirmation of what has been said above

convinced only in dialogue. For this reason he finds it tedious to be "preached at". When he hears a speech, a lecture, which has something to say to the problems which concern himself, he is not lacking in interest, indeed he makes an effort to understand. But when the content of the speech to which he is expected to listen has absolutely nothing to do with his problems, he is not interested nor can he understand. The language of the minister and of the Church has this character for him. He knows from the start that it will deal with the soul's salvation and a teaching which claims to be the Word of God. But both these are remote from him.

At this point we come upon the deeper reasons for his rejection of us. What interests the modern man is on the one hand the problem of his own personality, his search for self-discovery, the question how he can deal with his personal problems. This is the reason why our generation has such a lively interest in all the questions of psychology. And, on the other hand, the problem of moulding the forms of society in which he lives—the so-called social problem. But a Church which meets him only as an institution, which exists for the sake of this so-called Word of God and is organized exclusively for this purpose, which accordingly neither includes him in a fellowship nor has anything of importance to say to the problem of creating fellowship, is suspect in his eyes from the start. For this reason he cannot hear even its *Word*. Its claim to speak in God's name appears to him entirely unfounded and therefore unjustified. A Word of God would surely "find" him in his problems and his needs. It would surely be a Word which would help him to understand himself, and which would have something decisive to say on the problem of fellowship.

Here man's question coincides with the question of faith. The Word which bears witness to Jesus as the Christ is the Word of the love of God revealed in Jesus Christ. It is at the same time the Word in which man finds his true self, and in which the true fellowship, the brotherhood of the Ekklesia, has its foundation. This Word is a word spoken from fellowship and calling into fellowship. In faith man comes from isolation, from the absence of fellowship, to himself, and precisely in so doing to fellowship. Thus it is at the same time the Word which genuinely integrates personality and the Word which genuinely creates fellowship. For this reason it can be made intelligible only by, on the one hand, taking man seriously in his confused search for himself, for personal integration, and, on the other hand, by being spoken out of a fellowship which becomes visible as such behind the preacher, and receives into itself the man who is seeking fellowship.

This is why preaching which is not backed by such fellowship, but only by an institution, is unconvincing. Thus the crisis of preaching only makes fully manifest the crisis of the Church which is not Ekklesia. Thus the preaching of the gospel as the *Word* in which man finds his true self cannot be severed from the *being* of the Ekklesia as fellowship. The Word of the love of God must authenticate itself precisely by taking man seriously in his questioning about himself, and seeking not to evade him, but to reach him through his questions, in living dialogue. But it must also prove itself worthy of belief by being not only a Word "from faith to faith" but also a Word from love to love, from fellowship to fellowship.

Where this is grasped, the "Word of God" cannot any longer be preached in an authoritarian manner and faith demanded of man, and it must not only become clear to the hearer in earnest discussion and common commitment that "*I* am the man intended by this Word", but also that "He who says it to me places himself under this Word, at my side." Preaching thus becomes a creation of fellowship, in which the preacher in his Word invites the hearer into the fellowship from which he himself has received his Word. But this is just what does not happen in the Church in which preaching is the sole centre, and which does so little to give expression to fellowship either in the worship of God or in workaday action. The lack of fellowship in the institution "Church", its tearing asunder of "communication-of"[1] from "communication-with", of speaking from being, is the deepest reason why so many people today turn their backs upon it.

(3) THE CONDITIONS FOR OVERCOMING THE CRISIS

If in conclusion we were once again to test our results by examining the example of the American Free Churches on these four points just indicated, which show the causes of the crisis within the European Churches, we would discover that the Churches of America do not show the marks which are characteristic of the European Churches; that, on the contrary, both in the creation of fellowship and in the awakening of a universal sense of responsibility for the service of the gospel they are an example to us. On the two last-named characteristics, above all, rests the astonishing popularity of the American

[1] Cf. Ch. 2, p. 26, note referring to Hendrik Kraemer

(Free) Churches and their integration with life. So in conclusion we must say: the European (Protestant) Church is experiencing a situation of crisis because its renewal at the Reformation in these four respects did not manage to recover the New Testament understanding of the Ekklesia, and showed itself unable or unwilling to try seriously to undertake the task of continuing reformation in these respects.

We have already indicated the quite different danger which, in contrast to those of the Protestant Churches in Europe, threatens the American Free Churches; namely the toning-down of the gospel in the interests of popularity. So we see that the Churches of America and Europe have decisive lessons to teach each other. It seems to be the special gift of grace (*charisma*) of European theology to grasp conceptually the gospel in its uniqueness, in its non-identity with all the truths of reason, as it seems to be the *charisma* of American Christians to translate faith into action and to embody the fellowship of faith in a true human fellowship; and that not only in the relations between man and man but more and more also within the conditions of social, economic and political life. I mention one thing only, the equality of women with men, not only in society generally but above all in the Churches. Without the tremendous contribution of the women of America to the work of the Church and missions, the achievements of the Church, its financial and personal sacrifices, would not even be thinkable.

In this mutual exchange the Americans have indeed hitherto shown themselves more willing to learn from the European theologians than the European Christians have been to learn from the example of the American Churches. A true ecumenical outlook would show itself by a genuinely mutual exchange in which the intellectual arrogance of the European theologians would be shamed by the exemplary spirit of willing self-sacrifice in the American Churches, and the too self-confident pragmatism of the Americans would be challenged and corrected by the penetrating analyses of European theology and the loyalty of the European Churches to the Confessions; so that the acute crisis here and the secret, yet insidious, dilution of the Churches' vital power in a democratic society would be checked.

Hitherto we have spoken only of the Protestant Church. The Catholic Church has experienced no crisis either here or there: neither on this side nor on that side of the Atlantic does it know secularism, the loss of its true nature in worldliness. On the contrary, both here and there it is on the offensive, and is protected by its structure from confusion with rational social structures. This does not mean, however, that it has more loyally preserved the gospel of Jesus Christ. That the contrary is the case, that from the beginning its particular tendency was to substitute the sacerdotal for the truly evangelical element, and that it was only able thus to preserve its legal ecclesiastical structure, we have already sufficiently shown. But especially in a time when as never before all the foundations of life have been shaken, men are inclined to grasp at what is ostensibly eternal and unshakable, and seems to offer security, sparing them the trouble of thinking critically for themselves and relieving them of the need to make their own decisions. In the sacred system of Church law they believe they can find this eternal security. But the truth of the message of Christ is so intimately bound up with criticism of everything human, that this reliance on the sacred institution cannot in the long run achieve its end. It is precisely the man who has been truly possessed by the gospel who will inevitably perceive something of this compromise and feel suspicious of the totalitarianism of this hierarchical system.[1]

The more vital his love and his faith, the more inevitable will be his protest against this "holy" totalitarianism and its fundamentally unholy attempt to control the grace of God. In so far as the deepest insights of the Reformation slowly dawn upon the Roman Church, there will also awaken within it a realization of the incompatibility of sacerdotalism with true holiness, of the totalitarianism of ecclesiastical law with the freedom of the children of God.

When the Churches of Protestantism more and more transcend their false "churchiness" by the true holiness of God-filled humanity and when within the Catholic Church genuine faith revolts against the false "churchiness" of the totalitarian structure, this knowledge on both sides can lead to the disappearance of the conflict between the Confessions. That would be the true Ecumenism, where Catholics and Protestants were

[1] This, it seems to me, is nowhere more powerfully expressed than in the attitude of Simone Weil. On one side she came very near to the Catholic Faith, which had evidently been put to her in a very "evangelical" manner, but on the other side, on this one point—the State-like character of the Catholic Church—she felt an invincible repugnance, which she expresses in no uncertain terms. Cf. Simone Weil, *Gravity and Grace*, London, 1952; Perrin and Thibon, *Simone Weil As We Knew Her*, London, 1953; Karl Epting, *Der geistliche Weg der Simone Weil* (The Spiritual Pilgrimage of Simone Weil), 1955, and *Das Unglück und die Gottesliebe* (Misfortune and the Love of God), 1953, with a foreword by T. S. Eliot. What she was looking for was—the Ekklesia. I know few books which are so profound an expression of the spiritual crisis of our times, and bear witness to such an "existential" Christian faith

ready to confess that not the sacramental institution of the priestly Church and not the theological preaching of Protestantism, but Jesus Christ alone and His Ekklesia, the fellowship of the children of God destined for the freedom of faith and love, is the truth that is identical with grace.

CHAPTER 8

THE SEARCH FOR THE NEW FORM OF THE CHURCH

(I) NEW STRUCTURES WITHIN THE CHURCH EXPRESSING THE SPIRIT OF THE EKKLESIA

THE nineteenth century brought forth a number of movements which, springing for the most part from the Free Churches of England and America, transcended the limits of their Church or denomination. In so doing their whole aim was the service of the Churches, but they sprang from a realization that the Churches were not equal to these new tasks, and that principally for the reason that within their institutional structure they were not able to offer the fellowship or create the organs for action that were necessary.

Of this kind was the movement of "Home Missions" which was in Germany associated with the name of Wichern, in Denmark with that of Grundtvig. The part of Wichern's programme which in the end was realized fell very far short of his original idea. For his intention was nothing less than the rebirth of the German people in the spirit of love and service. He was the first person to recognize that the new situation of the Church was a missionary situation. For this reason he called his movement "Home Missions" in contrast with "Foreign Missions"—the Missions to the heathen. But from the beginning he refused to have his work made a part of the official work of the Church, knowing that subordination to Church leadership must act like a strait-jacket on the living forces which he called into life. The spirit of *diakonia*, of service of the brethren, required new organs for its expression. Grundtvig's motives were similar; his intention was to bring fresh life to the Danish people from the living Word, from "fellowship in the living Word". He despaired of his Danish Lutheran Church because "the Word of the Lord had departed from His house". To bring about this renewal he made use of the "Peoples' University".

About the same time as these two typically continental movements there came into existence in England the Young Men's Christian Association, which soon spread to every land, and today has attained great significance especially in non-Christian Asia. The Y.M.C.A. has been just as significant a force for the spread of the Christian spirit in the last fifty years as the Foreign Missions of the Church, if it has not surpassed them. Characteristic of it is the predominance of the lay element and correspondingly its lack of emphasis on preaching and cultus, its practical activities of love and service, its examples and ideal of Christian character, of Christian personality, its transcendence of race-prejudice through action, its cultivation of fellowship with young people of the most varied religious, social and cultural origins. The corresponding branch on the women's side, the Y.W.C.A., has had almost as significant a part to play, especially in the non-European world where at first the idea of the equality of women with men was almost unknown. It is true that the movement itself in the United States is in danger of becoming through a process of secularization a mere middle-class club, while in Europe, on the other hand, in close contact with the Church, it sets itself principally to the task of youth evangelization. This evangelization meets with the same hindrances as those which Church evangelism encounters, and thus it reaches few beyond the groups who are still on the edge of the Church.

An offspring of the Y.M.C.A. is the Student Christian Movement, which, under the distinguished leadership of John Mott, has made a singular contribution to the awakening of faith and the diffusion of Christian life among the intellectual *élite* of all lands, and has placed men and women of great spiritual distinction at the disposal of the Church as active lay members. We must not conceal from ourselves the fact that recently, through its assimilation to the Church, this movement has been in danger of losing precisely this function of stimulating lay people to action.

Of course all the revival movements of the nineteenth century come into this category. They mostly took their rise from individual dynamic personalities (Chalmers, Finney, Vinet, Moody, and others) and at first extended their efforts beyond all the frontiers of the Church, and in disregard of them created new forms of evangelization. They emphasized the elements of pastoral conversation so much neglected by the Church, and the element of brotherly fellowship as necessary for the spiritual growth of new converts, and by so doing brought back something of the spirit of the Ekklesia to the Church. They made the Churches realize that in our times the traditional form of preaching is no longer adequate, especially in relation to those who are estranged from the Church.

The fact that the task and theme of "Evangelization" is

today recognized throughout all the Protestant Churches as one of their most urgent tasks, while a hundred years ago hardly anything of the kind was heard, is a sign that the Church is beginning to awake. Within these movements certain new methods for the diffusion of the Word have been devised; methods which the Churches, more or less against their will, have adopted, without which in fact their work would no longer be possible—camps, short vacation courses, conferences, retreats, corporate Bible study. The Free Churches of the United States especially have taken the lead and acted as pioneers in the creation of new forms of activity. It was they also who first created the "socialized Church" and who made the Church accessible to the world and at the same time intelligible to the men of today. H. Fosdick's "Riverside Church" is a Church in which today the world and the Church encounter each other. That is the arm of the Church outstretched to the world. On its own side the world, without knowing it, is in search of the Ekklesia inasmuch as it is seeking for fellowship, brotherhood.

(2) THE WORLD IN SEARCH OF FELLOWSHIP

The nineteenth and twentieth centuries have been dominated by the problem of fellowship. Since the overthrow of feudal authoritarianism, including that of the compulsory Church, and after the brief phase of liberalism, the socialist movement has come irresistibly to the front. In the pre-Marxist and Marxist socialistic communist utopias the "*idée force*", the dynamic behind world history, is the idea of the classless society. It is true that the fundamental thought of Karl Marx, especially as it comes to light in his utopian eschatology, is at bottom not that of socialism or communism but an anarchic individualism stemming from the philosophy of the Enlightenment. But the part of his thought which was historically influential was not this individualistic utopian eschatology, but the idea of a classless humanity, the idea of a universal condition of humanity, a kind of idea of the Kingdom of God without God.

Although Marxism professed to be "scientific" it was those of its ideals which were not at all scientific, but humanist, which made it a power of the first order in world history. It was, so to speak, a humanist Messianism without a Messiah, the faith in a future brotherhood of man which thrilled the peoples. It was these powerfully emotional and irrational ideas overlying the economic and political system which imparted their dynamic to the whole and made socialism into a religion without God. The word "comrade" was descriptive of a reality of a spiritual and emotional character. "We seek the new, and better, more brotherly humanity"—that was the watch-word of this socialist-communist movement. Without knowing it, Marxism, so long as it was a movement, drew its power from a conception of man rooted in Christianity and from a hope for the future nourished by Biblical sources.

Only when the movement neared its first practical realization in the communistic state of Russia, only as the transition was made from Marx to Lenin and further from Lenin to Stalin, and gradually the Messianic enthusiasm gave place to cool power-politics, was it realized that the goal was now no longer that new brotherly classless humanity, but rather the total State which calls itself the Communist State. The system had taken the place of the spirit; the institution, the totalitarian State, had replaced the enthusiastic movement; the word of command had ousted co-operation. Soon the hitherto enthusiastic socialist or communist was bound to see that together with his ideals and expectations he had been betrayed to a power system which must prove the fundamental contradiction of those ideals.[1] Of fellowship there was no trace, for there is nothing that more radically denies fellowship than the "communist" totalitarian State, which would far better deserve the name of "terroristic State Capitalism" and which is far more hostile in its opposition to all humanity and fellowship than was the individualistic capitalism of the early nineteenth century.

There are still, especially in Asia and Africa, millions of people who experience a *laissez-faire* capitalism with its grim exploitation of the weak and defenceless which has been outdated in Europe, America and Australia. This alone they know in reality, Communism they know only in the form of idealizing propaganda which corresponds to their wishful thinking and is directed at this. The intellectually mature proletariat of the West, especially of America, has recognized with horror this totalitarian pseudo-communism and disavows it, but has unfortunately not yet clearly understood that the social programme of Marx *must* lead of necessity to this terrifying pseudo-communistic Total State, and therefore *cannot* realize the goal of that classless humanity which had been intended and hoped for. Non-Marxist socialism, however, is disorientated and without foundations. The less prejudiced

[1] Cf. V. Gitermann, *Die historische Tragik der sozialistischen Idee*, 1939

among these socialists are beginning to look to the U.S.A. where labour and management are beginning to understand the community of their interests, even though on single issues a hard struggle is still being waged for economic vantage-points. But conferences are held, there is mutual respect even where there is difference of opinion, there is an attempt at mutual understanding. Thus new paths are beginning to be opened up. It may indeed take a long time before the old methods of conflict on the one side and on the other are laid aside. But by and large we can say—and this is true more or less of the whole West—discussion is taking the place of force, compromise is replacing the struggle for power. More and more it is being recognized that even the other fellow, the opponent, is a human being, and his rights are being fundamentally respected. In this way entirely new prospects for the solution of social problems are being opened up.

But the nineteenth century was not only the century of the socialist movement, but also of associations and clubs. Much fun has been made of this by writers on culture or Church theologians, but without justice. For all this is a manifestation of nothing less central than the search for fellowship. The object of interest is not so much singing or activity in games as a comradeship which modern man can hardly any longer find in his everyday work and in his home in the great city. People look for the meeting of man with man, free from that division into social classes which the life of the worker brings with it. Freemasonry also, the Rotary Movement, and similar Brotherhood Movements, are an expression of the same longing and desire for fellowship, where one can talk intimately with one's friend,[1] where one is received simply as a fellow human being and brother. Similarly the world-wide Scout Movement is not designed in the first place to satisfy the need of youth for physical exercise and eagerness for adventure. It is rather that here boys learn what responsibility for each other means, and they learn it as a rule much better here than in the Church organizations for young people—just because here the boys bear the responsibility themselves, younger and older ones being placed in quite concrete relations of mutual service, and freely allowing themselves to be so.

From the standpoint of the Ekklesia one might say, all this is a poor substitute for the Ekklesia. True, but it is not a poor substitute for the *Church*. For it is precisely the fellowship,

[1] Literally "where one can say 'Thou' "—a practice restricted in German-speaking countries to close relatives and intimate friends. (TR.)

which people find everywhere in these associations, that they have not found in the Church, and that is why they have turned their backs upon it. For this reason even the *Word* of the Church is strange to them, and—because it speaks continually of love, but lets so little of it be seen—unconvincing. The Church's proclamation of Christ, its preaching, is for the average man of today a word of doctrine emptied of its social meaning, a word without relevance for himself in his everyday relations. This is why those men who have seen this crisis, and know their share of responsibility for it, have sought new ways to come into conversation once more with people who are outside the fellowship, and to show them afresh the significance of the Biblical message for their everyday life.

(3) BETWEEN CHURCH AND WORLD

In very recent times two movements have come into existence which diverge very markedly from the preaching Church, and which are characterized by a new insight into the brotherhood of the Ekklesia. Both movements have already exercised a significant influence: the so-called Oxford Group and the movement which has created the Evangelical Academies in Germany and other Church Lay Institutes like Boldern (Switzerland), Kerk en Wereld (Holland) and others.

A quite new, singular phenomenon which is hard to place is the movement which, originating with Frank Buchman, was earlier known by the name of the Oxford Group Movement, but today describes itself as Moral Rearmament (M.R.A.). It stands on both sides of our distinction inasmuch as—especially in its origins[1]—it can be regarded as a movement from the side of the Church for the renewal of the Ekklesia, and also as a movement from the side of the world in search of true fellowship. In any case it has that characteristic which Gabriel Marcel, one of the most significant philosophers of our time, emphasizes[2]—the interweaving of intimacy and world-wide scope of the society—as that which we have named the paradox of the social form of the Ekklesia.[3] No one can be indifferent to the impression made by those twenty "testimonies" which, spoken by Africans, Japanese, Indians and Westerners, from former dyed-in-the-wool communist trade union leaders, from

[1] Cf. my book *Die Kirchen, die Gruppenbewegung und die Kirche Jesu Christi*, 1936. (E.T. *The Church and the Oxford Group*, London, 1937)

[2] Gabriel Marcel, *Un Changement d'Espérance*, 1958

[3] See above, pp. 27 ff.

business men, eminent statesmen and intellectuals, all bear the same witness:

> Through taking the law of God in earnest, through being still and listening for His voice, and through being open to our fellow man, our life has been changed, we have been given the gift of a peace, a joy and an inner freedom which makes us able to love in every man our fellow human-being, and thus to bridge the differences of cultural level, of race, class and nationality, and to overcome our hatred of personal enemies or the members of a certain group of people.

As Christians we can only say, "Here God's Spirit is at work". On the other hand the decisive thing, confession of Jesus Christ and witness to Him, seems to be missing. But anyone who knows something of the inner life of this movement is aware that Frank Buchman himself possessed, and that his innermost circle of fellow workers possess, a living faith in Jesus Christ crucified for us, and in more intimate groups openly confess that this is the source of their power. Ever and again in conferences and international gatherings one finds that people who at first knew nothing of Jesus Christ and experienced as Buddhists, Muslims or atheists the transformation of their lives, step by step in fellowship with these Christian friends of theirs learn to know Christ, read the Bible and begin to live in prayer, without thereby losing contact with their own religious national community. What is public in the Church, the proclamation of Christ, is here not public, is, so to speak, merely whispered in the ear; what here on the other hand is public, is what is never or seldom spoken of aloud in the Church, the changing of one's own life.

Therefore this movement is at first something strange for the Church Christian, and only with difficulty to be expressed in terms of the traditional categories of faith and the Church. On the other hand, here actually happens the thing which the Church has always declared necessary: the transformation of life by love in response to love. Here a fellowship is created which is not unlike that of the brotherhood of the Ekklesia. At the very least we must acknowledge in this movement a very close approximation from the side of the world to the true fellowship which we have seen to be the nature of the Ekklesia.[1]

The organizations known as "Evangelical Academies" and

[1] For a number of years I took an active part in this movement, to which I owe much. But since it transformed itself into M.R.A. and set up a new ideology as its programme I have withdrawn from it, without losing close contact with it

described as Church Institutes for Laymen are clearly an effort to bring the gospel once again into touch with the life of contemporary man by entirely new methods. Men who knew from experience how completely large masses of the population have become estranged from the Church, and who realized that the word of the official preacher and the theological specialist is no longer capable of bringing the Christian message to our generation, have taken the urgency of this situation to heart and have begun to invite members of the same profession to conferences, at which definite themes with special interest for the group concerned are treated by competent speakers and then discussed by all the participants. While this practical discussion constitutes one pole of the conference, the other pole is the illumination of the same problem from the standpoint of scripture and Christian faith.

Experience shows that many people take an interest in such conferences and are ready to spare time for them, who neither have, nor desire, any contact with the preaching of the Church. In this way they are awakened to a new interest in the Biblical message, since here the place of the sermon is taken by a conversation with two poles: "The world of my profession and the Biblical message." Discussion of Biblical texts which have a clear relation to the realities which these men are meeting in daily life, has turned out to be a form of appropriation which answers far more closely to the spiritual maturity, the critical thought and the democratic self-consciousness of contemporary man than the experience of being preached at. The form of the conference also satisfies the modern need for fellowship far more than the preaching services of the Church.[1] So it happens that

[1] A quite singular phenomenon which is guided by the idea of the New Testament Ekklesia is the *Mukyokai*, the Christian non-Church movement in Japan. It was called into being by the Christian publicist and university evangelist Kanzo Utchimura, who died in 1930, and is the only genuinely Japanese Christian group or movement. Led by prominent laymen, it actually exists only in individual larger or smaller Bible study groups, in which every Sunday a leader expounds the Bible in a simple sermon, and there is singing and prayer. The message, which is diffused by little periodicals, is simple New Testament faith, of a specially Pauline type. There is a minimum of organization, and no organized connection between the separate groups, nor is there Baptism or the Lord's Supper in the traditional form. The Word of scripture alone, vitally expounded by a leader filled with the Spirit, is acknowledged as the foundation of the Ekklesia. There are no regulations to ensure continuity. In spite of this, not only has the movement survived two generations, but has even spread over the whole country, and has captured a number of leading men of the Japanese nation, who on their part have formed Bible study groups.

The relationship to the existing Churches founded by Foreign Missions and to the Church Council which came into being during the second world war is,

the people who meet each other here, and speak together, experience something of the true fellowship which comes from faith in Jesus Christ.

In this connection the idea of the "para-congregation" must also be mentioned, which was for the first time discussed in the ecumenical preparatory studies produced for the World Conference in Evanston in 1954. In his book *Die Kirche in der modernen Gesellschaft* (The Church in Modern Society) H. D. Wendland speaks of the para-congregations as new forms of congregation. They originate alongside of and outside the local congregations, and are orientated to perform a particular service, as, for example, the Student Communities. The aim is that through the formation of such cells of Christian life new Christian communities should be built up in the world.[1]

At the close of this chapter we wish to sum up the different aspects of our problem as follows. From the side of the world men are seeking fellowship without rightly knowing what it is. Still less do men know that true fellowship can be found only in Christ. The preaching of the Church is as a rule not able to show this to men. For many, a prolonged personal contact with true Christians is necessary, that is, with people who witness to

in general, a friendly, in part even a co-operative one. The exposition of the Bible is prophetic rather than fundamentalist or biblicist. Yet the movement is characterized by an absence of fanaticism, and by its marked moral levelheadedness and discipline. It is understandable that the members of the *Mukyokai* are of the opinion that in their movement the New Testament Ekklesia has found its Japanese expression. Certainly there is here very little sign of any tendency to develop into a *Church.* The organization consists in the unchallenged spiritual authority of the individual leaders, who are not by any means theologians but deeply experienced in their knowledge and exposition of the Bible.

When we ask the question "What guarantee is there for the continuation of the movement?" we are told "God will see to that, as He has done in the past." So long as the individual groups are not only wholly independent but without organized connection, the danger of development into a Church is small and the danger of disorder and schism which must be present has not yet materialized. Cf. my essay in *Evangelische Theologie,* 1959—"Die Nicht-Kirche Bewegung in Japan" (The non-Church Movement in Japan)

[1] *Die Kirche in der modernen Gesellschaft,* 1956, pp. 220–35. This book is not so impressive as one might have expected, because its theological foundation remains encumbered by the outworn categories of Lutheran dogmatics. I may refer to the fact that without knowledge of the para-congregation, I realized the necessity in Japan of organizing those who were sympathetic to the Christian Faith, but were inclined to be repelled by the Church, *in a preliminary form of Church,* which at the same time afforded the possibility of further training in faith. I also began to realize this idea in action, but was hindered by language difficulties and lack of time from realizing my idea on the scale I planned. Only a comparatively small group of people was formed which was composed both of Christians and non-Christians and continues to exist as a group sharing responsibility for the Evangelical Academy which is in process of creation

their faith less by words than by actions[1] in order to make others accessible to the Word about Christ. Jesus Christ is not only active in the Word which preaches Him, but He bears witness to Himself in the love and fellowship bestowed by Him, whose secret source He is only gradually recognized to be.

What preaching isolated from the fellowship of the Ekklesia is no longer able to achieve, to bring men in contact with Christ, can perhaps be achieved by the Christian fellowship which does not at first utter its witness to Christ aloud. Differently put: this genuine Ekklesia, which as such is both fellowship with Christ and brotherhood, will realize that because of the century-long separation of faith and love, of fellowship with Christ and human fellowship, the way to win the men of today is not at first to speak the message of Christ, but merely to *live* it. This would be a reversal of the hitherto customary way from faith to active love. And that would mean: not first preaching and Bible study, but first genuine disinterested service of our neighbours, and only afterwards—when the other person asks "Why are you so different and why do you act so differently from the others?"—the witness to Christ, the revealer of the love of God and the founder of true loving service of our fellow men. This is not a programme but a way which is suggesting itself, though not yet clearly; a venture of Christian love which can realize itself in the most divergent new manifestations.

We might provisionally describe this way as "The Ekklesia on the march", a phrase in which this expression "on the march" includes within itself a great variety of possibilities and which therefore should certainly not be rendered as "The new form of the Ekklesia." In using this concept, let us remember that being "on the march" belongs necessarily to the nature of the Ekklesia, since its consummation is still a matter of hope. There is in truth no other Ekklesia than the Ekklesia on the march, the journeying Church (*ecclesia viatorum*); for faith itself is something provisional, something which *is* already, and also is not yet. But the more institutional it has become, the more the Church has obscured this provisional character and has stood in the way of this insight both through its theological dogmatism and its claim to be a sacred institution. So it is high

[1] This way is not new; quite the contrary. It has always been followed by individual missionaries, men genuinely filled with the Spirit. Thus Paton, the missionary to the New Hebrides, showed himself to the cannibal islanders, before he began to preach, simply as a helpful comrade and thus won their trust and opened their hearts, so that they would receive and understand the gospel of the love of God. In the same way, Frank Buchman emphasized as the fundamental principle of all evangelization: "First be good friends"

time that the Church should allow this question to concern it, even if this means that it should be itself called in question. The age of the self-confident Church, which believes that it knows the way and possesses all that is necessary to lead men to Christ, is over.

The fact that such a search can be observed not only among Protestants but also just as much on the Catholic side is the sign that life in Christ is neither dead nor petrified, but is pressing on to new manifestations. To the outsider the Church seems more rigid than it is. But it must have the courage to confess this provisional character before the world also. To do so would simply be to take the principle "*semper reformanda*" seriously, a principle which it has always recognized, especially since the Reformation.[1] For in all its search for a new form, it is certain of one thing: that the foundation is laid in Jesus Christ, the goal is the Kingdom of God. But what lies between that divine origin and this divine goal, it may confess in confident uncertainty that it does not yet know.

[1] H. Küng, the author of the book *Rechtfertigung, Die Lehre Karl Barths und eine katholische Besinnung* (Justification: the Teaching of Karl Barth and a Catholic Reflection) has emphasized in a lecture to the Theological Faculty of Zürich that the principle *semper reformanda* has always been affirmed also by the Catholic Church and its theology

CHAPTER 9

THE ESSENTIAL MARKS OF THE CHURCH ACCORDING TO THE APOSTOLIC WITNESS OF FAITH

In the course of this critical examination of the nature of the Ekklesia, it has become clear to us why the Reformers' doctrine of the Church was bound to remain to this day unsatisfactory and problematic. On the other hand, it is now very possible to reformulate the fundamental definition of the nature of the Church which was set forth as long ago as the third article of the early Church creed: "I believe . . . in one holy Catholic and apostolic Church, the communion of saints".[1] We are here enumerating these fundamental norms in the reverse order since we have already dealt with the description "the communion of saints".

(1) THE CHURCH IS "APOSTOLICA"

It is "built upon the foundation of Apostles and Prophets, Jesus Christ Himself being the chief corner-stone" (Eph. 2: 20). Only a fellowship of men which rests on the foundation of personal commitment of life to Christ can be called Christian—whatever its form may be. "What is true to Christ, that is apostolic." This revolutionary word of Luther's does not indeed define the whole content of the concept "apostolic", but it touches the heart of the matter. The apostolic character of the Church rests primarily upon the fact that "it is concerned with Christ", that is, upon its essential spiritual conformity with the fact of Christ, as it is handed down to us in the apostolic witness. Nay, more, it rests upon the dynamic exercised by this fact of Christ. But in order to comprehend wholly the concept of apostolicity a second element must be included in it, the element of historical, spatio-temporal proximity of the witness to the event of revelation itself. The Apostles are the eye-witnesses and the original witnesses of the revelation in Christ. The Church is apostolic only when it stands in historical continuity with this primitive Christian Ekklesia.

What Luther really meant by his definition is that in the apostolic Church everything depends on Jesus, the Christ. His definition does complete justice to this real intention, even

[1] Cf. Calvin, *Institutes* IV, 1, 2 and 3

when we take into account the contemporary problem of the nature of the Church. In fact, the one name "Jesus" would be sufficient. The Church is apostolic when it is loyal to Jesus, for in this name its historical origin is indicated as such. This name is, of course, also known to secular historical scholarship, and indeed to the world at large. But the apostolic Confession means always the Jesus of faith, not the Jesus whom everyone knows as a historical personality and perhaps values as a religious genius or a man of ideal character. In all our descriptions of faith this primitive creed must sound as an undertone; that the Apostles recognize in this historical Jesus the Christ of faith. He who *believes* in Jesus, is a Christian. And he becomes a believer, and consequently a Christian, only through the mediation of the chain of historical tradition which leads down to him from Jesus through the Apostles as original witnesses, and through the Church which has been built upon this original witness. The attribute of apostolicity is concerned to give decisive emphasis to this historical element in the concept of the Church.

Further, the word of the Epistle to the Ephesians with its additional phrase "and prophets" is significant, both in the newer interpretation, which thinks of the New Testament prophets, and also in the older one, which takes it to refer to the Old Testament prophets. It is not historical tradition as such which creates the Church, but only the Word which comes from faith, the spirit-filled, prophetic Word. And only *that* Jesus is the object of faith, who was foretold by the prophets of the Old Testament and who fulfils their promise. So this additional phrase "and prophets" indicates the unity of the sacred history upon which the Church rests. Each interpretation refers to an aspect of the Church which must not be left out of account.

The Church knows itself to be an instrument of the Holy Spirit. The Church is not a synagogue, where the letter of the Bible as such is the authority and content. *Who* Jesus is, as the Christ, cannot be apprehended save "in the Spirit". Secular historical understanding does not know of Him as the Christ. And likewise Jesus is designated "the Christ" as one who stands in a sequence that begins with Abraham and leads through Moses to Isaiah and the Psalmists and comes to its conclusion with Him. God has communicated and glorified Himself in a history (cf. Part Four, chapter 4), of which the Old Testament and the New are the original documents.

For this reason the ancient Church was right to repudiate Marcionitism, which wished to discard the Old Testament—as also today Adolf von Harnack's opinion that the Church would do well to renounce this book and acknowledge only the New Testament as its foundation and norm is generally rejected as erroneous. The Church confesses that the Jewish people and its history are the presupposition of the Christian revelation. Only in this totality of the Old Testament and the New is Jesus apprehended as the Christ, and only so can He be the foundation and corner-stone of the Church. Whether the Church showed the same wisdom in its repudiation of Montanism might be called in question. There was at any rate emphasized in it an element—the prophetic element necessary to the being of the Ekklesia—which was very early almost entirely lost in the Church and buried under a false conception of Biblical authority and the authority of the Church. In modern times the prophetic element has been too exclusively identified with knowledge of the political and ethical actualities. The call for the "prophetic Word" has been too much understood in the sense of guidance in social and ethical questions. But it is just precisely in this sector that the scope for it is most limited; for social ethics should indeed be specifically Christian in their motive, but are in their essence a concern for rational reflection.

When we say that the Church is apostolic, we mean that even in its organization it must orientate itself by the Ekklesia of apostolic times and take this as its norm. That since its early days it has not done this, and has increasingly failed to do it, was the thesis of our last chapter. That it should be willing once more to do this was the intention of the Reformation and the various Churches, Free Churches and Brotherhood movements which emerged from it. They are all apostolic in the sense defined above, namely, that their intention was to restore the Ekklesia of apostolic times. None of them has succeeded, but they are all to be judged as attempts to reach this ideal. We have also already seen that every one of them in fact emphasized an aspect of the original Ekklesia, whether it was the apostolic Word, or the apostolic freedom, or the brotherhood of the Ekklesia. Because of this endeavour we have to acknowledge them as apostolic, although essential elements are lacking in them, or deviations in matters of essential importance have taken place in them.

However, the word "Apostolic", which was introduced only late into the Creed, was understood at the time when this occurred in a sense strange to the thought of the Apostles, in fact partly in conflict with it. There is in the original idea of the Ekklesia as we find it in Paul not the slightest trace of the thought of guaranteeing the fidelity of tradition by the legitimacy of episcopal succession. As we saw above, the idea of the Ekklesia was nourished in a very different soil. The Apostolic Succession in this sense is not at all Apostolic, but has absorbed into itself the political and worldly element of legitimate succession in office. We have already described how this Succession, understood as a guarantee for the reliability of the tradition of the apostolic *kerygma,* has failed of its purpose. The legitimate successor in office has very often turned out to be a betrayer of his cause, as a disloyal disciple of the Lord, as a shepherd who has led the flock into the desert instead of "beside still waters". But, on the other hand, this principle of Apostolic Succession has also had great advantages, and shown itself of value in the storms which the Church had to endure in the Middle Ages. Only thanks to this Apostolic Succession of bishops, and through the vigorous organization of the episcopate, was it possible for the Church to maintain itself through the confusions and upheavals of the time and to protect the gospel entrusted to it. So we must not be too severely critical of this false interpretation of "apostolic"; in all our criticism we must never forget this great debt of gratitude.

The critical principle contained in the concept "apostolic" is, however, directed not only against the Catholic but also against the Protestant Churches. For these have given an entirely different interpretation of "apostolic" which was nevertheless secular in character and just as calamitous in its consequences as the other. They have confused faith in Christ with an aprioristic faith in the Bible and thus have laid a great burden on the Church. Post-Reformation theology made no use of the critical principle contained in Luther's word "(Only) what is true to Christ is apostolic", but declared that the Bible as a whole was God's Word. We must indeed concede that by so doing they added a certain necessary supplement to Luther's too one-sided identification of the doctrine of justification with the revelation of Christ. For God's self-communication does not begin with Jesus Christ, but finds in Him its culmination. The Old Testament too is God's Word in so far as it is the deposit of this self-communication. Both these things Luther knew intuitively, but he was not yet able to formulate them completely.

For this reason scholarly Biblical criticism is an essential to the truly apostolic Church, as is also a regularly advancing and self-critical theology. Luther's thought, that the Christian community is called and authorized to test and to judge the preaching and doctrine of its commissioned teachers, is completely true to the apostolic faith. This community, which was founded by the Word of the Apostles and the prophetic expositors of the apostolic Word, is at the same time justified in keeping watch over the apostolic character of preaching and doctrine, and, indeed, obliged to do so. That is the "hermeneutic circle" to which the knowledge of apostolicity is forever bound. Thus, the true Church is always a self-critical Church within which the element of criticism is actually regarded as belonging to the prophetic office. "For it is time that judgment should begin at the house of God" (1 Peter 4: 17).

A Church which believes itself infallible is therefore never a genuinely apostolic Church. This is true above all with respect to its institutional form. The New Testament idea of the Ekklesia, which on the one side is completely lacking in the institutional element, and which on the other is inseparably bound up with the thought of brotherhood, is the sharpest critique conceivable of a Church which reckons its institutional apparatus to be essential to its nature, and, consequently, the sharpest critique of a false "ecclesiasticism". But this critical norm is applicable also to all dogma and to all the confessional writings of the Church. Only a Church that is ready to acknowledge this is genuinely apostolic. But what the social form of the Church would have to be in order to be genuinely apostolic, is a question which could be answered only by keeping in view at the same time the Ekklesia of apostolic times, the present, and the eschatological future.

So the concept of apostolicity, rightly understood, is not only fundamental but in the highest degree a critical principle. One might even call it a revolutionary principle of the Church. What is apostolic is not determined from the beginning, as orthodox Protestantism believed. This concept includes among other things scholarly Biblical criticism, which seeks for the truly apostolic interpretation of the New Testament. But further it has not stability in the sense of the Catholic Churches, who believe that they can guarantee apostolicity as a matter of Church law, through the principle of the Apostolic Succession. Thus this concept in its fundamental critical significance is the first criterion of a Christian Church.

(2) THE CHURCH IS "CATHOLICA"

Unfortunately it has become almost impossible for us Protestants to set free the concept of Catholicity from the sense given it by the Roman Catholics, while the Reformers never let there be any doubt that in their Reformation they had no other aim than the restoration of the genuine Catholic Church. Catholic means universal, dealing with the whole. It is true that this concept has from the beginning suffered from an ambiguity. Does it mean "actually spread over the whole world", or "intended for the whole world or for humanity"? In the former sense the Church even today is not Catholic, since even now there are peoples who have never heard the gospel, among whom no Church has ever set foot. Therefore we do not understand the concept as an empirical one, since the actual expansion of the apostolic Church could not be affirmed without critical reservations; we understand it teleologically and normatively. Man was created by God for the Ekklesia; that means his God-given destiny is to belong to Christ. Man as such, to whatever race, whatever class, whatever religion he may belong, whatever cultural level or whatever moral qualities he may have attained—must be regarded in the light of Christ as destined for the Ekklesia.

The word "catholic" thus reminds us of that word of Jesus about the "Father in heaven, who makes His sun to rise upon the evil and the good, and His rain to fall upon the just and the unjust" (Matt. 5: 45). The truth in Christ, His grace, and fellowship in Him are meant for all without qualification.[1] This would mean nothing else than that life in the Ekklesia is at the same time the true human life, the true humanity, though here we must at all events remember that the Ekklesia —even in the thought of the Apostles—is only the vanguard of the coming Kingdom of God. The Ekklesia of history is, as we have already said, only on the way to its goal. But in it, or rather in its foundation, Jesus Christ, this goal has been revealed—and realized, if only as yet in a provisional form.

This means, further, that the Ekklesia is meant for the *world*. The message of Jesus Christ and the life intended by it and based upon it is nothing sacred, not something contrasted with the profane character of the world, but quite simply the true expression of man's nature and of humanity. It is perhaps this that Dietrich Bonhoeffer meant with his "non-religious interpretation" of the gospel, and left behind as his legacy. Thus the "secularism" of which so much has been spoken in the last decades is, rightly understood, not something which as Christians we should lament and oppose, but the goal of the gospel. The Ekklesia is distinguished from all religions or

[1] See below, p. 184

cultic fellowships by the fact that it abolishes the antithesis between the sacred and the profane. We have already seen[1] that just this is one of the things which the Lord's Supper is intended to express. The Ekklesia, we could say, strives towards complete "worldliness"; the Christian cannot be "worldly" enough.

Here indeed a dialectic reveals itself which is not easy to comprehend. In the first place the Ekklesia is the *new* humanity, it is what sharply severs and distinguishes it from the "world" as the old humanity. "Be not conformed to this world" (Rom. 12: 2); "Love not the world, nor what is in the world" (1 John 2: 15), or as was said in the recent struggle for the liberty of the Church: "Let the Church be the Church, oppose co-ordination by the State!" The Ekklesia as *catholica* is the new humanity which has indeed every human being in view, but at the same time stands in opposition to the "World". But the transcendence of this opposition is its goal, its route of march. The Church must not sever itself from the world but make approach to it, enter into it. Forgetting its character as the Church, it must as Ekklesia so enter into the world as happened when in Jesus Christ the eternal Son of God became flesh. And in order to do this it must lay aside its sacred garments.

This is what distinguishes the Reformed understanding of the Ekklesia from the Roman Catholic. In the former the identification of Ekklesia and Church is denied; in the latter it is not only emphasized but made the foundation of the whole of theology and the Church. This antithesis, however, is not actually so great as in theological theory; the Roman Catholic Church also is involved in the search for a form, and the Protestant Churches also have their institutional sacred character. It means, however, that both the static and the dynamic elements of both Churches, their present character and their movement towards the goal, are activated by the dialectic of Ekklesia and world. Inasmuch as even the Roman Catholic Church is not content with its present character but measures this by the standard of the ideal Ekklesia of faith and seeks to shape itself in accordance with that ideal, inasmuch as it also acknowledges the principle "*semper reformanda*",[2] it is also a form of the Ekklesia. And conversely the Churches of the Reformation continually take themselves too seriously in their already established form, and thereby petrify into Churches in the wrong sense.

So far as the Church is conscious of being on the march it accepts self-criticism in the light of Christ and thus seeks not

[1] See above, pp. 60 ff. [2] See above, p. 116, n. 1

so much itself as its service to the world. This standpoint is important not only in relation to its understanding of the meaning of "catholica" but, as we shall see, in relation to its understanding of the meaning of unity (*Una*). But what transformations the Church on the march may yet experience in its character as Church, no one can yet foretell.

The "Catholic" nature of the Church was always the strongest missionary motive. "Go ye into all the world and preach the gospel to every creature" (Mark 16: 15). But missions also have been overtaken by a crisis, and here too this crisis indicates a false conception. For the words "preach to every creature" have been too much understood in terms of our tradition. What *we* call missions are very different from what the Word of Jesus means, for our conception is stamped by the false concept of faith. True faith is essentially bound up with love, and therefore also with the will to begin by understanding the other person. On the mission field it is evident that "communication of" must be bound up with "communication with".[1]

But what is true of missions in the customary sense must far more be true of "home missions", of the task of proclaiming the gospel in "Christian lands" and building the Ekklesia. Here Bonhoeffer's enigmatic word about the non-religious interpretation of the gospel becomes a programme to which we have hardly yet set our hands. Here we have something quite different from a problem of language and from a popular and more contemporary form of preaching. What is here at stake is the knowledge of the connection between gospel and humanity, between Ekklesia and true humanity, between faith and life in the world. But how could the Church be *catholica* without this understanding? The religious concept of the Catholicity of the Ekklesia is thus a radically critical principle of the Church. The seriousness with which it allows the principle "*semper reformanda*" to cause it concern will be the criterion whether, and to what extent, a Church is "*catholica*".

(3) THE CHURCH IS "SANCTA"

This description has no more place in the New Testament than have the two terms we have just considered. True, the Ekklesia of apostolic times is the *communio sanctorum*. The members of the community in Corinth—certainly not saints in the common sense of the term—are addressed as *Klētoi hagioi* (called to be saints). They are this because Christ has laid His

[1] See above, p. 26, n. 1

hand on them and placed them in His service. They are sanctified by having received the Word of reconciliation through Christ in faith (John 15: 3). It is all the more remarkable that Paul never speaks of a holy Ekklesia. True, Ephesians 2: 21 described the Christian community as a "holy temple in the Lord" and Ephesians 5: 27 indicates to it its task of becoming "holy and blameless". Paul obviously shrinks from using the word "holy" of anything other than persons. He acknowledges no holy "It", above all no holy collective, no holy institution.

There can, however, be no doubt that the Apostles' Creed thinks of the Church as an institution. The expression *communio sanctorum,* which was especially clear and important to the Reformers, had already at the time when it was included in the Apostles' Creed a neutral sense, referring to the means of salvation in the Sacraments. Thus it must have meant participation rather than communion, and the phrase *sanctorum* would have to be understood not as genitive of *sancti* (saints) but of *sancta* (holy things).[1] Through this displacement from the personal into the neuter and material realm (means of salvation) the concept lost its New Testament sense. In the New Testament *Koinōnia tōn hagiōn* is the "fellowship which we have with each other" through Him who binds us together through His love, and not *koinōnia* in the sense of participation in sacred things (*participatio sanctorum*). This latter concept is entirely absent from the New Testament, as indeed is also the whole sacramental concept.

At this point, however, the Protestant Church has something to learn anew, for the sacramental concept has deeply penetrated it and has obscured the meaning of faith. To a large degree the sacramental concept has restored to credit the Church's understanding of itself as the holy institution, the dispenser of the Sacrament, and has thereby endangered the revolutionary achievement of the Reformers. The Church must decide whether with the Apostles it is to think of itself in personal categories or with the Catholic Church in sacramental categories. There is no third possibility. It is in fact impossible to place an equal emphasis on "Word and Sacrament". One of the most urgent requirements of a Church that wishes to be apostolic in the New Testament sense is that it should be freed from sacramental thinking. That only by such a procedure would Baptism and the Lord's Supper regain their true significance, we have already shown in an earlier discussion. The Apostles were not concerned with the

[1] Cf. in this context Ch. 2, p. 27

administration of the means of grace but with the ever renewed establishment of the Ekklesia-brotherhood on its foundation, Jesus Christ. When we look back on the history of the Church and especially when we read the New Testament with unprejudiced eyes, the century-long discussion about the elements must be described as the search for an answer to a falsely formulated question.

Ecclesia sancta can then only mean: a Church which is founded on the sanctifying act and word of God in Jesus Christ which can be received only in faith. When the Word of Christ and faith meet, the presence of the Holy Spirit is experienced, and it is He and none other who sheds abroad the love of God in our hearts. The apostolic witness knows nothing of any other infusion of grace. And the Holy Spirit is primarily a speaking Spirit—the interior Word of God in us, assuring us that we are God's children and claiming us for the service of our brother. The Church as a *sancta ecclesia* is known by nothing else than this, that here men are present who allow this incredible Word of God's love in Christ to be said to them, believe it, and obey it by passing on the love bestowed on them to their fellow men in acts of love.

It is true that such a simple brotherhood, or a Church marked by the ideal of such a simple brotherhood, is lacking in that "numinous" element that attracts many to the Church of the Sacrament, and which from primitive times has been bound up with the priesthood, with the temple separated from the profane world, with the altar and the offering of sacrifice. Certainly an impression of the numinous is given even by the original accounts of the Ekklesia. But it is no longer characterized by the element of the sacred but rather by an awareness of a divine Presence which the natural man could not understand but which even he could not mistake: the presence of the Holy Spirit in the Ekklesia. Even if the account of Pentecost given in the Acts does not exactly correspond to the historical reality, yet, like the Book of Acts in general, it reproduces the impression which was made by the Ekklesia and its missionaries. That is the truly numinous thing: the presence of the living God in His people, which is not only "numinous" but also in a singular manner genuinely human at the same time.

(4) THE CHURCH IS "UNA"

The greatest, at least the most clearly visible, problem of contemporary Christendom is hidden in the smallest, most unassuming word of the apostolic Creed: "one". For the fact that there are many Churches seems to give the lie to this assertion. And yet we must agree with the Apostle's word, that the Body of Christ cannot be divided. The Ecumenical Movement of our day has arisen from a perception of this contradiction. This is, at any rate, its deepest spiritual motive. Let us frankly acknowledge that it has also roots of a worldly and pragmatic kind. But how far, in spite of this schism of the Churches, can we speak of the *one* Church?

In general, Protestantism accounts for this unity by referring to the Invisible Church, the Church of faith; but, by so doing, it surrenders the Church as a social entity by declaring not merely the *plurality* of Churches but also their deeply-grounded *differences* to be, in the last resort, unimportant. And indeed this explanation of opposition—for example the confessional opposition between Catholic and Protestant—as being in the last resort not fundamental, is offered both on the Roman Catholic side and on the Protestant. Official Catholic teaching leaves room, though admittedly very little room indeed, for the possibility of regarding individual Protestant believers as Christian brothers, while the distinction we have just referred to between the Visible Church and the Invisible enables Protestantism to be more generous. The Roman Catholic Church had a great advantage over Protestantism, inasmuch as it could appeal to the fact that this distinction was unknown to the New Testament which conceived of the Ekklesia as it came into existence, in Corinth and Thessalonica and so on, as the Body of Christ. In fact, as we have shown in detail, the Ekklesia of apostolic times is not an invisible entity. Here Catholicism is right. But neither is it a Church, least of all the most "ecclesiastical" of all Churches, the Roman Catholic Church. Here Protestantism is right. Rather is it the brotherhood of sinners bound together by Christ, men who are holy through faith.

But the claim of the Roman Catholic Church that *it* is the *Una Sancta* is already made questionable by the fact that long before the Reformation, namely, since the year 1054, there have been two Churches: the Roman, and, alongside it, the Greek Orthodox, which could say with some justification that it was the elder of the two twin sisters. The Roman Church could only maintain its claim to be the *Una Sancta* by throwing the blame for the schism on the Greek Orthodox Church.

The Protestant Churches are faced by the same difficulty. Their union is impossible, because they embody irreconcilable, antithetical formative principles. It will never be possible to unite the Baptist or Congregationalist Churches with the Episcopalians, because in the one case and the other the formative principles and ideals, that of the autonomous congregation and of the Church under central leadership, stand in irreconcilable conflict with each other. This insuperable hindrance, both in the Confessional conflict (Catholic-Protestant) and in the denominational one (Baptists-Episcopalians) lies in the fact that in both cases the institution is identified with the Ekklesia. Such an identification is, however, neither necessary nor justified. The Protestant Churches all recognize the primitive form of the Ekklesia as the New Testament ideal, which is implied in the understanding of faith, that is, in Christology, and is normative for the Church.

But, as we have seen, the Ekklesia itself is certainly not a Church in the institutional sense, but a brotherhood resulting from faith in Christ. If this fact were acknowledged, at least by the Churches which sprang from the Reformation, the stumbling block caused by the multiplicity of Churches and the spiritual reasons for having one Church would disappear. Interest would turn away from the form of the Church and towards our common service. Each Church would see that its special form can very well be regarded as a special means for accomplishing our common service. Institutional organization would be regarded from the first as of merely relative importance. When every Church sees that it *is* not the Body of Christ, but only *serves* to build up that Body, the differences are made relative, and are freed from the pressure of the New Testament Ekklesia-norm. Each Church could then very well regard the others as so many instruments or vessels which serve the one purpose, the creation of true fellowship in Christ, of true Ekklesia.

The multiplicity of such instrumental institutions would then not be regarded from the start as an evil, but could just as well, and with more justification, be reckoned as of positive value, as different means serving one end. They could be compared with different types of forces in one army, which each has its own way of functioning, which also "march apart, but strike together"—that is, trying each in its own manner, as Zwingli put it, under the one "Captain" to be obedient to His command and, above all, to make known in the world the glad tidings of reconciliation. This functional, instrumental conception of all Church organizations would bring with it a great measure of generous toleration. Each individual Church would have a modest estimate of its own value, and room would be left for the practical justification of its individual character. The Baptist and the Congregationalist could concede also the relative advantages of the Episcopalian system, and the Episcopalian the advantages of the system of autonomous congregations. Even the very fruitful service of a formation like that of the Japanese non-Church movement could then be appreciated. For in it also the message of a Redeemer is the central thing.

Thus we come to *this* solution of the ecumenical problem: the really lamentable thing is not the existence of different Church bodies, but the failure to acknowledge the Ekklesia as a spiritual brotherhood which is not an institution. If theological reflection and, above all, renewed serious study of the New Testament witnesses to Christ have once made this clear, then the way is open to a common understanding of our unity—namely our unity in Christ, without our having recourse to the concept of the *ecclesia invisibilis*. The institutional form, the Church, does not belong to the *essence* of the Ekklesia. But as we men are constituted this is necessary as its covering, its shell and its instrument. And here the form of the Church which from time to time has taken historical shape will have to be tested in respect of its usefulness, with an eye on the concept of the Ekklesia as apprehended by faith.

It is only on this basis that a truly ecumenical conversation is possible, when we have been freed from the burdensome task of forming *one* Church, which is the Ekklesia. The wish to give an organizational and legal form to the *Una Sancta* is the error of Rome and leads along the road to Rome. But Rome too—as precisely the Protestant can see—should be included in this conversation, regardless of the fact that it is the peculiarity of the Roman Church to believe in its identity with the Body of Christ. Since there is within Roman Catholic theology an unmistakable process of appropriation of Reformation insights, we must not give up the hope that some day a genuinely brotherly conversation between the Roman and non-Roman Churches might take place. But the *union* of these two partners in the discussion is indeed an eschatological hope.

But as far as the ecumenical conversation between the non-Roman Churches is concerned, the theological recognition of the non-identity of Ekklesia and Church—which we have striven to reach in this book—would lead beyond the antithesis between theological narrow-mindedness and worldly pragmatism. Our pluralistic view of the Church problem does not arise from considerations of convenience, but has been won from the theological knowledge of what the New Testament describes as the Ekklesia. Jesus Christ calls all Churches into His service by calling them as Churches to penitence. That faith is possible only in the Ekklesia—that is the truth that Rome represents over against us Protestants. But that the Ekklesia is nothing else than the fellowship in faith and love of those who believe in Jesus the Christ—that is the knowledge which we Protestants represent over against Rome. How far such knowledge is possible depends in the last resort on our understanding of the first word of the Confession of Faith concerning the Church: *Credo*.

(5) "CREDO"

The way we understand faith determines our understanding of the Church. Taken on purely linguistic grounds, the Apostles' Creed leaves open the question as to how the relationship between faith and the Church is to be understood. Is it to be interpreted, "I believe in the Holy Spirit and (in) the Holy Church" (*credo in sanctum spiritum et in sanctam ecclesiam*) or "I believe (that) the holy Church (exists)" (*credo sanctam ecclesiam* (sc. *esse*))? Linguistically, both are possible. The Reformers interpreted the formula in the second sense, saying that it was not possible to "believe in" the Church in the same way as one "believes in" God and Christ. Earlier forms of the Apostles' Creed betray something of the uncertainty on this issue, and indeed, something of its grounds. They read, "I believe in the Holy Spirit and I believe through the holy Church" (*credo in sancto spiritu* and *credo per sanctam ecclesiam*).[1]

There is a similar ambiguity in the case of the additional phrase "(*sanctam ecclesiam*) *communionem sanctorum*." Is it the *sancti* or the *sancta* (the sacraments) that are here meant? Here also the Reformers made an important decision, by taking *sanctorum* to mean the saints (*sancti*) and interpreting the term personally, not sacramentally. It was significant that of them all Luther seized upon this additional phrase as an actual definition. It was *that* Church, he said, which was meant which consists only of holy persons, of those who were made holy by faith in Christ, "the holy Christian people", "the

[1] F. Loofs, Symbolik, 1902, *In sancto spiritu als Formulierung des gallischen Taufsymbols. Das "Credo per sanctam ecclesiam" als die Formulierung des älteren afrikanischen Taufsymbols*, pp. 12 and 13. ("In the Holy Spirit" as formulation of the Gallican Baptismal Creed. "I believe through the holy Church" as the formulation of the earlier African Baptismal Creed)

congregation of the holy". The Roman Catholic Church has given the contrary answer to the question: the Christian must in fact believe in the holy Church, and this is by no means identical with the congregation of the faithful, but stands over against them as the dispenser of holy things—*sancta*. Communion should then rather mean participation.

We have sufficiently demonstrated in the preceding chapters that in the Ekklesia of the New Testament it is always those called to be saints—the *klētoi hagioi*—and never anything else, who were described by this word. They are called to be saints by the Word of Christ that is given to them and that dwells in them through the Holy Spirit, and as such they are called the Ekklesia. Their togetherness, their fellowship, is "in Christ"; therefore it is *Koinōnia pneumatos*, fellowship through, or in, the Spirit; at the same time visible as a fellowship with one another and invisible in the foundations of this fellowship with one another in Christ, in the Spirit. We can, however, very well understand that an Augustine, after he had begun to conceive of faith in the Pauline manner, could no longer simply accept "I believe in the Church", (*credo* (*in*) *ecclesiam*) because in the interval the Ekklesia had turned into a sacramental institution, and, even more, into a Church which since Constantine's edict of tolerance was no longer persecuted but privileged, and since the time of Theodosius had even been declared obligatory by the State. In his difficulty Augustine could see no way out but to make the distinction between an *ecclesia invisibilis* and the one which had become only too visible.

This distinction then, as we saw, played an important part in the Reformation also, not in Luther but in Zwingli and Calvin. By this means it was possible to call both the very heterogeneous entities—the Church as known to faith and the Church as an institution known to everybody—by the name of "Church". That this distinction itself neither was drawn nor indeed could be drawn in the New Testament Ekklesia, we have already shown.

But even in the lands of Luther's Reformation the question of the definition of the Church as known to faith and as a social structure was a continuing problem. The Confession of Augsburg, composed by Melanchthon, and read but cursorily and approved only with reservations by Luther, concealed the problem under a facile formula: "The Ekklesia is the congregation of saints in which the gospel is rightly taught and the Sacraments are rightly administered" (*Est autem ecclesia congregatio sanctorum* (genitive of sancti) *in qua evangelium recte docetur et recte administrantur sacramenta*). Here both the element of brotherhood and the institutional moment seem to be happily conjoined. But in reality this formula shirks the decision which was so massively taken in the further course of Reformation history by the Church government set up by the State. The Church is henceforward the institution in which correct doctrine is preached and the Sacraments are rightly administered—supposedly following New Testament example. The correlation of Word and Sacrament as of equal importance is, as has been shown above, not understandable on New Testament authority, but only in the light of the history of the Church.

This correlation, however, was made easy for the Reformers, this time including Luther, because they found and were able to adopt the formula "visible Word" (*verbum visibile*) put at their disposal by Augustine as the correct sacramental concept. But they did not notice that the distinction between an "audible Word" (*verbum audibile*) and a visible Word (*verbum visibile*) was merely psychological, relating only to the form of the Word. But this was not sufficient foundation to bear the weight of the sacramental concept. It was, however—at least as far as the Lord's Supper was concerned—easier to rest content with this, inasmuch as in this Sacrament the spoken Word, Jesus' Words of Institution, were of central importance.

Thus in the Reformation the faith which depends solely on the Word of God had, in fact, won the victory—yet not completely, but burdened with a twofold disadvantage. The Ekklesia had, falsely, partly identified itself with an institution which was known from its thousand-year-long history and was known as the Church. And this had principally happened—which is the second point—because also this Church believed that it must be the administrator of Sacraments. Thus the Ekklesia had once again become a sacramental institution, although the concept and not only the term "sacrament" was alien to the New Testament and had a quite different origin.

But this Sacrament, since it was founded only on the psychological difference between *verbum audibile* and *verbum visibile*, was from the first not really credible as a Sacrament. It could not be a Sacrament in the authentic sacred and Catholic sense, and in the sense of the Protestant Church it was not essentially different from the Word of Christ. The retention of the equal co-ordination of Word and Sacrament has rendered difficult of access this half-sacred Church which yet did not desire to be sacred. The living community has for a long time ceased to understand the Lord's Supper as a Sacrament, but has looked on it in the way that the Lord's Supper was regarded in the Ekklesia: the fellowship feast of those who are bound together by faith in God's act of reconciliation in the Cross, and by hope in the return of the Lord.

But as the Sacrament of this Church could no longer be understood as such, so neither could the institution; in particular, the clerical office. The more time passed, the clearer it became that this official and institutional character of the Church hindered the creation of Ekklesia. The crisis of the Church, of which we spoke above, has its cause above all in these two ambiguities which obscured men's understanding of the Ekklesia. Both, however, can be removed, but only by our learning anew what the New Testament means by *pistis*, faith. This is the task to which we now apply ourselves in Section II. For it must emphatically be repeated that the understanding of the true nature of the Church, that is, of the Ekklesia, depends on our understanding of the word "credo".

Section II

THE NEW LIFE IN CHRIST

CHAPTER 10

THE EKKLESIA AS PRESUPPOSITION OF FAITH

I

THE revelation of God in Jesus Christ is God's self-communication to mankind. In this revelation God has made known His own nature as self-bestowing love (*agape*). Charge is laid upon the Ekklesia to bear witness to this love. It is there to make this witness. At the same time this witness is the basis of its life. Christ has communicated Himself in such a way that He did not give the Ekklesia the Word alone, but His life also, and made it His Body through His Spirit. This life of His cannot but manifest itself as life-creating power. The Spirit who is at work in the Ekklesia expresses Himself in active love and in the creation of fellowship. Christ has not only revealed the love of God; He has at the same time bestowed it.

The Ekklesia does not only *know* that God is love. That would be mere *gnosis*. The Ekklesia also lives from the love of God—it lives indeed, even though only in an imperfect way, *in* the love of God. Jesus Christ is not only the "Truth"—He is at the same time the "*Life*". Not only in the Word about Him, but through the power of His indwelling Spirit, through its *existence* in Him, the Ekklesia is the Body of Christ. Faith in Christ is not only the answer to the question "What is true?" It is at the same time the answer to the question "What is fellowship, and how do we attain to it?" The Spirit who is active in the Ekklesia expresses Himself in active love of the brethren and in the creation of brotherhood, of true fellowship. Thus the Ekklesia has to bear a double witness to Christ, through the *Word* that tells of what He has bestowed upon it, and through the witness of its *life*, through its being, which points to Him as its vital source.

II

These two testimonies of the Ekklesia through Word and life corroborate each other, and neither is fully effective without the other. The Word of Christ is truly effective and credible only where it is accompanied by the life-witness of the Ekklesia. The life-witness of the Ekklesia is possible only where Christ's Word dwells actively in it. In regard to both testimonies the Ekklesia is the precondition of the birth of faith. If we ask, "How can a man come to believe?", the answer must be, "Through the proclamation of the Word of the love of God in Jesus Christ." But this Word can awaken true faith only when it is proclaimed by the Ekklesia, the brotherhood, in which alone it is vitally present. Only through the Word of Christ which the Ekklesia has received, can faith come into being.

The gospel of Christ is a Word "from faith to faith"—more precisely, a Word from the fellowship of faith leading to the fellowship of faith, and for this reason it is credible only where it is accompanied by the life witness of the Ekklesia. Without this it is unintelligible, unworthy of belief. When it is not backed by the love of those who speak it, it is a self-contradiction. Only that word of the love of God in Christ, which has as a commentary the love, the fellowship, the brotherliness of the Church that proclaims it, can have the power of a real witness. The Word of the witness presupposes his trustworthiness.

The misunderstanding of the Ekklesia as the Church, as a sacred institution, corresponds to the "misunderstanding of faith", through which faith was misunderstood as affirmation of doctrine or of facts.[1] In this manner correct doctrine became the object of faith, and through this displacement the unity of faith and love was sundered. At the same time as the priestly sacramental institution there came into being "orthodoxy", the belief in true doctrine, and the guarantee of this belief by Church creed or dogma. The misunderstanding does not consist in the establishment by the Church of a creed, a norm of doctrine and faith, but in the replacement of witness by this regulated doctrine and assent thereto, which is described by the same word "faith", and which takes the place of trusting obedience to the Christ who meets us and is present in the Word that bears witness to Him. However, we cannot deal with this in detail until we have shown what *pistis*, faith, means in the apostolic witness. Only this is now already clear: the distinction between faith in the sense of a faith which is believed (*fides quae creditur*) and a faith by which we believe (*fides qua creditur*) would have been just as unintelligible to the Apostles and the first Christians as would have been the distinction between an *ecclesia invisibilis* and *visibilis*. True faith is

[1] See below, Ch. 13, pp. 176 ff.

indivisibly both, faith in Christ and existence in Christ. As witness given in the power of the Spirit, the Word of Christ is never merely abstract doctrine, and faith is never faith in this doctrine, orthodoxy.

He who receives the Word of witness—through faith—is at the same time united with the Ekklesia and incorporated into it. But, as we saw in an earlier context, it can be the other way round.[1] A man is laid hold of by the life of the fellowship, moved by the love which he experiences there; he "grows into" the brotherhood, and only gradually learns to know Jesus Christ as the Church's one foundation. His way to Christ is through the fellowship; through receiving human love he comes to believe in Him from whom this love originates. As a rule the Church has reckoned only with the first possibility, and acknowledged this way, the way of instruction, as the only one. But since both the Word that bears witness to Christ and the love created by it have the same source, the second way, which leads through fellowship, through reception of the Spirit of love, to Christ as the source of this Spirit, is just as much to be reckoned with as a possibility, although true faith comes into being only through the unity of Word and Spirit, of truth and fellowship, of knowledge of Christ and the heart-felt experience of love. The "unclassical" way from the brotherhood in Christ to Christ as its originator is indicated in the story of Pentecost. It was not only the Word of Peter which led the bystanders to penitence and to faith; they were made ready to hear it by their astonishment at the astounding existence of the disciple band. In the accounts given in Acts it seems always to be the Word of the Apostle that creates faith. But in the letters of the Apostle himself we learn how it was only in conjunction with his loving presence that his Word opened men's hearts.

The one thing, the message of Christ, must have the other thing, love, as its commentary. Only then can it be understood and move people's hearts. True, the decisive thing is the Word of witness to what God has done. But this Word of witness does not aim merely to teach, but also to move the heart.

It is not the abstract Word of the Church's teaching, but the Spirit-filled Word of witness, behind which stands the reality of the brotherhood in Christ, which has the power to create living faith. Only the life-witness of Christians and of their brotherhood, above all, the readiness of the witnesses to die for their faith, makes the rapid expansion of Christianity understandable. The early Church still knew this and gave it

[1] See above, pp. 114 ff.

memorable expression in its saying "The blood of the martyrs is the seed of the Church"—"*sanguis martyrum semen ecclesiae*".

On the other hand, disproportionate attention to the content of doctrine contributed much to the early petrifaction of the Church, which was concealed only by the Constantinian inflation and the Theodosian compulsory Church. Witness by word and by action belong together, and consequently so do the teaching and the loving Church. Therefore both propositions are true: "Only through the Ekklesia do men come to faith", and "Only through faith do men come to the Ekklesia." If we say the first, then the Word of Christ is already implicit in the Ekklesia-fellowship, for it was created by the Word and is sustained by it. If we say the second, then the Ekklesia is already implicit in the Word of witness which creates faith, since it is indeed the Word of the love of God.

But if the Ekklesia turns into the Church as institution, the unity of Word and life-witness is at once sundered. Orthodoxy takes the place of faith (*pistis*), and the moral imperative takes the place of love. The Church has indeed preserved a memory of that (lost) unity by placing the Sacrament alongside of the Word. But this does not enable it to restore the original unity. Because the Word does not stem from the fellowship, it is no more the power of the life-witness of the Ekklesia. It is indeed no longer the Ekklesia, but the institution that administers the Sacraments. The Word is no longer backed by the loving brotherhood. The place of the power of the Spirit is now taken by the authority of the Church. The Word has become an authoritative Word of doctrine, and since the end of the fourth century this authority has been at one and the same time the numinous *auctoritas* of the whole college of bishops and the authority of the State which is bound up therewith. The law of the State now demands orthodoxy. It is clear that by this the essence of faith is fundamentally altered. The faith required by this Church is no longer the *pistis* of the New Testament.

III

So let us turn back again to the Ekklesia. In it the self-communication of God in Jesus Christ has become reality, inasmuch as it is received in faith. The Ekklesia lives from and in the love of God bestowed in Christ. In that love the Ekklesia has its existence as the human fellowship which is rooted in the love of God. It is charged and commissioned to bear witness to this love. The Lord uses its Word of witness to continue His work of self-communication. The Ekklesia thus becomes an instrument, a means, in the hand of God for the building of His Kingdom, for the establishment of His Lordship among men.

Thus, in this sense, it is a *means to an end*, not an end in itself, for the end is the perfected Kingdom of God. But at the same time the Ekklesia is not only means to an end but an *end in itself*, inasmuch as it is the Body of Christ and thus God's self re-presentation. In it Christ is present through His Word and His Spirit. In the celebration of the Lord's Supper, as through the "Word that dwells richly in it", it becomes ever and again His Body. *Agape* is the bond that holds together the members of the Ekklesia. "That we . . . speaking the truth in love, may grow up into Him in all things, which is the head, even Christ: from whom the whole body fitly joined together and compacted by that which every joint supplieth, according to the effectual working in the measure of every part, maketh increase of the body unto the edifying of itself in love" (Eph. 4: 15, 16). Here we have a description of the Ekklesia which summarizes the essentials in figurative language. In its love individuals are bound together in fellowship with Christ and in brotherhood at the same time. The hidden root of this union is faith, its visible fruit is love. This union with Christ—and in Him with God—came into being through faith. Through the love which faith lays hold of and receives as the love of God, faith finds its outer expression as union with the brethren.

The witness to Christ in the Word creates the faith that binds the individual to the Ekklesia as the fellowship of believers. The Word of Christ takes the isolated man out of his solitariness and binds him, when he becomes a believer, to the congregation of believers, *ek pisteōs eis pistin*, from faith to faith. It is therefore in fact impossible to speak of faith without at the same time speaking of the Ekklesia from which alone faith comes and in which alone it finds its realization. For only *that* faith counts which shows itself effectual in love. The isolation of the believer, Christian individualism, is a contradiction in terms. Faith is existence in fellowship, as it is also at the same time personal existence. On the other hand, it is not existence "in the Church", since mere existence in the *institution* of the Church is neither fellowship nor personal existence. Church membership is no guarantee that our life is a life "in love". Therefore, aloofness in relation to the Church institution and unwillingness to co-operate with it, the so-called individualism of the unchurched, is understandable.

And similarly the "faith" which stems from the Church and not from the Ekklesia, from doctrine and not from witness, is not in itself living faith. The Church, which as institution is not a fellowship, not a brotherhood, is for the believer truly only that "external support to faith" (*externum subsidium fidei*), that *school* of faith that Calvin calls it.[1] Or else it is the sacred institution which administers saving grace in the Sacrament and "outside which there is no salvation". It is the Church that supports with its authority the word of doctrine about Christ so that men first believe in the Church and through her the Bible. "I would not have believed the Scriptures, if I had not been moved thereto by the authority of the Church" (Augustine). This heteronomous faith is no more faith in the New Testament sense than is the faith in the letter of scripture required by the Orthodox Protestant Church.

We would mistake the meaning of these critical distinctions were we to draw the conclusion from them that there could be no vital faith within this Church. Catholic theology teaches that faith on authority should be regarded as a step on the way to true faith, just as Reformed theology regards mere faith in the Bible as a prelude to true faith, which rests on Christ Himself. But this distinction between Church and Ekklesia was necessary in order to set forth clearly the true relation of faith and the fellowship of faith. Not by starting with the Church, but only by starting with the Ekklesia can we understand this bond that unites faith to the *fellowship* of faith, just as only from this standpoint can the essential togetherness of faith and love be understood.

[1] *Institutes* IV, I, 5

CHAPTER II

FAITH AND UNBELIEF

> The one true deepest theme of the history of the world and mankind, to which all other themes are subordinate, remains the conflict between unbelief and faith.
>
> —Goethe[1]

WHEN Goethe wrote these words, he was hardly aware of the fact that this insight is possible only within the Christian tradition. For it is only in Christianity, not in the other world religions, that faith has so central a significance. Neither in Islam nor in Hinduism nor in Buddhism is the relation to the divine conceived of as faith. Paul was the first to use this word to describe the right relationship to God, and by so doing he gave it an absolutely dominating position in religious language. What he declares about God, about Christ, about the new way of salvation in Christ, he says at the same time about faith as the event through which alone these realities are present to us. Before him, no one spoke thus about faith. As the final issue lies between God and nothing, so does it lie between faith and unbelief.

It is his great rediscovery of this significance of faith—as opposed to a general and widespread misunderstanding of faith as the affirmation of the truth of certain doctrines—which makes Luther the greatest Reformer. When one speaks thus of faith and unbelief, one conceives of faith as existence, as a way of life, not merely as a certain content of consciousness or a special form of consciousness. Man *exists* either in faith or in unbelief. By speaking without qualification of faith and unbelief, that is to say, without specifying further who or what is the object of faith, Goethe shows that he is thinking from the standpoint of a Protestant tradition. The man who speaks thus of faith is speaking from the standpoint of the Reformers' understanding of the Bible, even when he does not know it himself; he is speaking indeed from the standpoint of Jesus Christ. It is one thing—as we shall make clear in the next chapter—that only the Bible, or to be more exact, only the New Testament gives us the *possibility* of saying this. But that we are under the necessity of saying it, of saying that faith and unbelief constitute a full expression of the problem of humanity

[1] Goethe: *Notizen zum Westöstlichen Divan*

—that is another thing. The historical anchorage of faith which we have indicated by the name of Jesus Christ is at the same time the foundation of the unconditionally human character of man, and the character of mankind as such, of the true humanity of man's existence.

We come nearer to our theme when we ask: "What *are* faith and unbelief?" In posing this elementary question, our intention is not to seek for a general concept of faith of which Christian faith might be just one historical variant or specification—as the theology of the nineteenth century tried to do. We must rather turn to the Bible, where alone faith has this dominating position, and ascertain what it understands by faith in distinction from unbelief and in contrast to it, and why in this concept the decisive characteristics of human existence are expressed. The concentration upon the most elementary and central points which this inquiry forces upon us will, as we shall see, prove significant and fruitful also for our later reflections about the nature of faith.

I

In the sentence, "I believe in Jesus the Christ", what is the significance of the words "I believe" in relation to human existence?

(*a*) Whatever else may be said about it, faith means, in relation to human existence, the knowledge that I do not belong to myself, but that I have a master, that I "belong to another". This knowledge that I belong to another reveals that the consciousness of belonging to oneself, of independence, which the natural man takes for granted, is false, is a denial of the truth and a lie. Before he believes, that is, before he is brought into subjection through Jesus the Lord, a man does not know this. He has indeed always had a certain inkling of it, but this inkling is ever and again obscured by the natural instinct of self-assertion, of self-protection and of self-reliance. His self understands itself as a free self, with its rights to freedom, as a self independent in its freedom and with no one to thank for this freedom; a self, therefore, that owes accountability to no power or authority, a self that is its own master. Experience of the world may call in question this claim to be one's own master—since in its etymological source the "self" is identical with "mastery".[1] It may do so by the pressure of force and circumstance, and this claim to independence may also appear to be denied by inter-personal relationships of actual subjection or

[1] F. Kluge, *Etymologisches Wörterbuch der deutschen Sprache*, 17th edn., 1957

slavery, yet these experiences are not sufficient to break the original claim to autonomy. For in face of the powers of nature, man asserts his claim to be autonomous through a feeling of inner superiority, and, in face of conditions of bondage, through a feeling of their injustice. In morals, too, in religion and in philosophy, man remains his own master. Only when the living God encounters him—and encounters him in such a manner that his self recognizes itself as a self fundamentally powerless and, precisely in its claim to autonomy, evil and sinful, does this mad longing for autonomy collapse, and he recognizes himself as a sinful creature. The faith which subdues him in the encounter with Jesus is at the same time the disclosure and the removal of this deluded craving for autonomy. In this encounter the decision is taken "Thou or I?" But faith is the decision: "*Thou* art the Lord, I belong not to myself but to Thee."

This *admission* that we belong to another is something quite different from the factual domination by nature to which man continually feels himself subjected. For this domination lacks what might take him inwardly captive, what might deprive him of the feeling of his superiority. These powers are indeed stronger, but that does not make them superior or higher. So he can indeed fear them, but not bow before them in reverence. Still more clearly is this the case where the domination is of a social and political kind, to which man continually falls victim. For here, if anywhere, the feeling of real inferiority is absent. "Let them have dominion and compel me—yet they do not reach my soul."[1] Here, in the innermost fortress, man's autonomy is unassailed; absolutely victorious. Only when He encounters us who is not only superior in power but before whom we must inwardly bow down, whose claim to Lordship is one not forced upon us, but one freely to be affirmed, only then is our claim to autonomy at an end. Jesus' claim to be our Master overwhelms our claim to be our own masters. This inward submission to conquest the Bible calls "faith", and He from whom this claim comes, to which absolutely no refusal can be made because here superior power is partnered by truth and inward superiority, it calls "The Lord".

Why do we say that this happens only where man encounters a definite historical person? The first answer to this is "It *is* simply so, it happens in fact only in this historical encounter." But this first answer does not cover the whole ground. When we

[1] This is roughly the mood and the central thought in Epictetus' *Handbook on Morals* and his *Discourses*

reflect on the rise of faith, it becomes clear to us that a real event which transforms existence can occur only on the plane of real events, that is, of historical events. For apart from real history, from the events that impinge on my existence, there *is* no reality that in the strict sense transforms existence. Neither thought—including imagination—nor any product of the will is capable of transforming my existence from independence to dependence. All that I *think*—even the highest, most ideal and truest thoughts—can, as something that *I* think, only confirm my autonomy. I am the master of my thoughts. So long as I am alone with my thoughts I am unchallenged and undisturbed in my autonomy. In the same measure I am out of touch with reality. Reality begins where I am "disturbed" in my thinking and dreaming solitude by what is outside of me, what is not me, where my thoughts encounter resistance. But nature, which is impersonal, cannot disturb this solitude, for I can include it too in my thought and become its master through thought. It is, on the contrary, what lies beyond me as the source of independent speech and will—the Thou, which really "disturbs" me and thus calls in question my autonomy.

For this reason history, the sphere of the persons who encounter me, is my reality. But these have not the power to break my claim to autonomy, since they are my equals. My autonomy would be broken only if in a human Thou the Power were to encounter me before which I must inwardly bow, freely acknowledging its unconditional superiority to me, which I must know and acknowledge as unconditionally higher than myself. Only where a human Thou—a historical person—meets me with the claim of the divine Person and Lord, can the autonomy of man be "really" broken; only here does the transformation from autonomy to dependence *take place*. And it is just this real event which is described in the Bible by the word "faith".

(*b*) And yet this dependence, this acknowledgment of the divine Thou to whom I belong, is not the decisive thing that the New Testament says about faith. Its message of Jesus the Christ is not merely a message about His Lordship, His claim to sovereignty; it is above all a message about the new character of this claim to sovereignty, namely the message that this claim is a bestowal and an assurance. The claim to sovereignty does disclose to me the delusion and dishonesty of my claim to autonomy. But I could not be moved to surrender the self-protection and the pride that are bound up with the claim to autonomy and so to leave the secure ground on which I stand, if, to make up for the loss of this foundation, a new foundation were not placed beneath my feet, a new being opened to me which frees my self from care about itself. The life for God which is required of me would not overcome the life for myself which is implicit in autonomy, unless this claim were at the same time the promise that God is for me.

Only through the promise of the Lord which secures for me, instead of the deceptive "foundation" of self-reliance, a more solid foundation, or rather the one absolutely sure foundation that can carry me, the life with God and the reliance upon this eternal foundation—can I surrender the (false) security. Only thus does autonomy collapse, only thus do I dare to recognize it as a lie and acknowledge God as my Lord. Only by dependence being revealed to me as a dependence upon God does the transformation *take place* from self-dependence to dependence upon God, only through the assurance of grace do I become truly a man who depends on God.

Through the assurance of the Lord, God's favour towards me, the word "dependent" gets its full meaning and at the same time its full reality. Through the assurance "You belong *to* me" the Lord places me at His side, not only under Him but beside Him. *That* is the new foundation that is laid under my feet and upon which I can securely stand, and for which I gladly exchange the earlier one, because it ennobles me. This assurance bestows on me a new being, a being which has its foundation entirely in His bestowal, and thus is entirely beyond my power of disposal and yet becomes wholly my own—is given *to me* as absolutely as it belongs to the Lord—through His kingly bestowal. Only now have I become one who wholly belongs to God because my dependence has become dependence upon God. It is not the word of demand which annihilates me, but the word of assurance that creates me anew, which makes the change from autonomy to dependence a reality.

(*c*) But even with this we have not yet comprehended the whole of faith. When man receives a new being through the assurance of God, he knows that this new being is not only something new, but at the same time the restoration of his original being. The Word of assurance is not only a Word that creates what is new, but at the same time a Word that restores. Only by means of it can faith become full certainty. For that claim of man to autonomy which was our starting point was not wholly false; there was also an element of truth contained in it, which had, however, been turned into an unrecognizable and lying delusion. This truth was that man's self was really made by the Creator for lordship over things and made to belong to God—to live at God's side.

But this element of truth, which is at the basis of all idealistic philosophy, which understands the self as superior to all that is impersonal, was so corrupted by the deluded misunderstanding of the self as autonomous, uncreated and self-originating, that it could only serve to intensify this lying claim to autonomy. For the true self of which we spoke, which was created by God and destined for fellowship with God, has its source not in itself but in the loving and gracious will of the Creator, and can only find itself again in the assurance of the Lord. In faith in the Lord's gracious Word of assurance it is recognized for what it is in its original nature: man's primal selfhood whose foundation is the Word of the Lord, a selfhood which is at once freedom and responsibility. Only because trustful, obedient faith is at the same time this self-knowledge, can it become full certainty.

Thus what is actually at stake in faith and unbelief is nothing other than the issue between dependence and independence, and therefore at the same time between true and deranged humanity. Only in faith is man's being known as a being of the self received from the Thou; that means, as a historical being. Only thus has our self come to its true self and been freed from deception, because the Lord encountered it in history in His challenging claim and the bestowal of His assurance. Only now does it know that it is a true self only through the "Thou" and this truth means that its ground is not in its autonomy but in the love bestowed upon it.

Thus at the same time its true being and its true humanity are given to it. For only as a loving self—instead of a dominating, self-assertive self—can it be truly human. But it cannot become a loving self by its own efforts, but only because it is "first loved", by having its origin in the creative love which is bestowed upon it. Faith is not only the restitution of man, but at the same time reintegration into the (lost) unity, into wholeness, yet a reintegration that is at the same time freedom and responsibility. This true humanity is at the same time man's unity with the human race. The self that through faith knows that it is chosen is at the same time called to be a member of the eternal Kingdom of humanity.

II

But what is unbelief? Why does man not hear and acknowledge the claim and assurance of the Lord? What else could unbelief be than the will to assert one's autonomy? Unbelief does not indeed see it thus. It is quite unable to see itself as unbelief, but understands itself as an *inability* to believe and a *duty* not to believe.

An *inability* to believe: Unbelief uses objective truth as a pretext for this inability. If we confine ourselves to the dimension of objective truth—which is identical with impersonal truth—then the claim of unbelief is wholly justified. For the Lord who confronts us with His claim and assurance is not present in the realm of objective truth. A *duty* not to believe: God as objective truth, God as a bit of the world, becomes an idol. Confronted by idolatry, unbelief does in fact stand up for the dignity of man. We must not believe in an idol, for an idol does not make a man a servant, it makes him servile, a slave. Here faith agrees with unbelief.

But what unbelief does not recognize is the occurrence and the motive of this displacement of the question from the dimension of historical encounter into that of objective truth. This motive is nothing other than the will to maintain autonomy. "Were there gods, who could endure not to be a god?" The claim to autonomy, resentment, the arrogance that cannot bear not to be God oneself, are the reason for unbelief. The flight of man from historical reality into the dimension of objective truth is caused by his refusal to face God's claim, for if he did so it would be an end of his autonomy.[1]

By laying claim to this autonomy man misses his chance of achieving true humanity. The autonomous man is in the strict sense of the word the *in*human man. For by missing his integration at the point where alone it can happen—namely in the *Word* of God—he becomes disintegrated man, who has fallen both from his own wholeness and from fellowship. The claim to autonomy cannot but find its expression in the claim to domination. The man who is not founded in love is also unable to love, he must seek to achieve domination. His fellow man becomes his opponent, the rival whom he resists; human history becomes the history of fratricidal wars—as indeed it has been from the beginning until this day. Historical experience shows that in truth the conflict of faith and unbelief is not only the deepest problem but the central theme and the crucial issue for mankind. For what deeper issue could there be than the establishment and the realization of the true humanity of man? And what is more frightful than the man who possesses indeed

[1] From this standpoint Kierkegaard's total rejection of all theistic proofs as "an affront to God" is understandable

in his reason the whole equipment of humanity, but uses it, not to realize his destiny and his true humanity, but to set up human systems of domination, in which men misuse their fellow men as mere means to their ends, and thereby enslave and dehumanize them?

III

Our account has made the apparently monstrous assumption that faith in the sense of dependence on God and trust in Him alone occurs only and solely in faith in Jesus Christ. This assertion invites the contrary assertion (*a*) that before the encounter with Christ and outside its scope there is religion which has in it something of the character of faith, (*b*) that especially in the religion of the Old Testament faith in the sense of obedience and trust is to be found, (*c*) and that finally even a man without religion does not have to be without further question a man filled with consciousness of self-sufficiency. These three objections must necessarily be taken into consideration and tested, if our thesis is to carry full conviction.

(*a*) We begin with the question of the non-Christian religions. We cannot content ourselves with a reference to the fact that in none of them is faith assigned so central and dominating a position as is the case in the Christian Faith. Certainly this fact is of great significance. But it is not merely a question of religious terminology. The point is that the structure of the relationship to God is wholly different. Neither of a Muslim nor of a religious Hindu or Buddhist can it be said that he "lives in faith" or that he knows that "the choice between faith and unbelief is the decisive question". Even in the Bhakti-religion of Hinduism or in Amida-Buddhism, which are acknowledged to be nearest to the Christian Faith, the relation to the divine is something quite different from the trusting and obedient acceptance of the divine claim and promise. Here too the encounter with the historical Revealer is lacking and for that very reason there is lacking this claim and assurance which is the correlate of faith. Therefore these religions cannot be characterized as forms of faith.

On the other hand it would be just as wrong to deny on this account that there is any real relation to God in these religions, and to regard them as mere intra-psychical phenomena. Judged indeed by our own criterion of the unbelief, the autonomy and the self-reliance of man, such a negative estimate appears impossible and unjust. For wherever a man kneels in worship before a power which appears to him a divinity, his autonomy and his self-reliance are called in question. He "bows" before a "higher power". His submission is indeed neither that of radical dependence upon God nor is it the obedience of absolute trust. His self-sufficiency and his self-confidence are not entirely uprooted, but they are kept within bounds. Yet the claim to autonomy continues to be made, even if it were only in the form that the religious man approves of his own piety and finds his assurance in it, or that he trusts his mystical practice to secure him the right relation to God.

Thus we can agree neither with the orthodox belief that all non-Christian religion is superstition and illusion, nor with that of the relativist school of the history of religions, that all religions including the Christian religion are variants of one and the same fundamental religious phenomenon. Both are wrong, because in all religion there is present something of reverence for the divine Power, and thereby the autonomy of man is at least kept within limits; but on the other hand this independence of man still asserts itself because man secures himself through his religion and even uses the divine Power for his own purposes. Only where the relationship to God is understood as absolute surrender to God and at the same time as unconditional trust in God, is it understood as faith, so that faith acquires the sense of dependence upon God alone, thus becoming the true form of existence in general.

(*b*) Although Christian faith *essentially* comes to perfect expression only in the New Testament, yet from the beginning the Christian community acknowledged that the faith of the people of Israel, as the Old Testament bears witness to it, was something necessarily bound up with the Christian faith. It did so by using the Old Testament as its own Bible, and regarding itself as the heir of the Old Testament people of God.[1]

It is precisely in relation to the Old Testament conception of faith that our criterion of faith as dependence on God shows its correctness, since here faith covers the totality of the existence of the man who depends on God and belongs to Him, and thus is conceived of as obedience and trust. In the Old Testament faith begins to occupy the dominating position which it later holds in faith in Christ. Faith is man's answer to God's claim and assurance. Yet this trusting obedience differs

[1] This theme is treated more fully in my book *Revelation and Reason*, Ch. 7. Yet there the sharpness of definition is lacking which has become possible through the introduction of the double concept "God's claim and assurance", and through concentration on the question "What is the essential nature of faith?"

from that of faith in Christ inasmuch as there the relationship between claim and assurance is not yet clear. The claim and assurance are present only in the form of prophetic speech, not yet in that of personal historical encounter. In so far as faith can be confused with the piety of man, it is not yet the radical antagonist of self-sufficiency and self-trust. This does not happen until the New Testament, where witness is borne to the identity of the Messiah and the Servant of God, of Him who in His Person asserts God's claim to Lordship and at the same time in His self-sacrifice not only reveals the love of God, but also gives it as the new life. Only from this standpoint can the real meaning of the Old Testament be understood. Seen from the standpoint of faith in Christ, Old Testament faith appears on the one side as the same, but on the other side as the yet imperfect form of New Testament faith.

(*c*) But how does it stand with the irreligious man? Can we rightly describe his existence by the concepts "self-sufficiency" and "self-reliance"? *Is* the unbelieving man without qualification a self-sufficient and self-important man? Even as an unbeliever, man knows of the Categorical Imperative, of a spiritual Power that limits his own will. He knows thus that he does not simply belong to himself. In all the moral law there is something that limits man, and sets a bound to his caprice. No one lives wholly without consciousness of responsibility. Certainly this moral law is a thing which is conditioned by human concerns, so that the positivist philosophy was able to conceive of responsibility simply as the essence of the requirements which society makes of the individual. But conscience can indeed demand of the individual precisely that he should not conform, and can thus isolate him from his people or from his times. The moral law is autonomous, it is not *in the last resort* dependent on the claims of society, and as autonomous law it requires of the individual that he should obey it in its mysterious commands. Thus in the moral law man has an authority confronting him, which calls in question his self-sufficiency and challenges him to deny it.

But this autonomous moral law proves to be not only the denial of man's independence but at the same time its most dangerous form. The man who, in consciousness of his moral autonomy, identifies the ethical law with his own innermost will, his "true" self, who not only acknowledges an autonomous law but under the concept of autonomy identifies the law-giving authority with himself, with his deepest or authentic self, finds in the ethical consciousness his highest self-justification and self-confirmation. Because he must affirm the ethically good, he believes himself in his heart's core to be good. This is the ambiguity of the ethical as it is recognizable from the standpoint of faith: it condemns the empirical man, saying of him, with Kant, that he is radically evil, and it justifies him at the same time as the transcendental self, which is identical with the ethical law, and thus is itself the legislative authority. In the question about the character of evil (whether it touches "myself" or only one side of me), and in the question about the origin of the "moral law" (whether it be a law of reason or the claim of God); thus, in the question whether man can justify himself, or can be justified only through God's assurance—here it is decided whether we have to do with man's claim to autonomy or with the Lordship of God.

For this reason we cannot equate morality with faith, however closely related to faith it may be through the consciousness of responsibility and the moral imperative. For it is the decisive point in the birth of faith. According as a man answers the question whether the self will accept responsibility for evil or not, whether a man will admit evil as his own act or regard it merely as the act of some impersonal element that is not identical with him, so will his decision be made whether to acknowledge the ethical law as God's claim, as something coming from outside of man, or to regard it as his own law, namely, a law created by himself. If it is a power over him, then the ethical law is God's commandment, and what he thought was autonomy becomes theonomy, and his moral consciousness becomes faith in the sense of acknowledgment of the divine claim, a claim that makes an end of his autonomy.

The autonomous man who recognizes himself as such in the encounter with Christ, and who acknowledges this claim to autonomy as rebellion against the creative will of God, is thus one who already in his autonomy was in one way or another called in question. Faith must thus bring this questionable status fully to light by unmasking it as declension from God, as sin (Romans 1: 18 ff.). Thus, in faith, penitence is implicit, like the reverse side of a coin that necessarily belongs to it. And this means the acknowledgment that already before his encounter with Jesus Christ and apart from it the man had some kind of knowledge of his dependence on God, but denied it to preserve his autonomy. Thus no "guiltless" person encounters Christ but a man who through this encounter becomes aware that his previous existence was unbelief, and that means rebellion against God. Only in the encounter with

Jesus Christ can the unbeliever recognize himself as such, since outside this encounter he uses religion or morals to protect him against the judgment of God and "makes his boast" of it. Only when Christ is known, can man really understand that the final choice is between faith and unbelief, and why it should be so.

CHAPTER 12

FAITH ACCORDING TO THE WITNESS OF SCRIPTURE

(1) FAITH IN THE WITNESS OF THE OLD TESTAMENT

As has already been said, it is by no means self-evident that the fundamental religious relationship should be described as faith. On the contrary this is nowhere the case except in Biblical religion. In the other higher religions there is either no equivalent for the religious concept "faith" or, if there appears to be such a concept, this "faith" nowhere plays a decisive central rôle. It is indeed true that *pistis* "became the watch-word of the propagandist religions of late antiquity"[1] (180). It is, however, still an open question whether this use of religious terminology was adopted from the Bible or from Christianity into the Hellenistic mystery religions. Indeed, it is true even of the Old Testament that "the utterances of the Old Testament about faith do not occupy the place of greatest prominence" (182).

I

We will inquire first of all into the history of the word "faith" in the Old Testament, as it has been made accessible to us today in the *Theological Dictionary of the New Testament* through the united labours of Biblical theology and philology. The problem of faith in the Old Testament is very much complicated by the fact that there is no *single* word of the Hebrew language which is the equivalent of *pistis*, but a whole series of words, and further, the word which the Greek translation renders by *pistis* (*pisteuein*) cannot be said in its Old Testament usage to have a sense absolutely identical with its New Testament equivalent, closely though the two may

[1] *Theological Dictionary of the New Testament* (*ThWb*) VI, pp. 174–230. This great corporate work of New Testament critical and historical investigation of the science of religion and philology seems to me something of the utmost significance in contemporary theology. The first part of the article *pistis*, which deals with the Old Testament, composed by Arthur Weiser, is excellent. On the New Testament part, see below under note 1, p. 162. The numerals in brackets following the quotations refer to the article *pistis*, *pisteuo*.

(An English translation of the greater part of this article appeared in 1961 under the title *Faith*, edited by P. R. Ackroyd, published in Great Britain by A. and C. Black Ltd. and in the U.S.A. by Harper and Brothers)

approximate, and however unmistakably and decisively the New Testament usage may have been influenced by this term in the Old Testament.

The different verbal roots which have a more or less clear relation to New Testament *pistis* are the following:
batach: to be secure, free from care;
chasah: to seek refuge;
qawah or *qiwwah:* to wait for, to hope for;
yachal: to hope, to hope for.

Above all, however, *aman* or *he'emin*—the only word which is rendered in the Greek translation by *pistis, pisteuein,* but which, like all the roots mentioned, can be just as well used in a profane sense as in a religious one and means "to put trust in, to trust in, to rely on what is reliable".

If we were to depend on statistics alone the result would be that this word was definitely less important than others, and that would imply a relatively small use of the actual concept of faith. "*Aman* or *he'emin* = *pisteuein* takes only the fourth place" (183).

"The usual translation by 'firm', 'secure', 'reliable' has only an approximate value" (184). The word *he'emin* is "A formal concept, whose content in each case is differently determined by the special subject" (184). "The nature of the Hebrew spirit further requires that this relation between concept and reality should be seen, not in the abstraction of logical thought, but always in living proximity to practical experience" (184). "The fulfilment, the realization of God's Word" (185), is indeed one of the fundamental religious meanings. In similar fashion the Old Testament speaks of God's *'emeth* and *'emunah.* "The fundamental meaning here also is 'the essential'—'that which makes God God' "—usually rendered by 'faithfulness'. The word *he'emin* describes "the attitude of man that corresponds to the divine claim as it is made from time to time, and is not limited only to single acts, but applies to the whole of man's relation to God" (185).

The Old Testament "uses . . . *he'emin* only for a personal relationship" (186). "The reciprocal relation between God and man belongs to the nature of faith, and indeed in such fashion that, even where faith means human activity, man is never the one who initiates this reciprocal relation. . . ." "God is the true originator of the relationship between God and man" (187). "If God's claim is under consideration . . . then faith means the acknowledgment of the claim and the obedience of man; if the emphasis is on God's promise, then *he'emin* expresses the acknowledgment of the promise and the power of God to fulfil it" (185).

But there are further possibilities implicit in the formal character of *he'emin* "especially in the direction of covering the general relations between God and man" (187). "Thus the Old Testament usage of *he'emin* points in the direction of taking God as God with absolute seriousness" (188). Not to believe, to be unbelieving, consequently means to "fall away" from God (188). From this—and from other facts—it follows "that the locus and origin of the religious use of the root word *aman* is to be sought in the Old Testament tradition concerning the sacred Covenant of Yahweh" (188). "To the extensive exclusiveness there corresponds an intensive one, in the sense that the concept of *aman* includes the totality of the expressions of human life within the relationship to God" (188). "Faith means . . . a relationship to God which includes the whole man in the totality of his outward behaviour and his inner life" (188).

It is in particular important that the word *he'emin* is also used in an absolute sense and thus comes especially near to the New Testament concept. This is the achievement of Isaiah. "For Isaiah the problem of the possibility of existence, the question of faith and life becomes the focus of interest" (189), and this "prophet's conception of faith . . . on its side goes back to the . . . personal encounter of the prophet with God" (189). Faith is "for Isaiah a special form of existence of the man who is bound to God alone" (189). "In faith itself there is a special mode of being, and the stability of the people of God" (189). "For Isaiah faith is the only possible form of existence, which radically excludes every other independent attitude of man or conjunction with anyone else than God" (189–90).

"In spite of the lessened frequency of the use of *aman* as a matter of mere statistics, the significance of the roots *batach, chasah, qawah, yachal, chakah* . . . has been assimilated to the sense of *he'emin* as an expression for the exclusive relationship of a personal nature between man and God" (190). "Where the word *he'emin* is used, the tendency to expand so as to cover the widest possible range of values is unmistakable" (190).

"The question as to the origin of the powerful religious dynamic which has used the root *aman* to express the peculiar character of Old Testament religion in its different stages" (190) is to be answered by saying that "it is from the beginning most closely connected with the special character of the religious structure and thought forms of Israelitic Yahweh-religion" (190). "The point of origin of this old linguistic usage of *aman* is to be found in the membership of the Covenant with Yahweh and its sacred tradition" (191). It is therefore a highly significant observation "that the majority of the passages in which the Old Testament uses *he'emin* refer to the relationship to God of Mosaic times" (191). "The Old Testament saw in the relationship described by *he'emin* the special religious relationship of the people of God to Yahweh" (191).

In reference to the other word roots, which express a sense somewhat similar to *pisteuein*, we must comment as follows:

batach means to be in a condition of security, to feel secure, "yet a broadening of the range of meaning can be ascertained in the direction of an approximation to the meaning of *he'emin*" (192). "Here a decisive turning point can be determined in the use of *batach* for the whole attitude of faith. It is to be found in the influence of Isaiah on the formation of religious terminology" (192). "Isaiah filled the word (*batach*) with the content of his own concept of faith" (193).

chasah means the "condition of security, or the act which strives to reach this condition" (193).

Especially significant is the meaning of the word *chakah* = to hope. "This waiting and hoping is faith, which does not see and yet hopes" (195). "The heightened energy of a 'nevertheless' uttered out of a final struggle for certainty lies implicit in this tension of faith" (195). "For this reason the second Isaiah knows . . . that it is God Himself who gives man such power to believe" (196). "Especially in the Psalms the word 'hope' is used for the whole relation of man to God in general" (196). "The changing use of the most different verbs to express the relation to God is the clearest proof of the fact that the usage of the language in the Old Testament flows from the most varied tributaries into one stream" (196). The Greek translation and the New Testament "have in fact seen things in their true light when they attached their concept of faith (*pisteuein*) to the Old Testament root *aman*" (197), where *he'emin* "includes in itself the exclusive and personal reciprocal relationship between God and man" (197), and where it is in fact decisive that the *aman*-concept "became the expression of this specifically Old Testament relation to God which was cultivated within the Covenant tradition" (197).

II

What was here simply taken over from the work of historical philology and critical historical theology can perhaps be systematically or dogmatically interpreted in the following manner.

(*a*) The concept of faith does not yet in general have the same dominating position in the Old Testament which is given to it in the New Testament witness of the Apostles (especially in that of Paul and John) but it is on the way towards it. The reason for this twofold result must now be discussed.

(*b*) But faith is without question a reality which relates to and determines the existence of man as a whole. Faith or unbelief is the decisive question of human existence, both of the individual man and of the peoples, i.e. of humanity. Man *lives* either in faith or in unbelief, and whether he is the one or the other is decisive for the healthy or unhealthy character of his life.

(*c*) The Old Testament uses "faith" to describe man's relation to God in its most central aspect. Therefore faith has a thoroughly personal meaning; the person of man in its relationship to the Person of God, who has manifested Himself to him. So far as faith relates itself to the "Word of God" it is not the logically intelligible content of the Word to which faith attaches, but the God who manifests Himself as worthy of trust in His Word. The human act of faith corresponds to the divine act of self-manifestation and is caused and elicited by it.

(*d*) This divine act of self-manifestation is essentially of a historical character. God manifests Himself in His "acts" which as such, as revealing Him, are communicated and made intelligible or handed down through the witness of the prophets. To the fact that God, who has revealed His name as Yahweh, is Lord of history, the God who intervenes with power in the destiny of His people, indeed creates it, guides it, and ever and again proclaims His name as the Ruler of history, there corresponds on the side of man that man should answer this mighty and self-consistent action of God with obedience and trust, with an obedience that is free and joyful, and a trust that, answering to this character of the divine self-manifestation, is unconditional, does honour to the revealed Name and gives Him His due as Lord. In this sense there is nothing which corresponds so closely to the self-manifestation of the divine Will as this "faith". The fundamental significance of this faith is trust and the acknowledgment of the power of the Lord. Therefore, faith has always in it an element of fear as reverence and of love as the joyful affirmation which is involved in trust.

(*e*) From all this it is clear that in the creation of the right relation to God—the relation which is constituted by faith—the initiative comes from God. He "calls" forth faith by His Word.

He creates it.[1] Faith is the answer which corresponds to God's self-manifestation and is caused by it. Even in the Old Testament concept of responsibility this correspondence of divine Word of summons and human answer can be shown in its positive as well as in its negative characterization. The man who answers God through faith is the true man, man as he should be. The man who does not give this answer is the perverted man, who is falling away from God or has fallen away from Him, the sinner. And indeed it is solely the negation of this (obedient) relation of faith to God, which constitutes sin. "Against Thee only have I sinned" (Psalm 51:4). Conversely the opposite of sin is not virtue, but faith, the trusting and obedient relation to God.

(*f*) If now we ask finally why in the Old Testament the concept of faith does not yet have the central and unconditionally dominating position which is given to it in the New Testament, we must first refer to the fact that God's self-communication has not there reached its full realization. The historical and the personal have not yet become one. God reveals Himself on the one hand in historical acts, on the other hand in the Word of the prophets. What is the relation of these two to each other? Does God's self-manifestation take place in these historical acts or in the prophetic Word? The prophetic Word is indeed nothing other than the declaration and explanation or interpretation of what God has done or will do. This interpretation is an authoritative and inspired one, for it is God Himself who speaks to the people in the Word of the prophets; but historical act and prophetic Word are not yet one. But in the New Testament Jesus Christ, the Lord, is Himself the act and the Word of God.

It is exactly the same with the unity of God's claim and assurance. The prophet does both; he claims Israel for God and he assures Israel that it is God's people. Indeed the claim of God results from the creation and the election, that is, from the gift which precedes the claim. Dependence is at the same time a belonging to God. But in fact the claim very much predominates, and therefore the prophetic message is above all the declaration of judgment, not good news—god-spel, eu-angelion—because human disobedience calls God's grace in question. Not until the New Testament does the gift of salvation stand unmistakably in the first place, and the character of the claim takes its colour from it. "Let us love, for He has first loved us" (1 John 4: 19).

[1] Indeed one may say that the expression "call forth" has its origin in the Old Testament conception of faith

From this a third point can be derived. Faith is so far not yet genuine faith, to the extent that the religious man does not place his confidence radically outside of himself in God alone but makes his own piety the ground of his confidence. The prophets did indeed shatter the false security of the Temple and the religious cultus but not the security of man's own "righteousness".

Finally there is still missing the Ekklesia which bursts asunder the national fellowship and distinguishes the secular law of the State from God's own will. In the Old Testament God's people is both the people into which every Israelite is born and the people of a State who can think of their Messianic king only as a monarch filled with the inspiration of God.

What is still missing in the Old Testament understanding of faith can be formulated according to the Reformed theological tradition thus: the three offices (*munera*) by which the work of Christ can be described are not yet concentrated in one person: the prophetic office (*munus propheticum*) the kingly office (*munus regium*) and the priestly office (*munus sacerdotale*). Correspondingly there is not yet present a complete unity of faith and obedience.

From all this the historical character of faith becomes clear in the sense that it can become perfect faith only when the historical self-communication of God has really and perfectly happened. In the Old Testament, faith is on the way to become complete faith, but this goal is not yet reached because the perfect self-communication of God does not occur until the Christ event.

EXCURSUS: MARTIN BUBER'S TEACHING ON THE APOSTLES' MISUNDERSTANDING OF FAITH

In his book *Zwei Glaubensweisen*[1] Martin Buber has in an unprecedentedly sharp and forcible manner indicated that there is a complete difference between what is understood in the Old Testament as faith and the Apostles' conception of faith. Since Buber adduces his arguments in a thoroughly original, disinterested manner which is also the result of penetrating and scholarly investigation of the Bible, one would have expected that Christian theology would have seriously taken up the challenge of his book. As far as I know, however, with the exception of an article by G. Schrenk, "Martin Bubers Beurteilung des Paulus" (Martin Buber's Criticism of Paul) (*Judaica* 1952, pp. 1 ff.), this has not so far happened. It is the more necessary for me to give Martin Buber an answer to his serious question, because through his teaching about the two dimensions I/Thou, I/It, he has performed such a tremendous service to theology, which Karl Heim was the first to appreciate as a "Copernican Revolution". While Buber's I-Thou philosophy has meantime found a large measure of acceptance and its great significance has been acknowledged, this is not equally the case with Ferdinand Ebner, who was the first to draw attention to the problem of the solitariness of the self (cf. *Das Wort und die geistigen Realitäten*, The Word and Spiritual Realities). It appeared in 1921, a year before Buber's *Ich und Du* (I and Thou) but was at first unknown to the latter. As early as *Die Mystik und das Wort*, Mysticism and the Word (1924), we alluded to Ebner, without ourselves having yet fully grasped his significance. On the other hand, Karl Heim, referred by us to Ebner, received from him the decisive stimulus for the personalism of his doctrine of dimensions and freely admitted the fact. Here, however, we must treat of Buber's *Two Types of Faith*.

This book, relatively small, but pregnant with exegetical knowledge and knowledge of comparative religion, has a threefold aim, and correspondingly a threefold theme: to make the religious message of Judaism understandable in the light of the Old Testament, to illuminate the message of Jesus as a phenomenon belonging to this world of faith, and to prove the theology of the Apostles—above all the theology of Paul and John, which according to Buber forms the foundation of Christianity—to be an alien thing, separated from that world of faith by a great gulf.

Everything that Buber writes on the first two themes can be accepted even by the Christian reader with unmixed gratitude. His picture of Old Testament faith can be approved—at all events with one very important qualification which we now proceed to mention—

[1] E.T. *Two Types of Faith*, Routledge and Kegan Paul, London, 1951

by every Christian Old Testament scholar, and valued as a contribution to the understanding of the Old Testament. What he says also about the connection of Jesus' teaching with the proclamation of the prophets will be confirmed by the Christian New Testament scholar, though here indeed with an even more important qualification. But the picture that Buber outlines of Paul's and John's understanding of faith, and of their theology, makes them in fact appear representatives of another kind of faith, which is not only in irreconcilable contradiction to the Old Testament witness concerning faith, but also to any personalistic understanding of faith whatsoever. Although in his preface Buber declares that he has not the slightest intention of engaging in apologetics or polemics—and anyone who knows Buber will believe that this is completely true—yet the exposition of these theses about Pauline theology is so logical and impressive that his book, without intending it, amounts in fact to a major attack upon Christianity.

The radical conflict between what Buber calls the faith of the Old Testament and what he understands by the theology of the Apostles is quite evident to himself. "Here not only Old Testament faith, and with it the living faith of post-Biblical Judaism, is in opposition to Paul, but also the Jesus of the Sermon on the Mount, although from different motives and with different intention" (p. 25). This thesis is not in itself new. It is the thesis of the "liberal theology" of the nineteenth century which conceived that there was a radical conflict between the faith of Jesus and the teaching of Paul. Buber here cites in his support the latest researches of the New Testament scholars, especially Bultmann, who himself regards the teaching of the synoptic Jesus as really belonging to the Old Testament, and further he cites the New Testament scholars who believed that Paul and John must be understood as radically influenced by Gnosticism. "Again the boundary line must be so drawn that Israel and the tradition of the primitive Christian community as far as we can understand it from the Synoptics stand on the one side in respect of their kind of faith, with Hellenistic Christianity on the other side" (p. 25). "When we consider the synoptic conversation with the disciples (Matt. 16: 13 ff.) and the Johannine conversation (John 6: 66 ff.) as two stages of one journey, we immediately perceive what was gained on this journey, and what was lost. The gain was the most sublime of all theologies, the price paid was the loss of the simple outlook of the primitive Biblical man, which was in touch with the situation and found eternity not in the super-temporal Spirit but in the depths of the real moment. To this side the Jesus of the genuine tradition still belongs, but not the Jesus of a theology" (p. 32).

"The difference between this 'It is true that the God of the world is our King' and that 'we believe and know' is not the difference between two expressions of faith, but between two kinds of faith" (p. 33). In the Old Testament, faith is trust and obedience; in gnostic Christianity it is faith in a theology which interprets the fact of Christ. By "fact" Buber means the historical event of Christ. That this *fact* is the content of faith makes—in Buber's opinion—the Christian faith a faith in facts, a *fides historica*. But a faith in facts is not a faith of trust; it is a "belief that . . ." By an "interpreting *theology*" Buber means in principle the proposition: "This Jesus is the Christ, the Redeemer." Thus in his opinion the Christian Faith becomes faith in a mythical gnostic doctrine. Through both, through the relation to historical event and through this dogmatic content, the structure of faith is completely altered. The place of personal surrender in trust and obedience is taken by a theoretical "conviction that". Through the citation of certain gnostic doctrines which are in fact to be found in Paul, this contradiction is made even more pointed.

Is it really a contradiction? *Is* the faith that Jesus is the Christ a theology (of a gnostic stamp)? This is the point where we find a distinction not between the faith of trust and "belief that", but between Jewish faith and Christian faith. Put in another way, here is decided whether one acknowledges Christ as God's plenipotentiary, trusts Him and obeys Him, or whether one is "offended at Him" (Matt. 11: 6). When Peter confessed Him as Messiah he did not accept a theology, least of all a gnostic theology—he knew the Only Son and bowed before Him. It is precisely this which is astonishing: that no instruction about Jesus the Christ preceded his confession of Christ. What we here perceive as faith in Jesus stands wholly within what Buber means by faith, security in God, trust and obedience.

We have indeed already indicated by our two "qualifications" that Buber's understanding of faith is not identical with that of the Old Testament, but that *one* essential element is missing in it. Buber's concept of faith does not make it clear that even Old Testament faith is an answer to God's action in *historical events* and in the prophetic Word. Further—and this reservation is even more significantly important—Buber will not admit that Jesus believed Himself to be the bringer of the Kingdom of God (whether one calls Him Messiah, Christ, Son of God or Lord, Kyrios)—and at the same time the suffering servant of Isaiah 53. If Buber has jibbed at the first—as the Jews did—the second, in connection with the event of the Cross, was far more unacceptable to him. But this is the heart of the Pauline Gospel, which is not indeed to be believed as his teaching or theology, but which refers to that event in which God encounters man, and which only he who knows himself to be a sinner can understand in trustful obedience as God's self-communication. (In this connection a conversation with Martin Buber has remained in my memory as significant. We spoke about sin. He opposed sharply the New Testament concept, above all, the Pauline concept of sin, because he saw in this a slur cast upon man's responsibility to himself and his freedom. But here the decision is made, whether one can believe in Christ, accept Him and His reconciliation as the Word of God.)

Christian faith, too, has thus no other structure than Old Testament faith, except that God's rule over history, in which He makes known His own nature, has gained in the historical event of Jesus at one and the same time the significance of self-revelation and of self-surrender. But Buber's confusing of the Pauline and Johannine interpretation of the fact of Christ with a doctrine to be believed, is the more easy to understand in the case of Buber the Jew, because the Christian Church has itself given him occasion for this misunderstanding. Only in most recent times has theology begun to distinguish between the *kerygma* which awakens faith and the doctrine which is to be believed. Thus Buber's sharply pointed thesis about the "Two Types of Faith" confirms in our opinion the importance of the task to which we shall apply ourselves in the next chapter.

(2) FAITH IN THE WITNESS OF THE NEW TESTAMENT

I

As we have seen, the New Testament's understanding of faith is the fulfilment of the Old Testament's understanding—the Old Testament is here a preface to the New. On the other hand, we must say of the Judaism of that day that in it the Old Testament concept of faith is essentially altered. True, "the Judaistic concept of faith contains the same structural elements as that of the Old Testament, but there is, however, a great difference."[1] "As a result of the canonization of tradition in the 'Scriptures', obedient loyalty takes on the character of obedience to the law, i.e. it is no longer true loyalty to God's action experienced in history in confidence in His future action therein" (*ibid.*, 201).

For *primitive Christianity*, however, it holds good that "*pistis* has become the dominant description of the relation of man to God" (205). Here continues the indissoluble unity between what Jesus says, and what He is, or what God does through Him, and therefore to believe means—even in John—"nothing else than to believe in Jesus" (205). We would add for the sake of clarity, to believe in Jesus as the Christ or the Kyrios or the Son of God. "That the word *believe* means for them *obey*"

[1] *ThWb* VI, p. 201; "Faith in the New Testament", compiled by R. Bultmann. Here also I simply reproduce in quotation the results of the investigation which seem to me important. I am, however, not so sure as in the Old Testament part that this description of faith, which results, is quite just to New Testament *pistis* and *pisteuein*. It seems to me here—in contrast with Weiser's representation of Old Testament faith—that Heidegger's terminology is too uncritically employed as a means of interpretation

(206), is the common witness of the New Testament. "Above all, Paul emphasized the character of faith as obedience" (206). He creates the untranslatable expression, which however emphasizes precisely what is decisive: *hypakoē pisteōs*, which we do not merely translate "obedience of faith" but which in addition allows the etymology of *hypakoē*, "hearing from below", to echo through it.[1]

In the Synoptic Gospels this *pistis* is above all related to the miraculous power of God manifesting itself in the Person of Jesus. In this connection even Jesus already uses *pisteuein* in the absolute sense: "If ye have faith as a grain of mustard seed . . ." (Matt. 17: 20). Faith means here trust in the helping power of God. "In Paul the meaning of *pistis* as trust in general is less frequent, yet it is found where Paul describes the faith of Abraham as trust in God's miraculous power" (207). "*Pistis* is trust in the fulfilment of the divine promise" (207). As in the Old Testament there is a close connection between faith, trust and hope. "The paradox of such hopeful trust . . . directs itself to the unseen . . . not only in so far as this is the promised future, but also in so far as it is the heavenly reality, which is not perceived by the senses, but can only be believed [*sic*] in faith" (207). "Even where in specifically Christian usage *pistis* means faith in Christ, the 'hopeful' character of faith is retained, but now indeed in such a manner that hope is . . . named alongside of faith" (208), and the fundamental togetherness of both is emphasized "that your faith is at the same time hope in God" (1 Peter 1: 21). "That the Old Testament significance of faithfulness is a component in *pistis*" (208), is shown by the connection of *pistis* and endurance (*hypomonē*) and the expression *tēn pistin tērein*—to hold fast the faith—just as also *apistia*, unbelief, is called unfaithfulness.

More precisely, faith is the acceptance of the Christian *kerygma* and therefore saving faith. Further, the "primitive Christian *kerygma* is the message that there is *one* God, and at the same time the message about Jesus Christ, His Son, and of what God has done through Him" (209). "*Pisteuein eis* . . . to have faith in, looks primarily to what God *has done*, not to what He will do" (209). The chief content of the Christian confession of faith is: Christ is Lord. Therein lies already implicit the acknowledgment of the miracle of His resurrection.

[1] *Translator's Note:* Here there is in the German, though less perfectly than in the Greek, a play on words which cannot be rendered in the English. *Glaubensgehorsam*, "obedience of faith", resembles *hören* (to hear) as *hypakoē* (obedience) does *akouo* (hear)

But this miracle is not to be believed in as a believed fact, but rather as a "fact of salvation, by virtue of which Jesus became Kyrios" (210). "So we preach and so you have believed . . . that Christ died for our sins" (210). Above all, the faith of Christians consists in the fact "that Jesus Christ is Lord" (Phil 2: 11) that Jesus, the Christ, is the Son of God. The words *egō eimi* "I am He" are the centre of faith in Christ, and the New Testament knows no other faith than faith in Christ. More precisely, the content of faith is the love of God to us revealed in Christ (1 John 4: 16): "A shortened expression of this saving faith is the formula 'believe in" *pisteuein eis* . . ." (210–11). "With this meaning *pistis* and *pisteuein* can also be used in an absolute sense" (211).

It is in fact worthy of note that "the relationship to God in the New Testament is almost never described by *pisteuein eis*. Conversely, the formulations describing our relation to God which we meet in the Greek translation of the Old Testament . . . are never applied to the relationship to Christ" (211). "Faith in Christ as the acceptance of the *kerygma* about Him" (212), means the understanding that "this history happened for us" (212). It "signifies faith in Christ Jesus and thus in fact a personal relationship to Christ analogous to the relationship to God, and yet different from it. . . . Faith in Jesus Christ is in its original and authentic sense not obedience to a Lord whom we already knew, but rather it is only in faith itself that the existence of this Lord is known and acknowledged. . . . Only in the *kerygma* does the Lord meet him, and he believes on the strength of the *kerygma*" (212). The message "never becomes a mere piece of guidance and information, which as soon as known might become superfluous; it remains always the ground of faith. Together with the Christ event God has appointed the *logos tēs katallagēs* (the Word of reconciliation). For this reason faith in the *kerygma* and faith in the Person mediated by it are inseparable" (212). *Metanoia*, repentance, goes together with *pistis* (213), "The hearers are summoned to repent and to believe" (213). "Correspondingly *apistia*, unbelief, is the rejection of the *kerygma*" (213).

In relation to the Old Testament we must say: so far as *pistis* in the New Testament is a faith in God's Word, there is formally speaking no difference from the Old Testament (216). "But the Word of God has received another character" (216). "It is so bound up with God's act that this act is only disclosed in this Word" (216). "God's act is His Word, so that John . . . can describe Jesus as the Logos, 'the Word'. . . . For this reason *pisteuein tō logō tou theou* (believing the Word of God) becomes *pisteuein eis Christon*" (believing in Christ) (216). "So far as faith itself is faithfulness, it is not faithfulness in relation to God's gracious acts in the history of the people (of Israel) but faithfulness to God's saving act in Christ, the only 'name' in which there is salvation" (217). The obedience of *pistis* "is not obedience under God's commands, which require justice and righteousness for the national life, but the 'obedience of faith' to the one way of salvation, which has been disclosed in Christ" (217).

"In everything *pistis* shows itself as the act by means of which man forsakes the world in answer to God's eschatological act in Christ and turns radically towards God" (217). "As such . . . *pistis* dominates life completely. It is just for this reason too that the absolute use of *pistis*, which, with the exception of Isaiah 7: 9 and 28: 16, is still strange to the Old Testament, and which begins to be found in Judaism, is so predominant" (217). With special reference to the witness of *Paul* on the subject of faith, "*pistis* is not a psychological attitude of man, but primarily the acceptance of the *kerygma*, i.e. submission to the way of salvation determined by God and disclosed in Christ" (218). In making confession of faith, "the believer turns away from himself, and confesses Jesus Christ as his Lord" (218). "If *pistis* is the believing acceptance of that which the *kerygma* proclaims, yet it is not reducible to a *fides historica*—a belief in historical fact" (218–19). "The acceptance of the Divine Grace is *hypakoē*, obedience" (219). "The knowledge communicated in the *kerygma* and appropriated in faith thus includes at the same time with the knowledge of God's deed in Christ a new self-understanding of man" (219). "But that trust —and also hope—belongs to faith, is shown by the use of *pepoithenai*" (219), to be convinced and certain. "To be in the faith (2 Cor. 13: 5) to stand in the faith, (1 Cor. 16: 13; 2 Cor. 1: 24) . . . means, to belong to the Lord and to the grace disclosed in Him, and proclaimed in the gospel" (219).

The contrast with the Jewish understanding of faith can be clearly seen from this. "Since salvation—as in Judaism—is described as *dikaiosynē*, Paul reaches the conclusion, paradoxical for Judaism, that *dikaiosynē* is bestowed on *pistis* as a gift" (220). "Only on the ground of his *pistis* and never on the ground of his works can man stand before God" (220–21). "From this it becomes completely clear that *pistis* is man's absolute surrender to God" (221). "And indeed a surrender, to which man cannot by any means come by his own decision—

for then he would remain in the sphere of *erga*, of works—but which can only be surrender to God's grace, and thus only an answer to God's act" (221). "But it is just as clear also, that this surrender is a movement of the will" (221). "In Paul the active character of *pistis* is expressed by his understanding *pistis* as obedience" (221). "The Spirit is bestowed on the believer, but *pistis* is not the gift of the Spirit" (221). Faith is thus this "paradox, that *pistis* as movement of the will is the denial of the will itself" (221). It is "action in the highest sense of the word, but also the opposite of every work" (221). *Pistis* is "the fundamental life-attitude which determines all individual behaviour" (222). It is "the eschatological attitude of man, made possible by God's eschatological act, the attitude of the new man" (222). This eschatological character of *pistis* is marked by the fact that the words "in faith" correspond to "in the Lord" and "in grace" (222).

In contrast to gnosis it is precisely this that is decisive, that faith is not already "in itself eschatological fulfilment" (222). "In *pistis* there is not realized as in the gnostic understanding of knowledge the finality of an eschatological existence" (222). "As it continually refers back to what God has done in Christ, so on the other hand it is continually orientated towards the future, to that which God will do" (222). "Faith is man's self-understanding under the divine grace of forgiveness" (223). "It never permits man to escape the concrete situation of his historical life" (223). "Therefore, constitutively, as hope belongs to *pistis*, so does *phobos*, fear" (223). This fear "means that the believer 'knows' himself 'before God' or in the sight of God" (223). "If in contrast to Judaism *pistis* is characterized as a Christian condition of being by its 'no longer', so it is distinguished from gnosis by its 'not yet' " (223). "Christian being in *pistis* is thus the paradoxical eschatological being within historical existence" (223). "In so far memory is an essential part of faith" (224), and also "The surrender of self-reliance, which claims to be master of one's own existence" (224). "It is not that an old possession once at our disposal has been exchanged for a new one now at our disposal; rather does the change between then and now mean the surrender of every will to possession, as radical surrender to the grace of God" (224).

The Johannine understanding of faith is different from the Pauline in so far as "the occasion of the Johannine statements about *pistis* is not, as in the case of the Pauline statements, the question of the *way* to salvation. John is striving to attain the right conception of salvation itself, and for this his characteristic description is not, as in Paul, 'righteousness' but always 'life' (225). To believe is to forsake the world, for the world does not know what salvation, life, really is" (225). "That a man should forsake himself is the primary meaning of faith. It is man's self-surrender, his turning towards the unseen, to that which is not at his disposal" (225). "The act of faith is not an act or transaction in the world, but a happening rooted in the transcendent, an act or gift of God Himself" (226). "In fact these statements say that the phenomenon of faith cannot be understood as an event in the world, but only as a miracle, and thereby they characterize faith itself as an act of forsaking the world" (226). "Jesus chose His own out of the world, so that they are no longer 'of the world', i.e. they no longer belong to the world". This "forsaking of the world" is not an act to be freely performed by man himself, to perform which Jesus' Word would merely supply the occasion. . . . "Rather is the forsaking of the world conceived of radically, because God is thought of as One who acts in His freedom: the forsaking of the world only becomes a possibility for men through His revelation" (226).

"But it is precisely the revelation which is the stumbling-block: the invisible becomes visible, and visible in a manner impossible and improper according to human standards. In the flesh God's Son has come, a man, whose parents . . . are known, who does not answer to all that Messianic dogma, (i.e. worldly conceptions of God's revelation) demands" (227). "He claims to be more than Abraham. . . . In fact, only in faith can the truth of this Word be known" (227). "The forsaking of the world must not be understood as flight from the world but as conversion, the shattering of worldly standards" (227). " 'The world' is for John not a natural magnitude, not, as in gnosis, a sphere, which surrounds man with a fate-like compulsion . . . it is rather a historical magnitude and power, which is constituted by the men who turn away from the light, from God, and in whose authority and might each man participates by his own conduct" (227). "The revelation is for this world the offence, since it calls this world in question; it is the judgment of the world. And faith is the act of forsaking the world, in that it is the overcoming of this offence, in that it surrenders man's independence, positively it is the laying hold of the revelation which encounters us in the Word" (227).

The conception of the Johannine faith as "gnosis" overlooks the fact that John's formulations serve precisely to distinguish his teaching from gnosis. "The believer has life 'only' in faith. He is not deified." "The direct vision of *doxa* (glory) remains reserved for a future existence outside of the world." "The act of faith thus does not place us in a condition of world-renunciation, but is an act of forsaking the world" (228). Man must "abide in Him". "To him who abides the knowledge of the truth is promised" (229). Thus John, unlike the gnostics, cannot set *pisteuein* over against knowledge. "As far as their objects are concerned, *pisteuein* and knowing are not distinguished. Faith, like knowledge, is directed to the fact that the Father has sent Jesus" (229). "All faith must also become a knowing. . . . In knowing, faith comes to itself; knowing is thus a structural moment of genuine faith. Let us remember further that the relationship of the Son to the Father is never spoken of as one of believing, but only as one of knowing, and it will be clear that this intertwining of faith and knowledge describes the human faith which must result in knowledge, without ever reaching a definitive condition of mere gnosis" (229).

One other thing is of importance for John's witness concerning faith: the conjunction of faith and love. "To the unity of faith and action corresponds the content of the commandments, in so far as the action required by them is nothing other than love." "Faith knows Jesus as the revealer of the divine love" (John 3: 16). "It is itself the reception of His love" (230). "But the reception of the love bestowed on us in the sending of the Son lays on us the obligation of brotherly love" (230) (1 John 4: 7–21). "By this shall all men know that ye are my disciples, if ye love one another" (John 13: 35).

II

What then is faith, according to the witness of the New Testament?

(*a*) It is without question faith in Jesus as the Kyrios, the Christ, the Son of God. These three expressions have exactly the same meaning. Thus even Peter (Matt. 16: 16) confessed his faith in Jesus, and thus the primitive Community confesses its faith—whether it uses the word "faith" or not—in Jesus as the Lord. This faith is at the same time an acknowledgment which transforms existence, and the knowledge that in this historical Person, in the historical event which took place in the life and death of this Person, God Himself meets man as sovereign power and manifests Himself to him. The apostolic community possessed this knowledge already before the death of Jesus, without the interposition of a message about Him.[1] Of itself it already made, so to speak, the discovery, that Jesus was—the Lord, the Christ-Messiah, the Son of God.

This faith, then, was by no means mediated to it through a *kerygma* about Him, a message about Christ, nor by His own teaching about Himself. Rather was it His Person, His actions, the authority with which He taught, the unconditioned nature of the love with which He loved, and admittedly also His reference to Himself as the one in whom the Kingdom of God had drawn near, that exercised an inner compulsion on them, so that they recognized that the power of God's Lordship was present in Him and could not help confessing their faith—"Thou art the Son of the living God."

(*b*) This faith was in the first instance the acknowledgment of His divine authority, His claim to Lordship. In this acknowledgment there was, however, already implicit a transformation of existence. For he who has a Lord is no longer the same man as before, when he had not yet this Lord. "All things are become new" because "I" no longer belong to myself but to Him. The identification of the claim of Jesus with God's claim to absolute Lordship did not, however, constitute the full depth of the transformation. This transformation was brought about rather by the fact that Jesus had taken upon Himself the death of the Cross. This event was at first a frightful shock to their faith in Jesus. It was only the miracle of the Resurrection—whose character we are no longer able to establish in detail, but which they with one consent described as an encounter with the One who had risen from the grave—which not only gave them back their earlier faith in Him as the Son of God but lent a new meaning to this divine Sonship.

Through the Easter event and after it they saw and understood His Lordship in a light in which they had not hitherto seen and understood it. The faith which they now confessed on the grounds of the Resurrection was a new faith. For now they not only understood His claim to Lordship but, at the same time, that He had given His—divine—life for them. Whether now for the first time they remembered the words of this Lord which he had spoken "during His lifetime" and above

[1] This is a decisive difference between Rudolf Bultmann's New Testament exegesis and the author's. Bultmann will not admit of a faith in Christ before the Resurrection of Jesus, and treats the Synoptic statements to this intent simply as theology of the community, while in our *Dogmatics* they are regarded as genuine in the sense of a tradition which must be acknowledged as historical. Here Bultmann's sceptical judgment of the sources seems to be an aberration from sound critical historical scholarship

all on that last night when He was with them, or whether these words had not yet really been spoken at all at that time—the decisive thing was that now they knew that He had given Himself, His life and His blood, for them. They saw Him now as the Suffering Servant of God, of whom Isaiah had spoken. This uttermost proof of divine love they now recognized in the light of the Resurrection as the decisive self-manifestation which was at the same time God's self-*communication*. And this Son of God they proclaimed henceforward as God's act creative of salvation and His Word of deliverance. He Himself, as the Crucified and Risen One, was to them God's Word and Act. And this was the *eu-angelion*—the good news—which they proclaimed and spread abroad.

But the hearers who had not seen Jesus face to face, and had not, like them, experienced His Resurrection, believed in Jesus, the Son of God, who encountered them if not physically at least spiritually, in this same proclamation.

(*c*) This faith is not, as may be thought, primarily trust in the *messengers*, and only then, on the ground of this trust, the faith that Jesus is the One they proclaimed Him to be. Rather was it the case that in hearing the message, Jesus as the Christ, as the Lord, as the Son of God, as the One who loved with a divinely perfect love, took possession of their hearts and overcame them. This experience of being overcome, not by mere power, but by a spiritual power which laid hold of them in the claim to Lordship and in the power of love, in God's assurance to them in Jesus Christ—this inner compulsion, which was at the same time a privilege, they named "faith". When they said "I believe in Jesus as the Son of God, the Lord" they meant the same thing as they found defined "in the Scriptures" as the trustful, obedient, reverent relationship to the God of claim and of bestowal—as faith.

(*d*) The proclamation of Jesus, the Kyrios-Christos, was developed especially by the Apostle Paul into the full *kerygma* of Christ, but was of such a kind that this witness was approved by the other original Apostles; that is, men who had hardly even heard of Hellenistic gnostic doctrines or been touched by them, but whose thinking was entirely determined by the Old Testament and contemporary Judaism. If they did not agree with him in everything, it was not his proclamation of Kyrios Christos that roused their opposition, but his teaching about the law. The proclamation of Kyrios Christos, that Jesus was the decisive saving act of God, was their common confession of faith.

Their faith was directed not to a doctrine but to Jesus Himself, as in this proclamation He had taken possession of them as the truth and the reality of God, and as He was Himself present to them in faith, and bore witness to Himself as the living Lord. Jesus Christ "portrayed before their eyes" (Gal. 3: 1) through the *kerygma* of the Apostles was He who through His claim to Lordship had asserted the claim of God in a new fashion. And it was the same Jesus also who revealed and gave to them the inconceivable love of God as the new reality in which it was now their privilege to live, as God's assurance and *gift*, as God's nature, as His existence-for-us. Through the proclamation of Paul this self-bestowing love was received by the Ekklesia as the first, most important and fundamental thing. Faith is now above all the hearing and obedient, trustful acceptance of the assurance of God who thereby admits man to His own Being, and only thereby makes him really His own.

This is not a special "content" or "object" of faith. Rather is the apprehension of this Jesus-Cross-Resurrection event a being apprehended by the gracious God who is present in His self-communication. Faith is not a vessel which can be filled with any content one likes; it comes into being always simultaneously with its "content", with this self-manifestation of God. Only Christ-Cross-Resurrection faith is complete faith—meaning, only this has the characteristics of faith fully developed. For it is wholly "obedience" and it is wholly "trust" and includes as its negative reverse side "penitence", *metanoia*, just as in Old Testament faith there was always bound up with trust an element of fear, even of mortal dread (Isaiah 6: 5). For this reason only this faith is "adult" faith, because here man wholly turns to God and depends on Him, on God's action and God's giving.

(*e*) And now we must add one more, last point. In faith itself God's self-communication finds its completion. For here and only here, in this event, which God alone brings to pass in man, does God's self-manifestation, self-revelation and self-communication reach its goal. For God wills to be glorified in His creature, in man, and so to communicate Himself to him that man should wholly mirror back God's glory and kindness (2 Cor. 3: 18). Only when God's being for us and man's being for God become one, does that happen which is the true purpose of God's self-manifestation that He should be glorified in the creature and be known by it as the loving God and loved in return.[1] When we set faith and revelation over against each other as "content" and knowledge of this content, we fail to do

[1] Cf. *Dogmatics* I, Ch. 14, "The Holy"

justice to what happens in faith. Faith and its content are no more susceptible of separation. Faith is itself what revelation has in view. "*In ipsa fide Christus adest*", "In faith itself Christ is present" (Luther). The certainty that we are the children of God is nothing other than God's own speaking in us, what the New Testament calls the presence of the Holy Spirit. "The Spirit bears witness with our spirits that we are the children of God" (Rom. 8: 16). Here God alone speaks; man has no more to say, he has only to listen to this "speaking of God within him". When man does nothing but listen, that is, when he is content to let God Himself speak, then God achieves His purpose in him. Thus here, in faith in Christ and His Cross and Resurrection, "the righteousness of God", His true Lordship, is realized.

To this assertion by God of His kingly rule there corresponds on the side of man nothing other than the "hearing from below"—the *hypakoē* of *pistis*. When man accepts this assurance of God as what alone counts, and receives this assurance from Him, he becomes in a final sense obedient. For what else should obedience be but unity with God's will? Here trust and obedience are one, just as the assurance of God includes His claim within itself.

(*f*) Faith as acceptance of the self-communication of God in Jesus Christ is the perfecting of Old Testament faith. For this already was directed to the will of God which manifested itself in His revelatory acts. The new thing in comparison with the Old Testament is only this, that this self-manifestation is no longer mere self-*manifestation* but self-*communication* above all through the self-surrender of the Cross and through God's self-representation[1] in the Holy Spirit. In the New Testament, Word-revelation and historical revelation are one, because Jesus is the bestowal of God's gracious and sovereign Word of Love, God's incomparable deed. "He that spared not His own Son, but gave Him up for us all, how shall He not with Him also freely give us all things?" (Rom. 8: 32.)

(*g*) To this self-communication of God there corresponds the double act of acceptance and self-surrender which takes place in faith. Only he can accept the One who was crucified for us, who knows and acknowledges the necessity of this "for us", who thus sees himself judged and put to death on the Cross of Jesus, who knows himself as the one in whose place Christ had to suffer this death. This is possible for him only because in Christ a new existence, namely eternal life in fellowship with God, is offered and given to him. The frequently-used expression "shock

[1] See Translator's Note on Ch. 1, p. 4

to one's existence" says too little. In this *mortificatio,* more is included; the most radical judgment on "the old man" which removes not only all our own security but, especially, all our self-justification—all *kauchema,* all boasting. It would, however, be wrong to conceive of all this psychologically. Rather is all shock that is experienced in our consciousness, all emptying, all humiliation, transcended from the first in the historical happening on the Cross, and infinitely surpassed by what happened for us there. By believing the "for us" contained in the message of salvation, we have already renounced the attempt to reproduce it adequately in ourselves. It is just this which faith means by "going out beyond itself" (Luther), that only "there" do we have "the righteousness of God". Faith contains in itself the knowledge of the discomfiture of our selves which happened there.

(*h*) But even more important is the positive element, the new security, the new personal dignity, the encouragement, the restoration of the divinely given, original, true selfhood, the restoration of the image—(*restitutio imaginis*)—the new pride of the man who is summoned from nothingness, from the death of the old man, to the status of a child of God (as John says) or of a son of God (as Paul says) and is created in obedience to this summons. Just as deep as is our penitence at the Cross, so high or rather infinitely higher is our exaltation through identification with the Exalted One. This is the *plerophoria*—the full assurance—of faith which corresponds to the *eu-angelion*—the good news. This joy, this pride founded in God, this security founded in God—this is the fundamental note of the gospel and of faith.

From this now we can understand the fact why, in the first place, in the witness of the New Testament—especially in Paul—the revelation in Christ or the grace of Christ on the one side and faith on the other side are not only inseparably bound together, but are given exactly the same dignity, and why in the second place the word "faith" is so frequently used in an absolute sense. As concerns the first point, we can for example prove our contention with a reference to the central passage, Romans 3: 21 ff. While Paul here is speaking of the new revelation or of the new way of salvation, which God has opened up in Christ, he speaks just as often of faith as of Christ. There is indeed no Christ outside of faith—since only for faith is Jesus the Christ, and only in faith does the work of Christ come to fulfilment. Therefore Paul alternates between speaking of "justification by faith alone" and "through Christ alone". One might actually say, faith and Christ are synonymous, at any rate in the sense that "to have Christ" and "to believe" are one and the same thing.

And from this there follows now the second point, the absolute use of the word "faith". The clearest instance of this is Galatians 3: 23, "but before the faith came . . . which should afterwards be revealed". Here there could just as well stand "Before Christ came". Indeed, the faith of the New Testament is nothing other than faith in Christ, and therefore it can be spoken of without addition, in an absolute sense. But from this we may again draw the first conclusion, that equal importance is given to the meaning of the word "faith" as to the meaning of the word "Christ", and that the emphasis on faith as the decisive thing in the New Testament must not be regarded as a piece of human self-importance. For faith consists precisely in thinking not oneself, but God's self-communication in Jesus Christ alone, important. Faith is indeed precisely the end of *kauchema*, of self-importance. On the other hand faith is nothing other than the knowledge that *God* thinks us men to be of the utmost importance. This "humanism" is implied in God's incarnation in Jesus Christ, and to reject this humanism would be nothing less than to reject Christ.

Merely as a matter of statistics it can be ascertained that Paul and John ascribe the same importance to faith as to Christ. In the decisive passages, where the theme is salvation in Christ, the word "faith" or "believe" is *invariably* found. "God so loved the world . . . that whosoever believeth in him . . ." (John 3: 16). In the section of the Letter to the Romans which contrasts the new way of salvation in Christ with the old way of the law (Rom. 3: 21–31), the word "faith" or "believe" occurs no less than nine times, as if Paul had wished to say "The one is not without the other, Christ is not unaccompanied by faith, only for faith is Jesus the Christ." For this reason Paul can actually call the coming of Christ the coming of faith (Gal. 3: 25).

(*i*) When we hear the message of Christ and let it be told to us, and told in such a fashion that we have no longer anything more to say to it, but have simply become listeners—when we hear thus—we believe. This hearing and faith are one and the same thing. But we can hear this message only through the witnessing Word of the witnesses. Thus the Word which creates faith is at the same time God's Word and man's word, Word of the Spirit, and *paradosis*, tradition. The Word about Christ is at the same time spiritual and historical. This double character refers back to the Incarnation of the Word. Only the Jesus of history can be the Christ. But faith grasps the duality not as a duality but as a unity. The Jesus of history *is* the Christ, the Son of the living God. The achievement of a genuine understanding of the nature of faith from the New Testament is the principal task of theology, and only when this has been done shall we be able to give Martin Buber a convincing answer.

CHAPTER 13

THE MISUNDERSTANDING OF FAITH

(I) THE WORD FAITH

WHAT the New Testament calls *pistis* and *pisteuein*, and what is represented in the Old Testament by a number of words which all contain the element of loyalty and trust, of confidence, of security and of obedience as their decisive element, this faith which always refers to God's speaking and active Person and personal and total commitment on the part of man, is rendered in the European languages by words which very much obscure this historical personal character. As early as the Latin translation a cleavage is noticeable since the substantive "belief" and the verb "to believe" are taken from quite different fields. The substantives *fides, fiducia* have in them something of the personal content of *pistis* and *pisteuein*, but from the verb *credere* we could hardly guess anything of this nature, much less that it could be used as an equivalent for *pisteuein*. Without use of a commentary a Latinist would translate *credere* as "giving credit to" an assertion, a doctrine, or a report; that is, as an expression belonging essentially to the sphere of intellect. A man believes (*credit*) a statement or a fact, but the relation to a person as such—if it was ever implicit in the word—has disappeared from it, at least in later Latin.[1] Quite a lot of explaining must be done if we are to make the substantive *fides* or *fiducia* cover the same ground as the verb *credere*.

The translation of the New Testament into Latin—and, let us add, the use of the Latin Bible in the Catholic Church—has therefore made no small contribution to the development of the tragic misunderstanding of faith. But the same thing is true more or less of all the languages of Western Europe, in the shaping of whose Christian vocabulary the Latin tradition has been a formative influence. Thus, for example, in the Romance Languages we find the duality of *credere* as a verb, (*croire, credere*) and *fides* as a substantive (*foi, fede*). In English indeed the verbal roots are different; the substantive is "faith" (*fides*), the verb "believe". But the dualism is of exactly the same kind. German is the great exception, because it takes the substantive

[1] The earlier assumption that *credere* must be derived from *cor-dare* (to give one's heart) is today regarded as incorrect. (According to a personal communication from E. Risch, the Indo-Germanic scholar)

and the verb from the same root: *Glaube, glauben.* But since German had no substantive alongside of *glauben* with the meaning of "trust", as had the Latin (*fides, foi, fede,* faith), the intellectualistic transformation of *pistis* and *pisteuein* was here most radical. But, on the other hand, because the verb and the substantive come from one root, the restoration of the Greek *pistis-pisteuein* concept by means of explanation, namely by Luther's explanation, which restored to the word the full Biblical content of *pistis,* could also be most easily accomplished in the German language.

But still today, in spite of the Reformation, we stand in the shadow of this displacement of meaning which has lasted for many centuries. We theologians must not deceive ourselves about its enormous extent and depth. Like the average European, the average speaker of German understands by faith something which belongs to the intellectual sphere, namely an assent to statements and doctrines as true, and further, an assent on the grounds of authority. Against this linguistic usage all the better teaching which comes from the Reformation as to what the Bible means by faith, finds it difficult to make headway. The case is like that of the word "Church," which has just as fatal a connection with the Catholic concept of a holy institution and in spite of Reformed teaching to the contrary continues to have this meaning. We allow for this fact by making in the following pages the distinction between "*pistis*" and "belief in doctrine" (*Lehrglauben*), corresponding to the distinction between "Ekklesia" and "Church". Moreover, these two misunderstandings are not accidental parallels, but are most closely bound up with each other. Belief in doctrine belongs to the Church as an institution, just as *pistis* belongs to the Ekklesia. It was the same struggle for security which led the developing Church to create the episcopal office as a result of which it became a hierarchical institution, and which led it to create dogma as the essence of "what is to be believed", as a result of which the concept of *pistis* was calamitously transformed into an intellectualistic "*credere*". From this time onwards the Christian is the man who believes what the Church lays down for him *ad credendum.* The more one believes such doctrines or facts, the more perfect a Christian one is.

The fact that the Bible understands by "faith" the totality of existence of those who belong to Christ, now has a doubly fatal result in consequence of this shift of meaning. The man who has this faith—in the sense of assent to the sum of the *articuli fidei,* the articles of faith laid down by the Church or taught in the Bible—is a member of the Body of Christ, a believer, one whose relationship to God is altogether in right order. The obvious fact that this belief in doctrine has absolutely nothing to do with the life of love—while the Apostle clearly declares that only such faith as shows itself effectual in love is genuine—was quietly ignored or, in Catholic doctrine, an attempt was made to correct it by saying that faith must be supplemented by love; *fides caritate formata*. With good Biblical authority the Reformers rejected this teaching. But this only made the harm greater, since—and in so far as—the misunderstanding of faith as a false "belief in the Bible" continued to operate, and the whole weight of the principle "*sola fide*" was rested upon it.

(2) THE RÔLE OF WITNESS IN THE RISE OF *PISTIS*

(*a*) That Jesus is the Christ, that in Him God addresses us as Lord and reveals and promises His Lordship to us and makes known this Lordship as the Lordship of His self-bestowing love, this is the theme of faith, this is faith. Such faith in Jesus the Christ existed already before Easter—even though in an imperfect form—and that means before Jesus was preached as the Christ. Thus already before Good Friday and Easter the disciples acknowledged Jesus, though not yet distinctly, as the Christ, the Son of the living God, and Jesus indicated to them that this was a revelation of God.[1] It is thus not true that faith could originate *only* through witness, through the preaching about Jesus as the Christ. It originated rather in the disciples through the impression made by His Person, His life and His teaching about the Kingdom of God—that form of teaching which we find in the Synoptic Gospels. This historical event itself, Jesus, was thus primarily the power that created faith. No historical scepticism must be allowed to cloud this truth for us. Jesus Himself is the primary reason for faith in Christ.

It is certainly true that for the full revelation, both of God's Lordship and particularly for the revelation of the character of this Lordship as the love of God, something further had to happen. The historical event of Jesus does not include only what precedes His death but it is above all this death itself and

[1] This passage is assailed on critical grounds. But this makes no difference to the (unassailable) general picture of Jesus. There can be no doubt that He regarded Himself as the man in whom God's Kingdom had not only drawn near, but had "arrived", i.e. had begun. He is therefore more than a prophet; He is more than anything that had preceded Him. He is, even if in a sense not yet understood by the disciples, the Messiah and the Servant of God. The revelation of God's Lordship as self-communication became intelligible and certain to them only after His Resurrection

Jesus' Resurrection from the dead. It is no accident that in the gospel account the story of the Passion is by far the most fully reported part of the life of Jesus and in it there is a perpetual undertone of reference to the death on the Cross. But to recognize the death on the Cross as the decisive revelation of Jesus as the Lord is possible only for the man who knows of the Resurrection. For without this last event in His history the penultimate event would have been at the same time the conclusion, the end of the influence of Jesus on the world. Without the Resurrection we would know nothing of Jesus. He would have sunk into oblivion and His name would be unknown.

We owe the fact that we have the Gospels to the completeness of this historical event of Jesus Christ, above all to the fact of Easter. Thus then all the Gospels, inasmuch as they are first-hand accounts of the life of Jesus, are at the same time witnesses to Easter—even if there were no accounts of Easter in them, as in the case of Mark.[1] They are at the same time witnesses of the completion of the revelation on the Cross. A Christian faith without our Easter faith is a contradiction in terms. For, without Easter—no Gospels! In the Easter witness of the Apostles there is implicit, at the same time, *in nuce* the message of the Cross, which then Paul, wholly at one with the rest of the Apostles and with their consent, was the first to make intelligible to us men of a later age in his doctrinal witness to Christ, declaring it to be the self-communication of God, as salvation and as the revelation of the new way of salvation, the *dikaiosynē theou*—the righteousness of God.

We need no philosophy of "the historical character of existence" to do justice to this fundamentally simple fact—that faith in Christ in the first place is dependent upon the event of Jesus.[2] It is not the *kerygma* about Jesus as the Christ

[1] It is agreed that the present account of Easter in Mark was added by a later hand. The "genuine" end of Mark 16: 1–8 contains only the report that the women saw the empty tomb, and that an angel gave them instructions to tell Peter and the other disciples to go to Galilee, whither the Lord would precede them. The different accounts of the Easter event itself cannot be harmonized. The true Easter event was evidently something like what Paul experienced outside Damascus, to which he bears witness on several occasions. He saw, the Lord "appeared" to him. This is what he says also of Peter and the other witnesses, of whom at the time when he wrote 1 Corinthians (about 56–57) the majority were still alive. Clearly there was unanimity of the witnesses to this effect

[2] In his famous book *The Christ of the Indian Road* the British missionary Stanley Jones tells how in India it is not the doctrinal witness to Christ but the gospel stories that awaken faith. They have plenty of doctrines and discuss them endlessly. It is the simple story about Jesus which opens men's hearts to Him and creates faith

that is the foundation of Christian faith, it is Jesus the Christ Himself. We men of later times can indeed only know about Him through this *kerygma*. But in this *kerygma* the Gospels, which tell us of the Person and story of Jesus, have a place of the very highest importance. It was a great loss for Christendom that the Gospels were thrust into the background by *doctrine* about Christ, because the significance of Jesus was not so clearly expressed as by a Paul or a John.[1] This is the case even in Luther—who laid such decisive emphasis on the humanity of Jesus, as the foundation of faith in Christ—in so far as he treated the Gospel of Mark somewhat contemptuously on the grounds that it merely told "the stories" about Jesus, but did not give us doctrine about Him. The development of faith's genuine knowledge of Jesus as the Christ "starts very gently and leads us to Christ as a man" (Luther).[2] But seen from this standpoint, we would have to give the Gospel of Mark the first place among the New Testament witnesses. For it is after all the oldest of them all and therefore, so far as the historical event of Jesus is concerned, the most reliable.[3] For everything depends on this: the historical event of Jesus—in contrast to pious legends, which only too easily became myths—is the foundation of Christian faith. Witness to Jesus is in the first place narrative witness, which, however, as witness about Jesus the Christ, the Risen One, is always at the same time *more* than "history".

[1] Here the author must himself say *peccavi*, when he thinks of the small interest which he showed in his book *The Mediator* for the Jesus of History. I have for a very long time recognized the justice of the criticism which at that time P. Althaus made of me on this point (*Theol. Lit. Zeitung* 1929) and am completely in agreement with what he says in his book *Das sogenannte Kerygma und der historische Jesus* (E.T. *the So-called Kerygma and the Historical Jesus*, Oliver and Boyd, Edinburgh, 1959). Here a genuine understanding of Martin Kähler confronts a misinterpretation of Kähler. Kähler's book *Der sogennante historische Jesus und der geschichtliche biblische Christus* (*The so-called Jesus of History and the Historical Biblical Christ*, E.T. London), which appeared in 1892, is still a vitally relevant work, and its principal thesis has been taken up even by the more thoughtful of Bultmann's scholars. Cf. for example Käsemann's statement: "Nor can we cancel the identity of the exalted Lord with the earthly Lord without falling a prey to docetism, and robbing ourselves of the possibility of distinguishing the Easter faith of the Church from a myth" (*Z.Th.K.* 1954, p. 141). It is precisely this criticism which we have made of Bultmann (see above, p. 169). G. Bornkamm expresses himself in exactly the same way in his book *Jesus von Nazareth* (1956) (E.T. *Jesus of Nazareth*, Hodder and Stoughton, London, 1960)

[2] *W.A.* X, I.2, p. 297

[3] It is this which Bultmann refuses to recognize, and which constitutes his docetism. It is an expression not of scholarly criticism but of scepticism to say that "of the life and the personality of Jesus we can know almost nothing" (*Jesus*, 1926, p. 12). The secular historians are of an entirely different opinion on this matter; cf. Ed. Meyer, *Ursprung und Anfänge des Christentums*, 3 vols. 1920–3 (Origin and Beginnings of Christianity)

Even Mark begins his account with the words "the beginning of the gospel of Jesus Christ". Therefore we must in the first instance learn in Mark's school if we want to know who Jesus the Christ is, just as certainly as we only learn from Paul what faith is. When we grasp this we shall no longer play off the Pauline word "We know Christ no longer after the flesh" (2 Cor. 5: 16), and with it the doctrinal witness to Christ, against the narrative witness of the Gospels.[1] The fundamental *kerygma* is the report of Mark, whose intention is to reproduce as faithfully as possible the historical event of Jesus Christ. For precisely this is the feature that distinguishes Christian faith from all other religions; that it is faith in a historical person as the self-communication of God.

The *primary* witness runs thus: this is what Jesus the Christ was like, thus He spoke, thus He acted, thus He suffered. It is *kerygma* as narrative. To evade this is docetism. For this reason Paul's recourse to *paradosis*—tradition—and to the many appearances of the Risen Lord are entirely of a piece with his full and clear witness to Christ. We have to thank the "Form Criticism of the New Testament" for at last delivering us from the fatal antithesis of history and eternal truth. In fact the "accidental fact of history", Jesus, who has caused offence to the philosophers of all times, is the centre of Christian faith, and not the "Christ idea" that is championed against Him. If the Church had not early forgotten this, in spite of its fight against gnosis and docetism,[2] then the disastrous transformation of faith which made Church history so tragic would never have occurred.

(*b*) But the witness to Jesus the Christ is not *only* a narrative, an account, telling what He was in His earthly existence, what He said and did. It is at the same time an explanation of what this life and this death mean, seen in the light of the Resurrection. *Doctrine* as *kerygma* takes its place alongside the *narrative*. But this doctrine is no more mere doctrine than the narrative is mere account. Paul's teaching is authorized by the fact that "God revealed His son in me" (Gal. 1: 16). This statement about himself by Paul must be placed alongside Peter's confession.

[1] This is of course a reference to Rudolf Bultmann's views. "To wish to know Christ no longer after the flesh" does not mean to have no longer any interest in the historical Jesus, but to know Him no longer in a "fleshly" manner, that is, in this case merely historically or more generally, as a mere man

[2] In all traditional Church doctrine a certain docetism is noticeable. The humanity of Jesus is not taken really seriously. Paul says quite naively "a son of David" (Rom. 1: 3). Only later does the conception of the Virgin Birth appear, which really does make Jesus' humanity questionable. But the Virgin Birth is the content of the preaching of none of the Apostles, least of all John's

In the latter case Jesus received the confession of Himself with the words "For flesh and blood hath not revealed it unto thee, but my Father in heaven" (Matt. 16: 17). Here Paul says it himself and thus this doctrinal witness is to be understood as a knowledge of Jesus as the Christ bestowed by the Spirit of God, the knowledge of the self-manifestation and self-communication of God.

But this doctrine has no other purpose than to explain who Jesus really was: the Son of God, even in His earthly existence before Easter; the man, therefore, for whom "it was not possible that he should be holden" by death. Thus this doctrine does not find its ground and its goal in itself, *but is always a pointer to Him*, the historical Jesus, who through the Resurrection is the first born from the dead and our contemporary. Thus it is not confined within itself, not meant as "doctrine in itself" but as a pointer to Him, the Jesus of whom the gospel narratives tell us, and whose portrait they mediate to us. To portray Him "before our eyes" (Gal 3: 1) is the aim of the apostolic preaching, and we may not by-pass it to construct a conflict between the preaching of Mark and that of Paul. Paul the missionary's portrayal of Christ before men's eyes must have also included the story of Jesus as the Gospels depict it; only, in the letters of Paul to the Christian communities, that is, to people who were already believers in Christ, it is, above all, the *meaning* of this history which is thrown into relief for us. It is as if Paul, the teacher, had read the Marcan account underlining only the most important things in red pencil. In a like manner in His last meeting with the disciples, Jesus Himself, while dividing the bread and in giving the cup, had in brief words explained the meaning and significance of His impending death.

When the historians whose theme is primitive Christianity so often played off Jesus against Paul, they forgot that Paul was continually surrounded by men who had seen Jesus in His lifetime, and who had been with Him day by day. How could they have accepted the Pauline Christology and given Paul the right hand of fellowship if his teaching had been something incompatible with their own picture of Jesus, or even if it had merely seemed to them something unfamiliar? Their judgment was rather "Yes, this is what He was, this was why He had to suffer death on the Cross, this is why He rose again." The unity of the teaching about "Christ, the Son of God" with the narrative about Jesus, as they had experienced Him, was *the* decisive thing about the *kerygma* concerning Christ. John found the most perfect expression for this: "The Word became flesh." With this formula, too, he built a bridge between the Old Testament self-manifestation of God and God's self-communication in Jesus the Son of God.

Thus on both sides, on the side of the preaching narrator Mark and on the side of the preaching teacher Paul, it is not the narrative as such and not the doctrine as such which create faith, but both of them in their *unity*. For the "object" of the narrative is indeed a man, in fact the only truly human man, but at the same time this man is He who was "declared to be the Son of God with power according to the spirit of holiness by His resurrection from the dead"[1] (Rom. 1: 4).

(*c*) But the witness is not only a Word of narrative and a Word of teaching, but an authoritative Word of the man who has himself recognized this crucified One as the living Lord and has received from Him the love of God. He knows himself to be commissioned by Him to pass on this love to others through his Word, but also through his own existence, through his life. Therefore it is a Word of life spoken out of a fullness and warmth of love that immediately convinces the hearer of its truth. So Paul reminds the Thessalonians not only of *what* he had preached to them, but, just as much, of *how* he did it. "We were gentle among you, even as a nursing mother cherishes her children; so being affectionately desirous of you, we were willing to have imparted unto you not the gospel of God only, but also our own souls, because ye were dear unto us" (1 Thess. 2: 7, 8). But it is also the truth for which he himself stands security, in readiness to give his life for it as a sacrifice (*martyria, martys*). Both these things are in Paul's mind when he contrasts the *pneuma* (the Spirit) of the New Testament preaching with the *gramma* of the Biblical letter, the written word. The spiritual existence of the messenger makes men ready and able to receive the message. The self-dedication of the Apostle overcomes the resistance in the hearts of the hearers. The wholly new quality of love creates an understanding for the love of God which has revealed itself on the Cross, for it is one and the same love (1 Cor. 13). Trust in the messenger opens hearts and makes them ready to trust the message.

Here also the saying holds good: *omne vivum ex vivo* (all life comes from life). The Word that is to create living faith must itself come from a vital apprehension by the love of God.

[1] Here Luther's translation seems to me even to improve on Paul's formulation: "and mightily proved to be a Son of God according to the Spirit". For already before Good Friday and Easter He had been recognized by some disciples as the Son of God

But this vital element cannot be comprehended in any doctrine. In contrast with it doctrine is an objective "article of faith" which in its content may agree with the witness, but can waken no faith, because it has in itself no longer this personal sympathy with Christ and concern for the hearer.

(*d*) Lastly, the Word of witness is not the Word of an individual but a Word spoken from fellowship, the Word which because it bears witness to Jesus Christ at the same time bears witness to a fellowship, to the brotherhood of the Ekklesia, which has its origin in Him. When it speaks of the reconciliation which has taken place in Him, it speaks at the same time of the Kingdom of God, of God's reign in love, as something already in process of realization. Where the witness is true and vital, it creates Ekklesia, the brotherhood that tears down all barriers which otherwise divide the historical and earthly world of men: the barriers of race, of class, of nationality, of sex. To bear witness to Christ means to bear witness to God's reign in love, a rule that is already present where He is.

The Apostle never speaks as "this individual", he speaks always as "one of those who . . ." As his gospel comes from faith "*eis pistin*"—to faith—so is it a Word from Ekklesia to Ekklesia. For it is the Word about the new man, and he is, in distinction from the old, the man in whom the "we" has taken the place of the "I". Because the witness really in the highest degree, in an unconditional manner, is himself united with his witness, and therefore—as we have just said—stands surety for it with his own existence, it is at the same time the Word for humanity which concerns all, includes all, without distinction. To bear witness to Christ means to bear witness to the new humanity, and that not as an idea, but as a reality. This is the Ekklesia, the brotherhood in which absolute humanity has begun to come into being; the Kingdom of God in love, namely in God's love, which in this brotherhood is life. The Word of witness is not a Word of the Church, but it *is* a Word of the Ekklesia, just in the same way as it is a Word of God. How could it bear witness to the reality of Christ if it did not at the same time bear witness about the realization of His will that has now already begun, that will in which "God for us" is correlated with "us for God"? That the one becomes the other—precisely this is the presence of the Holy Spirit. Therefore, just as the witness issues from faith to faith, so also is it the Word that issues from love to love, from brotherhood to brotherhood. It is the only genuine word of togetherness, recognizable by the togetherness of the new humanity that has begun to be realized in the Ekklesia which comes from this togetherness and aims at this togetherness (*Wirheit*).

To be a witness means to be a man in whom this meaning of the message is manifest in everything that he says, in everything that he does. The Kingdom of God in Corinth, the Kingdom of God in Galatia, the Kingdom of God in Rome, stands behind him and sends this Word, in order that elsewhere this reality of the Kingdom of God should come into being. For this reason the word "We" is not only inseparable from the Word of witness, but refers in a special measure to Him in whom this new divine humanity is present. For this reason He is the Christ because this togetherness became real for the first time in Him, the new humanity, which is new because it is humanity whose origin and goal is in God. One has not received the Word of witness as the Word of Christ unless one recognizes and loves in the witness the representative of this one thing, this new humanity identical with Christ.

All these elements in their conjunction make *keryssein*—preaching—an activity *sui generis*, which has only a remote relationship to the activity of teaching and learning. *Kerygma* is not narrative and yet there is narrative in it. It is not doctrine, and yet there is doctrine in it. It is not an authoritative Word of witness, which is to be believed on that account, and yet it is the Word of witness with authority. It is not a Word of the Church, and yet it is a Word proceeding from the Ekklesia and directed towards the up-building of the Ekklesia. All these elements find their unity in God's self-communication in Jesus, the Christ, and the intention of all of them is to point to Him. Indeed, in this *keryssein* God's self-communication, which has once for all happened in Jesus Christ, continues in order to make this unique event contemporary. Preaching shows itself to be living, spiritual *kerygma* by creating Ekklesia in which Christ is present in power.

(3) THE CAUSE AND FORMS OF THE MISUNDERSTANDING OF *PISTIS*

The fatal displacement in the interpretation of the word "believe", which we have already discovered in the linguistic usages of the modern languages, can be seen in the isolation of the separate elements of witness.

(*a*) The narrative witness to the life of Jesus is conceived of as a report of facts which as such are to be believed. Therefore one might call this form of misunderstanding of faith "belief in facts". This conception of faith still plays a disastrous rôle today.

In the Gospels we are not given an account of Jesus as a "historical personality" in whose historicity one must "first" believe before one can believe on Him as the Son of God. This historical Jesus is rather the product of an abstraction which the conscientious historian feels himself compelled to make for the sake of the objectivity of his account. But the gospel narrative on which the historian is dependent as the only (considerable) source of his knowledge, in order to fill up the gap in his historical continuum which would otherwise remain unfilled, namely the origin of Christianity, has quite a different intention. Its aim is to bear witness to Jesus the Christ. But it is not this Jesus to whom the Gospels bear witness as the Christ, as the risen, living Lord, the Son of God, that interests the historian, but only what he can guarantee as an objective reporter. For this purpose he uses the Gospels as "source material" for his objective account. He abstracts consciously from the thing that is of the utmost importance for the evangelist—namely the witness to Christ and the Easter event which is fundamental to it, and uses as his "material" only what remains over when this abstraction has been made.

Thus the "historical Jesus" is the product of this objectifying abstraction, by means of which the narrative of the Gospels is estranged from its own purposes. The believer, however, does not make this abstraction. For in the narrative witnesses to Jesus the Christ, he is in penitence and trust encountered by one whom he recognizes as "the Lord", "Kyrios Christos", as indeed the narrator and witness intended to present Him. This is the origin and the meaning of his (narrative) witness.

Only when a man who believes in Jesus the Christ feels himself at the same time under an obligation to historical objectivity, that is, to this cultural task, does this abstraction of the historian, the so-called "historical Jesus", interest him. But the fact that this is possible, that when this abstraction has been made enough "material" is left to satisfy the purely historical interest, is interesting to him. It is indeed more than merely interesting to him; it coincides with his real interest—the interest of his faith—because, also for his faith, Jesus the Christ is a man, because for his faith too an event of history (namely the Crucifixion) is the decisive fact for faith, or saving fact.

Thus the interest of faith must make contact with the interest of the historian, otherwise it would not be the man Jesus, the incarnate Word, in whom or in which he believes. Indeed we may go further. It is certainly of interest to him that even the conscientious historian who aims at an objective representation should speak of a personality "that could not be invented", a personality "unique" in its humanity; and that this phenomenon which is unique in the objective scientific sense, and as such possesses only a relative uniqueness, should coincide with what he knows in his faith to be the absolutely unique event, of which the historian as such knows nothing.[1] This coincidence between what lies on the plane of history and of general human possibilities, and what can be known only to faith, has however been long appreciated by the believer before he became acquainted with this abstraction of historical scholarship. It is implicit for him in the name of Jesus, as the Christ of whom the (narrative) witness of the evangelist spoke to him. He always knew only the one Jesus Christ as his Saviour; he did not need historical knowledge for that. It was present in the witness to Him as a unity with this witness.

There can thus be no question of his having *first* to believe in a fact, and then on the strength of that being able to believe in the sense of *fiducia*. He does not owe his Jesus, the Christ, to the historian, but to the man who bore witness to him about Jesus as the Christ, so that in penitence and faith he recognized Jesus as such through the same Spirit in which He had been preached to him. Therefore his faith is not first a faith in facts, but, from the beginning, vital faith in Christ. The believer knows nothing of a faith in facts which would have to precede his genuine faith. It was the same Spirit of God that created the witness of the evangelist, that authenticated Himself to him, the hearer of this witness, when the witness created in him the saving faith which caused the *pro vobis*—the "for you" of the witness—to become the *in nobis*—the "in us"—of faith. The Jesus of the historian is unknown to him, the believer, for the Jesus whom he knows is none other than the Christ, his Saviour.

(*b*) The case of belief in doctrine is exactly similar. From the (doctrinal) witness to Jesus the Christ, the Lord crucified and

[1] Compare the great writer on ancient history, Ed. Meyer, whom we have already cited. In his work *Ursprung und Anfänge des Christentums*—(Origin and Beginnings of Christianity), 1920, he lays emphasis on the fact that imagination could not have invented the Person and story of Jesus. This, so to speak, is the side of Kyrios Christos that is accessible to the world. That on this question Gogarten has recently come to the support of Bultmann marks a change of opinion from his first post-war book, *Die Verkündigung Jesu*, 1946 (The Preaching of Jesus)

risen for us, in whom we believe because He shatters our autonomy and at the same time fills us with trust and obedience, there is isolated the doctrinal element which declares "Jesus is God's son—this must be believed." But the believer knows nothing of such an abstraction. He knows only the one Jesus Christ who encounters him in the witness to Christ, he knows Him through the Spirit whom the witness filled by Jesus Christ transmits also to him. How could he in this situation have believed in a doctrine? A doctrine that Jesus was the Son of God would not have had the slightest power to convince him. His faith was created in no other way than through that witness which in the unity of these elements, which all point to Christ, was able to lead him to penitence, to obedience and to trust. As the witness comes from the Spirit of God, so through the same Spirit it is made our own certainty of faith. "Doctrine in itself" would never have had the power to touch the heart's core (*radix cordis*), said Calvin. It is not a challenging Thou-Word of God, which calls "me" to repentance and makes "me" a child of God. Doctrine is an "It-word about something" which does not touch me in my existence, but concerns my understanding only. These two misunderstandings, belief in facts and belief in doctrine, have in the history of the Church and in its theology taken the form of belief in dogma and (aprioristic) biblicism.

(*c*) In place of the Ekklesia, the Spirit-filled brotherhood which stands behind the Apostles' witness to Christ, we have now the episcopal institution which puts forward a doctrine to be believed in; that is, prescribes it to man as a law of faith. This doctrine is the element of doctrine and narrative abstracted from the witness, the "facts which must be believed" and the "doctrine which must be believed" that explains their meaning. This doctrine and these facts could not alone awaken faith. One must "simply believe" them, in order to participate in the saving grace of the Church. Just as the Ekklesia has become transformed, namely into a priestly episcopal institution for procuring salvation, so has faith been transformed. It is no longer the conquest of the heart resulting from the encounter with the living Christ, no longer that event wherein the Spirit is transmitted from the Apostle to the hearer, an event which only faith can understand; it is rather blind submission to the teaching office of the Church. Once more the place of the *pneuma* has been taken by the *gramma* in the form of authoritatively prescribed dogma, which must be believed. Above all, faith has been transformed in the sense that it is given now in the first place to the Church and only through the Church's mediation to Christ. For not only the teaching about Christ, but everything that the Church teaches must be accepted in faith. This belief in dogma is the specifically Catholic form of the misunderstanding of *pistis*.

(*d*) In orthodox Protestantism an (aprioristic) faith in the Bible corresponds to this faith in dogma. The Biblical concept of faith which the Reformers had rediscovered was replaced in the post-Reformation period by a "faith" in the Bible backed by an equally formal authority, namely the authority of the Holy Book whose divine inspiration has to be believed "from the first". The Bible is inspired in every part, indeed in every letter, and therefore it is the infallible Word of God. Here also there has been a fundamental change, inasmuch as the believer must *start* by believing in the Bible as God's Word. The scripture principle of Orthodoxy runs thus: The Bible is the authority (*principium*) from which all the articles of faith (*articuli fidei*) are derived. Faith in it is given priority over faith in Jesus Christ and the *sola gratia* principle. This (aprioristic) Bible-faith is neither the *pistis* of which the Apostles speak nor the *emuna* of the prophets and psalmists. Rather is it a theorem about the Bible, which is not of Christian origin, but stems from the doctrine of the verbal inspiration of scripture which was taken over from Judaism. To believe in the Bible in this sense is to replace the Spirit by the letter.

Faith in the infallible Bible is no longer possible for modern man, unless he shuts his eyes to the facts which have been disclosed by Biblical criticism by opposing his theory of the infallibility of scripture to this criticism and making it his criterion of orthodoxy. Thus he is compelled to reject all critical scholarly investigation of the Bible from the outset as a work of unbelief. How did this utterly unbiblical conception of the nature of faith and this utterly unbiblical theory of the Bible arise?

While Luther had taught: "Christ is the Lord and King of scripture" (*Christus dominus et rex scripturae*), because he had won his understanding of faith from the justification of the sinner through the reconciliation in the Cross of Christ, and understood by the Word of God this Word of challenge that encountered him and created him anew in the Christ event, the polemic against Rome in post-Reformation times made the Protestant Churches look for an equally massive *a priori* authority. The Pope in Rome was countered by the "paper Pope". It appeared that the authority of the same Apostle who gave us the *sola fide* principle could be cited for this. For was it not in the Second Epistle of Paul to Timothy that the word could be found "For all scripture given by God is profitable for doctrine" . . . (2 Tim. 3: 16)? It was not yet known at that time that this letter is a writing of the second century. It is, however, no accident that it was the same pseudonymous author who formulated the Jewish Bible-principle whom we have already encountered as the first representative of an episcopal conception of the *Church*. Both views are the outcome of the same legalistic thinking.

Faith in the Christ who encounters us in the Spirit-filled witness to Himself, the creator and giver of this faith, has turned into the legalistic faith of the (Protestant) Church, which demands faith in the Bible as infallible Word of God. And this legalistic faith is supported by the argument that we must believe in the divine inspiration of the Apostles. The authority of the Apostles, which vindicates itself to the hearts of the hearers, has turned into the belief in the inspiration of scripture, a belief which now conceives of this inspiration as a formal legal authority.

Today there are but few theologians left who believe in the theory of the verbal inspiration of Scripture. In spite of this the completely different character of this so-called faith from justifying faith is not yet rightly understood. The error is not so much that its advocates do not see and concede the inaccuracies and human fallibility of the holy Book—that is the argument of the Enlightenment, which is indeed right, but does not touch the central point. The error is that through this (aprioristic) Bible faith, faith has been transformed into something fundamentally different from what the Bible itself means by *pistis* and *emuna*. The result of our reflections is thus as follows: Aprioristic Bible faith is not Biblical but stems from precisely the Jewish legalistic thought which was transcended by justifying faith.[1]

[1] There is not only this false, aprioristic, legalistic Bible faith but also a Bible faith in the genuine sense. On this point, see below, pp. 244–50: Reflections on the Formulation of a new Doctrine of Scripture

CHAPTER 14

THE PERFECTED FORM OF FAITH: THE JUSTIFICATION OF THE SINNER BY FAITH ALONE

THE Pauline doctrine of justification, especially Romans 3: 21–31, is the true centre and climax of the Christian message. The superlatives of Luther with which he has again and again underlined this are not subjective or time-conditioned or accidental. It is precisely his one-sided emphasis on justification which marks him out as the congenial interpreter of the Apostle Paul and as the one teacher who in all the Church is nearest to the mind of Christ. The view of Albert Schweitzer that the doctrine of justification by faith is a polemic against Jewish legalism, and thus only a "side-crater" while the true centre is Christ-mysticism, is wrong, if only for the reason that both these are one and the same thing. In justification the faith that is believed (*fides quae creditur*) is identical with the faith by which we believe (*fides qua creditur*).

The so-called objective element in revelation, the self-communication of God, and the subjective, existential character of faith as *pistis* in contrast to belief in doctrine meet here, exactly and mathematically formulated, as it were, by Paul, and completely coincide. In this knowledge of the identity of God's self-communication and man's self-understanding in faith there lies the possibility of transcending theological antitheses which have rent asunder the whole of the theology of the Churches since the post-Reformation period and continue to do so right up to the present day.[1] But this knowledge is at the same time —and this is relevant to our concern—the most personal experience of the man who has passionately struggled with God, and been subdued by Him.

What Paul and Luther call "justification by faith" is not a doctrine that is to be believed. It is rather God's personal assurance in which he addresses "me" in spite of my sin as His beloved son, an assurance that I ought to believe and can believe because it is based upon the reconciling act of His Son Jesus Christ; and in this historical event, which can be known by me in faith as the perfect self-communication of God, the self-bestowing love of God is revealed to me at the same time

[1] See Excursus following this chapter, on The Contemporary Theological Situation

as the depth of my own sin. The omnipotence of God reveals itself in the weakness of man, life in the form of death. For this reason my knowledge of God in faith as inconceivable unconditional love becomes at the same time my understanding of myself as a sinner.

Here, as nowhere else, happens what Calvin speaks of in the famous first paragraph of the first chapter of the *Institutes*, namely the perfect co-ordination of knowledge of God and knowledge of self, and therefore also the unity of God's act of revelation and human self-understanding in existential experience. Only by identifying myself with the crucified Christ can I understand what justification means. This identification means at the same time this paradox, that the self of the present moment looks entirely away from itself and looks wholly to the "It is finished" of history, to the crucified Son of God, and so not only becomes free of its own past, but gains its own being in the Word of God. This is its being, given to it in Creation, to which it is now not only restored but in which it experiences the love of God as its new, restored and completed, eternal being.

It is now necessary to clarify for ourselves in detail the Pauline doctrine of justification.

I

We can only understand what the expression "justification" means if we first pay attention to the negative side, which necessarily belongs to the positive, and at the same time stands to it in the reciprocal relation of ground and consequence; namely, the radical understanding of our sinfulness. Only the man who acknowledges himself to be a sinner can understand what is meant by justification. But how much he is a sinner becomes fully clear to him only through justification. The encounter with the crucified Christ tells a man first something about himself, namely, how it stands with him "before God".

Even apart from Jesus Christ man knows something of the fact that he is not what he ought to be. This is already implicit in the knowledge of an imperative. For by his distinguishing the "ought" from the "is" he acknowledges to himself that there is no coincidence, no congruence between the two, but that this distinction points to opposition in himself. This opposition he is as little able to remove as the difference between ideal and reality. He sees thus, even if only very indistinctly, that "things are not well" with him. He knows that he should be different. The "natural man", the man who is still untouched by Christ, does not, however, permit this knowledge to make real headway. He tries to explain the fact of "discrepancy" in the most harmless way possible by referring to the imperfection of all things, and thus excuses himself by saying that after all he is not perfect. Or, if the moral consciousness asserts itself more decisively in him, he will try to explain the discrepancy between the "is" and the "ought" by conceiving of the ideal as his "better self"; this, he thinks, stands over against the real as the lower self which, as a matter of nature and destiny, somehow clings to him. Thus he divides himself into two halves, and flatters himself that the better self is his truest self while the other, the lower self, is (so to speak) only its fatal shadow. In this way he denies his responsibility for the whole man, in order to maintain a good opinion of himself, in order to justify himself to himself.

But the natural man has in very recent times learnt an especially effective kind of self-deception. He has done away with the moral norm by conceiving of it as nothing more than an entity created by society for the self-protection of human life, or by thinking of himself as nothing more than a being of nature, for which no imperative exists. This manœuvre of his does not indeed entirely succeed, because alongside of this naturalistic theory the moral imperative remains as the real environment of his life in which practically he has his existence. Even when he conceives of man as "an animal", a complete emancipation from conscience is not possible for him. Above all, he desires to be treated by his fellow men with a respect and consideration which contradicts his theory, or at least can never be derived from it. In fact no man is emancipated from moral obligation, however much in theory he may assert that he is. But his theory must help him to excuse himself morally by blaming the "evil" in him on heredity, on the social environment, on education. As a matter of fact, however, he makes the distinction that is made also in the penal code, in civic morals and in all education, between "good" men and "bad"; and in so doing he always succeeds in counting himself as belonging to the "really" or "fundamentally" good.

This morality, however, without which in fact human life cannot continue, is as such an emancipation from God. As soon as man stands "before God" by understanding the ethical law as a divine command, these devices of self-justification are done with. For "in thy sight shall no man living be justified" (Psalm 143: 2). Indeed, fundamental and honest reflection on the ethical law ends with the judgment that there is a radical evil in man.[1] The philosopher reaches this conclusion by conceiving of man's will as a totality; that is, when he perceives that in the individual evil act there is disclosed an inexplicable "predilection for evil".[2]

But this acknowledgment shows itself to be really inevitable only where I am confronted with God's commandment; where, accordingly, every evasion becomes impossible. This is the witness of the Old Testament. Before the claim of the Lord man's self-justification is silenced. Here the judgment "You are evil" becomes the judgment "You are a sinner", i.e. a man separated from God, one shut out from fellowship with Him, a man who has no share in God's salvation and His life. But what Paul says about the situation of man, of man in the sight of God, refers not only to morality. Rather is morality included within the relationship to God. But because God is the Lord, there is no way to fellowship with God which disregards His will. Nothing whatever that man may undertake, neither sacrifice nor mystical practices, in short no human work, can obtain for him salvation and fellowship with God. "He has no honour in God's sight," nothing whereby he could justify himself in the eyes of God.

But man is unable permanently to bear this radically unfavourable verdict upon him of the divine commandment, for without self-respect he cannot live. So in fact he always evades this judgment. He takes refuge either in a kind of cynicism, acknowledging indeed the negative element but setting it down at the same time as a fact of nature: "That is after all the kind of man I am"—and thus disowns responsibility, but at the same time denies his own personal being, which is identical with responsibility. Or else he sinks into despair—unless he happens to turn to faith.

When Christ, the Crucified, encounters him, it is no longer the commandment that condemns him but God Himself, who in a real event, in the event of the Cross, shows him how it stands with him. The only really righteous man is crucified. He, the guiltless One, suffers the death of the rebel; hence, not because of *His own* sin, but because of *yours*. This, then, is how things stand with "you"—this is the kind of man *you* are. The

[1] Cf. Kant: "Religion within the Bounds of Reason Alone", Part I, III

[2] It must be granted that even the great Kant does not remain true to this insight, since in the course of his treatment of this radical evil he again rescues the better self by identifying it with the moral law, which is, he declares, *its* law (autonomy). Only when this concept of autonomy on which the identification rests, and which makes possible such a division of the self into a better self and an empirical man, is abandoned and the law is acknowledged to be *God's* law, is this autonomy, and with it also man's self-justification, abandoned

Cross, the gallows of the rebel against God's majesty, is what you have deserved. This judgment spoken from the Cross thus implies the absolute annihilation of our own moral and religious attempts to justify ourselves. We are reduced to nothing in the sight of God.

For this reason the message of the Cross is the stone of stumbling for everyone who is not ready to let himself be thus reduced to nothing. That is why man rejects this message—as an affront to human dignity—unless he believes that God really encounters him here, that through the Cross God Himself speaks to him. But when the miracle happens, and he believes, then he hears from the Cross not first this verdict of annihilation, but the unbelievable positive that God loves him, this sinner, this rebel, in spite of all he can do. Here man's self-knowledge as a sinner and the self-communication of God the merciful One are indistinguishably fused together, so that it is "not easy to see which of the two precedes and gives birth to the other" (*non facile est discernere utra alteram praecedat et ex se pariat*).[1] Only because there is bestowed on the man, whose existence is condemned as impossible by the divine judgment, a wholly new being, a new self-respect, a new pride in which he may again stand upright—only then can he dare to be so honest with himself as to accept the justice and truth of that judgment. And this other gift, this new "status" is simply the verdict of God, the assurance "In spite of all I love you, in spite of all I approve of you. Because I let myself be identified with the cursed blasphemer of God dying on the Cross, I am also identified with Him, the Son of God in whom God is well pleased". And conversely, the identification with the Son of God occurs only for the man who hears the judgment of the Cross as his judgment. Only through the one is the other true. So in the message of the Cross both are inseparably conjoined, the sinner's radical self-knowledge "Mine, mine was the transgression, But thine the deadly pain" and the acquittal of God, who says to me, "My son, in whom I am well pleased."

In faith in the Cross as what happened "for us", all moral and religious self-justification, all security of the feeling that we can stand before God—and that is what Paul calls *kauchema* (boasting)—is excluded, and so excluded that I cannot even save my "better self" from bankruptcy. For it is not my better self, it is God, that gives this verdict. Indeed it is the case that the man who in faith accepts this verdict as delivered upon him knows at the same time that even now his acknowledgment of

[1] Calvin, *Institutes* I, I, I

sin is never so profound as it really ought to be, that I must rather look on the Cross of Christ to understand what God thinks about my sin. So also self-knowledge passes beyond itself to Jesus Christ, to the real, historical event, in order to determine by Him the measure of sin. When a man looks at the Cross it is as if he stepped upon God's scales, in order to read from them the weight of his guilt. Of every knowledge of our sin that we can ourselves achieve it must be said: "You have not yet considered how great is the weight of sin" ("*Nondum considerasti quanti ponderis sit peccatum*"; Anselm). Luther's word is true even of this (negative) self-knowledge. It is outside of us and alien to us (*extra nos et aliena nobis*), meaning that even the self of self-knowledge is only truly to be known "there"; not in me.

II

But there is here implicit, as we have already said, a strange and wonderful dialectic. When I, the sinner, identify myself with the man who was crucified as a blasphemer against God, there also takes place a second identification, namely an identification with Jesus, the Christ, the Son of God. It is not the negative word "You are a sinner" that is the authentic message of the Cross. It is only the presupposition for your truly hearing also the authentic message, namely, "Although you are like this, God loves you." He says to you, "My child, My son in whom I am well pleased." What man all his life long has vainly attempted to reach through morals, through education and self-education, through piety and religion—peace with God, salvation, life in fellowship with God—God bestows this upon him in free and kingly grace. He bestows upon him reconciliation with God. He bestows upon him righteousness, that is, He makes him right with God. He quite simply declares "You are right with me."

How is this possible? How can God say something like this which is in contradiction with the empirical reality? We answer: Because God creates this other reality. What counts "in God's sight" is for *God* alone and no one else to say. But He says: "I assure you that, just as you are, you are right with me. I am the final authority that makes this decision. I love you, not because you are worthy of my love, but in spite of your unworthiness, simply because it is my will to do so." This love of His has no other foundation than itself. It is the unfathomable "flowing" love through which He "posits" me as righteous through His creative Word.

It is not caprice and not the preacher's habit of slipping into sermonic language which has caused us here to choose the form of direct speech. It is rather what is demanded by the theme itself. For here we have to deal with something which can be rightly said in I-Thou language, and which also can be understood only in I-Thou language. For we are speaking about the assurance of God. When a man believes this assurance, receives this assurance as God's own Word and allows God to say it to him, then it is clear that this is not a case of believing in (a fact) but an act *sui generis* which perhaps is most correctly described by the Greek *pisteuein en*, "believe in (a person)". In the event of Christ's Cross I hear God's call: "Thou, Son." One could indeed more correctly say: "In the name of Jesus the Crucified, the name 'son of God' is addressed to me." Faith is an act in which a man is purely receptive, in no way actively takes the initiative, and yet here his whole person is "summoned" to receive this new total character as a person. Indeed it is only in this act that man experiences what the total character of personality is, and only in this act is that totality present. Faith is the only act in which the totality of the person is "gathered together", while otherwise—even in the most passionate dedication such as is experienced in artistic creation or the passion of love—the totality is only an ideal, an intention, never a real achievement. For here alone man surrenders himself completely and here alone he receives a new personal being, a new person as his own.

III

But how does a man come to understand the Cross, this tragic event of history, as God's assurance? Certainly, that is the witness of the Apostles. But our inquiry goes behind the Apostles to the event itself. This faith does not simply rest upon the authority and trustworthiness of the Apostle. Rather does the word of the Apostle indicate the Person and act of Christ as the objective ground of its affirmation. The witness is not itself the ground of faith, it is true rather that faith is based on Jesus Christ Himself to whom the apostolic witness points. He who died on the Cross is He who speaks with divine authority and in whose action God Himself acts. The *kerygma* about Jesus Christ the reconciler includes in itself the picture of Jesus and the story of Jesus, in which Jesus is shown to us as the man who speaks and acts with divine authority.

Jesus had already confirmed the faith of the disciples in Him as the Messiah-Christ, the One equipped with divine authority, the "Son of the living God" (Matt. 16: 16 ff.), acknowledging it to be God's revelation in their hearts. And in just the same manner as He applied the Messianic promises to Himself, Jesus also understood the other word about the Suffering Servant of God as referring to Himself, and thus conceived of Himself as the atoning sacrifice through which God proclaimed His will to reconciliation. Jesus' sufferings and death were thus just as much God's act as His saying "But I say unto you" was God's Word. And this had all become a certainty to the Apostles through His Resurrection, after they had been cast into the deepest despair by His preceding death. In the power of the Easter fact they dared to proclaim Him, the Crucified, as the Son of God given up for our reconciliation. Through this proclamation of theirs the same certainty is bestowed on us, so that we also, just as we hear the authoritative Word of God in His earthly historical life, are able to understand His sufferings and death on the Cross of Golgotha as the authoritative act of God.

We believe, not *on the strength* of what the Apostles say, but thanks to our own insight which is bestowed on us by God *through* the witness of the Apostles. Fides is *autopiston*—bears witness to its own truth—so the theological Fathers tell us, meaning that our faith stands on no other foundation than that on which the Apostles also stand. Our knowledge of Christ is our own, not dependent on the authority of the Apostles, though it could not come into existence without the witness of the Apostles. We ourselves know that it is as they say, even if we could never have known it and seen it without their witness.

It is one and the same authority of Jesus which enables us to hear His *words* as God's Word and to recognize His *acts* and His obedience unto death as God's act. But this knowledge is made possible only by the fact that His whole life culminates in His obedience unto death. He is the only one who is able to say, "The Son of Man came not to be ministered unto, but to minister, and to give His life a ransom for many" (Mark 10: 45). Every one of His acts is an expression of this same will of God which He proclaims, and it is precisely the complete congruence of Word and action which gives us the certainty of His divine authority. Not only His words and His acts, but His Person in its totality and its mystery is authoritative Word, and His passion, death and Resurrection is God's act. He is what He knew Himself to be, the Messiah and Suffering Servant, who as the Messiah embodies the claim of God, and in His sufferings is the Servant of God, who bears for us the penalty of sin, "the chastisement of our peace" (Isaiah 53).

In order to make clear to us the meaning of the death on the Cross, Paul has used an expression or an idea from the Jewish sacrificial cultus—the sacrifice of the day of Atonement. But this expression is not the reality itself, for Paul, like the other Apostles, uses also other metaphors for it.[1] For us today in general the concept of the atoning sacrifice (*hilasterion*) is difficult to understand. That Jesus took upon Him the sufferings of the Cross for our sake we can understand even without this cultic figure. Here, in what happened on the Cross, the character of the whole Biblical revelation finds its perfect expression: that God reveals Himself and deals with us in history, that He communicates Himself in actions that speak and words that are acts. The self-communication of God as *revelation,* as the possibility of knowing Him is one thing: His self-communication as self-*surrender* and *gift of participation* in Himself, the *reconciliation,* is the other. But both are one in the death on the Cross, as it is proclaimed to us as an imminent event through the Word of Jesus, and as an accomplished fact through the Word of the Apostles. The God who speaks to us and deals with us not only proclaims in Jesus' obedience unto death that He loves us, but He Himself also removes out of the way the barrier that lies between Him and us, our sin, and gives us Himself, His love.

It is this event which makes the assurance of God tangible to us, which frees us from the strain of trying to do it ourselves, which gives us access to fellowship with God and makes us children or sons of God. For this is what the message of the Cross says to us: "I give myself to you, of my own free, unfathomable, eternal will of love."

IV

Why is this called the "justification" of the sinner? This expression, taken from rabbinic usage, means nothing but this: While we try in everything we do to assert ourselves and indeed even "in the sight of God", while thus all our action has self-justification as its final and deepest motive, we acknowledge "in Christ" the futility and impossibility of this self-justification. Righteousness, that is, unity with the will of God, membership in His Kingdom and participation in salvation, cannot be won thus. We are incapable of doing so, for between us and God there stands the imperative, which is understood as the claim of God. But on the other hand this righteousness is given to us

[1] See *Dogmatics* II, Ch. 11, "The Saving Work of God in Jesus Christ"

as a gift through Jesus Christ, when God promises us life at His side, life in fellowship with Him, as God's sons or children. Indeed, only when we grasp this do we see clearly how impossible our self-justification was. For it could not succeed, just because our true life is a life in the self-bestowing love of God. Self-justification is no longer *possible* for the man for whom Christ was nailed on the Cross. It is not *necessary* for the man to whom God says "You are my son." He has seen through the lie of the proud autonomy of the self, "the better self"; the ground on which he took his stand so long as he "relied" on his own achievements or his own rightness has been cut from under him. But God has given him a new "status" in its stead. His "security" is now what God gives to him, the God who raises him to the highest dignity, the dignity of being a son of God. This is the "righteousness which counts with God" because it is His own gift.

But now we can say more. Because a man places his reliance upon what God gives, by finding his new "standing" in the Word of God, in the Word of self-bestowing love; because he receives his personal life as a life in the love of God and knows and acknowledges that he receives it, he *is* the man that God would have him to be, namely the man who depends entirely upon God, and relates all his self-consciousness to God; the man who is righteous through faith. To live in faith—in this genuine faith—is the true humanity, the life that is pleasing to God.

God *declares* the sinner righteous; that is what justification means. Again it was a Latin word, *justificare*, which as translation of the Greek *dikaiousthai* stood in the way of the right understanding of the gospel. The Pauline word had been taken from the language of the law courts: a man accused is acquitted of guilt, declared to be innocent. The Latin speaker no longer understood this Hebrew terminology. He understood *justificare* as *justum facere*. Mediaeval theology thought that the event of this *justum facere* should be equated with the sacramental *infusio gratiae* (infusion of grace) occurring at Baptism. It was a decisive insight of Luther that he rediscovered the Hebrew and Pauline meaning of *justificare*, which had been completely buried and concealed by the Catholic sacramental tradition of many centuries, and at the same time thereby recognized the unbiblical character of the whole sacramental conception of grace. Justification is not an *infusio gratiae*, but God's declaration: "You are right with me"; and to let this Word of God be said to one and to accept it trustfully, is to believe.

Here both the Word of assurance, and faith, are clearly related to one another as nowhere else. For here faith really and exclusively is dependent on the Word, which against all empirical reality, supported by no experience, is in itself enough; the Word whose sole foundation is in God's affirmation of His purpose, and is only to be grasped in the event in which that affirmation is uttered. Indeed the Word is here God Himself, the divine Thou, that addresses me, and faith is nothing but letting this Word be spoken to me. This is the act of absolute receptiveness, and just because of that an utterly personal happening, because here a claim is made on the believing subject totally present in this receptive act.

Here as nowhere else the I-Thou relationship is to be found. The absolute Thou encounters the created self and gives Himself to it, calls the self into existence as a new self, a self well-pleasing to God, a self which is founded on the Word in which God calls. God gives Himself as the One who loves without a cause and man receives himself from God's Word addressed to him, as one who is loved without a cause. Man ventures forth from himself in unconditional trust on the God who addressed him with unconditional unfathomable love and declares him to be His own, His son, whose being He unconditionally affirms.

Here there is really nothing else but the Word, "the naked Word of God" as one might say, and the trust which "hears" this Word "from below" and repeats it obediently, the *hypakoē pisteōs* of the man who entrusts himself, who forsakes all security and takes shelter in the security of the God who opens His heart and communicates Himself in the Word, a pure venture of faith without any safeguards. Here there is nothing left of the autonomous self, which reserves for itself the last word, the last decision. Here the God who speaks has "the last Word" and for what He says there are no other grounds than *His* decision and His declaration of His will. This *voluntas Dei*, whose ground is in itself and nowhere else, is called election—the turning towards us of the *agape* whose foundation is in the eternal will and being of God.[1]

[1] The Catholic criticism of the "Fideism" of Protestant theology (B. Bartmann, *Lehrbuch der Dogmatik*, pp. 51 f.) is a valid criticism of a "faith that is purely a matter of feeling". But the critic does not realize that it is absolutely impossible by means of such psychological categories to apprehend the Reformation concept of faith, which is derived from justifying faith. The argument that we must first acknowledge that God *is*, before we can trust in Him, seems indeed evident to common sense, but stems from a rationalistic ontology which understands "knowledge" to mean "knowledge of the presence of an object" and thus equates God with an object. Greek ontologism and

This Word of God, in which man knows his new being, and in knowing *possesses* it, this Word is therefore the Word of the Creator, and this "new man" is none other than man as God created him. That he has his being only in God's Word of love and promise—this was the case right "from the beginning" of the Creation. Only man had forgotten, denied and lost this origin and true being of his. This is his sin. This is "reason's misunderstanding of its own nature" (Jacobi). Instead of being a receptive reason, whose foundation was in God, it had become a self-based, autochthonous and autonomous reason. Through God's Word and act in the Cross of Jesus—which first became recognizable through the Resurrection as His Word—God has given back and restored this lost origin. It was thus not a pure mistake when mediaeval man heard in *justificare* also echoes of *justum facere*. All that was wrong was that he wished to find the *facere* in something different from the Word of God. God shows Himself in His Word as a Person; He also creates us as persons in His Word which we answer in faith.[1]

In this Word we have our freedom, which is at the same time our responsibility. This unity of freedom and responsibility in God's act and Word—Jesus Christ—this is faith, and this faith is one with justification. We can just as well describe it as justification by faith alone or as justification by the grace of God in Jesus Christ, the Crucified. Paul too does this when he uses the two expressions interchangeably as having the same content.

V

Yet another expression requires explanation, the "righteousness of God" which is the leading motif in Paul's formulation of his doctrine of justification (Rom. 3: 21). Luther translated it

intellectualism rebels against Biblical personalism, and Greek rationalism rebels against the Biblical historical revelation.

But God is knowable only in His action, in His self-revelation. Catholic ontology refuses to abandon It-knowledge. It aligns God with impersonal being, which is known in the realm of It-knowledge. In contrast with this, Paul's theory of knowledge is identical with his doctrine of grace—God gives Himself to be known by giving Himself. To know God means in the last resort to be known by God, i.e. to be loved by Him and to let oneself be loved by Him (1 Cor. 8: 3). Knowledge of God is the same thing as the faith that receives God's love, and faith is nothing else than to become open for the divine love through divine love. The article "Kyrios Christos" needs no preceding article "God the Creator" The God who imparts Himself is the Triune God (see my *Dogmatics* I, Ch. 16) and God's self-communication is the same as His grace. The concept "self-communication" which includes the cognitive element (revelation, knowledge) and the element of salvation (grace, eternal life), and which is the Biblical concept of God, is therefore the formal as well as the material principle of theology

[1] Compare my *Man in Revolt*, pp. 103 ff.

by "righteousness that counts in God's sight" and thereby touched the heart of the matter. But at the same time he failed to do justice to Paul's thought. The righteousness of God is something different from, and more than, the righteousness that counts in God's sight. When, in spite of this, Luther translated the *dikaiosynē theou* thus, he did it in the knowledge that the word "righteousness" had suffered so disastrous a change of meaning through a misunderstanding which had persisted through a thousand years of history, that it could no more be used straight away in the context "righteousness of God". For Latin speakers could understand under *iustitia Dei* nothing but the righteousness of the judge who impartially rewards and punishes. But even our concept of righteousness is moulded by this *Latin* usage. The Pauline *dikaiosynē theou* however stems from *Hebrew* thinking. In Hebrew, Old Testament, usage the "righteousness of God" means the will of God who wills to assert his authority over the Creation as the Lord, and to establish His Lordship. The product of this will and this action is what is right.[1]

The righteousness of the judge is indeed included in this as one element, but in the sense that through His administration of justice God removes injustice and helps the vindication of the right. God's action as judge is not—as in our thought—conceived as that of the just judge who *finds* and perceives what is just, but as that of the King who *creates* what is just. This thought is now taken up by Paul. The divine action in Jesus Christ is the action through which alone God's purpose breaks through. Through Christ love is revealed, and in Him it is embodied, as the will of God, when man's own righteousness is known and acknowledged to be a lie. In faith in Christ the truth breaks through that God alone is the source of love, that is, of real goodness and true life.

We may say that in the Pauline expression "righteousness of God" the theocratic tendency of the Bible finds expression in a sense purified from all political Messianism. God's Lordship, identical with the love of God, is visibly vindicated only where man gives up his claim to autonomy and lets God take his place. And this is what the "righteousness of God" really means. The

[1] Cf. L. Diestel, "Die Idee der Gerechtigkeit im Alten Testament" in *Jahrbücher für deutsche Theologie*, 1860, an article which even today has not lost its significance and which was epoch-making at the time of its publication. The article *Dikaiosyne* by G. Schrenk in *ThWb* II, pp. 194–214, acknowledges the fundamental soundness of Diestel's principal thesis, but finds that it does not "exhaust" the Biblical—or, to be more precise—the Pauline conception of righteousness

emphasis here is laid not upon judicial righteousness, but on the effective kingly righteousness which also manifests itself precisely in the act of pardon which has always been the King's privilege. It would be a translation of *dikaiosynē theou* intelligible today if we were to render it "God's sovereignty", His will directed to the realization of His Lordship.

For this reason we have said that Luther's translation "the righteousness that counts in God's sight"—although it is in itself ingenious and touches the heart of the matter—fails to do justice to the thought of Paul. It has had a somewhat disastrous effect in the Lutheran Church because it places the salvation of *man* and not the purpose of *God* in the centre. Jesus Christ must be thought of as the highest revelation of the will of God to realize His rule as a rule of love, and not merely as the bringer of salvation. God's claim to Lordship is not impaired by God's gracious and loving promise, but receives a new meaning: "I (the Lord) am among you as he that serveth" (Luke 22: 27). God's Kingship receives its deepest significance in the Suffering Servant of God. He who sits upon the throne is "The Lamb of God". Man's existence for God has been transformed into God's existence for man.

The Kingdom of God, the *basileia theou*, is the rule of the love of God, the realization of His inmost will. It is precisely through justifying faith that this love comes to its most perfect and purest form of expression. One might say that only from the standpoint of justifying faith can we understand that God is pure love. For in this faith we apprehend that our security is founded in nothing else than this self-bestowing love. The self-bestowing love is, however, God's unfathomable love, whose origin and source is in God's will alone. Thus love is known to be the nature of God.

VI

But why is it called "justifying faith"? Justification is God's verdict which faith hears and accepts. It is only in faith that God's self-communication in Jesus Christ reaches its goal; when man repeats in his heart what God says to him: "You are my son; *you* are my son, because that is my will; you *are* my son, if you believe." *Only in the faith of man does God's righteousness come to its goal.* And conversely only when man repeats in faith the Word of God does he understand himself as God sees him and wishes him to be. The singular thing about man is that he is one who has a false or a true self-understanding. The singular thing about the relation of God to man is that the purpose of God's self-communication is to determine man's self-understanding, so that man's "This is what I am" should be identical with God's "This is what you are." In the achievement of this identity God's self-communication is completed as self-*communication*. Thus faith is the coincidence of divine self-communication and human self-understanding.

Where faith is understood only as self-understanding, it is misunderstood in the subjectivist sense. Where the revelation is thought of merely as an object of knowledge, it is misunderstood in the objectivist sense. Where God's self-communication is not identified with man's self-understanding, and indeed is understood in such a manner that the self-communication is regarded as the sole creative factor, then faith is *gnosis*, in which the heart and person of man is not transformed, where the man is not present as a person at all.

The coincidence of God's self-communication and man's self-understanding is the experience which Paul calls the operation of the Holy Spirit. He has in several passages himself spoken of this coincidence and equated it with the operation of the Holy Spirit within the spirit of man. "And because ye are sons, God hath sent forth the Spirit of his Son into your hearts, *who* cries Abba, Father" (Gal. 4: 6). "Ye have received the Spirit of adoption, whereby *we* cry Abba, Father. The Spirit itself beareth witness with our spirits that we are the children of God" (Rom. 8: 15, 16). The speaking in us of the Spirit who calls us children (sons) of God, and the joyful cry of our hearts "We are now the sons of God," are one and the same. This unity of God's self-communication and human self-understanding might rightly be described as "Christ-mysticism", *unio mystica cum Christo*, mystical union with Christ. The *pro nobis* ("on our behalf") of faith in the Cross is identical with the *in nobis* ("in us") which is one with the speaking of the Holy Spirit. Justification, that is, the "grace and truth"—that we stand before God no longer as sinners but as beloved children, is God's verdict, and to believe this verdict with the heart (Rom. 10: 9) and to know "This is what I am, this is the truth about me"—this is "justifying faith".

While the Old Testament still talks about God "justifying" *the righteous* (2 Chron. 6: 23) i.e. declaring him righteous, we are now told God justifies the *sinner*, and declares him to be His son, in spite of sin. It is only in faith that the Word of God reaches its goal, and proves its creative power by creating man anew. For this reason Paul can say both "righteousness of God" and "righteousness of faith", and he means by both of these one and the same thing. The importance for him of this identity between the righteousness of God and the righteousness of faith is shown most clearly in the central passage (Rom. 3: 21–31) where to all the decisive concepts that indicate God's action in Christ, he appends the word "faith": "an expiation—through faith", "the justifier of him which believeth in Jesus", "the righteousness of God which comes through faith in Jesus Christ". The law of works is contrasted with the "law of faith", and finally he closes with the formulation: "Therefore we conclude that a man is justified by faith." Thus faith is the "rightness" of our being as God created it in place of the righteousness we strained after and claimed through our own action. It is the man who gives glory to God alone, the creature in which the *doxa theou* (God's glory) shines reflected, it is what corresponds with God's will to self-realization and what is man's true being —a being utterly dependent on God.[1] This true being indeed necessarily contains in itself the hope of fulfilment, the "revelation of the sons of God" in the eternal future. Therefore to these words about the sonship of God achieved through the Holy Spirit by faith, Paul at once appends the eschatological prospect of the awaited fulfilment. Faith is the provisional form of what will receive its completion only in sight.

VII

Justifying faith discloses to us that all *religion* is a last and highest attempt of man to find his own security. Even the religious man—not excepting the Christian religious man—comes under the judgment of God, and can find his security no longer in his religious inwardness but only in that righteousness which is *extra nos et aliena nobis* (outside of us and alien to us); in Christ Himself. This is justifying faith. This exists only where the Cross of Christ is preached and believed in. Faith in justification is therefore what most sharply distinguishes Christian faith from all religion, and what most clearly distinguishes the Ekklesia from all cultic associations. Men know

[1] Thus it is not the "arrogance" of a doctrine of faith, in virtue of which "the Christian in the last centuries has begun to take himself seriously in a manner which is very far from appropriate to the seriousness of Christianity", which leads to this eulogy of faith. It is rather the Bible's own witness to faith, whose significance is still specially stressed by us Protestants as the origin of the Reformation, and certainly is not the discovery of a new theological school. Karl Barth thinks of this emphasis on faith as something which concerns only the "Christian individual" (Barth, *Kirchliche Dogmatik* IV, 1 p. 828; E.T. *Church Dogmatics*, p. 741). But we shall show directly in the discussion that follows that this matter concerns not the "individual" but, on the contrary, the Ekklesia

of grace even outside the revelation in Christ. But it is only the New Testament that speaks of that grace which acquits the sinner, and of that love of God which turns towards the man who is God's enemy (Rom. 5: 10). And it speaks of this grace as of a happening which is at the same time an event unique in the historical sense, and also unique in the sense peculiar to revelation-history. This unique event is the Cross of Jesus Christ.

If we ask why this one thing that is the centre of the Christian faith was revealed only in that one place in the story of Jesus Christ the answer must be; because it has pleased God to reveal Himself as the living, the holy and merciful One only within the history of the Jews and of Israel, which finds its culmination in Jesus, the Christ, the Messiah and Suffering Servant of God. It *is* so, and there is no reason for it that we can recognize in any way, except just that God so wills it, so that we may know that everything depends on this "accidental fact of history" which as such is the bearer *extra nos*, outside of us, of the grace which is utterly independent of man, and therefore the *reality* of God's self communication.

VIII

As the nature of faith is only fully to be understood in its relation to justification, so the nature and the reality of the Ekklesia is to be understood only in the same context. We say intentionally, the Ekklesia, not the Church. For only the Ekklesia which as the work of the Holy Spirit is the Body of Christ, is the "we" that corresponds to justifying faith.[1]

It is quite impossible to speak of the Ekklesia without at the same time speaking of faith. The Ekklesia is the communion of the faithful (*communio fidelium*). It is the brotherhood of those who experience their new life as at the same time a life with their brothers in Christ. It may indeed be said that justifying faith is the origin of the Ekklesia, although this concept was first created by Paul. The thing was there before the concept. The grace of God in Jesus Christ, the inconceivable self-bestowing love of God, which can be apprehended only in faith and which reaches its goal in man, is the same event through which man, the autonomous, the self-sufficient, the self-supported, man in his self-created solitude, becomes a member of the fellowship—of that fellowship which acknowledges in Christ the source of its life and has its reality in the Holy Spirit. The man who was hitherto self-enclosed and self-sufficient in the centre

[1] Cf. above, Ch. 13, 2 (*d*), p. 184

of his being is broken asunder and opened to admit the "Thou" by the assurance of God received in faith. He must also on his side impart to his fellow man what he has received through God's self-communication. For this he does not require a special "missionary vocation" but the "love of Christ constraineth us" (2 Cor. 5: 14). The love of God is the life element of the Ekklesia. From this love it ever builds itself anew according to the gift which is given to every man, and through the truth which is identical with grace (John 1: 17). Through this love it corrects and continually purifies itself, drawing upon the faith which has no dogma as its content—not even as its norm—but which ever springs free and direct from the witness to Christ through the Holy Spirit.

IX

One last question results from our previous conclusions. If justifying faith is the standard, the criterion of all faith, what can faith be beyond this? When we have said justification through Jesus Christ, have we not said everything? But what would be the relation to this of what we have always been accustomed to call "the remaining contents of the Christian Faith"? As Christians we believe in God, the Creator, in His providence and government of the world, we believe in the Kingdom of God and in eternal life. What happens to these "contents of faith" if the "You are mine" of justification is the authentic "content" of faith, or rather not the content, since it is Christ present in us in faith through the Holy Spirit who says this to us?

When the false concept of faith was employed, this question was concealed by the (Trinitarian) Creed, which seemed from the beginning to offer a far richer content of faith. But since we have seen through this false concept of faith, and accordingly have recognized justification as the centre of faith, the question about the "other contents" has become urgent. That this question is along the right lines Martin Luther the great theologian of justification makes clear to us. In a sermon on Peter's denial he says:

> No article of faith is harder to believe than the article which states, "I believe in the forgiveness of sins". The reason is that all the other articles are outside of us and do not come into our experience, do not touch us daily. But the article about forgiveness of sins gets right home to us; it enters into our continual experience and daily practice and touches me and you incessantly. We speak of the other articles as of matters remote, but we speak of the

article "I believe in the forgiveness of sins" not as a remote affair but as we speak of ourselves. When we believe and confess that God is Creator of heaven and earth, that Jesus Christ, God's Son, suffered and died, that there is a Holy Christian Church, and other things that follow in the Creed or Catechism, it all seems as if someone else were concerned. For everyone thinks: "That concerns Peter and Paul; who knows if it concerns me?" But forgiveness of sins does concern and touch me and you.

Thus all the other articles lead up to the single article on forgiveness of sins, and come together in this article, as it were in a circle. What does it profit me that God created heaven and earth if I do not believe in forgiveness of sins? . . . What does it help me that Christ was crucified and died and that the Holy Spirit came if I do not believe in forgiveness of sins? What God has done . . . all amounts to this, that we have forgiveness of sins. Therefore I say . . . the other articles . . . do not come into our experience. But if they are to come into our experience and touch us, *they must come into our experience in this article and touch us*, so that we all, I for my part and you for yours, and each man for himself, believe in forgiveness of sins. The article "I believe in the forgiveness of sins" touches us and comes into our experience and makes the other articles also touch us and come into our experience. For this reason it is the hardest article to believe.[1]

This Luther passage seems to us to be of fundamental significance because it illuminates like a lightning flash the nature of the unity of the whole of Christian doctrine. We shall try now to develop this point in our own words.

Luther refers to the fundamental and exceptional position of the centre of faith (justification), its precedence over "all other articles of faith", and postulates: "If the other articles are to come into our experience and touch us, they must come into our experience in this article and touch us." He means that they are to be expressions of faith, they must proceed from this centre and refer to this as their point of origin. The special thing about faith in justification is just the coincidence of God's self-communication and man's self-understanding, the identity of the objective-historical element of revelation and the existential-subjective element of self-understanding. This coincidence, however, means nothing less than a description of the fundamental form of statements of faith in general; namely that they must at the same time be related to history and be existential. Anything that has not this fundamental form is thus not a statement of faith at all.

This means on the one hand that all statements of faith must

[1] *W.A.* XXVIII, 271 ff.

be Christological, developed from the centre, Jesus Christ. On the other hand, they must be existential in the sense that man understands himself in them as given a new character. They must be not only statements about God, but at the same time statements about man. Classical forms of such statements are "I am the Lord your God", or "Fear not, for I am thy Redeemer", or "I call thee by thy name, thou art mine".

Let us take, as an example, faith in the Creator. There are doubtless statements about God, the Creator of the world, which do not satisfy this postulate; namely, statements of philosophical theism. But Christian faith in the Creator is at the same time Christological and existential; it is based on the revelation in Christ and at the same time it concerns "me", it gives a new character to my existence. Only when we *so* speak of the Creator as through this statement to explain what is given in the revelation of Christ (Christology) and also at the same time make a statement about ourselves (self-understanding) can we say, it is a statement of faith. Without this it would be mere cosmology or *Weltanschauung*. To this corresponds the fact that when we spoke of God as the Lord and Creator[1] we referred to the fact that Israel's faith in the Creator was first of all faith in Yahweh, the Lord; for it was only later that the knowledge of the Creator, as a consequence of this first faith, took shape, and not *vice versa*: and so for us the statement "God is the Creator of the world" is a statement about Him as our Lord and about ourselves who unconditionally belong to Him, and we encounter this Lord in Jesus Christ and not in our experience of the world. It is the faith in the Creator set forth in the prologue to St. John's Gospel, which identifies the Logos of the Creation with the truth and grace that is revealed in Jesus Christ.

From this standpoint the whole programme of Christian doctrine can be seen as an expression and unfolding of justifying faith. From the centre Christ-Cross-Justification radiate the statements which project the truth of Christ into the totality of human existence in the world, and always in such a manner as at the same time to do justice to the self-understanding of man as one who belongs to God. The self-communication of God in Jesus Christ is the theme of all Biblical doctrine and all faith, and precisely this is the Christian self-understanding of man.

This, we believe, is the significance of Luther's understanding

[1] See *Dogmatics* I, Ch. 13: "God, the Lord"

of justifying faith as the centre of the message of Christ and as the criterion of all faith, and it is this which is the fundamental plan on which our *Dogmatics* are built.[1]

[1] Part 1, "The Eternal Foundation of the Divine Self-Communication".
Part 2, "The Historical Realization of the Divine Self-Communication".
Part 3, "God's Self-Communication as His Self-Representation through the Holy Spirit".
Part 4, "The Consummation in Eternity of the Divine Self-Communication"

EXCURSUS: ON THE CONTEMPORARY THEOLOGICAL SITUATION

I

THE fact that we are able to append this "Excursus on the Theological Situation" to the chapter on Justification by Faith is an indication of the fundamental change that has overtaken the field of theological inquiry. Today the theme is no longer religion, as it was before 1920, but faith in the New Testament sense of the word. Indeed, it is the common characteristic of the most significant works in systematic theology of this new epoch that they all find their centre in the essential New Testament message, reconciliation in Christ and justification by faith alone; that is, in the distinctive message which differentiates Christian faith from all the other religions and is peculiar to it alone.

In this book also we must not ignore but must gratefully acknowledge the fact that the chief credit for this very significant change of front lies with Karl Barth. For when theology was in danger of losing itself in the history and psychology of religion, it was he who, first by the prophetic call to action in his *Commentary on Romans* and then by the intellectual labour of his monumental *Church Dogmatics*, brought it back to its true theme. If there were some others of us who from the beginning took part in this movement, yet we must take second place to him and confess that no one but this powerful, vehement and gifted spirit could have effected this transformation.

But the theological development continues. And here it seems that in a manner—at least in German-speaking lands—the Hegelian threefold pattern of thesis, antithesis and synthesis has been taking shape. Shortly after the inception but long before the completion of Barth's mighty work, a theological tendency of an entirely different character found favour, a tendency which had a contrary point of departure from that of Barth, though it was not in downright opposition to him. This was the theology of Rudolf Bultmann.

The vehemence of this counter-attack and the fact that it was really launched through one single essay, which, like a forest fire, set the whole of German theology ablaze, indicates clearly that an essential emphasis had failed to find adequate expression in Barth's theology. And in fact one might say that half of the truth had been left out of consideration in his theology: the subject, faith in the subjective sense.

While at the very beginning it had seemed as if he would be the man who would reap the theological harvest of Kierkegaard's powerful and revolutionary thinking, and while for a long time men thought of Barth—as they still do in America today—as the theologian who followed in Kierkegaard's footsteps, he very soon turned away from Kierkegaard and expressly repudiated Kierkegaard's main thesis, "subjectivity is truth". It seemed to Barth unnecessary to spend much time inquiring about the nature of faith. This was a result of his completely objectivistic conception of the *sola gratia* principle. He ridiculed the distinction made between "the faith by which we believe" (*fides qua creditur*) and the faith *which* we believe (*fides quae creditur*) as "a croaking of frogs". It seemed to him enough to know and set forth the truth of revelation as such. He was concerned about faith in the sense of the faith of the Church—the creed.

This objectivism is illustrated by a sermon about the two thieves on the cross, who according to the text of Mark (15: 27) died the death of criminals dumbly and without taking notice of the One who was crucified with them. These two criminals, who died without a single sign of faith, are praised by Barth as the first embodiment of the Church. The problem of appropriation, which by common consent is central in Kierkegaard and to which Calvin devoted the entire third Book of his *Institutes*, is hardly mentioned in Barth. He regards interest in the believing subject as mere pietistic subjectivism.

This tendency to an orthodox objectivism—more visible in Barth's case in his support of the post-Reformation scholastics, but in the case of some of his pupils more evidenced by a "theology of the Confessional writings"—had during the time of the Church struggle the value of a protective wall, when it was imperative to resist the onslaughts of the ideology of modern heathenism and the co-ordination of the Church with Hitler's totalitarian State. But this Church Dogmatic turned out to be of little use in the following period, when the problem of the Church in the West was no longer that of resisting an aggressive atheism, but the indifference of the masses to the Churches and to faith, and when it was imperative to win a hearing for the Christian message in a post-Christian world.

In this situation it became increasingly evident that a theology which has its point of departure in Church *preaching*, and whose entire aim is the communication of sound doctrine, is an anachronism. And we must add to this that Barth's lack of interest in the believing subject and his identification of faith with the creed of the Church had the consequence that he was unable to give any clear guidance in ethics, but changed from one extreme to the other. From his early indifference to all political matters he changed to his militant crusade at the time of the upsurge of the romanticism of the total State, and then again to a contrary standpoint, a political *laissez-faire* in the face of the fully developed cynical nihilistic total State of the East, linked with an unrealistic pacifism which advocates the defencelessness of the Western nations in the face of aggressive Communism

II

For all these reasons it was inevitable that after the end of the world war a violent theological reaction should set in. This happened, as we have said, in the form of the theology of Rudolf Bultmann; that is, on the part of one of the leading critical Biblical scholars, a man whose intention was to preserve the heritage of Kierkegaard and to do justice to his thesis "subjectivity is truth".

As a critical New Testament scholar Bultmann encountered the fact that in the New Testament there are present conceptions which are determined not by the *kerygma* of Jesus Christ but by the world-picture of antiquity and which on account of their mythical character are no longer intelligible to men of the twentieth century. In the light of this insight he wrote the epoch-making essay on the New Testament and Mythology which was destined completely to dominate German theological discussion for the last two decades. The demands of scholarly Biblical criticism, which had been restrained during the Church struggle, could now no longer be denied.

Here the philosophy of Heidegger, who had developed the thought of Kierkegaard into a philosophy of existence, was used by Bultmann as a formal instrument for the interpretation of New Testament concepts. He connected the problem of "demythologizing" with that of an "existential interpretation". The problem "What is faith?" was thrown into relief. Bultmann's concern was with faith as a self-understanding of man; a fact which had received striking expression in the title of an earlier book by him entitled *Glauben und Verstehen* (Faith and Understanding).

This then was the counter-attack on Barth's objectivism, made from the standpoint of the subject, the standpoint of faith. But this was also a new theology which had the power to bring the message of the Bible home to contemporary man. Yet here too there was a failure to do justice to an essential element. Barth's rejoinder was not unreasonable—that this theology was a pure subjectivism which dissolved the work and Person of Jesus into a *kerygma* about Christ and a subjective faith. As Barth's objectivism fails to do justice to the Biblical witness to revelation, so, on the other side, Bultmann's "subjectivism" fails to do justice to the reality of the historical revelation, as the Jesus of history disappears behind the believer's witness to Christ and the Old Testament sacred history has no longer any part to play. The question whether a historical event, a personality called Jesus, stands behind the Christian witness of the believing community, and whether the picture of this Jesus drawn by the Gospels corresponds to historical reality, was rejected by Bultmann as irrelevant and theologically unjustified, and the discipline of Biblical criticism was identified with the historical scepticism of the scholar Bultmann.[1] We have to do, not with Jesus the Christ Himself but only with a historical witness about Him.

[1] Cf. P. Althaus, *Das sogenannte Kerygma und der historische Jesus*, p. 10; E.T. *The so-called Kerygma and the Historical Jesus*, p. 19 (Oliver and Boyd, Edinburgh, 1959)

In the theology of Bultmann it is noticeable how the two postulates, that of demythologizing and that of existential interpretation, often pass over the one into the other, are even identified with each other. And yet they are of very unequal importance. Far and away the more important is the second one. In the demand for an existential interpretation we have to do with nothing less than the rediscovery of Luther's "Christ for me" ("*Christus pro me*") in the sense of the saying of Luther quoted in the previous chapter about forgiveness as "what finds me", what "comes into my experience". Here Bultmann has rediscovered the original meaning of the Pauline "I believe". On the other hand, the demand for demythologizing—which occupied a far more central place in the discussion—has reference merely to the influence of the ancient picture of the world upon the form of the New Testament *kerygma* which, we agree, must be "demythologized" in so far as it is no longer intelligible to us men of today.

Certain limits must be set to this demand, however, if it is not to lead to the dissolution of the Christian faith and its replacement by an existential *philosophy*. But in Bultmann, on the contrary, this postulate of demythologization is made repeatedly to serve the purpose of conforming to the idealistic or naturalistic self-understanding of modern man. Measured by this illegitimate and unrestricted criterion it is true that a great part of the essential content of Christian faith is lost. Thus the postulate of demythologization, contrary to Bultmann's true intention, leads to a rationalistic, typically "liberal" method of elimination and so to a serious impoverishment, even to a mutilation of the Christian message.

Two things are to blame for this confusion. First, Bultmann's too close adherence to the philosophy of Heidegger, in the belief that it is possible to use it as a purely formal principle of interpretation. This belief is a manifest error (cf. my essay *Christlicher Glaube und Philosophie der Existenz, Festschrift für Heinrich Barth*, 1960)[1] and Bultmann has thereby exposed himself to the justified criticism on the part of the philosophers, that his theology (or philosophy) stops half-way. The second point is, that Bultmann seems to have no inkling of the transformation of epistemology by modern physics. He is still living in the closed deterministic universe of the rationalist philosophy. Thus there enters his theology a rationalistic element which leaves concealed the mythical character of this rationalistic thinking, a character only disclosed by the most recent physics, and so replaces the Biblical mythology by the "science" which is in truth the mythology of the nineteenth century. (Cf. on this point C. F. von Weizsäcker, *Zum Weltbild der Physik*,[2] and Karl Heim, *Die Wandlung im naturwissenschaftlichen Weltbild*.)[3]

[1] "Christian Faith and Philosophy of Existence", in the volume of *Essays in Honour of Heinrich Barth*, 1960

[2] E.T. *World View of Physics*, Routledge and Kegan Paul, London, 1952

[3] E.T. *The Transformation of the Scientific World View*, S.C.M. Press, London, 1953

In relation to the Christian *kerygma* the result of this is that Bultmann confuses his own historical scepticism with scholarly criticism and attempts at the same time to do justice to two things—to this scepticism on the one hand, and to the Christian *kerygma* on the other. This was the purpose of his ingenious distinction between the historical and the historic.[1] The historical has nothing to do with faith, and on the other hand what Bultmann calls "the historic" can be apprehended only by faith. But this solution is in fact no solution at all, since the witness of the New Testament refers to that Jesus Christ who as Jesus is also the object of historical criticism, but who can only be apprehended as Christ by faith.

A somewhat similar tendency finds expression in the fact that Bultmann should think of faith *only* as a self-understanding of man, while in the New Testament it certainly *also* is this, but is in the first place a self-understanding which is identical with the historical self-communication of God. In this reduction to the subjective, to our understanding of ourselves, lies the subjectivism of Bultmann justly criticized by Karl Barth, and it has caused great embarrassment for preachers of the Gospel trained in the Bultmann school. But whence comes this isolation of the subjective moment in faith? From the fact that Bultmann does not relate faith to the historical Jesus Himself, but only to the believing *kerygma* about Him. He does this because his scepticism has disintegrated the Jesus of the Biblical narratives, since he is of the opinion "that we know practically nothing about His personality". So he asserts that faith has no interest in going behind the *kerygma* and asking about the Jesus of history, while, in fact, in the New Testament it is no exaggeration to say that everything depends on this unity of the historical Jesus with Christ. Bultmann has no right to appeal as he does to Martin Kähler as his predecessor. For in fact in his very important book *Der sogenannte historische Jesus und der geschichtliche biblische Christus* (E.T. *The so-called Jesus of History and the Historical Biblical Christ*) Kähler affirmed precisely this unity of the historical Jesus with Him whom faith calls Christ.

It can further be clearly seen on the one hand that Bultmann is not able to draw a clear line of distinction between himself and theologians who develop further than himself the logical implications of his views and transform his demand for "demythologizing" into a demand for "dekerygmatization" (M. Werner and others). On the other hand, however, we can note in his own school a welcome reaction from his own extreme scepticism and a return to the historical Jesus, from which we may expect a healthy correction of

[1] *Translator's Note:* The German nouns whose sense is here rendered by the adjectives "historical" and "historic" are "*Historie*" and "*Geschichte*" *Historie*, as understood by Bultmann, is history in the sense of a mere sequence of past events such as might be narrated dispassionately by a chronicler. *Geschichte* refers to the past at a much deeper level, as living on into the present and challenging me by its impact upon me to a life decision

Bultmann's subjectivism. (I am thinking here of scholars like E. Käsemann, G. Bornkamm, E. Fuchs, and a systematic theologian of the stature of G. Ebeling.)

As Karl Barth's objectivism ends in a biblicist orthodoxy, so Bultmann's subjectivism leads to a new form of docetism, that is, to a doctrine which denies that the Christ of faith was the real man Jesus of history. Further, the reduction of statements of faith to self-understanding results in a failure to do justice to the theocentric character of the Biblical proclamation, the message of the Kingdom of God. This deviation from the theocentric theme (the Kingdom of God) to the anthropocentric one (salvation) was, as we saw above, already implicit in Luther's translation of *dikaiosynē theou* as "Righteousness which counts in the sight of God." But it is very much more prominent in Bultmann. While, as Karl Barth continually and rightly emphasizes, the Bible is from start to finish primarily concerned with God, and only in the second place with man, Bultmann's primary concern is unmistakably with man, and with God only in so far as man understands himself in God. Interest in forgiveness of sins has in Bultmann, as in Luther, but to a far greater degree, swallowed up Jesus' message of the Kingdom and with it the whole Old Testament sacred history. But even the forgiveness of sins, that content of the Christian message which is retained in Bultmann's theology, is (as it were) left hanging in the air, since it is not rooted in a real historical event. The essential thing about forgiveness is that it has really happened. Without this it is a mere idea.

Above all, the discrepancy between the Biblical message and Bultmann's "interpretation" is visible in the way he conceives of hope. In Bultmann the term "eschatological" is again—in contrast to the Biblical witness—given a subjectivistic twist. In place of the message of the approaching Kingdom his eschatology consists merely of the "historic character" of man "understood in the radical sense" (cf. his *Geschichte und Eschatologie*, p. 49).[1] This is not an interpretation at all, but an elimination of the Pauline *kerygma* of the future coming[2] of Christ which is all the more serious because this future coming is for Paul most intimately bound up with the knowledge that we are the children of God (Rom. 8: 17 ff.). Justification of the sinner finds its completion in "the manifestation of the glory of the sons of God" (Rom. 8: 19). But this knowledge follows naturally from a true understanding of the central Christian message, the identity of God's self-communication with man's self-understanding; or, in other words, from the fact that justifying faith is itself the completion of the divine self-communication.

[1] English original *History and Eschatology*, the Gifford Lectures, Edinburgh, 1957

[2] *Translator's Note:* Here there is an untranslatable pun upon the German word *Zukunft*, "future", which literally means "coming towards" (Zu-Kunft)

III

We would, however, be giving a most one-sided picture of the "theological situation" if we were to describe it merely in terms of the Bultmann-Barth antithesis. Besides these two there are other outstanding theologians who, though sharing many insights with them, have a quite independent significance as interpreters of the Christian message. Friedrich Gogarten deserves to be mentioned first. In his earlier days a close collaborator with Karl Barth, he was "put on trial" by the latter at the same time as the author of this book, with the result that he took no part in theological discussion throughout the whole period of the Church conflict in which the rôle of undisputed theological dictator fell to Karl Barth. But after the end of the world war he wrote a series of important works which restored him to a place in the foremost rank of creative theological thinkers. With the exception of the first of these works, *Die Verkündigung Jesu Christi* (The Preaching of Jesus Christ), all these profess to be re-interpretations of Luther, which stress the decisive principles of the Reformation in Luther's thought.

His profoundly penetrating power as a thinker and the originality of his general outlook impress the reader. In particular, the breadth and range of insight into the problem "What belongs to faith and what to the world?" is of great importance for a right understanding of the gospel. It is a special characteristic of Gogarten's theology that it is thought out in continual engagement with the spirit of our times, which is represented in modern and most recent philosophy and in its conception of truth as a scholarly discipline. In this respect, as it appears to me, Gogarten has no rivals. His interpretation of law and gospel, drawn just as much from the New Testament as from Luther, is in its application to the realities of our contemporary world an entirely new one. This great originality and depth is, however, at the same time his greatest danger. The danger is that this view of the gospel should turn into an existential philosophy of Gogarten's own brand and thus lose its connection with scripture revelation and its true dependence upon it.

In this context what was said about Bultmann applies to Gogarten. In his latest publications he has let himself be led astray by Bultmann's historical scepticism. His first post-war books, "The Preaching of Jesus Christ" which we have already mentioned and "Man between God and the World" (*Der Mensch zwischen Gott und Welt*), are still quite free of this tendency, and therefore they are also his best. In the former he begins with the preaching of Jesus in the Synoptic Gospels and the Person of Jesus who can be recognized behind it; passes on to the Apostle Paul's preaching of Christ and turns finally to Luther's theology, which is, as he makes clear, a rediscovery of the Pauline understanding of Christ and of faith. In him also the anthropocentric tendency which we have already seen in Luther is noticeable, and yet his continued work on Luther protects him from Bultmann's extreme subjectivism.

Gogarten is a radically individualistic thinker, who in contrast with Paul does not keep in sight both faith and the Ekklesia-brotherhood whose foundation is in Christ. The consequence is that like most Lutherans he has no interest in Luther's *Deutsche Messe*, with its idea of a fellowship of faith which is not identical with the institution of the "Church" and yet is a visible entity (cf. *Die Verkündigung Jesu Christi*, p. 385). This weakness is deeply rooted in the separation between faith and love, whose inseparability is *the* decisive thing in the New Testament. In spite of all this, Gogarten's contribution to our understanding of the gospel is of the very highest importance.

A similarly imposing and important project is to be found in Paul Tillich's *Systematic Theology*,[1] which is at present carrying all before it in America among those who are not simply content to reproduce the theology of the past. In Europe his theological past tells at first against him. It is true that then he followed the line of Schleiermacher and Schelling and is therefore still suspected of making theology dependent on an idealistic philosophy. But Tillich has travelled a long way since he went to America. Since the appearance of the second volume of his main work there can no longer be any doubt that he means the Jesus of history when he makes Jesus as the Christ the central point of his thinking. Yet his ontological concepts give one a rather uncomfortable feeling. But as his work is still uncompleted we will have to confine ourselves to formulating our doubts about this system in several questions.

Has not Tillich co-ordinated his theology with a philosophy of existence and by so doing subordinated it thereto? Must not the abstractly neutral conception of God as Being obscure or repress the personalism of the Biblical concept of God? Is the antithesis between true being and the existence estranged from it really what the Bible means by sin, the rebellion of the creature against its Creator? And is the overcoming of this antithesis which Tillich portrays, the return of the estranged existence to true being, the same thing as the forgiveness of guilt and the creation of a new person by justification through faith?

We do not yet venture to answer these questions ourselves. But when the rejoinder is made that these ontological concepts are not meant for the believer himself or for the preaching of the gospel but serve merely the apologetic purpose of coming to an understanding with contemporary philosophy, we shall have to answer that to achieve this purpose it is not legitimate to alter the thing one is defending. Therefore our questions may be considered as the serious doubts of many Christian thinkers in relation to Tillich's imposing attempt to combine the logos-idea of Greek philosophy and modern idealism with Christian faith. Might it not be that precisely what is most admired as Tillich's strong point, namely the rigour of his

[1] University of Chicago Press, U.S.A., James Nisbet and Co. Ltd., London, 1953

method and the completeness of his system, is an indication of the incompatibility of this system with the offence of faith, the foolishness of the message of the Cross? One thing at least is clear, the God who speaks to us and who in this sense is personal is not identical with "Being", however true it may be that the notion of unconditional Being is a part of the Biblical concept of God. There can therefore be little doubt that the I-Thou-It philosophy of an Ebner or a Buber, which is itself drawn from the Bible, is more fruitful for theology than the philosophy of existence and its ontology, and this particularly in view of the fact that Tillich considers it important that Schelling and Marx and also Nietzsche should be regarded as representatives of this existentialism.

The theology of Karl Heim is a very significant achievement in its own field. Introduced by *Die Mystik und das Wort* to Ferdinand Ebner, the latter's and Martin Buber's discovery of the distinction and antithesis between the I-Thou dimension and the I-It dimension, which he felt to be a "Copernican revolution", stimulated him to develop his own very impressive "doctrine of dimensions" which is of the greatest significance for the debate between theology and the other disciplines. But his influence on theology has been comparatively small, perhaps principally because his thought was almost exclusively devoted to the apologetic problem. His belief was that the Church had already enough dogmatic theology, and that it was the task of the theologian in these times to open to men whose thought is determined by science the dimension within which it is relevant to speak of the human and the divine Thou; a dimension which, however, cannot come in conflict with scientific knowledge so long as the latter remains merely critical. Unfortunately he did not recognize that this implied a complete rebuilding of the structure of theology. For there results from his discovery a new understanding of faith which coincides with the Biblical understanding and which must inevitably revolutionize traditional Church Dogmatics.

It is clear that here he was hindered by his Württemberg biblicism, for which faith in Christ and faith in the Bible are the same thing, while in fact, as we shall see, they are very different things. The reason why German theology under the dominating influence of Karl Barth showed so little interest in Heim's work lies in the fact that it also failed to make this fundamental distinction. The lack of interest, however, shown by Bultmann and his school is perhaps in part due to Bultmann's concept of science, which is that of the age of rationalism, and which, as has been said, has remained untouched by the twentieth-century revolution in physics. A still more important factor here, however, may have been Bultmann's belief, which he shares with most of the exponents of the philosophy of Heidegger, that the latter has shown the problem of knowledge as Kant envisaged it to have neither urgency nor reality. (That this is not the case can be seen from the work of Heinrich Barth, *Philosophie der Erscheinung*, Part 2.)

In closing we must mention one more important figure whose achievement in contemporary theology has been to explain in an original manner the vital significance for today of Luther's heritage, Anders Nygren and his work *Eros und Agape*[1] which has already become a classic. By using this hitherto unnoticed pair of contrasted concepts Nygren has succeeded in illuminating with peculiar precision and clarity the difference between New Testament faith and a theology determined by Greek ontology. It is only to be regretted that his method of research into motifs which produced this highly significant result has not been applied to the other concepts of the New Testament, resulting in a general movement for the renewal of Lutheran theology. The almost universal adoption of his formula "*Eros-Agape*"—famous theologians have made lavish use of Nygren's concepts without one word of thanks or acknowledgment—is a proof that this further result was a real possibility.

IV

All these thinkers aim at a right understanding of the Christian message of the New Testament.

Karl Barth is right in his emphasis on the revelation of God the Lord, the absolute Subject, and His grace, on "By grace alone, Christ alone", "to God alone be the glory" ("*sola gratia, Christus solus, soli Deo gloria*"). This note of the Biblical message and of the message of the Reformers rings out nowhere so powerfully in modern theology as in his works. Christology is in fact the starting point and the foundation of theology. But theology must take the humanity of Jesus more seriously than is the case in the dogma of the ancient Church, or even in Karl Barth. It is not the God-man of dogma whom we believe in as the Christ, but the real Jesus as, thanks to critical scholarship, we learn to know Him in the Gospels: a Jesus free from legendary accretions, but also free from the preconceptions of Greek ontological theology. When justice is done at this point, then the Pauline equation of *solus Christus* with *sola fide* will also follow as a result. And this means that we shall come to a new understanding of the Holy Spirit and of faith which is not indeed in accord with old Church dogma, but is in accord with the New Testament witness, and throws into new relief the saying of Calvin we quoted earlier about the indissoluble connection between knowledge of God and knowledge of ourselves. But then it will also become clear that faith is not theology and that faith in Christ must not be equated with faith in the Bible.

Bultmann is right in his emphasis on man's self-understanding in the light of the *kerygma* of God's forgiveness in Jesus Christ. But this *kerygma* refers to the Jesus of history who lived at such-and-such a time and place, who hung upon the Cross, who really rose again, and was seen by the disciples and only because of this was proclaimed

[1] E.T. *Agape and Eros*, S.P.C.K., London, 1953

as the Christ. He is the same as the one whom the Gospels show to us as the Son of Man, who in His life and sufferings and death lived that life of love which in faith we recognize as the love of almighty God, the Creator of the world. The justification by faith alone which Paul preaches refers to no other Christ than this, and the forgiveness of sins which he places in the forefront of his message is possible only on the basis of this historical event which for the believer is infinitely more than a mere historical event, namely the self-communication of God. And this faith in Christ is at the same time the foundation of our hope, our certainty concerning the coming Last Things, the consummation of the creation, that eschatological message which Bultmann looks on as outworn mythology. The coincidence of God's self-communication and man's self-understanding is the centre of the Pauline theology, the experience of the presence of the Holy Spirit, who creates the Ekklesia. And yet according to Bultmann belief in this spirit is a relic of animistic ways of thinking.

Gogarten is right in his emphasis on the new understanding of the New Testament message and faith as Paul saw them, which we owe principally to Luther. He is right when he asserts that Luther not only discovered anew what faith means in the Bible, but that he at the same time reached a new understanding of what the New Testament means by "the world". This insight is, however, independent of contemporary philosophy and philosophy in general. On the other hand, it implies a new insight into that reality which Paul calls the Ekklesia, the visible brotherhood of those who are (invisibly) bound together in Christ. But this knowledge results only from faith in the Jesus to whom the gospel narrative bears witness, the Christ.

Tillich is right in his emphasis on the fact that the man who is "in Christ" has a new being, a being which became reality in the historical Jesus, as He is apprehended in faith, and which in faith transforms our existence into true being. But it is not the revelation of true being which is proclaimed to us in the gospel, but God's gracious approach to us, the rebels, which is made when the verdict of justification is spoken and which creates us anew when this verdict is received in faith. The address of the Thou, not the engrafting of true being into our existence, is the theme of the Bible and the content of Christian faith. And to set this forth in clear concepts intelligible to the man of the scientific age, not to replace this insight by an ontology which originates in the monologue-thinking of philosophy, is the task of theology today. Just because the "offence" and the "folly" of the Cross are its ground and its central content, faith in Christ will never allow itself to be represented as a self-enclosed philosophical system, and will always have to renounce that rigorous method whose true field is in the physical sciences.

Karl Heim is right in his emphasis on the truth which can be found and expressed only in the I-Thou relation. But this insight is important not merely for apologetics, nor indeed is its main significance to be found here. Rather is there implicit in it a new theology which must break free from the theology which is determined by biblicism and which therefore involves a reconstruction of theology and its release from the dogma of the Church.

Nygren is right in his emphasis on the *agape* whose sole source is in the will of God, which we have done absolutely nothing to deserve. He is right in his emphasis on the revelation of this *agape* and its communication in the bestowal of grace. But in this insight there lies the necessity and the possibility of a reconstruction of theology, which indeed in decisive matters is true to Luther's deepest insights, but which would exclude as alien to faith many things which Lutheranism has reckoned to belong to true doctrine and still does so today.

But it is not only these pioneers of a new understanding who are "right". Right, too, are all those who in discussion with them maintain already established truth, men like Paul Althaus who for decades with exemplary openmindedness towards the work of the others has pointed to Luther as the rediscoverer of the Biblical understanding of faith. Particular credit also must be given to the work of Biblical investigation itself, which precisely by its independence of systematic theology aims at liberating the New Testament witness about Christ and about faith from the prejudices of traditional dogmatics, and upon which, even though the dependence may not be directly mentioned, the work of these pioneers of the new knowledge is based.

All this makes one thing clear: that none of the contemporary theologies is the "right" one but that we are all on one journey to the goal; that consequently theology, when it rightly understands itself, is always "theology on the march". The Church and Christendom have to learn from each thinker, but will do well to avoid dependence on any special theology. The best of contemporary theologians all indeed aim, as we showed, at one point, Jesus Christ Himself; at the justification by faith alone which is to be seen in the Cross of the Son of God. But, just as even in the New Testament itself we do not have any one *doctrine* about Him, but a variety of types of doctrine which find their unity only in Jesus Christ, so it will also be the fate of all theology never to be *the* true and perennial theology (*theologia vera et perennis*). Rather shall we find that here also the saying holds good: "Only by the mouth of many witnesses is the truth confirmed."

In the science of Biblical criticism this knowledge has long since become the common possession of all who share in the work of research, and for this reason in that discipline it is taken for granted that men should listen to one another and learn from one another. Here the monologue is under suspicion, for such monologue-theology stems not from the Bible but from our Greek inheritance. All this does not mean that we favour an eclectic theology of compromise. Only the man who dares to follow his own insight will do a real service to the gospel. The decisive question in relation to this service will be: is this insight central, or peripheral? Even though the thing that the world specially admires is systematic unity and completeness, no one will succeed in embracing the whole truth of the gospel within his system, for each man sees only an aspect of it. The zeal of the theologian (*furor theologicus*) is not a holy zeal, for it springs from a concealed arrogance, a forgetfulness of his own creaturely status. The correctness of a man's theological knowledge will have to show itself by his willingness to learn from others, however determined he may be to hold to what he has learnt for himself.

V

I wish the view of Christian faith represented here, as arising from the perceived identity of justifying faith with the witness to Christ *for* us (*Christus pro nobis*), to be understood only in the light of what I have said above. Its specific nature may perhaps be defined under the following headings.

1. As in *Dogmatics* I and II, the supreme co-ordinating concept is that of the self-communication of God. There is more in this concept than in that of revelation. While the latter comprises God's work only in so far as it is covered by the aspect of knowledge, God's self-communication means at the same time that in Jesus Christ God gives man a part in His eternal life, and that this self-communication, received by the faith which proves effectual through love, transforms the existence of man. This is the truth which is identical with grace (John 1: 17).

2. Because it is seen that God's self-communication reaches its goal in faith, faith is co-ordinated with God's word of justification. God Himself speaks in man through the Holy Spirit. The word of justification "Thou art" and the word of faith "I am" say the same thing, "Abba, Father" (Gal. 4: 6, Rom. 8: 15).

3. Thus we transcend the one-sidedness of objectivism which does indeed confess *sola gratia*, but does not really confess *sola fide*, and also the one-sidedness of subjectivism, according to which faith is not concerned with the Jesus Christ of history, but only with the *kerygma* about Jesus Christ.

4. This insight, however, is made possible only by our drawing a sharp distinction between faith (*pistis*) and belief in doctrine and in the Bible, since faith arises from the witness to Jesus Christ, and not in the relationship to Biblical or Church doctrine. Doctrine is the abstract intellectual formulation of the doctrinal element in witness, while witness is a non-abstract, spiritual event.

5. This theology makes constitutive use of the results of critical historical scholarship. But it distinguishes critical historical scholarship from a historical scepticism which is incompatible with faith in Jesus the Christ, and which leads to a new docetism.

6. Here faith, precisely in its fully developed form as justifying faith, is always at once both individual faith and the faith which creates the Ekklesia as a brotherhood in Christ. Just because we take

our stand upon justifying faith, we are driven to make the distinction between Ekklesia and Church, and only from this standpoint can we do so. This distinction alone enables us to see in Christ not only the answer to the supreme epistemological question, but also the solution of the problem of fellowship.

7. By this apprehension of the Pauline understanding of faith, which does justice to the righteousness of God (*dikaiosynē theou*) in its Biblical "theocratic" significance, we are enabled to see God's assurance and His claim both in their distinctness and in their unity, and thus to recognize both the necessity of an ethic resulting from justifying faith and the necessity of an eschatology in the New Testament sense; an eschatology that looks with hope to the day when God will consummate that which for our faith is still imperfectly realized, the communication of Himself. From this it follows that this theology above all others must be aware at every moment of its incompleteness. It is thus particularly aware of its own nature as a "theology on the march".

CHAPTER 15

JUSTIFYING FAITH IN CHRIST AND THE CREED OF THE CHURCH

Now that we have realized that *pistis* in its perfect form is justifying faith in reconciliation through the Cross of Jesus Christ and not faith in the doctrine of justification or in any other Church doctrine or Bible doctrine, the question has become inevitable—"What is the relation of this faith to the content of Christian doctrine as it is defined in the Creeds of the Church and in dogma, in the Catechism or the Confessional writings (of the Reformation)?" The saying of Luther quoted above at the end of the discussion on justification, that all doctrine must "come into our experience" in this one point, in the forgiveness of sins, in order to beget real faith, tells us only of a *conditio sine qua non* of the existence of these other articles in the Confession of Faith. It does not tell us why it is necessary that such articles should exist at all. It tells us only that unless it has relevance "for me" a doctrine cannot be called a Christian doctrine, but it presupposes these other articles as something given, taken for granted. It tells us the existential sense in which they are to be understood. But whence do they themselves come?

We must also put this question to Paul, who says that he knows in the Ekklesia of the faithful "nothing but Christ and Him crucified". Is this "nothing but" to be understood literally? Surely not, since in fact there is a complete theology in his letters. But what is this theology's relation to the central point of justification? And it becomes even more obvious that we cannot take "nothing but Christ" literally when we think of the Old Testament, which the Ekklesia from the beginning justly claimed for itself also as the Word of God. So we are confronted by a problem that cannot be evaded: what is the relation of the totality, the wide sweep of Christian doctrine (as we find it, for example, in one of the classical catechisms) to that one central point, about which the Apostle asserts that he "knows nothing" he must preach "but this one thing, Jesus Christ and Him crucified"?

Schleiermacher was putting a similar question when he asked what was the relation between the Christian doctrine which confronts us in such a stately edifice and simple "pious feeling".

He justified this distinction of his in the famous letter to Lücke by the reflection that obviously a man can be a pious Christian without being a learned theologian. But this point of departure—like the resultant conception of Christian doctrine as "reflection on pious feeling"—cannot be accepted by us. Our point of departure is indeed quite a different one: faith in Jesus Christ, as we have depicted it in the chapter on justification. Christian doctrine must accordingly be nothing other than the unfolding of this primary datum, the exposition of this Confession of Jesus Christ, the Lord, of the first Christian Confession of Faith, which is the common theme of all the New Testament witnesses.

This primary datum, which is identical with the word quoted from Paul, contains in fact the whole of Christian doctrine. For the man who says "kyrios" means by this the One in whom God the Creator and the only Lord attests Himself to us as such. This historical event—the life, death and Resurrection of Jesus—is the happening in which God reveals Himself as the Lord and *becomes* our Lord. Seen from man's standpoint this happening is faith; seen from God's standpoint it is the testimony of the Holy Spirit within us. In the Son we know through the Spirit the almighty Father who creates us. We have described this assertion of Lordship by two simple words: claim and assurance. In this twofold Word of God believing man recognizes and possesses his (new) being as a being in the holy love of God, a being which is at the same time his original being.

For the Jew Paul this God was none other than He who had already manifested Himself as the Lord and Creator in the revelation of the Old Covenant. This is why the unity of this history, the inseparability of promise and fulfilment, means so much to the Apostles. For in Jesus the Christ the promise of the prophetic revelation came to its fulfilment, a fulfilment which alone held the key to the meaning of the title of "Christ" and the concept "Son of God" which is identical with it. Jesus *is* the Messiah Christ. But at the same time there was a new element in this fulfilment which had not before been connected in this manner with the Messianic expectation: God's self-communication through the sacrificial death of Jesus, this dreadful event of the Cross, which was transformed from a calamity to a liberating assurance only through the experience of the Resurrection. It was the awareness of a hitherto unimagined grace, of forgiveness of sins and the declaration of man's divine sonship, and this reconciling grace became through it absolutely central and primary. Now the first place was taken by the assurance of grace, in whose light also the Lord's claim must and could be understood anew.

He who speaks to man and deals with him is He who gives man a new being, no other Creator than He who in the beginning "calls into being that which is not". In the gracious bestowal of this word of love He reveals Himself as the God who in His love created man and destined him for fellowship with Himself. The man who hears the verdict of justification really as the Word of God knows now who *God* is in His inmost nature and who *man* is in the sight of God and what he will be through the consummation of that which was begun by the Spirit in faith. He knows now the incredible, never to be foreseen truth, that in God's sight he is identical with the "Son in whom God is well pleased" through whose self-bestowing love he has been given this new status.

In this Act and Word of God, through trustful and obedient hearing of this Word, the historical and the existential are one: it is what happened in the history of Jesus and what happens through penitence and faith. Objectively it belongs to sacred *history*, subjectively it belongs both to the present and to the future in the new self-understanding of faith. This identity of God's self-communication and man's self-understanding, this word that is at the same time "outside us and different from us" (*extra nos et alienum nobis*) and that we nevertheless know through faith as the Word for us and in us, as God speaking in us—this is Christian faith. Historical faith and "mysticism" are now one and the same. Henceforth the whole history and the whole subjective experience of man are seen in this one Christ through faith. Christ is now for the believer the central point of the world.

It was this God, this event, this Word of His that is also an Act, or this Act that is also a Word, that the Apostles desired to proclaim; nothing else. This was the *eu-angelion* which they desired to communicate to the whole world as the message of reconciliation and coming redemption. In this communication which was nothing but the human repetition of the divine self-communication, lay the task of the Ekklesia, which was indeed nothing but a gift. Henceforward their life was to live in this faith, and through it in this love, and to lead others to this faith was the goal for which they lived. This, then, is the faith which preaching has to pass on, and which doctrine has to unfold.

But *that* Christian doctrine which we know from the catechisms is very far removed from being simply an unfolding of this apostolic witness to Christ. How is the Apostles' witness of faith, especially that of Paul and John, different from that of later Church doctrine? In answering this question the critical New Testament scholar must first have his say. The aim of systematic Biblical criticism—at least today—is above all to let these texts speak for themselves, that is, to make clear what the Apostles themselves mean when they say "I believe in Jesus the Kyrios (Lord)". The criticism which it makes does not touch the apostolic witness to Christ, but the misunderstanding of that witness which in the course of the centuries of Christian history has overlaid the original meaning. This was made clear to us in Section One of this book in relation to the single concept "Ekklesia" which has nearly always been translated "Church", so that something entirely non-institutional, the brotherhood of those bound together by the reconciliation in Jesus Christ and led solely by the Holy Spirit, was equated with a sacred and sacramental institution. In this second section we have made the acquaintance of a second concept which has been just as disastrously misunderstood, the concept of *pistis*, whose meaning has been altered almost beyond recognition by the doctrinal tradition of the Church, and which now, thanks to the efforts of New Testament scholars, is at last reaffirmed in its true sense.

But if we ask wherein the difference between Christian traditional teaching and that of the Apostles consists, the answer, anticipating the result of the following inquiry, may be given shortly: The witness to the God who has communicated Himself in Jesus Christ, the fulfiller of the Old Testament revelation, is not identical with the teaching of Christian doctrine; and faith, as the Apostles understood it, is not identical with what is understood as faith in the so-called "Apostles' Creed". We begin with the latter, which is the foundation of dogma.

(1) THE APOSTLES' CREED

This *Symbolum Apostolicum* was not, as its name says and as was long believed, composed by the Apostles, but is the product of a long development which began in the middle of the second century, went through a number of materially divergent forms, and finally took the shape known to us about the end of the fifth century. We acknowledge at the outset its high value as the Creed that unites all the Christian Churches, and which above all rendered invaluable service in the struggle against the gnostic heresies, because it gives unmistakable expression to the truth that Christian faith is faith in the God who has revealed Himself through the Holy Spirit in the person of Jesus, as the gospel narratives bear witness to Him and as the Christian community acknowledged Him from the very beginning as *Kyrios Christos*. To this extent we can acknowledge the Apostles' Creed as an excellent expression of the Christian faith in the New Testament sense, saying in its brevity all that is essential.

But, over against this, we must describe it as not merely inadequate but as misleading, inasmuch as it names a series of "facts" of the life of Jesus which in part did not belong to the apostolic preaching; and above all because it represents these facts as facts to be believed, without making it clear that they are "salvation facts" as things that happened "for us". In this the Apostles' Creed led Christendom along a false path which we have described as "belief in facts" and at the same time it makes the confession of faith a "law of faith". Very soon appears the expression *lex fidei*,[1] a concept through which the glad message of the Apostles, which sets us free from the law, is itself turned again into a law. On the other hand, it says not a single word about one matter that was of such decisive importance to the Apostles from the outset in their preaching, namely that this Jesus stands in historic continuity with the Old Testament revelation and saving history. The element of saving *history* and the existential element receive in it only an inadequate emphasis.

This means that the words "I believe" come to have another meaning than they bear in the preaching of the Apostles. The Apostles' Creed does not say a single word about the thing that is the one chief concern of the New Testament, the love of God which comes to meet us in God's act of reconciliation. The forgiveness of sins, which, together with the message of hope concerning the coming of God's Kingdom, forms the centre of the Bible, is mentioned only in the third section—as an appendix, so to speak; the hope of the coming Kingdom appears only in the form of "return to Judgment", and eternal life as a last addition; it is not brought into essential and necessary relation with faith in Christ, does not inevitably follow, as it does in Paul, from justification by faith. If we had asked one of the Apostles whether he recognized in this formulation the central concern of his message, his answer would have been an

[1] F. Loofs, *Symbolik*, p. 13: "For we know that Cyprian was not only aware of a credal law (*symboli lex*) used in Baptism, to whose exact formulation he adhered, but also that catechizing in the faith (*interrogationes de fide*) and assent to the faith (*fidem dare*) were already customary in Africa at that time"

emphatic "No". The Apostles were concerned with something quite different, with the self-communication of God's love in Jesus Christ, His Act and Word as the foundation of our hope in the coming Kingdom of God. As the Apostles' Creed by enumeration of a series of facts to be believed caused *pistis* to degenerate into faith in facts, so by its failure to mention the act of reconciliation it favoured the wrong development of dogma along speculative lines.

(2) DOGMA

The early Christian theology which finally crystallized into the dogmas of the old Catholic Church concerned itself principally with two problems which are indeed indicated in the apostolic witness of faith, but yet are not its main concern, are not what the Apostles desired to proclaim to the world: the doctrine of the Trinity and the doctrine of the two natures of Jesus Christ.

As far as the dogma of the Trinity is concerned, we certainly do not wish to criticize it radically. We have indeed already indicated how the Apostles themselves acknowledged the Father in the Son and the Son in the Father—through the Holy Spirit. We gladly acknowledge that the theologians of that time did an outstanding service by the creation of this dogma. Yet the question thrusts itself upon us whether their concern was identical with that of the Apostles. We believe ourselves compelled to deny this. The doctrine of the Trinity has a different concern from the apostolic proclamation of Christ. The primary intention of the *kerygma* of the Apostles was not to speak of the ontological unity of the Son—and of the Spirit—with the Father, but to witness to something quite different: that God has communicated His love to us through the Spirit of faith in the Cross of Jesus Christ and thereby has promised to mankind a new goal of history, the revelation of the sons of God in His eternal Kingdom. That was their good news; the believing, obedient, trustful apprehension of *this* and being apprehended by it they called "faith". In it was also contained the message that "God was in Christ, reconciling the world to Himself" (2 Cor. 5: 19); what stood in the foreground was not the ontological unity of Father and Son but the *event* of reconciliation as an act of God in Christ, which we know through the Holy Spirit in faith.

Both the prominence which the theologians of the ancient Church ascribed to this unity, and the manner in which they sought to underline it, are alien to the mind of the Apostles. For this reason the Trinitarian dogma of Luther and the other Reformers has been felt to be to some extent an alien body in their teaching, although they never felt any reason to deviate from it or to contradict it. Nor is it now our intention to cast doubts on the truth of the doctrine of the Trinity. But what we do say most emphatically is that with its introduction the centre of interest was shifted from the gospel and re-sited elsewhere. A speculative ontology took the place of the existential soteriology based on saving history.

This may have happened at first with apologetic intent, and may so far have been justified. But it implied a fundamental transformation of faith in Christ, as the Apostles understood it when they gave their witness of faith to Him. The theme was no longer so much the message of the reconciliation accomplished in Jesus Christ, the vindicator of God's Lordship and the revealer of the divine love, no longer "salvation from the power of darkness" and participation in new being, in divine sonship through "the obedience of faith", but something static which had taken the place of that dynamic message. "Faith" consists no longer in participation in the love of Christ through faith, but in astonishment at the inconceivable miracle of the unity between the Person revealed and the Person who reveals; a faith which has only a remote relationship to the forgiving love of God.

This shows itself above all in the discrepancy between the New Testament witness to the Holy Spirit, and the manner in which the Spirit is spoken of in Trinitarian dogma as the third Person of the Trinity. In the New Testament the Holy Spirit is not something in which one must believe but the reality in which the believer lives; in which, above all, the Ekklesia lives. The Holy Spirit is not preached, as God's Act and Word in Jesus Christ is preached: He is rather there present wherever and inasmuch as the Word of the Apostles creates faith in the sense of the obedience of faith. There is not a single passage in the New Testament which indicates that men should believe in the Holy Spirit, or do so believe. The question that is asked is rather: "Have you received Him? do you live in Him?"

The theme of the Holy Spirit has always been an awkward one for the Church in its formation of dogma, while in fact the Holy Spirit Himself is present in the Ekklesia as the reality underlying all witness to Christ. The doctrine of the Holy Spirit is that part of theology which can be constructed only from the experience of the living Ekklesia. The doctrine of the

Spirit is the doctrine of that which proves itself as the power of the gospel in men's hearts and is the vital source of the Ekklesia and the origin of its character of brotherly love. The doctrine of the Trinity is not the unfolding of the contents of the apostolic *kerygma* but a doctrine which stems from an interest of a different kind. The Church which was absorbed by the struggle about the meaning of the term "*homousios*" is no longer the Ekklesia of the Apostles. It is true that individual Fathers of the faith in that epoch also wrote profoundly and with passion about the Atonement. But the main stream of the interpretation of the faith flows in another direction: towards belief in the miracle of the unity of the Person of the Redeemer with the Person of the Creator. A supra-rational ontology has ousted the apostolic message of salvation and faith.

A similar comment might be made on the second central dogma, the two-nature theory. This, in spite of its "truly man" (*vere homo*), does not take Jesus' humanity fully in earnest, since it does not expound the narrative witness of the Gospels about Jesus the Christ, but starts from the viewpoint of the divine and human *nature*, which is alien to the whole Biblical witness to Christ, and philosophizes about Christ's God-manhood. It is not God's approach to us in Jesus Christ, revealing and communicating God's Lordship and His self-bestowing love, but the metaphysical character of this mystery of Christ's Person, that it sets out to expound. The two-nature theory—like the Church doctrine of the Trinity—is not an unfolding of the apostolic confession of faith, but instead an ontological construction, perfect in its kind, but which directs faith in another direction than does the New Testament witness to Christ.

(3) THE CONFESSIONAL WRITINGS OF THE REFORMATION

The revolutionary advance made at the Reformation which resulted from the new understanding of the righteousness of God and of faith, found expression not so much in the official confessional documents—which were submitted to public authorities—as in the individual personal writings, in the sermons of the Reformers and above all in the Reformers' exposition of scripture. The confessional writings share only to a certain degree in this change and the nearer they stand in time to this revolutionary advance the more they do so. Yet in all of them we can trace a hiatus. They are all ambiguous, since on the one hand they are proof of the new understanding of the apostolic message, but at the same time conjoin with it the understanding of the ancient Church and of its dogma, without realizing for themselves the difference between the two. This shows itself above all in the fact that they unreflectingly take over the Apostles' Creed and in part also the other Old Church Confessions, and directly or indirectly express the belief that the new understanding of faith really concerns only the one article concerning justification by faith, while in the other articles their faith is identical with that of the Old Church.

The place where it emerges most clearly that the revolutionary new knowledge is a new understanding of the whole gospel is Luther's Schmalkaldic Articles and his two Catechisms, which all belong to the confessional writings of the Lutheran Church. Luther is the only man who sees plainly the deep cleft between the old and the new, and he expresses this insight in his Great Catechism and in the Schmalkaldic Articles. He is also the only one who, when he speaks about the Church, does justice to the element of brotherly pastoral fellowship as one of the constitutive elements of the Church: the mutual conversation and consolation of brothers (*mutua conversatio et consolatio fratrum*).[1]

At that time Biblical scholarship had not yet sufficiently advanced to make possible a clear demarcation between the new understanding of faith on the one side and that of the Apostles' Creed and Old Church dogma on the other. We take it therefore that the uncritical acceptance of the Apostles' Creed by the Reformers was due to a providential immaturity. We call it providential, for a shaking of the foundations common to the whole Christian Church might well have brought with it such an upheaval as even the powerful faith and genius of the great Reformers could not have managed to control. But by describing it as an immaturity we have already acknowledged the task set our own generation, and have made frank admission of it.

We see the task with quite special clarity from the passage quoted earlier from Luther.[2] One most important part of the theological repentance which this text preaches to us is that we must stand away (in a critical sense) from the confessions of the Old Church which are incorporated in the confessional writings of the Reformation, both the Apostles' Creed and its expansion in the Niceno-Constantinopolitan, the so-called Nicene Creed, and the so-called Athanasian Creed.

[1] This formulation stands in the 4th Part, "*De evangelio*". Thus the theme is not directly the Church. This theme is not one which is as such to be found in the Schmalkaldic Articles explicitly at all

[2] See above, pp. 208 f.

That these cannot bind our faith in any *legal* manner is an immediate conclusion from our earlier discussion. We have further sufficiently learnt how disastrous a factor formal, legal authority has been in the history of the Church and of theology. But we have also already seen the material difference between the formulations of these confessional writings and the preaching of the Apostles. While we fully concede that they give expression in classical form to genuine Biblical truth, we have at the same time acknowledged that their concern is different from that of the apostolic witness to Christ. But this is by no means true in the same manner and to the same degree of the confessional writings of Reformation times. Their central theme is once again that of the apostolic preaching. They do not deal with questions which were raised from an ontological interest in relation to the apostolic witness to Christ, but with *soteria*, with the message of salvation in Jesus Christ, which is at the same time the message of the coming Kingdom of God. They have recovered the understanding of the gospel as the message of God's approach to man.

But in so far as the "Apostles' Creed" is incorporated in these documents of Reformation times, or forms the framework in which theology unfolds itself, the two essentially different concepts of faith come into mutual conflict. The "I believe" (*credo*) of the Apostles' Creed means something different from the *pisteuo* of Paul, of the New Testament, and of the Bible in general. And this difference cannot be simply recognized as a difference in the "object" prescribed to faith, but in the very fact that here for the first time mention is made of an object or "content" of faith. The Biblical word *pisteuein* is characterized by the fact that it is directed towards the God Himself who speaks, and is open for Him. God does not teach theology, but gives Himself when He speaks. It is the fatal subject-object antithesis determined by Greek thought, which also lies behind the Old Church concept of the "*credo*". To have left this behind and thus to have recovered the Biblical understanding of "I believe" is Luther's achievement as a Reformer. This is the reason why Luther did not write a "Dogmatics". The "Dogmatics" which issued from his own discovery were Melanchthon's *loci theologici*[1] whose intention was to serve merely as aids to the understanding of the Bible, a kind of theological dictionary of the New Testament.

[1] This does not mean that Melanchthon's formulation of Reformation Theology is to be described as exemplary, but only its intention of being a theological dictionary of the New Testament

Calvin's *Institutes*, on the other hand, contains the doctrinal concept of faith of Old Church dogma alongside the Biblical personal one, and already bears the stamp of the fatal subject-object antithesis mentioned above as belonging to the Greek concept of knowledge. From our standpoint we can do nothing but register our sharpest dissent when faith is described as "knowledge corresponding to its object". God in His speaking to us is anything but an object, and the faith which consists in the reception of the divine love is something different from what we call knowledge.[1]

None of us today is yet able to say how a Christian doctrinal system would look which did full justice to the genuinely Biblical concept of faith and to faith in Jesus Christ alone, the crucified—and risen—Lord. But Luther's utterances quoted above on the "Article" of justification which "comes into our experience"[2] have confronted us inescapably with this task. A truly Biblical theology would further have to follow the advice which is contained in another passage expressive of Luther's intuitive genius. "Scripture begins quietly and gently and leads us to Christ as to a man, and thereafter to a Lord over all creation. . . . Thus I come gently in and learn to know God. But the philosophers and the men who are worldly-wise desire to begin from above. We must begin from below and afterwards come upwards."[3] This means that theology must be theology of experience, but here experience is not to be understood in the sense given to it in the theology of experience developed under the influence of Schleiermacher, but means the experience of the Word of God, and consequently a theology which is built up inductively instead of deductively. Today we do not yet have such a theology. Kittel's Dictionary of the New Testament is the most promising first step towards it. All of us are only moving towards this theology.

[1] Cf. on this point Ch. 17, "Faith and Knowledge", pp. 251 ff.

[2] See above, pp. 208 f.

[3] *W.A.* X, I, 2, p. 297. It is interesting that G. Thomasius constructed his "Evangelical Lutheran Dogmatics" from the central point of Christology (1886–8, 2nd edition). Karl Barth has also developed his Church Dogmatics on a Christological basis. But neither of them does full justice to what Luther means in the sentence quoted above, namely that the starting point should be Christ as a man. In Thomasius this failure is conditioned by the "latent docetism" of the Church doctrine of the humanity of Jesus, in Karl Barth by his beginning with the doctrine of the Trinity, i.e. "from above" instead of "from below"

CHAPTER 16

DOCTRINAL BELIEF AND BELIEF IN THE BIBLE AS THE VEHICLE OF *PISTIS*

I

WE have made clear in the preceding chapters what true faith is, in the sense of New Testament *pistis*, which finds its most perfect expression in the Pauline doctrine of justification. It is only from the standpoint of justifying faith that we can understand that faith signifies a new personal being, that in faith there lies the unity of truth and grace (John 1: 17), of freedom and fellowship, of God's righteousness and man's salvation. Above all, only of this faith can it be said that it proves itself effectual in love.

But who has this faith? Did the dockers of Corinth or the peasants of Galatia, to whom Paul wrote his great letters, have it? Or—if the assertion is true,[1] that as early as the second century the Pauline message of justification by faith alone was no longer understood—was there then since that time no more faith in the world till Reformation times? We must make our formulation here parallel to what we said about the Ekklesia and say that this faith is at the same time idea and reality. This idea of faith, or, as we put it today, this "understanding of faith" was certainly very early lost, and was replaced by a quite different concept, namely by the "faith" in the doctrine prescribed by the *lex fidei* as obligatory for belief.

But Catholic theology very early noticed that the relation between love and this faith in doctrine was not what Paul had depicted. And, therefore—carrying further what the Epistle of James had already said about faith—it described this faith as unformed faith (*fides informis*) which becomes true faith, namely faith perfected by love (*fides caritate formata*) only by the addition of love. For since unformed faith—the assent to the truth of Church doctrine, the creed—had no relation to love, such a supplementation by *caritas* was necessary. *Caritas* was enjoined as the highest virtue. Beside the creed came the moral imperative of love to God and neighbour to complete it.

[1] As is well known, this is the thesis of A. von Harnack in his *Lehrbuch der Dogmengeschichte* I, p. 106 (E.T. *History of Dogma*): "And yet we cannot speak of a general influence of Paulinism. Such a thing is not to be found. His thoughts were too unfamiliar for Paulinism to have been grasped and retained even in Paul's own Christian communities"

Further, the doctrine was set up that this *caritas* is infused through Baptism. Thereby sacramental doctrine was conjoined with dogma and *caritas* with the person of the believer.

This (in itself) understandable supplementation of doctrinal belief which in fact has hardly anything to do with love, was repudiated by the Reformers, and, from the standpoint of justifying faith, with full justification. This certainly had not been Paul's understanding of *pistis*. For him the connection between faith and love was a much more intimate one, one that was indeeed implied by the very nature of faith. For Paul, faith is indeed nothing other than the reception of the love of God. We can therefore understand the vigorous polemic of the Reformers against this doctrine of "unformed faith". What was at stake here was nothing less than the principle "by grace alone, by faith alone".

But now post-Reformation theology also failed to remain true to the Pauline Lutheran conception. It too added a supplement to it, by placing the words "by scripture alone" (*sola scriptura*) alongside the *sola fide* of justification. The first was called the material principle, the second the formal principle. This latter, however, as necessarily resulted from its character as formal principle, was understood as the formal *a priori* authority of scripture. This means that we must believe "from the outset" that scripture is God's Word, from which the conclusion necessarily followed that "everything that scripture says, teaches or narrates, is equally God's Word and therefore inerrantly true". Thus, without men's being aware of it, a *double concept of faith* originated: faith is in the first place faith in justification through Christ, and it is secondly faith in the Bible as the inerrant Word of God. In the first faith we have the centre of the gospel, the faith that is essentially bound up with love, but in the other "faith" we have something that has nothing to do with love. For what can "believing that everything recounted and taught in the Bible is true" have to do with love? This double concept of faith, however, has dominated Protestantism, unrecognized in its *quid pro quo*, more or less until the present day.

It seemed as if the principle "by scripture alone" could stand beside the principle "by faith alone" as possessing at least equal authority with it. But it only became evident that something here was not in order when the new Biblical criticism proved that in future it would no longer be possible to believe in the inerrancy of the Bible. It is therefore quite understandable that the denial of the inerrancy of the Bible, that is, the discipline of higher criticism, was condemned as a work of the devil and as the very principle of godlessness.

Thus we see that not only Catholic theology but also Protestant post-Reformation theology added "supplements" to faith. This double concept of faith, faith as justifying faith in Christ, and "faith" as belief in the Bible, is still operative even when the belief in the orthodox doctrine of the verbal inspiration of the Bible has long been given up. Only there is confusion about the origin, the nature, and the total disparity of these two things which are both given the same name, "faith". Christians are expected today, as formerly, to "believe in the Bible", only it is not recognized that then something totally different is meant by "believe". It has thus become the most urgent task of theology to make a clear distinction between these two meanings of "faith".

II

Our present task, however, is not to draw this distinction, but precisely the contrary. And indeed our present reflections about "Belief in the Bible as the vehicle of *pistis*" follow an exactly parallel course to our discussion in the first section of this book. There also, after first speaking of the misunderstanding of the Ekklesia as the Church, we dealt in a further chapter with the question of how this Church could still be the instrument and "shell" of the Ekklesia and said that its task was to change from the Church into the Ekklesia. This parallel is, of course, not accidental. How could it be, seeing how closely our understanding of the Ekklesia is bound up with our understanding of faith? Indeed we can go further and say that in both cases it was formal authority which caused the misunderstanding, the formal legal authority of the teaching office of the Church on the one side, and the formal authority of the Bible on the other. In the one case this formal authority led to the Papacy; in the other, to "the paper Pope". We shall confine ourselves in the first place to belief in the inerrancy of the Bible.

The formal element here is "Implicit faith in whatever the Bible says," faith in the Bible as an entirety, "blind" faith. This is the only way in which one can "believe in the Bible". But this faith is not the faith that the reader of the Bible experiences when he reads the scriptures, the faith which makes the Bible become the living and life-creating Word of God.[1]

[1] This fact is clearly evident in the work of the orthodox dogmatic theologian Johann Gerhard. Where he speaks of the *testimonium Spiritus sancti* he chooses passages like Romans 8: 16, Galatians 4: 6, where in fact the witness that we are the children of God is described on the one side as the witness of

The word of the Bible becomes God's Word only when God Himself speaks to us. What fills us with true reverence, with trust and grateful love to God is not the *a priori* axiomatic principle we have spoken of, but the real encounter with the God who reveals Himself to us in the opened scripture, who calls to us and speaks to us. That *a priori* doctrine is a theory about the Bible which the believing Bible reader—mistakenly—believes necessary in order to read the Bible rightly. But our joyful faith does not spring from this theory about the Bible, but rather from the experience that in this Biblical Word God Himself assures me through the Holy Spirit of His immediate presence, and makes me hear His Word addressed to me, so that it "finds" me here and now in a wholly personal manner, assuring me through judgment and grace of His love, and making me in Jesus Christ a child of God.

The theory about the Bible, however, is a generalization from the vital experience of encounter. There is indeed a certain truth behind this generalization from the self-authenticating experience of the intrinsic authority of the Word of God and of the faith which rests wholly upon it. There is a certain truth behind the conviction that everything that is to be found in scripture is to be believed. It is this: that the reader of the Bible can never know beforehand at what passage in the Bible this encounter will take place. In that sense he must in principle be ready and prepared to encounter at any place in the Bible the God who speaks to him. But he must not confuse this readiness to hear God speaking everywhere in the Bible with the general principle mentioned above, that everything which stands in the Bible is to be believed. For to do this is to transform the character of faith from an encounter into a general law. Faith in the God who speaks to us then becomes faith in a book. What the believer really lives by is something quite different: God's self-revelation to him as self-bestowing and forgiving love. Thus he possesses in the husk, the vehicle of belief in the "Bible", the truer living faith which Paul names *pistis*.

the Holy Spirit to Himself, and on the other side as the witness of faith. Of this witness it is indeed true to say what Gerhard writes about the experiences of the devout reader of the Bible, namely that in reading the scriptures and in meditating upon them the witness of the Spirit is received. But, on the other hand, it is mere doctrinaire theory to assert that this experience accompanies all reading of the scriptures. Here he confuses a (false) generalization from this theory with the experience of encounter with the self-communication of God. It is just this confusion which is the cause of the change from the Reformers' Bible faith to the orthodox belief in the Bible. His theory makes him claim as experience what, in fact, never was or can be experience

Thus it is important to see two things: on the one hand, the deep gulf which separates living faith in Christ and an *a priori* faith in the Bible, and on the other, the possibility that within the husk of an erroneous theory about the Bible there may be contained a genuine and living faith. But from what has been said it will above all be clear that we need a new formulation of the true doctrine of scripture, which must not be allowed to stand as a second principle alongside of justifying faith, or indeed to thrust itself into the primary position, but which will, on the contrary, take its shape from justifying faith or faith in Christ, as merely another expression of it. This principle might perhaps be formulated thus: Christian faith is faith in the Bible in the sense that the Bible alone is the place in which God speaks to us, judges us as through His Word, acquits us from condemnation, and imparts Himself to us as the self-bestowing love in which He creates us anew.[1]

III

We must now say something about doctrinal belief and belief in dogma similar to what we have said about belief in the Bible. The majority of those who in the past have proved themselves genuine believers by their discipleship and sacrificial love came by way of the Church catechism to this faith. In this sense even Luther set great store by catechetical instruction as the normal way of becoming a Christian, and himself wrote a catechism which is unequalled in the vitality with which it "teaches the faith". In this sense Calvin too looked on the visible Church as the school whose first obligation is instruction in the Christian faith. Although such doctrinal belief in itself does not amount to *pistis*, there is very often concealed beneath it the true faith which proves effectual in love. How is that possible? For the reason that even in doctrine there is hidden implicit the element of witness. Where faith is not simply enjoined as something to be believed, but where the believer is pointed to Christ as the true meaning of the creed, there the abstract thing, dogma, is transformed into witness to Christ. In Luther's catechism this character of witness is especially manifest.

Thus here also, while making a clear distinction between doctrinal belief as such, and faith in Christ, we must bear in mind the other point that within the husk of doctrinal belief doctrine may be transformed into genuine witness, and true faith come to birth.

[1] Cf. Ch. 18

IV

What we have up to this point been describing as doctrinal belief and belief in the Bible is, however, of positive value from an apparently quite different aspect. Doctrinal belief has a tremendous cultural, social and political significance. This does not of itself come within the scope of dogmatics. We must, however, make at least a passing reference to this aspect, because it has continual relevance for the discussion about the nature of faith and is especially important for Christians who are not theologians.

We know indeed—especially through the work of Biblical criticism—that there is no such entity as "Christian teaching" or "the Biblical doctrine", but only a multiplicity of theological views in which the witness to God's revelation is presented to us. Even the New Testament—not to speak of the Old—contains a series of, in some respects, widely divergent "doctrines"; for example, that of Matthew, of Luke, that of Paul and that of John, which as such cannot be brought to one common denominator, but none the less find their unity in the one Jesus Christ to whom all bear witness. Just as little is there one homogeneous Protestant teaching. But even the "homogeneous teaching of the Catholic Church", when more closely examined, is not a unity but a multiplicity of mutually divergent teachings, whose representatives in part vigorously oppose each other, while the central teaching authority of the Pope guarantees and gives the semblance of such a unity. In spite of all this the consensus in respect of Christian teaching is so great that one may speak of "the Christian teaching" as a homogeneous unity. In spite of all confessional and inter-confessional differences there is a great common corpus of "Christian teaching" which as such has not only been a decisive contributory factor to the cultural, political and social life of Western mankind but is also at work as a ferment in the life of the whole human race.

We mention the following doctrines, which in respect of their cultural or political and social effects have been of special and manifest significance: The monotheism and personalism of its concept of God, characteristics shared by the Jewish creed. The doctrine of Creation, in particular the doctrine of the creation of man in the image of God. The doctrine that God is love and the summary of God's commandments in the twofold commandment to love God and our neighbour. The doctrine of the Kingdom of God as the final goal of humanity and of eternal life as the goal of the life of the individual and of the nations.

So long as it was believed as doctrine, that is, so long as it was believed to be true in the sense of doctrinal belief, Christian doctrine has proved itself a factor of the highest importance in the cultural, social and political life of the "Christian nations". This corpus of Christian doctrine common to all had the significance of a common ideology. By binding together the historical and immanent with the eternal and transcendent it has had the result that on the one side the realm of earthly historical life was taken seriously, and that on the other side life was liberated by it from the emptiness of mere immanence. As a doctrine of the law and of a coming Judgment it has brought the individual man under a responsibility both in the highest degree personal, and at the same time extending to all humanity, and yet by its doctrine of grace it has moderated the rigour of a tense moralism. Through the doctrine of man's creation in the image of God, it has created a personalism which did not allow man to fall a victim to materialistic "realism" and yet at the same time protected him from an idealism which deifies man. It thus produced a humanism which by its acknowledgment of the love of one's neighbour vindicated the true humanity of life and at the same time by its requirement of love to God raised man above himself.

Politically it was of supreme importance that Christian doctrine did indeed affirm the State as an ordinance willed by God, but at the same time limited it by the thought that its borders and boundaries are defined by the God-given dignity of man and above all by the sovereignty of God. The Christian doctrine of man has also had a tremendous *social* importance because and in so far as it taught the equal dignity of all men and at the same time found a basis for their actual inequality in the concept of Creation. By so doing it created modern democracy and yet kept alive the sense of the necessity of authority. But above all in virtue of the fact that both the Church of the Sacraments and also the Church of preaching stood open to all men without distinction of race, or class, or sex, it has contributed much to the creation of a consciousness of human solidarity, to a "sense that humanity is one family", to the idea of a family of nations. These are only a few examples which might be further developed and supplemented in a "Morphology of Christianity".[1] Here they are intended only as a mere suggestion and sketch.

What has this to do with the theme "Doctrinal belief as vehicle of *pistis*"? Without calling in question what was said

[1] We adopt the use of this expression from the well-known work by W. Elert, *Morphologie des Luthertums* (Morphology of Lutheranism)

about the deep difference between doctrinal belief and *pistis*, this short digression into the territory of cultural science shows unmistakably that even belief in doctrine has a power of determining culture and society which must not be overlooked, and which may be reckoned to have worked effectively, though not solely, for good. What we have to do with here is not indeed faith in the sense of the Biblical witness, but a significant and influential ideology.

But we who have learnt to know Jesus Christ as the sole and sufficient ground of our faith have the task laid upon us of proclaiming true faith to the unbelieving world. This task must be undertaken in the strength of a faith whose foundation is in Jesus Christ and in no other authority.

Note

THE TRUE NON-APRIORISTIC BIBLE FAITH: REFLECTIONS ON THE FORMULATION OF A NEW DOCTRINE OF SCRIPTURE

The Reformation Churches' doctrine of scripture, which in its earlier (orthodox) form, namely, in its identification of the word of the Bible and God's Word, has proved to be untenable and incompatible with the Evangelical Faith, is intended to give expression to the fundamental truth that the Christian Faith, and with it the Christian Church, rests upon the foundation of the Bible word. In particular it asserts that this datum, the revelation of God which took place in a determined history, precedes all faith, although only faith is able to recognize the revelation history and saving history as such. Even justifying faith comes into being only when faith apprehends the event of the Cross as the event that took place once and for all, that is, apprehends that this event precedes faith and is its foundation, and as such comes to us only in the word of scripture, and that in this event in faith we see this revelation history and saving history come to its completion.

"God of Abraham, Isaac and Jacob—not of the philosophers." That is Pascal's legacy, which at his death was found sewn into his coat. This word of a man who himself was a great thinker points us to that revelation history which began in the grey dawn of the history of Israel and the Jews, and disclosed its true meaning and goal in the history of Jesus the Christ. There is always, indeed, a prophetic or apostolic word to interpret the event and make us understand this meaning. But the special character of this word is that it is never separable from the historical event. It is indeed just this unity of word and event which distinguishes the Bible from the books of other religions.

The pervading theme of the Bible, the concern of this Act and Word of God, is that in it God makes known His Name, that He manifests the mystery of His nature as being just this will to communicate Himself and create fellowship; that in this self-communication He also unveils *our* mystery, the mystery of our human destiny, and that in so doing He does not surrender but rather underlines the essential mystery of His own being. When God makes known to us His nature, He makes known His will that is identical with His nature, and in this act of manifestation He transforms the man who hears it in faith into another, "new" man. Already in the Old Testament this "hearing" which transforms a man's nature is described as "faith", but not until the New Testament does its significance become unmistakably clear. And precisely as this message, this "Word", can be heard only in conjunction with a real event, an event, that is, which takes place in space and time, so also it aims at just as real an event as its intention, its goal, and the realization of its purpose. It is thus not simply a word directed to our understanding—like, for example, the Greek *logos*—but its purpose is to achieve something through being understood.

This is true of the whole Bible, and of all its component writings. All unite in giving this peculiar significance to the concept of "understanding". In the New Testament, indeed, something new is added to this common content of meaning: inasmuch as the Son of God—Messiah—is no longer merely the expected One, but the One who has already come, so faith also, the hearing of the news of what has already happened in the Cross of the Son of God, has a new content. Faith itself is now the transformation at which the Word aims. Justifying faith is now itself what the Word intends; namely, a sonship of God which is not merely promised, but which by being believed is already a reality through the real presence of the Holy Spirit that speaks in us. This real presence of the Spirit is at the same time something already possessed and not yet possessed. Faith is inseparable from the certainty of the hope which awaits the consummation in eternity of our divine sonship. Therefore God's Word is not merely His self-revelation, but His self-communication, His truth which is at the same time the gift of a share in His own eternal life.

But this reality created in and through the Holy Spirit is not only an individual faith but a communal reality, the Ekklesia: the new people of God, the new humanity, a people among whom Christ is present and reigns as Kyrios, a people which is thus the vanguard of the coming Kingdom of God.

Not everything written in the Bible has this character of divine self-disclosure and disclosure of man's nature. Much of the Bible is narrative of the kind that is found in history books, chronicles and the annals of the nations. We are given information about secular affairs, and cosmographical, geographical, ethnographical, astronomical and zoological knowledge of every kind, corresponding to the intellectual stage of development of the time in question. But this "profane" material cannot be distinguished simply from relevant matter dealing with God or man. For right in the middle of information on purely profane matters the beam of divine revelation can break forth, while on the other hand it may not perhaps be visible in theological passages. Just for this reason it is not possible to delimit and earmark the "Word of God in the Bible" as such.

This has been the ever-renewed experience of believing Christians through all the centuries in relation to the Bible. They have heard the Word of God in reading the scriptures, in scripture as a whole, though not everywhere in scripture in the same manner. This is what their confession means in relation to scripture when they call the Bible the Word of God. It is in this way that this concept is to be understood, not in the sense of verbal inspiration.

And this was what was implied in Luther's rediscovery of the Biblical concept of faith, justifying faith in Jesus Christ. Because his starting point was the *experience* of faith in the reading of scripture and not an *a priori* doctrine of Biblical inspiration, he was able to believe so firmly in the Bible and yet at the same time to be so free in his criticism of the Bible word. His understanding of justifying faith had led him at the same time to a new understanding of scripture as God's word. When, like Paul, he realized the conflict between work-righteousness and the righteousness of faith, he broke through to a new understanding of scripture that set him free from the legalism of the Jewish conception of the Bible, which was indeed nothing other than the doctrine of verbal inspiration. The Word of God is Spirit (*pneuma*) not letter (*gramma*) (2 Cor. 3). The man who hears God speak to him in scripture hears the inner witness of the Holy Spirit. But the word of scripture which is to be accepted implicitly as God's Word is—law. His motto "Christ the Lord and King of Scripture" (*Christus dominus et rex scripturae*) cleared the way for a faith whose attitude to the Bible was at once believing and critical.

Thus, then, from his discovery of the *sola gratia* principle, Luther won an astonishing freedom of critical reflection on the Bible. This found expression particularly in his introductions to individual books of scripture, of which the introduction to the Epistle of James is the best known. Whether in other respects Luther was right or not in his judgment on this Epistle is no matter for discussion here. His criterion "(Only) what deals with Christ, that is apostolic" *is* the decisive criterion, even though he may himself have understood it in too narrow a sense. He means by this, expressed in our terminology: Only God's self-communication to me is God's Word. It is the Lord in Person who makes me His servant and at the same time by His fatherly word "Thou" spoken in Christ Jesus makes me His son. God does not inform us *about* this and that. He opens His heart to me and in so doing He also opens my own heart. That is the meaning of "God's Word" as it encounters me in the Bible. It is an "I-Thou" word; it cannot be generalized, materialized or objectified. God's word is not a "something", an objective thing in itself, rather is it a transitive transaction, an assurance and claim. The Bible is not "in itself" God's Word, any more than faith "in itself" is faith. But in this correlation of God's Word and faith, God's Act and Word —that which has happened—is always the primary and begetting agent, and faith is always the secondary and begotten element.

That in this self-manifestation there is always contained God's will and purpose to bring in His Kingdom, his claim upon man for Himself, is perhaps not quite so clear in Luther as his knowledge of grace. But if we understand the saying "What treats of Christ" in this sense of assurance and claim, then we have given precisely *the* criterion of what God's Word in the Bible is. The so-called formal principle, namely, *that* God speaks to us in scripture, has become identical with the material principle, *what* God speaks to us in scripture. Herein is also included the proviso that we have not to decide how God makes known His will. The contingency of the manner of revelation, which is identical with the contingency of the historical event, is thus as frankly acknowledged as is the content of His revelation.

It is perhaps this which could especially be learnt from Calvin rather than from Luther. On the other hand, there are no grounds whatever for asserting that Calvin alone, and not Luther, was concerned to assert the unity of the Old and the New Testaments. Luther's unremitting exegetical labours on Old Testament writings, especially his expositions of the Psalms, refute such an assertion. But what does indeed distinguish Luther from Calvin is the different value he places on the Old Testament Law. We agree with Karl Barth's assertion, that there is always law included in God's Word, in so far as nothing different is meant by this than the claim which is included in God's promise. Luther did not deny that there is a genuine Word of God included in the Law (*torah*) of the Old Covenant, nor would we today call this in question, in view of the knowledge which the critical study of the Old Testament has newly given to us.

God's will to have an obedient people is not the law which Paul describes as the *nomos*, which stands in antithesis to Christ, but is the will of God which is decisively to be known in Jesus Christ, the righteousness of God. It is precisely through justification that God creates for Himself this obedient people, the Ekklesia, and it is precisely for this reason that Christ is called the Lord. The Ekklesia belongs to justification as its correlate, the fellowship born of the Spirit of those who have received God's love and dwell in it, even if in such a manner that this life is in continual conflict with "the old man". In our opinion Zwingli has been unjustly neglected on this whole question. He has in general the same free conception of the Word of God in scripture as Luther, except that in his work the *sola gratia* principle is perhaps not so firmly grasped as in Luther. On the other hand, he paid more attention than Luther to the *people* of God, new-created by the Word, and therein saw more clearly than Luther God's "theocratic" will to bring in His Kingdom; that is, the claim on God's people implicit in their knowledge of Christ, even in social and political concerns. In this matter the last word has not yet been spoken. New disclosures are to be expected from research into Luther's and Calvin's and Zwingli's writings, which will show that the Reformers are nearer to each other than had been thought, and which above all will open new perspectives of the knowledge of Christ and the scriptures. (We think of scholars of the Reformed Confession like E. Dowey, A. van Ruler and his pupils.)

On the other hand, in one respect the picture is decisively clear; Calvin stands much nearer to the theory of verbal inspiration than does Luther. He thus represents already a much more orthodox standpoint, which hardly leaves room for critical Biblical scholarship. This holds good less for Calvin the Biblical exegete and preacher than for Calvin the dogmatic theologian. For this reason "scriptural proof" plays a much larger part in his works than in Luther's. Certainly Calvin also is thoroughly permeated by the genuine Biblical *pistis*-concept and this dominates his thinking about adoption, about life in the Spirit, about *libertas Christiana* and is nearly everywhere present in his exegetical writings. From the knowledge that he gained from Galatians and Romans of the certainty of adoption (which is identical with the witness of the Holy Spirit within us) he formed the concept of the self-authenticating clarity of the Word of scripture. But then he generalized this, making it a universal law, transforming its application to the words of the Bible as such. Thus he became one of the fathers of orthodox biblicism. He has the double concept of faith of which we spoke; faith as experience of the Word of God and faith in scripture as authoritative Word of God. The essential difference between these two concepts eluded him—as it did the later orthodox theologians and many of our contemporaries. Without being conscious of so doing he can equate the one with the other, and here, as we showed above, the passage in 2 Timothy 3: 16 plays a disastrous part.

Thus we arrive at the problems which underlie the contemporary discussion on hermeneutics. These scholars are doing the work which in other disciplines is called investigation of fundamental principles. These have, however, one common characteristic, that they are in a high degree abstract. Thus even this hermeneutic discussion is concealed in a terminology so specialized and abstract that it is accessible only to a few. And yet the problem to whose clarification all these efforts are dedicated is a simple and central one: In what sense can we understand the Bible as God's Word? We have too much respect for the work being done in this field to attempt prematurely to anticipate the result of these inquiries and ourselves formulate the new doctrine of scripture which results from the knowledge of justifying faith. For this reason we have set forth our thoughts merely in the form of "Reflections on the formulation of a new doctrine of scripture" But two points are in any case established.

1. The Bible is the pre-condition of all faith, that which alone makes it possible. And the whole Bible at that. Therefore neither may Luther's saying "What is true to Christ", that is, the understanding of God's Word as the Word of the grace of Christ, lead us to separate the Old Testament and the New from each other—a tendency of German theologians since Schleiermacher and Ritschl, and today a very clearly marked characteristic of Bultmann. Nor may John's word "They" (the scriptures) "are they which testify of me" (John 5: 39), be developed into a Christological exposition in the manner of Wilhelm Vischer, which inevitably does violence to the text. Rather must both things be kept in view together, the unity of the Testaments and the difference between the Testaments. Modern critical and historical Biblical scholarship has made not only the difference but also the unity clearer to us than could be known at the time of the Reformers and yet up to date no one has been able to formulate this unity of the Testaments without falling a victim to the orthodox levelling tendency, nor has anyone been able so to do justice to the difference between the Testaments as to avoid the evolutionary relativism characteristic of the nineteenth century history of religions school.

It is clearly to be seen that the decisive category is in fact the one which was employed to master the problem as early as the days of primitive Christianity: that of promise and fulfilment. But at the same time it has become clear to us that these concepts must be understood in a broader and profounder sense than was then given to them, in that not merely individual passages but the whole of saving history and revelation history is seen in this light. At this point we expect the decisive clarification to come from those who are working on the problem of hermeneutics. But this work should not be confined to scholars of the Lutheran tradition and theologians of German origin, for whom the antithesis between law and gospel is primary, in order that justice should be done to the revelation of the Kingdom of God and the "theocratic" viewpoint of the Old Testament.

2. It is equally clear that we can never return to the old doctrine of scripture, and that not only on grounds of scholarship, but just as much, or even more, for reasons of faith. For that doctrine of scripture was—Jewish legalism. This is shown with unmistakable clarity by 2 Corinthians 3, where faith of the letter and faith created by the Spirit are contrasted with each other. It stands out most clearly, plain enough for all to read, in Luther's introductions to holy scripture, where we perceive that heart-warming conjunction of Bible faith and critical freedom of which we have taken note.

We must therefore postulate a doctrine of scripture of a kind that will really make clear and do justice to the unity—let us say it even more clearly, the miraculous unity of the revelation history of the Old and New Testaments—but which will at the same time establish the theological legitimacy of the scholarly critical study of the Bible which is everywhere proceeding; that is, acknowledge this study as something which is not only compatible with the faith of a Christian, but is directly demanded by it. Meanwhile we must content ourselves with acknowledging that everything which is said in this work of ours has been drawn from the one source of holy scripture, and indeed as from a unity which is for us the great miracle of history.

CHAPTER 17

FAITH AND KNOWLEDGE

Is faith knowledge? Modern man feels it very strange that this question should even be asked. Most people indeed are convinced that faith and cognition, faith and knowledge, are contraries, that they are at least essentially different things which bear no comparison. We believe only what we cannot know, but what we know we do not need also to believe. This conception manifestly contradicts the Biblical conception, for there the injunction "Know the Lord" perpetually recurs. This injunction makes it clear that the Biblical and modern concepts of knowledge lie on different planes. In order to clarify our minds about this difference it is necessary first to interrupt our theological inquiry and enter the field of philosophical epistemology. For it can hardly be doubted that our contemporary concept of knowledge has been created by philosophy. It is the product of Greek philosophy and the modern science which has sprung from it.

I

The ideal of knowledge—or the idea of knowledge—which underlies it, is that of "objective knowledge". Knowing objectively is equivalent to apprehending the object as it is "in itself", that is, without admixture of subjective elements. In order to know, one must—to use an expression of the astronomer—"cancel out the personal equation". This ideal of knowledge originated in the realm where nature is the object—as was the case in Greek philosophy, especially in its origins, and as it is once again in the science of modern times. The model of such knowledge is the science of physics[1] which is just as objective as it is exact, i.e. capable of mathematical representation, and whose object is correspondingly subjectless, approximates to a pure object, a thing, whether it be the material element

[1] It has not escaped the author's notice that even physics today can no longer be called in the epistemological sense a purely "objective" science, owing to its having become since Einstein "perspectival", since its statements are always relative to a definite "system of reference". But in spite of this it is strictly objective, because this "system of reference" itself can be represented in exact mathematical quantities and to that extent is identical for every cognitive subject, that is, free from all "subjectivity". Cf. on this point Karl Heim's most important book *Die Wandlung im naturwissenschaftlichen Weltbild* (1951), especially pp. 79–112. (E.T. *The Transformation of the Scientific World View*, S.C.M. Press, London, 1953)

or the abstract mathematical formula, the law of nature. The question now is, whether this objective knowledge is the ideal for all knowledge in general; that is to say, whether this objectivity can be and must be transferred to other fields, in order to reach valid knowledge.

This problem is now the subject of furious debate in the field of biology, the world of animate matter. One party, the causalists or mechanists, affirm the objectivistic ideal of knowledge, averring that real advances of knowledge are made only when this ideal is strictly pursued and the object is apprehended thus, as an objective thing and by means of causal categories as in physics. The other party, the vitalists, affirm that in this manner the real object of biology, the organism, is lost to sight, because its characteristic peculiarity is just precisely the non-mechanical element, since biology has to deal with wholes which are distinguished from mechanisms by the fact that here—confessedly in a manner which is inaccessible to our knowledge—the whole is prior to the parts, that is, cannot be put together as the sum of its analysed parts. This totality which is different from a mechanism is what constitutes the concept of an organism. In all definitions of organic and living entities this "mystical" entity called "the whole" recurs in concepts like "*self*-movement", "*self*-direction", "*self*-reproduction", and so on. In these words there is contained a "subjectual" element[1] which is taken from the self-perception of men and used to describe the essential peculiarity of organic and living things.

In face of the arguments of the mechanists the vitalists appeal to the fact that it *cannot be questioned* and is *in fact unquestioned* that in higher organisms such a subjectual element must be assumed to exist, or refer on their side to the indispensability of animal psychology and the advances made in this discipline, which could not function without concepts like "instinct", "behaviour" and even, in higher animals, "intelligence". There will be few today who assent to the truth of Descartes' view that animals are mechanisms. Knowledge in this field is then not possible without a kind of participation in the object, which is entirely lacking in physics. The organism, the world of living matter, cannot be apprehended unless man recognizes something of himself in his object.

The totalities in biology may be more and more questionable

[1] As Brunner has here coined a word of his own I have taken the liberty of coining a new word—subjectual—to give his sense in English, a word which is meant to refer to the world of subjects, without having the pejorative sense of unreality inevitably attached to "subjective" (Tr.)

the lowlier the organisms become with which it has to do, but there can be no doubt that man is a totality which cannot be apprehended without such a subjectual element. There has indeed been no lack of attempts to apply the ideal of knowledge in physics to the knowledge of man. Since Democritus an atomistic psychology has attempted to split up the soul of man into atoms and to conceive of its unity as built up from summation according to mechanical laws of association. The physiological psychology which in recent times tried to apply vigorously this objectivist ideal of knowledge was, however, soon recognized as a way that led to results of little value, and its measuring appliances stand unused today in scientific museums.

Objectivism then made a new attempt in the guise of "behaviourism", which appeared more promising. Man was regarded as a living being that just like others has its "way of behaviour" which can be objectively studied. But even the leading concept of this school, "behaviour", indicates that we must deviate from the consistently objectivist line in order to apprehend man. For "behaviour" is a concept which is taken from our experience of ourselves, and even more than the concept of organism contains within itself the totality of a directing factor. But even so, this kind of psychology soon comes to its limits, namely wherever it has to deal with what is the peculiar characteristic of man and his behaviour, with the mind and the manifestations of mind—with culture. This behaviourism today enjoys only in America, the land of its origin, a reputation which we admit is not inconsiderable. But in Europe it is repudiated as the untimely offspring of an already outworn naturalism or biologism. It has been demonstrated that man in his humanity cannot be known thus.

The same fate has overtaken objectivistic sociology. After Auguste Comte, its founder, had defined this science as the physics of the formation of human groups, it departed step by step from this ideal of knowledge borrowed from physics, and replaced this objectivist method by a method of knowledge which ascribes a decisive significance to subjective concepts such as "interests", "values", "consensus" and "mind". Max Weber's Sociology of Religions took a great step further, when he asserted that the religious motives were decisive and powerful factors in the shaping of society and culture. Thus he was a pioneer in a development of sociology which takes over the concepts of a newer philosophical anthropology, above all, that of man's "self-understanding" For the way in which man shapes society, law, morals and culture corresponds to his self-understanding.[1]

But the adoption of the concept of self-understanding means the total surrender of the objectivistic ideal of knowledge. When it is acknowledged that man is the being who understands (or seeks to understand) himself, and whose peculiar being consists in this understanding of himself, this manner of knowing, namely the act of *understanding*,[2] is identical with its object, the man who understands himself. Knowing can now no longer consist in the exclusion as far as possible of that which the knowing subject contributes to his "object"—the "personal equation"—but, on the contrary, it can come into existence only by the knowing subject finding himself again in the thing known. His understanding reaches just as far as this rediscovery of himself takes place; knowledge is here possible only as it is accompanied by an act of self-understanding, and thus by a maximal participation, and not, as in the case of objective knowing, by a maximal self-exclusion.

II

A further decisive step in the transformation of the concept of knowledge was taken by psychiatric psychology. The psychiatrist has realized that he can help his patient only when he, the doctor, stops trying to look at the other as an object whom *he* must know, even if it were in the way of understanding him. Rather does he achieve success when he

[1] As long ago as the publication in 1931 of the *Handwörterbuch der Soziologie* by A. Vierkandt, the sociologists represented in this volume, such as Geiger, Mannheim, Michels, Tönnies, L. v. Wiese, etc., had an outlook on sociology which, by reason of its taking into consideration mental and subjective elements, was very different from that of Auguste Comte. This holds much more of sociologists of very recent times like H. Schelsky, D. Riesmann, H. Freyer, A. Gehlen and, above all, Rosenstock-Huessy, in whose work philosophical and anthropological categories like W. Dilthey's "understanding" or Heidegger's "self-understanding" or even theological categories play a significant part

[2] It is significant that the two thinkers who have done most to vindicate the independence of the mental sciences over against the material sciences, Wilhelm Dilthey and Heinrich Rickert, have each of them developed and so placed at the service of theology one of the viewpoints which are constitutive for the concept of *pistis*. Dilthey has contributed the view of understanding as identification with the object, Rickert the view of historical knowledge as apprehension of the uniqueness of historical occurrences in contrast with the knowledge of the natural scientist in conformity with general laws. These concepts are already taken for granted today as thought-categories, but before these two thinkers they were not yet present—not at least as fundamental categories. Of course both of them have their antecedents in the history of modern philosophy, and are always used by historians in practice, although generally without the consciousness of their epistemological significance

allows the patient to *communicate himself.* Knowledge is thus here no longer the achievement of the knowing subject alone, but the result of a communication. The mystery of the concrete person "discloses itself" only through an effort of mutual co-operation on the part of doctor and patient. Here it is no longer a case of knowledge through understanding, but of understanding through self-communication.

But this knowledge presupposes that we know something else. Man understands himself only when he takes into consideration not merely what he *is* but also what he *ought to be.* The contrast between "is" and "ought" is the thing which most profoundly distinguishes man from all other beings. Only when he understands that obligation, responsibility, is just as much a part of his being as his factual and empirical condition is, does he understand himself as a man. This sense of obligation confronts the psychiatrist in a concrete manner in the phenomenon of his patient's consciousness of guilt. What is spoken of here is no longer, as in idealistic philosophy, obligation in the abstract, but concrete obligation, obligation which the patient in this way or that has failed to meet, and guilt. This feeling of guilt is the principal hindrance standing in the way of the patient's self-communication. This is why psychiatry in its Freudian beginnings attempted to remove this "guilt complex" by explaining it as the mere product of social convention. But it was very soon evident that this "explanation" not only caused the complex to disappear, but called in question the personal status of the patient. There was a danger that such "treatment" would cause man to lose his true humanity, because there was a risk that he would lose his personality along with his responsibility. Such a cure was indeed no cure, but a destructive amputation, although it might give subjective relief. The instrument by which it was performed was simply objectivism, recourse to causal explanation.

If guilt, responsibility and obligation are objectively explained, namely as the product of mere social convention, then conscience too is "recognized" as a mere product of education. It is then nothing more than the experience which human society has had of what is useful to it, and which now confronts me as what society demands of me. But when I "recognize" that, I am set free from its imperative, because now I know how this imperative came into being. Because I have discovered the mechanism, hitherto unknown to me, through which so-called conscience originates, it has lost for me its normative and mysteriously imperative power. It is now unmasked as a mere utilitarian rule of society; its authority to command and accuse is set on one side. In future I shall myself examine whether it is in my interest to act in obedience to its "commands" or whether I serve my interests better by acting otherwise. When conscience has been "seen through" and "explained" thus, it has ceased to be for me an authority which I should obey. It has been dissipated through explanation just as a child's fear of Santa Claus[1] is dissipated as soon as he perceives "that it is only father who has dressed himself up like this". The objective and so-called scientific explanation has destroyed what it should have explained.

But what is the nature of *understanding*? Can the psychiatrist "understand" the guilt of whose burden the patient tells him? Certainly he can do this in the sense that he himself also knows these "pangs of conscience", can thus identify himself with the patient, recognize himself in him. But then he himself is also a guilty man, and is confronted by the same question as his patient: "What is guilt, and how am I to get rid of it?" Thus the question about guilt—and the question about responsibility which underlies it—is not capable of being understood by him either. "Understanding" is a faculty which envisages only the phenomenon, without being able to comprehend it, to escape from the pressure exercised by it. The problem of the nature of guilt, the origin of this mysterious accusation, remains unanswered.

III

But perhaps, now that the naturalistic objective explanation has shown itself not to be a real clarification, but rather a falsification, idealistic philosophy can take us further at this point. Kant's philosophy, indeed, recognizes obligation as the fundamental phenomenon of morality. Kant calls it the Categorical Imperative. He leaves us in no doubt that it is not only a reality, but that the whole dignity of personality depends upon it. Obligation is for him a reality of a frankly numinous character. But on more exact conceptual analysis it proves to be an essentially more sober reality. It is in fact the law of my reason, the law of autonomy. I myself as a rational self am the author of this obligation. I myself dictate to myself. My rational self dictates to my empirical natural self. Thus a division enters into the self, the division between a self identical with the law and a self not identical with it. This becomes specially

[1] *Translator's Note:* In Germany and Switzerland the part of Santa Claus is taken by a man who comes dressed up bearing a sack, and who speaks very roughly to the children before he gives them gifts

clear when the phenomenon of the evil will, the will that deviates from the law, comes in sight. Here Kant is inexorable. If there is already evil in my will, then the "inclination" to it, the "propensity" to evil must have been hidden in me even before the evil act. At this point the philosopher acknowledges the kinship of his teaching with Christian doctrine. It is not an accommodation to his Christian environment, but an expression of the most stringent and sharpest conceptual analysis, when he speaks of "radical evil."

But the critical reader cannot avoid asking "Which, then, is true?" The elevating and inspiring word about autonomy, or the sombre depressing word about radical evil? Who is it now that is responsible for this evil? Is it the empirical natural self that Kant thinks of as subject to the law of causality? In that case, it is not conceivable how this natural self can be evil, since it lacks the freedom necessary for responsibility. Or is it the rational self, the intellectual self? But this was declared to be identical with the law. This question shows that idealistic ethics has got into a self-contradiction. It also is unable to comprehend or explain the phenomenon of responsibility, which becomes especially evident in its negative form as guilt or evil. Philosophy thus stands on the same boundary to which understanding led us. One obtains a glimpse of the problem of responsibility and guilt, but it is not possible to say what it is.

Or does the existential philosophy perhaps lead us to our goal? It speaks of a "call to authenticity". But it perceives that as a rule this call is not obeyed, since man remains at the impersonal level of "One"[1] and is not ready to be summoned forth from it by this call. But it is neither able to say whence this call comes, nor why it is not obeyed. It has not worked out with such precision as Kant the doctrine of obligation, of responsibility. But at any rate it does not take us beyond that threshold where indeed we get a glimpse of obligation but neither know whence it comes nor how we are to be liberated from the negative aspect of responsibility, guilt.

So man's own thought takes him thus far: he must affirm responsibility, man must admit his guilt, but further he cannot come. He can neither explain nor comprehend the source of responsibility, nor can he unburden himself of guilt. At this boundary line faith comes into being. This is not to say that it

1 *Translator's Note:* In the existential philosophy of Heidegger, a large part is played by *das man*—"one"—the inauthentic conventional mode of personal being from which the call of responsibility summons us back to authentic being, the existence unto death

originates *from* the knowledge of this boundary. We saw indeed that neither (objective) explanation nor (subjective) understanding leads to more than the glimpsing of just this boundary. Thus the liberating answer cannot come from our own act of knowledge. But this answer—so faith tells us—has come *to* us. Faith indicates a point in the reality of man's world, that is, in history, where this liberating answer has happened. This point is the revelation, Jesus Christ. Faith is the relation to the historical revelation, to Jesus Christ.

IV

In the encounter with this reality the thing happens of which we have spoken earlier. The first thing that happens is that now it becomes clear whence this "call", this obligation, this responsibility comes. What we have described up to now in these words is really the claim of God the Creator, who, as the Creator, declares that we belong to Him. It is thus indeed correct to speak of responsibility; it is indeed much more correct than we of ourselves knew. "Responsibility" must be understood literally. Only then is it really understood: as being called to responsibility, as having to give an answer, or having to give account to Him who alone has the right to call us thus to account, to "the Lord" who created us. When we come "before Him" and this happens in faith, this responsibility in its negative form becomes much clearer to us, not merely as "radical evil", not merely as obligation that we have failed to meet, as guilt, but as sin, for so it is called when we stand before God. But this realization annihilates us. For sin means lostness, severance from the salvation of God. Faith entirely confirms what man's own knowledge tells him of guilt and evil. But it underlines this negative, it radicalizes this judgment, it leads it to the end, to the bitter end. To stand before God now means to stand before the Crucified, of whom we know that though innocent and not a criminal He died a criminal's death. Thus He died, not for Himself, but for me. This I learn from the Cross, and affirm it in faith, because my own conscience must assent to it.

But now—as we saw—a second thing happens in faith, which I of myself am utterly unable to learn: this same Christ, the crucified, has risen from the dead. This is now *said* to me, communicated, and at the same time I am told: this resurrection also is for your sake and as through it He was revealed as the Son of God, so will you also be revealed as the son of God. This is now said to me, or promised in the sense of: "This is what you *are*, really and truly". This is the word of justification through which alone faith in the full sense comes into being as the acceptance of this communication. In this acceptance it consists, it *is* this acceptance.

Is faith then knowledge or is it not? Calvin says boldly "faith consists in knowledge, not in ignorance" (*in cognitione non in ignoratione fides constat*) and Karl Barth, agreeing with him, says even more downrightly "Faith is the knowledge which corresponds to its object". We have made a long detour up to this point in order to make clear to ourselves what kind of knowledge faith cannot in any case be. It is poles apart from what is usually meant by objective knowledge. For it comes into being not by the exclusion, as far as possible, of the subject, but on the contrary only when the subject is totally engaged, fully present, and committed—as indeed it is not an object that he knows, but the Absolute Subject. Further, it is not knowledge of the same kind as understanding. It comes into existence only at the boundaries of understanding, where we indeed know ourselves to be responsible, but do not understand whence the call comes that makes us responsible. And yet it is a self-understanding, namely the self-understanding which results from God's self-impartation. This takes place where the same God who declares that I belong to Him and that I am guilty, at the same time forgives my sin and guilt and promises me sonship.

This "knowledge" is also of a singular kind in this respect, that it can be won only through the self-knowledge that I am a sinner, and that in contrast with other knowledge it is not of a general character but is "strictly personal communication", that it can only be heard and expressed in the form of an I-Thou communication. It is thus much more like the acceptance of a communication than an act of knowing, for in it Another communicates to me the mystery that only He knows—namely that He loves me—while we, when we speak of knowing, do not think of this word as having any relation to love. What we call knowledge and what we understand by fellowship or love lie on two quite different planes. But faith has to do with just this communication and faith is nothing but the trustful acceptance of this communication in wonder and gratitude.

On the other hand it is knowledge of the historical kind. For I must come to a quite definite place in history to be able to hear this communication. But in the moment that I hear this communication, this historical point is transformed into pure, most immediate presence, and this Thou is transformed into an "I". "I am thine and thou art mine." When I "believe" it, that is, when in trust I let God say to me "Thou art mine", I know: "Now I am His." Now God says His word "Thou" in me. This exchange, this communication in the most personal sense, is faith.

V

To the question: "Is faith knowledge?" our first answer would have to be "No: it is not the same thing as everything else that we mean by knowledge". It arises only where all knowledge is at an end, both objective knowledge, "explanation", and also the subjective knowledge that we call understanding. It arises only where there are no more "objects" of any kind, but also where the process of understanding—of understanding the Thou or understanding ourselves—has come to its unsurmountable boundary. But there, just at this boundary—in the knowledge of guilt which I cannot understand, and which is now deepened into the knowledge of sin—we come to a new understanding of ourselves, but to an understanding which we do not achieve by our *own* resources, as one says a ship is travelling under its own power; to an understanding "under the power of another", to a self-understanding which has greater similarity to the act of being summoned and receiving a gift than to the act of knowing an object.

Our knowing is always a taking of something in possession for ourselves, an inclusion of something in our property. But faith, as we saw above all from the prophets' utterances about themselves, is a being apprehended, a being overpowered, a being challenged or elected. Subject and object of knowledge here actually change places. The believer is the one who is known, and God is the knower. This being "known of God" is in Biblical usage always the same as being loved. To be known or to be loved by God—this is indeed what is given to us in Jesus Christ. It is the love of God which communicates itself as that which God is. Therefore it is not knowledge at a distance, *theoria*,[1] but a call and a bestowal, through which we ourselves are transformed. The truth that is meant here is thus not truth of the kind that one *has*, but of the kind that one is—or better, *in* which one *is*. To be in the truth—that is the manner in which truth and therefore also knowledge is spoken of in the Bible. This knowledge is not merely cognitive, but it transforms our existence.

And yet faith is knowledge, true self-knowledge, which comes

[1] *Theoria*, like *Idea*, means observation, and this presupposes that distance from the object which is characteristic of knowledge of nature

into existence only when what I already know about myself—that I am responsible, that I am guilty—is taken up into this knowledge, confirmed and radicalized by it. And only when that happens, when I recognize myself as the rebel hanging "there", do I see behind this crucified man the risen Son of God as the true reality. It is the "for me" of the Cross that causes the veil to fall and the Son of God to appear manifest. "We saw His glory".

Thus Calvin is right when he says in the first sentence of his *Institutes*: "Our wisdom, in so far as it ought to be deemed true and solid wisdom, consists almost entirely of two parts, the knowledge of God and of ourselves. But as these are connected together by many ties, it is not easy to determine which of the two precedes and gives birth to the other". It *is* thus right to say "Faith *is* Knowledge". This twofold answer to the question, its affirmation and denial, is expressed with wonderful simplicity in the words of Paul, in which he concentrates in small compass everything that we have said about the difference of faith and knowledge, and about the foundation of faith. "Knowledge" (in the usual sense) "puffeth up, but charity edifieth. And if any man think that he knoweth anything, he knoweth nothing yet as he ought to know. But if any man love God, the same is known of Him" (1 Cor. 8: 1–3).

One more point must be emphasized in closing, although it can be developed only in the context of eschatology. All the knowledge of faith is provisional, partial, not definitive. Just because true knowledge is that through which alone we ourselves become true, faith and its knowledge, through which alone true being is promised to us, is not yet final. For "it hath not yet appeared, what we shall be". Since the transformation at first lays hold of the invisible core of personality, the very self in the act of faith, and does not yet affect the man as a visible whole,[1] the knowledge of the truth in faith cannot yet be final. Here, too, Paul has said what is essential with final clarity. "For we know in part. . . . But when that which is perfect is come, then that which is in part shall be done away.... For now we see through a glass, darkly; but then face to face: now I know in part, but then shall I know even as also I am known. And now abideth faith, hope, charity, these three; but the greatest of these is charity" (1 Cor. 13: 9–13).

[1] See Ch. 19, on the New Birth, pp. 269 ff.

CHAPTER 18

THE CERTAINTY OF FAITH, AND DOUBT

I

THE certainty of faith has received its grandest expression in the words of Paul, "For I am persuaded, that neither death, nor life, nor angels, nor principalities, nor powers, nor things present, nor things to come, nor height, nor depth, nor any other creature, shall be able to separate us from the love of God, which is in Christ Jesus our Lord" (Rom. 8: 38, 39). Yet this certainty is of an entirely different kind from the rational certainty of objective knowing. The latter rests on the evidence of the principle of identity, which is the fundamental principle of logic, or on the certainty of sense-perception. It is the certainty which the autonomous solitary self possesses in itself, or in its encounter with the "It", the world of things. But the certainty of faith is that of the theonomous self, whose certainty is founded, like its own being, not upon itself, but upon God, which consequently "rests" in God.

Whence comes this rest, and what is it? It is comparable to the manner in which the pendulum comes to rest in the vertical position, a condition which is reached through the cessation of the swing from one point to the opposite point. The rest of the pendulum is the rest of non-eccentricity—and this is, speaking in a figure, the certainty of faith. When the self has found its true centre, its being, in God, it comes to rest. "Our hearts are restless until they find their rest in Thee, O Lord" (*cor nostrum inquietum donec requiescat in te, Domine*; Augustine). It is thus always a having come to rest, not a being at rest.

Because faith cannot be proved, and because its foundation is invisible, it is always exposed to the suspicion that it is baseless, and thus capricious or illusory. Proof has its justified place in the realm of objectivity, of natural knowledge. Here there is the certainty of perception, of that which is immediately given in perception, which receives further confirmation from the perception of others and through the repetition of experiment. Or there is the certainty of logical proof; that is, of what is in the last resort rationally derived from the principle of identity.[1] The more anything partakes of the character of impersonal

[1] This is an insight which we owe principally to the philosophy of Eberhard Grisebach

being, the character of an object, or of the formally logical, the more susceptible it is of proof. The most perfect examples of proof are to be found in the realm of pure quantity, in mathematics, in which this method was first developed. Proof by experiment never leads to absolute certainty, only to practically absolute certainty, which, however, is only the highest probability.

Faith, as we have seen, is poles apart from this objective knowledge. For it is pure knowledge of the subject, and indeed depends upon the self-communication of God, the Absolute Subject, to the human subject, posited as relative. It can therefore have nothing to do with rational certainty; neither with the certainty of sense-perception, nor with the derived certainty of what has been proved. Faith is "a confidence in things hoped for, a conviction about things which are not seen" (Heb. 11: 1). It is the certainty which arises in the encounter with the God who communicates Himself, and it is "based" on this encounter. Objective knowledge and its certainty, on the other hand, is the world of abstraction, the It-world, the world without God. When the self "encounters" this world and knows it, no real encounter takes place. For the knowing self is infinitely superior to its objects. It embraces them all. On the other hand, because it is the unencountered self, it is also the solitary self.

But the believer recognizes that this solitude of the self is the lostness which follows when the self has made this abstracting objectifying knowledge the criterion of all truth, has set itself up as master of the world, and withdrawn itself both from God's Lordship and its responsibility to its neighbour. But to the believer life in the self-bestowing love of God has been revealed as his true and divinely created life. And this love as it encounters him in Jesus Christ is at once the basis and the fulfilment of his responsibility. Believing in this God who encounters him in Jesus Christ, God's Act and Word, man knows his Creator and home, in whom he "rests" through faith. In Him he has rediscovered his centre and rests in Him as his truth, which is no longer solitude and lostness but the fulfilment of his responsible being as an existence in love, and at the same time the end of all solitude and lostness in fellowship with God. The believer knows that life without God is the rejection of the destiny for which we were created, a life abnormal, deformed, estranged from its true being and displaced from its centre.

Therefore faith rejects absolutely every demand for proof as a piece of arrogance on the part of autonomous man, as the demand that we should find a place for God's Lordship within that abstract impersonal world and subordinate that Lordship to it. Not only *can* faith not be proven, but it *must* not submit itself at all to this insolent demand of autonomous reason.[1] Even to wish to prove God is to fall away from faith, an act of unbelief. Faith is already in its right place and established as it ought to be, namely in the Word of God, in which it rests. Faith finds its foundation in Jesus Christ, in the self-communication of God which takes place in Him. It rests in the self-bestowing love of God which is the fulfilment of all responsibility.

Doubt, on the other hand, stems from vacillation, from oscillation between reliance upon God and the autonomy of reason and its demand for demonstration or proof. Only the believer can doubt, but he can do this only by forsaking his standpoint, his centre, which gives him rest. To doubt is to cast furtive glances at the contrary possibility. The doubter is in fact just such a man as the Epistle of James describes (James 1: 8); the two-minded man, the divided soul, the unstable man who vacillates from the one side to the other, the soul that does not *continue* in the Word of God.

This doubt must not be confused with Descartes' method of doubt, nor with scepticism. Descartes' method of doubt consists simply of the rational method of obtaining certainty which is entirely legitimate in science. But scepticism is always the end result of the rational process of knowledge, namely the insight that this certainty is in the last resort not certainty, and that at the end of this way there stands the conclusion "I know nothing for certain" since neither logic nor perception leads to final certainty. The desire to prove everything ends in the inability to prove anything. The sceptic doubts not merely God and the moral law, but also science and reason itself. But that is not our present subject. The doubter, on the other hand, is the man who has become uncertain in his faith. He has become uncertain through not remaining in the encounter with God, through being at one and the same time a believer and a doubter. He is correctly described in German as a *Zwei-fler*.[2]

II

But we cannot honourably avoid the question whether there is any faith at all that is not tempted and disquieted by doubt. We have indeed already answered this question by saying that faith is not a position secured once for all, an assured possession. The certainty of faith is not a condition of rest but is continually renewed in the encounter with the living Lord, in

[1] Note Kierkegaard: *Philosophical Fragments*, Oxford, 1936, p. 31

[2] Kluge, *op. cit.*, p. 512. (Here there is an untranslatable pun in the German between *Zweifeln*, to doubt, and *Zwei*, two.) (Tr.)

hearing the Word of God, and in laying hold of the divine sonship offered to us, in the trusting obedience of faith. Faith has ever and again to fight with temptation, and is therefore fundamentally something that is coming to be. "Faith is not a being, but a becoming" (*non in esse sed in fieri fides constat*; Luther). "Not as though I had already attained, either were already perfect, but I follow after, if that I may apprehend that for which also I am apprehended of Christ Jesus" (Phil. 3: 12).

On the other hand, the saying so much quoted recently, "Lord, I believe; help thou mine unbelief" (Mark 9: 24), is not the expression of faith. No Apostle speaks thus of faith. These words are rather an expression of the beginning of faith, of faith extricating itself from unbelief. We shall not understand this rightly until we have learnt the cause of unbelief, and the relapse from faith into unbelief. But the believer knows well that he must continually struggle in order to retain his faith. Faith is not a condition (*habitus*), not a virtue, but an act. We are continually returning from unbelief, from godlessness, to faith and can obtain the certainty of faith only through the act of abiding, through "dwelling in Him". Faith is "the actuality of response", the actuality of hearing and answering. Because the negative reverse side of faith, the knowledge of sin, is ever and again the presupposition of faith, faith is continually reborn through daily repentance. For coming to God is always at the same time a coming to ourselves, and this can happen only through *mortificatio*. That we should come to ourselves through coming to the Word of God is the paradox of the bestowal of freedom as a gift, of integrity, completeness and self-hood in the Word of God. But it is here that faith rests, this rest in the Word *is* faith, in contrast with vacillation between life in the Word and life apart from it.

In unbelief, however, we are cleft by the contradiction between our empirical being and what we ought to be. In unbelief, therefore, there is no possibility of attaining wholeness, of integration. This is achieved only through faith that lays hold of the life in the centre which God offers, a life in His Word. That we should ever and again return from unbelief and let ourselves be ingrafted in the Word—this act of seeking refuge is faith, it is the continual renewal of the health, completeness and integration of man, in nearness to God through life in the Word by which He calls us to His side. For this reason faith must continually be won afresh in the struggle with unbelief. It exists only as the fight of faith, as a continual transition from unbelief, from the desire to rest in oneself, to life in the presence of God. To the question: "Is there certainty of faith?" the correct answer is: "No, *there is* not certainty; *He gives* it" (Karl Barth). It is not an object that we discover, but the act of apprehending and letting ourselves be apprehended. It is a *passio*—something that is done to us—a being called, and an *actio*, our answer, our act of apprehension.

III

But what is the cause of that declension, which constitutes doubt? The cause of this doubting is not only man's desire for autonomy, but rather experience of the world which contradicts the message of the love of God. Men doubt, because it is not the love and righteousness of God that rule in the world, but on the contrary lovelessness, cold unscrupulous cruelty, injustice. This it is which causes doubt to arise in them about the truth of the Word of God, of God's righteousness and His love, and so undermines their faith and makes it falter. For how can all this be compatible with the word, "God is love"?

We may not lightly pass over this question. On the contrary, the believer accepts it. He confesses that this is always his own question too. So long as we live in this earthly and bodily world, faith has always the character of "nevertheless I believe". There is no other faith than this. But how can we "nevertheless believe"? Is faith perhaps a blind faith, the faith of a child, who does not yet know the reality, does not see it as it really is? It is indeed right to say that faith rests solely and wholly in God's Word, in which God speaks in love to man as the Lord, but this is not everything that is to be said. We must note on the authority of the New Testament message of faith itself, how and where God speaks to us as the loving Lord.

For the Word in which God speaks to us decisively and encounters us in love, the Word in which He speaks to us sinners as His children, the Word of justifying faith, is spoken in the Cross of Jesus Christ. But this Act and Word of God stands in relation not only to our guilt but also to our experience of the world, to what we suffer in it and from it. The senseless cruelty which encounters us in the world is neither ignored nor denied nor treated as harmless by this Word, but is taken in most deadly earnest, is indeed affirmed by the sacrifice of a life. Only thus could God's deed and Word, the verdict of justification, be uttered; through Jesus Christ taking on Himself in suffering these things, so appallingly contrary to the will of God, which we experience in the world: death, and this world's thoughtlessness and cruelty. Thus He affirmed their reality and made manifest their enmity to God and to love. Through this dreadful thing that God allows to work out its fury against His Son, He has revealed to us His love and glory as our true being, namely as the divine Sonship of the Crucified. The superficial aspect of reality is not the true reality, not the reality as God created it, but it is only the veil, the covering which conceals the reality from our sight but in such a fashion that the love and the "righteousness of God" is in spite of all made manifest as the true reality. The Resurrection of Jesus from the dead is God's answer to that question which is most fiercely insistent in the Cross of Jesus.

There is nothing more realistic than the message of the Cross; realistic in the first place in its relation to "me", the sinner, the rebel against God, but realistic also in relation to the history of mankind, which is brought with me to the bar of this revealing judgment, and realistic finally in relation to the world and its horrifying aspects and its suffering. Thus, in order to believe in Christ, we must not look past the terrible reality but look directly at it. To believe in Christ means thus to penetrate with God Himself through this terrible reality and, in spite of all, to trust in the love of God. All talk of the love of God which does not rest upon the Crucified can from this vantage point be recognized as sentimentality. "Nevertheless" is certainly the word of faith, but it is neither the faith of naïvety, which does not know the reality, nor the obstinate faith of the fanatic, who refuses to see it. It is the realistic "nevertheless" of the man who recognizes in this most frightful event of world history—an event in which the Son of God, who teaches nothing but the reign of love and embodies it in His Person, is murdered with senseless cruelty as a blasphemer against God by the religious leaders of His people and the judicial authorities of the supreme world power—the love of God, the Lord of the world and His victory over the powers of darkness and of death (Col. 2: 14, 15).

Thus his "nevertheless" is rooted, not in an illusion which disregards the character of this world's realities, but in a recognition of all its devilish wickedness. But it is founded upon the Creator's Word of love. This is most clearly to be heard in the Cross itself, because in the Resurrection of Jesus God has made the true reality, the divine Sonship of the Crucified, shine forth and penetrate the darkness, and has done so in such a fashion that He condemns sin through the Cross, but justifies the sinner and calls him to his eternal life as a son of God. In Jesus Christ the Crucified the wickedness of the world is more clearly visible than in any other event of world history, but in Him there is even more clearly visible the love of God as the origin and goal of the world, as my origin and my eternal goal. To see these matters in this light is to believe in Jesus Christ.

Doubt, on the other hand, is a "faith" which does not keep true to this insight, but allows itself ever and again to be so impressed by experience of the world that it is led astray from Christ. Who does not know this temptation? Who does not find it understandable, all too understandable? The unbelief into which the doubter falls back is indeed the condition of the "natural man", from which he emerges only through the divine summons, and therefore it is the condition into which he is apt to sink back. The unbelieving way of life in the world is what is regarded by unbelief as self-evident and certain, while faith seems to it something unnatural, like the attempt of the earth-bound to fly. Therefore relapse into unbelief lies very close to faith. Therefore faith is a continual struggle, like a man's keeping himself awake when he is continually tempted to fall asleep, and this struggle consists wholly and solely in awakening and entering into the light of the truth in Christ. Faith is holding fast to the Word, watching and praying in the temptation to give up the struggle and become earthbound. To live in this struggle is what Paul calls "walking in the Spirit" and what is described in John as "dwelling in Him".

And yet faith does not say "Lord, I believe, help Thou mine unbelief", but "Thanks be to God who giveth us the victory through our Lord Jesus Christ" (1 Cor. 15: 57). The doubt which arises from our negative experience in the world can be truly overcome only by *that* faith which at the same time bears within it the hope of seeing the final victory. For without this it would not have the power to bear the strain of this "nevertheless". Faith in the Crucified is always at the same time the hope of the world of the Resurrection.

Faith knows no other theodicy than the Eschatological Hope. For it breaks through the veil we spoke of, and shows that it is not the true reality. But faith as hope is the knowledge of that manifestation of glory which alone removes the cause of declension from faith, the cause of doubt, and makes manifest the love of God as the true reality in the face of all doubt. The faith which contains in itself this hope, which indeed is almost identical with it,[1] is the faith which has passed through death unto life and the certainty of the eternal goal which is promised to faith.

[1] See below, Ch. 1 of Part Four, pp. 339 ff.

CHAPTER 19

REGENERATION AS A SPECIAL ASPECT OF JUSTIFICATION

I

UP to this point, following Paul, we have spoken of faith in Christ under the figure of justification, an expression taken from the field of jurisprudence. In addition to this, however, the New Testament uses another figure for exactly the same thing: regeneration. We must therefore treat of this, not as an independent theme, but only as a second aspect and a second linguistic expression. For the meaning of this word, which is not used by Paul at all, and only seldom in other New Testament writings, is simply what we described by the words "justifying faith". And indeed the first, Pauline, expression is the more appropriate, because it makes clear that it is the I-Thou Word of God by which the new person is created. But we have reason, in spite of this, to deal with the new birth; above all, because this concept has played a disastrous part in the history of theology and the Church, in that the figure was not understood as a figure but in the sense of a natural process. In this way the I-Thou happening, the Word of God, which is received through faith, became something like a natural process, detached from the Word and faith.

Because in the New Testament the expression "regeneration" means the same fact, the creation of the person through God's historical self-communication, it stands in strict relation to the historical fact in Jesus Christ. But if the figure of birth or begetting is understood in the sense of a natural process—and this danger lies near at hand—then both the historical character of God's self-communication in Jesus Christ and faith are lost. The thing that it emphasizes (if rightly understood) in a specially impressive way is the *totality* of the new creation of the person. This cannot indeed be more trenchantly expressed than by the figure of birth or begetting. One other thing could be said in favour of this expression as over against that of justifying faith, namely that it gives stronger expression to the character of the new being of the person as *life*. Jesus Christ is not only "the Word" but also "the Life", and conjunction with Him is not merely a self-understanding, but life in His love.

Further, this figure brings out more clearly than the figure of justification the efficacy of the creative Spirit of God. The Spirit of God does not merely speak, He also creates, creates what is new, creates life, yet not in disregard of Word and faith, but through them both.

The danger of the naturalistic misunderstanding has become actual in the Roman Catholic doctrine of Baptism, which conceives the Sacrament of Baptism in an objectivist sense, as if the Holy Spirit or grace were "infused" into the baptized person through the act of Baptism. This falsely literal conception of regeneration is, however, by no means confined to Roman Catholic doctrine. There is, for example, nothing essentially different from this in the way that the Lutheran Harless expresses himself: "The man, however, who has received the Holy Spirit (through Infant Baptism) already possesses life in God, and does not have to wait to receive it through faith."[1] So far can adherence to the Sacrament of Infant Baptism lead astray even an otherwise loyal champion of the teaching of Luther! But indeed similar words written even by Luther himself might be quoted. However the question may be answered whether in New Testament times there was Infant Baptism or not, one thing is established beyond all doubt: that the baptismal *doctrine* of the New Testament is orientated not to Infant Baptism but to Adult Baptism, and never separates baptismal grace from the faith that receives it.

Paul's baptismal teaching gives especial prominence to the personalistic moment, when it speaks of dying and being buried with Christ as the meaning of Baptism (Rom. 6). Only by dying with Christ can we receive the Word of new life, our adoption to sonship on the strength of God's Act and Word in the Cross of Jesus Christ. He came to bring the true life to men. They come short not only of the glory of God, of the true honour in the sight of God and the "splendour" that belongs to the life of God, but they also come short of life itself. For sin is not guilt alone, but also at the same time death[2]. Sin is disintegration, decay. The man who separates himself from God, separates himself at the same time from the

[1] Harless, *Christliche Ethik*, p. 230. It is gratifying that recently P. Althaus has spoken out very decisively against the "faith of infants" (*fides infantium*) (*Theologische Literaturzeitung*, 1959, pp. 866 ff.). But then there remains only the alternative of Harless, or we surrender the view of Infant Baptism as the sacrament of the bestowal of the grace of Christ. Althaus is right in his emphatic comment "Certainly: the Word of God is creative. But where God wills to deal with man, it has personal character, and performs a personal act" (p. 868)

[2] See below, Ch. 6 of Part Four, esp. pp. 381 ff.

source of life, and thus falls a victim to death. When, instead of having the Word of God as the centre of his existence, he makes himself the centre, his personality decays, disintegrates, he loses true life. "Ye, who were dead in trespasses and sins . . ." (Eph. 2: 1).

To the eyes of the world, this assertion appears a monstrous exaggeration. The men whom the Church calls "unregenerate sinners" *do* live, live intensely, are busy, active, and creative, have passionate emotions and display tremendous energy in the domination of nature and the creation of culture. What then is the sense of describing this mighty reality "man", the fighter and pioneer, who valiantly wins the struggle for existence within a world full of dangers and obstacles, as one who lacks life?—this man who, though thrown down a thousand times, continually rises again, who though overwhelmed by the reverses of fortune as by an avalanche, continually works his way out, asserts himself and goes his way, who in genuine creative power brings forth amazing works of art and scientific and technical achievements? We must be aware of the monstrous character of the Biblical assertion in view of this manifest fact, in order rightly to estimate the boldness of the assertion "dead". What are the grounds of this Biblical judgment?

II

We shall begin with a comparison taken from a field familiar to everyone. We know that there are men going about who look the picture of health, are full of vitality, but the doctor knows that they carry the seeds of death within them. Death has secretly devoured the root of their vital powers. This is the parallel of that word "dead" which in the New Testament precedes the word of regeneration. God, the Lord of life, who sees our inner hearts, says of all of us what the doctor thinks of those candidates for death: "sick unto death". What is this mortal disease?

This question is the theme of one of the profoundest books of Sören Kierkegaard, *The Sickness unto Death.* With inexorable psychological insight he analyses in this book the nature of the sickness unto death in the multiplicity of its manifestations. Fundamentally, however, it is always the same: despair. The phenomenon of despair is familiar to us, but as an exceptional condition. Kierkegaard, however, shows that the apparent exception is the actual condition of all men, even of those who in appearance directly belie it. To be a sinner and to despair are one and the same thing, for the sinner is the man who is living in revolt against himself and in revolt against God.[1] But the man who lives in revolt against himself does not really live as a self. His self has disintegrated, is in process of decay. The man is "sick unto death".

But man cannot himself extricate himself from this revolt. For everything that he undertakes is infected with it. Only the Creator can overcome the revolt. He does it in the fact of reconciliation in Christ, when he cancels the revolt through His assurance which is accepted in faith. The self is restored to soundness through justification by faith. The revolt is removed by the forgiveness of sin, and man's original, integrated, undivided self is bestowed upon him once more, when he is declared to be the child of God, the son of God, and this declaration becomes an inner reality as a result of the identification of the self with the self of Christ. "I live, yet not I, but Christ liveth in me" (Gal. 2: 20). This happens through the witness in us of the Holy Spirit. "The Spirit itself beareth witness with our spirit, that we are the children (sons) of God" (Rom. 8: 16). We have now a share in the true, eternal life and are integrated in God, the foundation of our lives. Thereby "we have passed from death unto life" (1 John 3: 14)

But if we only look deep enough, it is not only in the case of the individual but in that of humanity that experience confirms the verdict of the New Testament. True, man has magnificent achievements to his credit. But nearly every one of his inventions is used by him as an instrument of war and slaughter. His empire building, in which is manifested his urge towards an ever more widely embracing unity of mankind, is at the same time an unremitting sequence of war, enslavement, exploitation and the desecration of man. What makes man great at the same time makes him dangerous to his fellow creatures. Not only the history of States but also the history of culture shows this picture which Jakob Burckhardt has drawn of Greek culture. Whatever man undertakes turns out inevitably to be a source of death as well as of life to him.

But reconciliation is healing, reintegration of the disintegrated. For when God reconciles us with Himself, He removes the rift that separates our being from His being, our life from His life. When through forgiveness of guilt that contradiction we spoke of, sin, which is enmity against God, is removed, the contradiction in man is also removed and thereby the unity of the person is restored, whose inner discord is the "sickness unto

[1] This is the chief theme of my book on the doctrine of man, as appears even from its title *Der Mensch im Widerspruch* ('Man in Revolt')

death". The reconciliation is faith's anticipatory grasp of redemption, which we await as the completed realization of the divine Will for our salvation. For this reason the hope of that coming event is so bound up with regeneration that an Apostle was able to say "Blessed be the God and Father of our Lord Jesus Christ, who according to His abundant mercy hath begotten us again unto a lively hope through the Resurrection of Jesus Christ from the dead" (1 Peter 1: 3). For only that life which is fulfilled in the coming of the glory of the Lord is a truly integrated life, and therefore also is a life in God set free from death; only this is life eternal.

III

But how is rebirth related to the fact that even the believer, the justified man, is a sinner? Faith is that event through which sinful man, in spite of his sin, is declared righteous, that event in which he receives the new personal being. Therefore this new being is at first limited to the fact of faith. In faith man possesses the new being. This statement must be qualified on both sides, namely against the misunderstanding that man can only believe in the new being and does not really possess it, and against the misunderstanding that with this new being the empirical being of man has also already become sinless. The one view is a misunderstanding of the teaching of Luther, who always emphasizes that the new man is *outside* of us, in Christ, and that we have a share in his being only through faith. But Luther would never wish to deny that the new man is our new reality, and that consequently rebirth or justification is a *creative* act of God. But admittedly he emphasizes at the same time that this new being does not come into evidence as such, that empirically we are still sinners, and that it only becomes empirically visible in the strenuous battle for sanctification.[1] On the other hand, the doctrine of perfectionism is to be rejected, which says that the new man is already an empirical datum, consequently that man actually becomes sinless through faith. This perfection is just as false as the pessimism which denies the renewal of the person outright.

Here we are shown once again how necessary it is strictly to distinguish personal being from all empirical being, from all being in the world. The person is a reality, but—to speak with Luther—it is only the "little point" in us which has the splendour of eternity. And yet this little point is nothing less than our new personal being. Regeneration consists in this, that in this

[1] See below, Ch. 21, pp. 290 ff.

invisible core of personality the great, eternally decisive change takes place, that "Christ is formed in us" through the death of the old man and the creation of the new, and that from this origin something new, even if only relatively new, comes into visible existence also.

But this integration which ends the disintegration does not happen without at the same time necessarily taking the form, not merely of an integration of the person, but of an integration into the fellowship, or an integration of fellowship. Through the Word of Christ which is proclaimed to him—in whatever way this may happen—the solitary man, who is most profoundly isolated by sin from his fellow man, is incorporated into the fellowship of faith of the Ekklesia and thus becomes a member of the new humanity. This also happens in a corresponding personal event, in a two-sided act. In the New Testament this act is Baptism, and just for this reason it is so intimately bound up in the New Testament witness with rebirth. In early Christian times, when a man was apprehended by the witness to Christ, when Christ apprehended him and made him turn towards Himself in faith, he became a member of the Ekklesia through Baptism, through the double act of entry and incorporation. The act of submitting to Baptism and causing oneself to be baptized, of being submerged and of submerging oneself, is the appropriate symbol of admission to the Ekklesia, since in fact it occurs through the death, the annihilation and the repentance of the old man. Through Baptism the spiritual and *personal* event becomes at the same time a spiritual and *social* event.

But when the Ekklesia developed into the Church, and when this symbolic two-sided occurrence of reception and confession developed into the *Sacrament* of Baptism, the spiritual and the social elements were torn asunder in such a manner that we can hardly recognize in them the original intention. The Ekklesia which had grown into the institutional Church was quite unable to make clear in its Sacrament of Baptism this connection between spiritual personal event and social incorporation. An institution is certainly not a fellowship and a magical rite is certainly not a personal event. What Church Baptism, however, was intended to express—though its means of doing so were entirely inadequate—was this: that the new creation of the person is at the same time creation and incorporation into the true fellowship, the Ekklesia. For sin as personal self-isolation from God is at the same time self-isolation from one's fellow man. When through faith in Christ sin is removed, and man's heart is opened to God, it is opened also to his fellow man; life for oneself is replaced by life for one another, by the will to fellowship and the capacity for it. Thus regeneration means two things: that we become our real selves, and that we become capable of real fellowship. The faith through which we are born again includes the knowledge that the creation of a true self is identical with the creation of a true capacity for fellowship.

CHAPTER 20

CONVERSION[1]

THROUGHOUT the whole of the Old Testament there is maintained a continuous and clear correlation between divine revelation and human responsibility, God's faithfulness and human trust, God's claim and human obedience. This correlation finds its most pointed expression in what we have described as the "divine conditional".[2]

"*If* thou wilt hearken to the law of the Lord thy God . . . and walk in His ways . . . *then* thou shalt live . . . and the Lord thy God shall bless thee. . . . But *if* thine heart turn away so that thou wilt not hear . . . *then* I denounce unto you this day that ye shall surely perish. . . ." (Deut. 30: 16 ff.). This holds good not only of the Mosaic Law but also of the great prophets.

[1] The problem of conversion should first be seen as a linguistic one. The central concept of the prophetic teaching of the Old Testament is the concept of conversion (*shub*) in the sense of turning away from one's previous ways and turning to God. The New Testament has two words for what is meant by "conversion"—*epistrephein* (a turning to Christ) and *metanoia* (repentance, conversion). The theology of the Reformers equates *conversio* (the equivalent of *shub*) with repentance. But even in the theology of the Reformation itself "repentance" can hardly be understood as an equivalent of what the Old and New Testaments mean by conversion, since it is mostly used merely in the negative sense of "acknowledgment of sin" and thus hardly includes in itself the active moment in faith, namely the "laying hold of Christ" or "putting on the new man"

This linguistic fact brings a historical fact into evidence. Conversion to Christ is not a real possibility within the Constantinian Church situation, since there everyone is a baptized Christian. This is the reason why conversion is hardly mentioned there. This at once becomes clear when comparison is made with the situation in the Free Churches of America. Here the concept of conversion is central, because the man who turns to the Church turns thereby at the same time to Christ. It is thus not only a theology different from that of the Reformers, but the historical reality, which has here kept the concept of conversion true to its Biblical sense. What I have written later in this book about the double aspect of the Epistle to the Romans as a missionary document and as an exposition of apostolic theology must be seen against this background of the different Church situations. The more the situation in Europe also is seen to be a missionary situation, the more will theology be forced to take the Biblical concept of conversion seriously. In his otherwise attractive and well-balanced book *Die Bekehrung in reformatorischer und pietistischer Sicht* (The Reformers' and the Pietists' Views on Conversion), Althaus seems to have done less than justice at this point, because as a typical Lutheran he presupposes Infant Baptism as the normal beginning of life in the Church while the "pietists" (who, like Wesley, Finney, Spurgeon, Moody, etc., are also the great evangelists of modern times) take as their starting point the new situation, that the attachment of the great masses of the population to the Church *is only fictional*

[2] See *Dogmatics* I, Ch. 22, "The Eternal Divine Decrees and the Doctrine of Election"

"*If* ye seek me, *then* ye shall find me, when ye shall search for me with all your heart, *then* I will be found of you" (Jer. 29: 13). This same "divine conditional" is evident also in the great word of Isaiah, "*If* ye will not believe, surely ye shall not be established" (Isaiah 7: 9).

Now this correspondence of God's gracious will and man's trustful obedience seems to be abandoned in the Pauline and Johannine proclamation of the reconciliation in Jesus Christ, of unconditional grace, of *sola fide*. Is it perhaps the case that Martin Buber's[1] thesis is right?—that in the apostolic preaching faith is spoken of in a manner which denies this "divine conditional", this personal correspondence, because another "mode of faith" is posited instead of faith understood as a dialogue, a mode of faith in which the human subject is allotted only the function of assent to a "theology" as true, and thus is eliminated as a responsive subject?

When we think of the Church's Catholic sacramental doctrine or of the orthodox Protestant doctrine of the Bible, or of the fact that in the orthodox Confession it is in fact asserted in plain words that in the reception of grace the human factor plays only the part of a block or a stone (*truncus et lapis*), this elimination of the human subject certainly does mean the destruction of continuity with the Old Testament concept of faith. New Testament faith then seems in fact to be "another mode of faith" while nothing is left of the dialogue character of personal correspondence of which we have spoken. This is chiefly evident, one might continue, in the fact that in the Reformation Churches there is no longer mention of conversion, of change of heart, but only of the repentance which results from the bestowal of grace. The central word of the prophetic preaching, "*shub*" ("return!") would thus have been eliminated not only from the language of faith but also from its doctrine, in favour of a divine monergism, in which nothing of the dialogue-character of our relation to God is left. Once more we have to face this serious question of the great Jewish philosopher and interpreter of the Old Testament.

In fact, not only in modern pietism, but in the whole of scripture, conversion means the turning away of man from the previous way and life of his own choosing, and a turning to the will and way of God. But it is not only the Old Testament that speaks of this act of turning away and turning towards, but also the New Testament—and indeed not only the Jesus of the synoptic narratives, but also the apostolic witness to Christ.

[1] See above, Excursus, pp. 159 ff.

I

Let us at first confine ourselves to the Old Testament. The word *shub*—in the Greek translation *metanoia*—is not only something moral and negative, the turning away from a godless course of action which contradicts the divine law. Neither is it a mere "change of mind", a translation which is very popular today and yet for all that entirely inadequate. What is meant is rather the total act of the person which turns away from everything of its own in the past and turns to God. Conversion means thus in fact the personal corresponding event of which we have spoken. At the culminating point of the Old Testament this divine conditional takes a form which brings it very near to the Pauline doctrine of justification: "If thou wilt return, O Israel, saith the Lord, thou mayest return unto me" (Jer. 4: 1). "Only acknowledge thine iniquity, that thou hast transgressed against the Lord thy God" (Jer. 3: 13). In connection with this prophetic knowledge the insight also breaks through "For in thy sight shall no man living be justified" (Psalm 143: 2). Above all, at that point where Israel has reached the nadir of its national existence, where its people "sat down by the waters of Babylon and wept" (Psalm 137) in the Babylonian exile, the holiness and sovereignty of God are most powerfully proclaimed, and at the same time the mysterious word is spoken of the Servant of God, who is the Suffering Servant, the "man of sorrows" who "hath borne our griefs", "was stricken for the transgression of my people" and "made his life a sacrifice for sin", who "bore the sin of many and made intercession for the transgressors" (Isaiah 53). The prophet who spoke this word that can hardly be understood[1] within the context of the Old Testament was the same man who, exactly like his prophetic predecessors, challenges Israel to repentance and says "Look ye to me and be ye saved" (Isaiah 45: 22). Only here the call to repentance has a new meaning: "Return unto me, for I have redeemed thee" (Isaiah 44: 22).

Here we stand on the threshold of the New Testament proclamation, not only in virtue of this call to a change of heart which so remarkably foreshadows the grace of Christ, but also because of the fact that here it is no longer Israel alone that is summoned, but "the races of the earth, whom I called from the beginning" (Isaiah 41: 4). We ask, is this not the same call with which Jesus began his work, "Repent, for the Kingdom of Heaven is at hand" (Matt. 4: 17), the same with which Peter cried out on the day of Pentecost to the crowd of spectators

[1] See above, p. 3, n. 1. Introduction to *Dogmatics* III

in Jerusalem, "Repent, and be baptized every one of you in the name of Jesus Christ for the remission of sins" (Acts 2: 38), the same call with which Paul as an "ambassador for Christ" summons us, "Be ye reconciled to God. For He hath made Him to be sin for us, who knew no sin, that we might be made the righteousness of God in Him" (2 Cor. 5: 20, 21)?

Admittedly this call has changed decisively from the prophetic call: what the prophet only promises in the enigmatic word about the Servant of God—the New Covenant, the Covenant of forgiveness (Jer. 31: 31 ff.)—is now fulfilled. This Covenant *has* been concluded because the Servant of God has appeared who "bare the sin of many". And just for this reason the call to change of heart is now "Be ye reconciled with God". And just because through the coming of this one Servant, Christ the Lord, the situation is changed, the manifestation of this new situation is also the central point in the call to repentance. This is what Paul means by his "But now . . ." and by the "righteousness of God" revealed in Christ (Rom. 3: 21 ff.). The question which is put to us by the Old Testament can only be "Has the challenge 'Be ye reconciled with God' a meaning that somehow has taken up unto itself the meaning of the word 'Return'?"

This question is to be answered with a clear affirmative. It has in fact assimilated the meaning of the word *shub*. For what are we challenged to do when faith is required of us in Him "who knew no sin and was made sin for us, that we might become the righteousness of God in Him"? The faith to which we are there summoned is certainly not simply a "belief that"—it is an existential happening, it is, in fact, precisely what Jeremiah means by "Acknowledge thine iniquity, that thou hast transgressed against the Lord thy God." He, the man who is summoned, is the man for whose sake the Servant of God was "pierced", whose guilt has stricken, "smitten", that Servant of God. This conversion (*Umkehr*) thus means nothing else than "I am crucified with Christ" (Gal. 2: 20). In this identification with the Crucified, man accepts the condemnation, he gives himself over to death, he knows himself as the one who is punished on the Cross. This act of *mortificatio*, of "repentance" is indeed no achievement, but it is an act of the self which must be present as partner in the "exchange" (Luther) in which we give Christ our sin and receive from Him His righteousness, the sonship of God, as a gift bestowed upon us.

Post-Reformation theology indeed denied this presence of the human partner, in order to prevent any possibility of man having any share of merit or any reason for self-congratulation, boasting, and it believed that it was necessary to surrender the rôle of the human subject as itself present, and to reduce it to the pure passivity of an object. But in so doing it completely destroyed the Pauline conception. When Paul says "believe" this act of *mortificatio* is always thought of as an accompanying one, as he also unmistakably showed in his "Be ye reconciled. . . ." And this is an issue about which the Ekklesia could not be in any doubt since Peter's sermon at Pentecost.

The religious Israelite "repented" by "returning" to the Lord who had made known to him His Fatherhood in the Covenant of Sinai and had chosen him along with his people as a partner in the Covenant. The Christian, that is the man who lets himself be summoned by the message of Jesus Christ, must travel a longer journey "back". To use a picture, the whole "film" of his life history, understood at the same time as the history of humanity, is wound back until he arrives at the very beginning of all, at the Fall from God's Creation. The history of humanity is represented as the history of Adamitic man who has estranged himself from his origin. There is no one who might be able to quit the ranks here. "There is none righteous, no not one" (Rom. 3: 10) "for all have sinned and come short of the glory of God" (Rom. 3: 23).

This return to the beginning is necessary in order that I may realize what Christ has done for me, what I owe to God. But I can return to this beginning only because the Word of the beginning, which I had lost, has come again to me. So here the prophetic call "*shub*" is radicalized and at the same time universalized. I must not only repent, I must die with Him, be crucified as the rebel and blasphemer against God in order to hear His word of grace. "Thus thou mayest return to me", "Thou art my beloved son", "This is the price of the costly pearl, which is so great that one must sell everything to acquire it." But then I hear "The price is already paid. You could never have paid it, it is too great for you." Dying with Christ includes the insight that what I would have to achieve is utterly beyond my power to achieve. Repentance, conversion, now consists precisely in the knowledge "He died for me"—and this is already faith itself. This is what Luther means when he says that there is nothing harder to believe than the forgiveness of sins. For this includes in itself the surrender of pride in myself, pride in humanity, pride in the autonomy of reason. All this self-congratulation, this pride in ourselves, is annihilated.

II

But the Old Testament word *shub*, change of heart, means not only a forsaking of the old way but an entrance on the new way. How is it in the New Testament? This entrance on the new way has its complete parallel in the Apostles' witness of faith. "Repent" now means "Put on the new man", "Walk no more after the flesh, but after the Spirit". As the prophet has already said "We are here, we come to Thee, for Thou art the Lord our God", so the challenge now is "Trust Him, and go with Him, now, after Him!" Faith "in" Christ is genuine only when at the same time it includes discipleship with it. But in the first place we must understand the first thing—faith.

When it happens that man returns to his beginning, he finds there his true God-created being. But this can never happen through our own action; it happens when we let ourselves be told "He has done it for you." Therefore this origin in Creation, this election to the Covenant, to partnership with God, can be perceived only in faith. In identification with Christ crucified there is already implicit identification with Him as the living Son of God. "Likewise reckon ye also yourselves to be dead indeed unto sin—rebellion, autonomy—but alive unto God through Jesus Christ our Lord" (Rom. 6: 11). "Let not sin therefore reign in your mortal body, that ye should obey it in the lusts thereof" (Rom. 6: 12). "Put off the old man with his deeds, and put on the new man, which is renewed in knowledge after the image of Him that created him" (Col. 3: 9, 10). The meaning of this is not—as the new gnosis teaches—that it is enough in Christ to know the new man, but that the new man is created in us, through the knowledge of Christ. Regeneration is the new creature (*kainē ktisis*) through faith, and this faith in Christ demands our active participation.

Further, it is on the positive side also an action of man to which we are summoned. Both the end of the old way posited in Christ and the beginning of the new way of repentance posited in Him is always something which calls for total activity on our part. At any rate it is just as necessary to emphasize this active side as the passive side, regeneration, and the active side of one and the same faith is conversion, both in the negative sense of a turning away and in the positive sense of a turning-to. Here, however, as was said above, we are not dealing with a temporal sequence, an order of salvation (*ordo salutis*) which begins with one thing, let us say regeneration, and continues with another, let us say conversion or sanctification. We are dealing rather with the different aspects of this one happening.

Discipleship, obedience, is bound up with faith itself as obedience of faith (*hypakoē pisteōs*). "The *materia* of faith is the will" (Luther), not the intellect; the person, not merely its thinking, nor yet, as is emphasized one-sidedly in the idiom of today, merely its self-understanding. What is essential is that you yourself should become another man, and that cannot happen without your help. Fear of Catholic Pelagianism, of work-righteousness, must not lead us to betray personalism, that is, the outlook that always bears responsible personal being in mind. In faith in God's creative Word in Christ we are created as the new person, as the son of God.

Paul too lays express emphasis on self-transformation. "Be ye transformed by the renewing of your mind" (Rom. 12: 2). That is very far away from the "rôle of a block or a stone", *truncus et lapis*, of the Confessional writings. The creation of the new man, in faith in the new created Word of God in Christ, does not happen without our presence as responsible persons, without the act of "self-transformation". We ourselves have also something to do here, whether this is labelled synergism or not. Conversion is the active voluntaristic aspect of this one event. We have already seen[1] that in this we must come to the frontier of our own being where we ourselves are not the ones who know or understand. Only at this frontier does the new thing happen which on the one hand takes the form of hearing the Word of Christ, and, on the other hand, of *giving* oneself over to death, as *letting oneself* be reconciled, as "*putting* on the new man, the man created by God". It is disastrous when the one aspect of passivity and cognition is emphasized and the other, the aspect of will and action, is neglected. In the Word of God as claim and assurance both are included. Only in the apprehension of both movements, that of claim and that of assurance, is the Word of Christ completely apprehended.

Here we have a happening on which the outlook of the theologian differs from that of the evangelist. The task of the missionary is, above all, as "God's fellow-labourer" (1 Cor. 3: 9) to proclaim the Word of repentance, because only through heart-searching, through the *shub* of which we have spoken, through coming to his own frontiers does man become ready for the message of forgiving grace. Therefore in the New Testament as a missionary document the call is always "Repent and believe". But for the theologian, who sees the whole thing in retrospect, the order is reversed. For he knows that this *shub* radically understood can only reach its goal in the strength of

[1] See above, Ch. 17, p. 260

the assurance of Christ, in the twofold identification with the Crucified and Risen One. In Paul, in the Epistle to the Romans, we find both orders of sequence. For even his Epistle to the Romans is both missionary gospel and theological word, whose purpose is to make intelligible the missionary event in all its depth. Romans 1–3 follows the order "repentance and faith", Romans 3–7 follows the order "faith and repentance".

"Before" and "after" become irrelevant where we have to do with the centre, with the God who lays claim to us in Christ, and who gives His assurance to us in Him. There, however, not only do "before" and "after" become irrelevant, but something different also happens. When at that boundary where the Word of Christ can alone become actual, man falls silent, he finds, when he turns from his own to what is bestowed upon him, that here God alone speaks. The hearing of the message of divine sonship is the speaking of the Holy Spirit. Conversion happens—or ends; it comes to its real climax in the exultant hearing of what God promises me in Christ. "You are a child of God, only believe it!" Faith as conversion is at the same time the end of the old—the end of the man whose centre was in himself—and the beginning of the new, the beginning again of the new God-created man; the end of my autonomy and the acknowledgment of my Lord and Creator. After my own speaking has come to an end, now Christ speaks in me, as the Holy Spirit. The "for me" turns into the "in me". The doctrine of conversion culminates in the doctrine of the Holy Spirit, who now, instead of man, is the spokesman.

It is once again the same paradox as everywhere appears where faith is the theme: the new life is effected on the one hand only through the repentance of man, and on the other hand only through the act and speech or the speech and act of God. Both are true: we must repent, and it is God alone who creates the new life. The personal corresponding event is both preserved and transcended when the Holy Spirit makes what has happened through Christ the truth for me, and truth in a double sense; truth about God, and truth about myself. And when that happens God becomes present in me and I become present in God. Therefore here also the temporal moment of "before" and "after" is transcended. Before the event the call of the preacher is unambiguously imperative: "Repent, be ye reconciled, believe in the Lord Jesus" (Acts 2: 38; 2 Cor. 5: 20, Acts 16: 31) or "Accept the invitation to the feast and make no excuses!" (Luke 14: 16 ff.), or "Open the door to Him who knocks, and desires to come in unto thee and to sup with thee" (Rev. 3: 20). *After* the event the word is: "It is a pure gift, He alone has done it" (Rom. 5: 1). *In* the event, however, both elements are present in unity, "I am Thou, and thou art I."

It is remarkable when we start from the viewpoint of the Apostles' Creed, from Trinitarian dogma, that prayer is not made in the Ekklesia for the gift of the Holy Spirit, any more than "He is believed in."[1] The primary reason for this is doubtless that the primitive Christian Ekklesia was so filled with the Holy Spirit that the request for Him was not an urgent need. But the decisive reason is as follows. The reception of the Spirit depends on man's doing what he is commanded to do: "Repent, and ye shall receive the gift of the Holy Spirit". The Holy Spirit is given in the same manner that God calls man to repentance. Only through the imperative "Repent" do we come to the indicative of faith, of the new life "in the Spirit". For this reason faith itself is called the obedience of faith. Faith itself is answer to the Word that bestows the love of Christ. Even faith in the forgiving mercy of God stands under the imperative: "Believe!" But when this faith arises, then it recognizes itself as God's speaking in us. I am not free to believe or not to believe. I must not wait until faith is bestowed upon me. From this it is intelligible why when Luther was in temptation his only help was in the First Commandment, the imperative "Believe!" Faith itself, the event that the Holy Spirit, God Himself, speaks in me (Rom. 8: 16), this transcendence of the Subject-Object antithesis, this mystical event, which is yet nothing other than faith in Him who has given Himself up for us, and therein communicates Himself to us—this faith cannot come into being except through our being challenged, commanded to believe.

III

So paradoxical is this happening that all our thought-categories fail to express it. God does not give the gift of the Holy Spirit in any other way than through the repentant act of our will, an act in which I and Thou become one. Therefore the Holy Spirit is not believed in. He happens in faith. Prayer is not made for the Spirit, but He happens when men hear and obey. This is how Martin Buber's question is to be answered. The answer is to refer to the Holy Spirit of whom it is said in John

[1] See above, Ch. 15, p. 232. (The passage Luke 11: 13 does not contradict this, for there this request is spoken of before the outpouring of the Holy Spirit)

7: 39, "He was not yet given", but in whom the personal correspondence, the dialogical relation at the same time comes to its fulfilment and loses its character as dialogue. For precisely that is what is meant by "Christ in me" which in faith in "Christ for us" becomes the experience of the Spirit that speaks in me.

But the reception of grace must not be thought of, as orthodox Lutheran doctrine conceives of it, as an event in which man is present purely passively as an object handled, *truncus et lapis,* and not as a subject. Rather is it the act of identification with the Crucified in the knowledge of His identification with us sinners. This double identification is entirely misunderstood when it is conceived of as a mere "operation", as a kind of causal event, a natural happening. It is true that the Lucan account of Pentecost and the Johannine words of Christ about rebirth seem to suggest this. In both cases the gift of the Spirit is compared with a natural force, with "a sound from heaven as of a rushing mighty wind, and it filled all the house" (Acts 2: 2); or with the blowing of the wind whose sound you hear but cannot tell "whence it cometh and whither it goeth" (John 3: 8). But this analogy from nature is in both cases corrected by Luke's words "Repent and be baptized every one of you . . . and ye shall receive the gift of the Holy Ghost" (Acts 2: 38) and through the continuation of the words of Christ in John, which culminate in the supreme evangelical word about the love of God who "gave His only begotten Son that whosoever believeth in Him should not perish, but have everlasting life" (John 3: 16).

This is made clear beyond all doubt by the fact that life in freedom, the freedom of the children of God, is contained in the witness concerning the Spirit. Life in the Spirit is life in the power of Christ, life in Christ, and this itself is freedom. "And where the Spirit of the Lord is, there is liberty" (2 Cor. 3: 17). How is there freedom here? When man knows himself as one whose life depends upon the self-bestowing love of God, he becomes truly himself. Through faith his false off-centre self is brought back to its true centre and thereby "integrated" and becomes a self that understands itself. This is the culminating point to which the doctrine of conversion leads, the doctrine of man's repentance and his return to his origin which in truth does not lie in himself, to knowledge of the true freedom, which is at the same time the true freedom's bestowal.

As a new understanding of God and a new self-understanding

follows from faith, so also there follows a new understanding of freedom. For the "natural man", freedom is the same thing as independence. For faith, freedom is complete dependence on God. For the unbeliever, freedom is the primary thing, which is founded on nothing else and can be founded on nothing else. For faith, freedom is secondary, it is founded wholly on something else (on God). For this reason the thought which makes the self and its freedom its starting point must deny God, the Lord and Creator. For (so man argues) if there were a God, He and His creative power would be primary, and man, the created being, would be secondary, that is, not free. The atheist who makes this absolute concept of freedom his starting point, like, for example, J.-P. Sartre, must then for the same reason deny all moral obligation, and must thus become a nihilist. The thought of freedom as lack of restraint leads finally to nihilism. Conversely, if we make the thought of God our starting point, the understanding of freedom as lack of restraint is impossible. For freedom as the primary thing, freedom without qualification, absolute freedom, that is the nature of God. But the freedom of man is freedom *through* God, freedom *in* God, freedom in dependence on God. This freedom is identical with subordination and consequently with responsibility.

The denial of this dependence on God in the name of freedom, this protest of freedom against the divine constraint, is the very essence of what faith calls sin. Conversely, faith consists in the acknowledgment of this dependence on God Himself, and acknowledges that precisely this is its freedom, because it knows itself as a being founded on God. The arrogant assumption, the usurpation of absolute freedom is the original rebellion of the creature against its Creator. Its consequence is the disintegration of the creature, which by the very act of falling away from its origin, its centre, loses its true selfhood. Faith is therefore identical with return to our origin in Creation, to dependence on God and subordination to Him.

To the "natural man" who understands himself as his own master, depending only on himself and bound only by his own will, i.e. to the autonomous man, this concept of freedom is unintelligible. Here we come to the decision: I or Thou—either I am my own master or Thou art my master. This decision is faith. In faith man understands himself (once more) as God's creature; indeed, in faith he not only understands himself thus but he becomes thus, the son of God, begotten by the Word of God. Therein he lays hold of his "authenticity", which means that being which the Creator designed for him in love, that being for which he has been destined from eternity. But this happens in the act of turning away from himself and turning to God, an act that is possible for him only in the Act and Word of God, in the Cross and Resurrection of Jesus Christ the Son of God who is perfectly obedient to God and who bestows himself wholly and freely in love.

This does not entirely escape even the man who does not indeed believe, but yet admits his responsibility. But this responsibility is taken fully in earnest only when it recognizes itself as responsibility before God. And it is acknowledged and affirmed only when its negative reality, guilt, is fully acknowledged. It is through this acknowledgment that the double identification of which we spoke is realized, in faith in the Cross of Christ suffered for us and in identification with the Son of God through the Word of the Holy Spirit spoken in our hearts. When God speaks thus within us, God's self-communication is completed, for this indeed is its intention, a created being that wholly reflects God's glory and His love, that lives by His love and in it (2 Cor. 3: 18).

Thus in faith we have to do not merely with a new *understanding* of freedom, but with the realization of freedom. Anybody can assert this freedom and postulate it. But only the man who has been set free from self-centredness of sinful man can "live freedom", the man who possesses it not in his "ego" but in the "Thou" of God. All other freedom is, in fact, mere bondage. But the freedom of the sons of God is the only real freedom because it is freedom from self. Now indeed it is only in its beginnings, a seed which will "only then" appear fully when "that which is in part" shall be done away. We cannot "choose" this freedom, it chooses us; it is the bestowal of grace, which communicates itself to us in the Holy Spirit.

The freedom rooted in faith in God's promise is identical with life under God's Lordship and in God's love. Just because it is God's bestowal, it can be realized only in man's completely free act, when we lay hold of God's Word in Christ. The apprehension of Christ is the other side of being apprehended by Him. Just this unity of turning back and being turned back is the radicalization of what the Old Testament means by repentance. So closely are God's work and man's interwoven. It is the same happening which is the continuing theme of this whole book—the correspondence on the personal plane which is completed in God's self-communication and in the faith of man.

IV

But conversion must be understood in a much more comprehensive sense still. Discipleship, going after Jesus, following His way, belongs to conversion. But the way of Jesus is always the way to man, the way into the unfriendly world. He was the friend of tax-gatherers and sinners. To enter upon this way; that is what repentance (*metanoia*) means, the extraversion of introverted piety. Only seldom have Christians recognized this way as their way, through fear of the world. Their legalism has once again set limits to their freedom which they had received through Christ. The man who is really converted by Christ is the man turned towards the world. The end of conversion is the complete worldliness of the man who lives in Christ, the worldliness of the man whose security is in Christ. The world has as yet experienced little of this true freedom in Christ, since only seldom have Christians reached this last point, this breakaway from legalism. And yet it is clearly the way of Jesus, to which He challenges His disciples.

But it is not only this description of the goal which at first strikes us as startling, but this direction of attention to mankind in general which is new. True, when we think of the Old Testament we see that it is not completely new. For it is the Prophet of the Exile, the so-called Second Isaiah, who takes all the nations of the world into his ken. But he does so rather in the sense that all the peoples of the world are summoned by his call. But now every believer is interested in the world of the nations, he knows himself called to dedicate himself to the goal of the coming Kingdom. If conversion is really to be repentance (*metanoia*) as Jesus Christ understood it, it must prove its authenticity by taking the whole of humanity within its concern, as well as by converting men from introversion to extraversion.

We do not refer here merely to the missionary interest. A Christian without such an interest is a contradiction in terms. We refer also to active participation; enlistment in the band of those who wish to win the world for Christ is the consummation of the "change" in which conversion consists. This alone makes it clear to us how falsely negative and falsely individualistic is the traditional interpretation of the words "Repent and be converted." The Christ who calls us to be His disciples calls us to this way, which will probably always be a way of the Cross. "Zeal for thine house hath eaten me up" (Psalm 69: 9)—this is a word that must always be kept in mind when we think of repentance and conversion. How much more positive, how much more full of content and how much more worth while this conversion becomes, when behind this word that has grown so unattractive this great goal becomes visible: Repent, for the Kingdom of God is at hand, become men of the Kingdom of God, men with an interest in the world and in humanity! It is thus that we must understand the freedom of the Christian man, which is given to us when we turn to Christ. Only this great goal corresponds to the divine sonship which is bestowed upon us in justifying faith.

What then is conversion? It is just this turning in upon oneself, this turn right-about, this return to God. It is thus really the event of which the prophets were thinking, but whose utterly radical character they were not yet able to understand, because the decisive event had not yet happened. Man must really get out of himself, but this is precisely what he cannot himself do unless it happens in the reality outside of him, which is at the same time his reality and the reality of God. Only in this movement out of himself towards God does man find his true self, and with it his liberty, in unconditional dependence on the Power that created him.

CHAPTER 21

SANCTIFICATION

YET once again the work which Christ does through the Holy Spirit is seen under a new aspect. We have already represented it as justification, as regeneration, as conversion; now we shall represent it as the work of sanctification. The New Testament speaks of sanctification in a twofold sense: in the one sense as a work of God, and in the other as a task of man.

(1) SANCTIFICATION AS THE WORK OF GOD

Holiness is God's fundamental nature, what distinguishes God from everything that is not God. God is the Holy One, who has made Himself known to His people as such, and therefore can be called "The Holy One of Israel".[1] God's holiness is His will to be acknowledged as God alone.[2] God sanctifies that which in itself stands in conflict with this will, by taking it out of "the world" and setting it apart for Himself, drawing it into His realm and claiming it for Himself, making it serviceable to His aim and purpose.

In this sense, in the New Testament, "sanctification" can be used as the concept which embraces all God's action, in which also justification, regeneration and conversion are included. In this sense the members of the Ekklesia, the body of Christ, are called simply "the elect saints", where Paul uses the concept "sanctification" as equivalent for justification. "Ye are sanctified, ye are justified in the name of the Lord Jesus, and by the Spirit of our God" (1 Cor. 6: 11). When the Christ, "the Holy One of God" (Mark 1: 24, Acts 3: 14), has taken possession of a man, this man is a "saint". A saint in the New Testament sense is a man who is specially "marked" by the Cross of Christ. It is "the blood of Christ", that is, God's Deed and Word in the event of the Cross, which has the effect of "cleansing us from all sin" (1 John 1: 7). It is the Holy Spirit who sanctifies. He alone can effect sanctification. The whole of Christian existence

[1] Rudolf Otto, *Das Heilige*, 1917 (E.T. *The Idea of the Holy*) had important insights but the decisive Biblical message that God is the Holy One escaped him

[2] Cf. *Dogmatics* I, Ch. 13, "God, the Lord", and Ch. 14, "The Holy"

as such is the work of the Holy Spirit and, as such, is sanctification.

Beside this all-embracing concept of sanctification, however, the Bible has also a narrower one which is distinguished from justification, and this specific concept has passed over into the theology of the Reformation. Sanctification stands alongside of justification as a second thing, which is not identical with justification. And this is the specific difference, that sanctification, in contrast to justification, is not thought of as a unique event which as such brings into being the new creature, but refers to the manner in which gradually, step by step, by those processes of growth characteristic of all things, a sinful, unsanctified man grows into a sanctified man. Sanctification then corresponds to the gradual growth of the new man as it proceeds under the progressive influence of the Holy Spirit. Thus the action of the divine Spirit within the temporal process in its human, temporal aspect is what is meant, in contrast with justification which declares man righteous as a totality and at one moment.

For man, after all, like all created beings, is subject to the law of process, of growth, of more and less. This aspect is especially congenial to contemporary thought, which views everything under this aspect of process. On the other hand, it is for the same reason suspect in the eyes of the theologian whose thought is based on justification. And yet this outlook is undoubtedly of Biblical origin. Indeed, we may say that it is a quite particularly clear expression of Biblical thinking: God the absolute and eternal enters into the sphere of relativity and takes up His dwelling in the temporal. The living God is the God who, without ceasing to be the Lord of time and the Lord of all creatures, interests Himself in temporal and relative things, and even devotes Himself to them. So then it is not astonishing that the New Testament says so much about growth and increase—of knowledge and of obedience and love—about the goal which the believer approaches.

This means, of course, that a tension is created; on the one side the Christian is the man who is apprehended by Christ and apprehends Him in justifying faith, who all at once and once for all is united with the Holy Spirit and reconciled; on the other hand he has yet to become what he already is through the acquittal of justifying grace—"Ye *are* clean through the Word which I have spoken unto you" (John 15: 3). But we only understand this gradual process rightly when we start with the other element, the "once-for-allness" of justification, and do so indeed by saying that in faith, in the centre of his being, man *is* already the new creature, but in the periphery of his existence, in "experience", in what is visible, he has not yet that character. There he is a sinner who is indeed justified as a sinner, but who must yet empirically become that which God already sees him to be.

Yes, even faith itself has its "measure". "To every one of us is given grace according to the measure of the gift of Christ" (Eph. 4: 7). There is a "measure of faith" (Rom. 12: 3). The non-empirical transcendental concept of faith which is presupposed in justification by faith is combined with an empirical concept, which acknowledges the diversity of gifts and the differences in growth which spring from the reality visible to us and compel our attention. It is precisely upon this variety of gifts and this difference of measure that the Ekklesia rests as a fellowship of mutual enrichment and mutual service (1 Cor. 12; Eph. 4: 12–16) Whoever is united to Christ through faith certainly has the whole Christ. And yet, alongside of those who are already strong and, as it were, advanced in faith, there are others who are still weak and only beginners.

But even where sanctification is spoken of in this second fashion as something in process of growth, its meaning remains the same; it signifies always that what does not yet stand at God's disposal should be put at His disposal, should be made His property or instrument. Precisely thus has it been "set apart" and at the same time cleansed from what is unprofitable for this service. Sanctification thus stands in contrast to the world that is estranged from God, to the world as it is "without God". The world as it is "in itself" is the realm of what is alien to God, severed from Him, sinful. Sin is theft, outrage against God's property, the misappropriation and diversion of what originally belongs to God into a realm of our own. This realm of our own, in contrast with the realm of God or God's property, is the world in its negative sense. And sanctification can consist in nothing else than restoring this misappropriated property again to its lawful owner, that it should be restored from serving our own purpose to serving God's purpose.

Hence it is understandable that the concept "sanctification" in relation to the world is a double concept, and therefore one that can easily be misunderstood. On the one hand it negates—namely the world in itself, on the other hand it affirms the world, and lays claim to it in the name of Him to whom it belongs. Sanctification means simply the restoration of the original world, the world created by God and for God. But it can happen only through the power of Him who "so loved the world that He gave His own Son" in order that He might take it into His hands again.

Certainly in the sight of God sanctification is an indivisible unity, and in its character as justification through Jesus Christ a unique and total event. But as a matter of experience it is accomplished in the individual man in a series of acts, as it were by means of forward thrusts by God into man's sinful nature. God wins back for Himself, step by step, starting from the personal centre, the heart, which has heard the Word of justification, pressing forward into the "surrounding territories" towards the periphery, by taking control of the various sectors of human feeling, thought and will, and even reshaping his unconscious self. This is the truth which is enshrined in the Catholic mediaeval concept of the saint. These are in fact people who are so filled by God's Holy Spirit, that their holiness is visible to everyone and unmistakably evident. And yet such a man is precisely the person who perceives with an exceptional clarity the infinite distance that still separates him from his goal.

If *this* concept of sanctification has been less prominent in Protestantism than the other one, in which it is identified with the justification of the sinner, that is intelligible when we recall the front on which the Reformers were fighting. And yet, for all that, this emphasis has been unjustifiably one-sided. Although all men without exception stand in need of divine forgiveness, yet that does not mean that they are all to the same extent involved in estrangement from God. As everyone who is free of theological prejudice knows, there are degrees of approximation to the goal of complete union with the divine will and of transparency to the divine light. It seems to us that in preserving this clearly Biblical insight, Catholicism—eastern as well as western Catholicism—has an important advantage over Protestantism, although on the other hand the declaration of sainthood by the Church, canonization, is something problematic, above all because the great majority of those officially recognized as saints—both in earlier and in later times—were people in "holy orders" so called. The true saint will prove his discipleship in Jesus first and foremost by not severing himself from the world, but by the special intensity and concentration of spirit with which he seeks to give expression to his unity with God in an outpouring of loving service to his fellow men. Perfect love of God has become perfect desire to share the lot of one's fellow men. It is true that he has ever and again the urge to leave his fellowship with men and to be alone with God, but even so God calls him ever and again out of this solitude to be with his brother men.

Such true Christian saints do exist in Protestant lands also,[1] although they are hardly ever described as such. Their hallmark is the complete naturalness with which they praise the grace of Christ in their lives and give expression to it as love and service. And it is especially wonderful when they are hardly conscious of the extraordinary power of the Holy Spirit which shines forth from them. There may therefore be such saints living in entire obscurity of whom the world knows nothing; true saints just because in them the Holy Spirit shows His power in their simple naturalness and humanity. But they are certainly all people who know themselves before God as sinners in need of forgiveness. It is just the "everyday saint" who is an especially clear example of what the New Testament means by sanctification.

But there is one point in particular where we Protestants have reason to think again. Our all-too-onesided emphasis on (theological) knowledge, or on growth in it, has led to an intellectualization of the Christian faith. For *that* knowledge for whose growth the Apostles pray is not in the first instance theological knowledge, but a knowledge that finds its expression in love.[2]

In their training of Christians the Protestant Churches have created a Biblical and theological knowledge which is indeed necessary for the Church, but which has but little importance from the standpoint of sanctification.

At this point a problem becomes visible to which our attention was first drawn by modern psychology: the rôle of the unconscious. It is from this region, hitherto little known to us, that the true dynamic of human historical life comes. The comparison with an iceberg, of which by far the greatest part lies under the surface of the water and is therefore invisible, suggests itself forcibly. Therefore the influence of the Holy Spirit in this zone of human life is especially significant. Granted that the Holy Spirit penetrates into the heart of man through the *Word* of God heard in faith. But when the influence of the Word is confined to the zone of hearing and understanding it cannot really create a man anew. The New Testament tells us of a transforming power of the Spirit which sanctifies "through and through" (1 Thess. 5: 23) and therefore also is

[1] Cf. Walter Nigg, *Heimliche Weisheit*, 1959
[2] Cf. Ch. 17, "Faith and Knowledge", pp. 251 ff.

manifested in phenomena which are not at once intelligible to us rational men of the twentieth century and which are judged as non-existent by the rationalists.

It is therefore high time that theology should turn its interest to these psychological realities and powers which have been disclosed to us by depth-psychology. Disregard for this reality has had the result that hitherto, theology and the pastoral care which is under its direction have found themselves confronted by irrational phenomena with which they are quite incapable of dealing. The older theology, before the Reformation and also the theology of the Reformation, had a much less prejudiced attitude to this side of reality. For it took into account the *secret* operation of the Holy Spirit which necessarily escapes all formulation in theological concepts. A mutual exchange between depth-psychology and theology is therefore urgently to be wished, if only in the interests of Biblical understanding.

It is true that the heart of sanctification is justification and that this comes only from hearing the Word of Christ. But this does not mean that it can come into being only where a clear consciousness of the significance of Christ is present. The Spirit of God begins His work at a point where man is not yet conscious of himself as a self, and genuine faith in Christ penetrates in its working even into the depths that are inaccessible to the light of consciousness. It is therefore impossible for theology as such to give a conceptual representation of *this* working of the Spirit of God, for that would be a contradiction in terms. But theology can at least indicate this reality and by so doing remove obstacles which would be placed in its way by a thought whose concepts are all too sharply clear, and which prides itself on this clarity. By so doing theology could most effectually counter one of the greatest dangers of our age: the splitting of the powers of the unconscious from the conscious, a great and menacing danger especially in the Protestant West.[1]

Perceiving the strict correlation between God's Deed and Word in Jesus Christ and faith, which is known to us as the inward witness of the Holy Spirit, we must insist that more attention than formerly should be paid to this mysterious operation of the Spirit. Sanctification is that operation of the Holy Spirit through which man in all the aspects of his existence becomes the property and instrument of the will of God, and

[1] Cf. C. G. Jung's important book *Gegenwart und Zukunft*, 1957. (E.T. "Contemporary Events" to appear during 1962 in *Civilization in Transition*, Vol. X of Jung's *Collected Works*, Routledge and Kegan Paul, London.)

the bearer of His light, whose purpose is to shine forth everywhere. Both the scriptures and the Ekklesia of all ages bear witness that this cannot happen all at once, but only through a lifelong process which never comes to its completion in this earthly historical world. Rather does it give a new expectancy and hopefulness to those who experience it, while at the same time giving them the certainty of the fulfilment of this hope beyond the boundaries of our history here on earth.

One last thing must be emphasized which has already been said in principle in the context of faith and Ekklesia, but which must also be reiterated clearly under the aspect of sanctification. The true disciple of Jesus is always a man fundamentally ready for fellowship and capable of fellowship. This is the reason why the New Testament quite specially speaks of the Holy Spirit in those passages where it is dealing with the brotherhood of the Ekklesia. For just this is true holiness as the New Testament understands it—a life of real fellowship both with our brothers in the faith, and also, in principle, with every man, and the universality of the hope of the coming Kingdom of God, a universality which embraces all mankind. All individualism as a religiosity directed to the salvation of one's own soul is a contradiction of the will of God revealed in Jesus Christ. What is at stake is the realization of the "theocratic" purpose of God in the world, a purpose which has been revealed in Jesus Christ.

(2) SANCTIFICATION AS THE TASK OF MAN

In faith we know that God regards us and accepts us, not merely as His subjects but as the sons who belong to Him. This acceptance in spite of what we are, this inconceivable adoption of the sinner as a son of God—to be willing to let this happen to us, and to believe this assurance—that is what the New Testament calls faith in the full sense of the word. By this acceptance of God's gracious assurance the door of our heart is opened to the Holy Spirit, or rather, the Holy Spirit is already speaking and working in this ability to believe it. This opening of the heart begins as soon as a man repents, that is, as soon as he begins to be honest with himself and to see himself as he really is in the sight of God. Repentance is at the same time assent to the divine will, as it is always already, even though obscurely, known to us from the law, from the revelation of God's holy demands, and in our conscience. The God who bestows Himself upon us in Christ is no other than He who lays upon us the requirements of the law. It is only in the unity of His assurance and His claim that God encounters us, only thus is Jesus Christ to be understood as the revelation of "the righteousness of God", only thus is the sonship of God promised to us in Him a real sonship of God. Therefore in the bestowal of the gift of faith there is always directly implicit the summons to obedience. With the indicative of grace, "You *are* this, if only you will believe it," there is always at the same time given the imperative of discipleship—"Be this!" To God's self-surrender in the Cross of Christ, there corresponds—on the personal plane of correspondence—the self-surrender of man to God.

This is the human, ethical side of the one happening, sanctification. The one must not be neglected or thrust back in favour of the other. "Cheap grace" (Bonhoeffer)—that is, the grace of forgiveness without the summons to do God's will, makes even grace unintelligible and ineffectual. Only in the unity of assurance and claim, of gift and task—only in the unity of, on the one side, our release from unfulfilled responsibility and from guilt, and on the other the responsibility which lies before us as the subjects of God—is our encounter with the Cross of Christ an encounter with the God who is and remains our God. As a result of the war they had to wage in their historical situation against the work-righteousness of the mediaeval Catholic system, the Reformers did not always assert this second truth with the same emphasis and clarity as the first. One might say that they treated the Epistle to the Romans as if it ended at chapter 11, while Paul in no way regards the discussions in chapter 12 and the subsequent chapters as an appendix. What has been said about the gift bestowed in Christ is followed in Romans 12 by what has to be said about discipleship, not "one storey down" but on the same level of importance. The ethics founded in faith are not an appendix to Dogmatics, but the other side of the same thing. They are the representation of the sanctifying work of God in so far as it is not merely a gift but a task given to man, the instruction as to what we ourselves must now do to prove that we belong to Christ, in order that we may ever more "grow into unity with the likeness of His resurrection" (Rom. 6: 5).

Certainly our transformation through Christ, the new life, is God's act alone. But our co-operation is included in this act of His. The indicative of grace is never without the simultaneous imperative of discipleship. The words of Paul that introduce the section on Christian ethics are these: "I beseech you therefore, brethren, by the mercies of God, that ye present your bodies a living sacrifice, holy, acceptable unto God, which is your reasonable service. And be not conformed to this world, but be ye transformed by the renewing of your mind, that ye may prove what is that good, and acceptable, and perfect will of God" (Rom. 12: 1, 2). We have already seen in the previous chapter that conversion consists in this self-transformation, that this is consequently no heresy—as it has repeatedly been labelled on the part of Lutherans—but clear New Testament Pauline doctrine. Man's transformation through the Holy Spirit does not happen without the presence and co-operation of the man himself. Sanctification is indeed God's work, for no one can sanctify but He who is Himself the Holy One. Nevertheless His work of sanctification, as the transformation of the self from self-dependence to dependence upon God, cannot bypass the self but must happen through the self, by laying claim to the self. Thus sanctification is in fact also the task of man. And that is how it is expressly described. "Follow . . . holiness . . . without which no man shall see the Lord" (Heb. 12: 14). "Let us cleanse ourselves from all filthiness of the flesh and spirit, perfecting holiness in the fear of God" (2 Cor. 7: 1). "For God hath not called us unto uncleanness, but unto holiness" (1 Thess. 4: 7). As the Apostle knows himself set apart for apostolic service, so must all believers know themselves as "elect saints" who have their calling in the service of Christ.

The norm of this service is "Be not conformed to this world" (Rom. 12: 2). The character of this service is expressly described by the cultic word for divine Worship, *latreia*, which characteristically is used by Paul only at this one place,[1] and precisely not in its cultic sense. In order that this service of God may be possible and "reasonable" it is compelled ever and again to return to the beginning, recalling what God has first done in Christ. In order that the sacrifice of our life may be a genuine one, well pleasing to God, it must arise out of the sacrifice which Christ has made for us. It must thus happen in correspondence with God's Act, just as we can only love Him truly because He first loved us (1 John 4: 19). The transformation through which our action becomes a sacrificial service of God consists in the first place of our letting ourselves be transformed through the renewal of our minds. Thus sanctification, in so far as it is our task, consists primarily in conversion in the double sense mentioned above, in turning away from our previous life, and in turning to the way of Christ. The "old leaven" must be

[1] In the second place where Paul uses this word, Romans 9: 4, *latreia* refers exclusively to Jewish religion

purged out that we may be a "new lump" (1 Cor. 5: 7). As we have already seen under the aspect of sanctification as God's work, this process is a gradual step-by-step process, although its ground and its direction are to be found in the unique reconciliation once for all accomplished in the Cross of Christ. We must take steps of obedience and discipleship towards the goal that has been shown to us in Jesus Christ. Sanctification consists in following His steps. To describe this the Middle Ages coined the concept of *imitatio Christi*.

This formulation can appeal with full justification to the New Testament. In the apostolic exhortations the words "like Christ" play no little part, and the challenge also to take the example of the Apostle as a model is frequent. When the theology of the Reformation tended on the whole to repudiate this thought, it was not without good historical reasons. There was a fear both of Catholic work-righteousness, and of a rationalistic conception of Christ as a mere example. But there is no intrinsic objection on the basis of faith in Christ to the thought of discipleship, nor even to that of *imitatio*. On the contrary, we are "to have this mind in us, which was also in Christ Jesus" (Phil. 2: 5); and the picture of His self-surrender on the Cross should certainly be the guiding pattern of the Christian life (1 Peter 2: 21), just as Christ in the scene of the washing of feet had set His self-humiliation in and for this service before the disciples as an example for them to follow. "A new commandment I give unto you, that ye love one another as I have loved you. . . . By this shall all men know that ye are my disciples, if ye have love one to another" (John 13: 34, 35). This is the rule of conduct for sanctification.

This commandment is at the same time new and old (1 John 2: 7, 8). It is old, because already in the Old Testament the commandment of love was known as the true significance and the summary of the whole law (cf. Lev. 19: 18). But it is new in this, that the word "love" has received a new meaning through the event on the Cross, and in that this commandment is no longer the first but the second thing, namely, the imperative that results from the indicative of the justification of the sinner. It is thus no longer a law but the description of what is already contained in the gift bestowed by God. "The love of Christ constraineth us" (2 Cor. 5: 14). This is the law written by the Holy Spirit in the heart (Jer. 31: 33) which no longer really needs to be enjoined upon the believer, but which itself results from the relationship with God re-established by Christ, of which he merely needs to be "reminded".

Thus the concept of sanctification and of sanctity is given a meaning radically different from what is called by that name in the field of comparative religion. Here we have not to do with abstinence from the world, not with world-denial as such, but with service of our neighbour. A saint is not a man who has as little as possible to do with the things of the world, but one who serves God and his neighbour in the world. Above all, a saint is a man whose face and not his back is turned towards his neighbour. He is a man in whom unworldliness has taken the shape of release from dependence on the world through dependence upon God alone, and who therefore no longer needs to find expression in a world-renouncing asceticism. "All is yours . . . and ye are Christ's" (1 Cor. 3: 21–23). The new ethic is subjection only to the will revealed in Christ, and liberation by the Holy Spirit who is shed abroad in our hearts as a result of this constraint. The disciples of Jesus are at one and the same time wholly bound, under the law of Christ (*ennomoi Christou*), and free from all other bonds that have authority and power in the world. "The Christian man is a free lord of all things—through faith." He is at the same time "a servant of all things—through love". He is free from the world through his dependence upon God alone. He is bound to the world, in so far as he can only serve men in the orders and social structures of the world.

The right understanding of sanctification as the task of man is principally threatened by two misunderstandings; those of moralism and of quietism. Moralism remembers that advance is made "step by step" but forgets that the whole is at stake in every step, namely "the putting on of the new man" "who is renewed in knowledge after the image of him that created him" (Col. 3: 10), in the knowledge of Jesus Christ as the Archetypal Image of Him who alone can restore the divine image in man. A sanctification which is cut adrift from faith in Christ can be nothing but moralism. This moralism is constituted by an inability to break free from the law, from general rules of obligation.[1] It was above all the doctrine of the Reformed Church which made an apparent link between the Doctrine of Justification and this moralism, this reintroduction of the law by the back door of the so-called third use of the law (*usus tertius legis*). There was a fear that without the restraint of the law man would again be released from all restraint, while in reality he is constrained once for all through faith in Jesus Christ as his

[1] See on this point the next chapter, "The Commandment of Love and the Law"

Lord. The New Testament knows nothing of a *tertius usus legis*.[1]

It is legalistic moralism that has lain like a blight on the history of Christendom. This moralism has robbed Christians of the glorious liberty of the children of God; a liberty which should have resulted in the Christian man's daring, in freedom from all other bonds than these which unite him to Christ, to choose new ways to travel in each new situation, ways which would have infuriated the moralistic Philistine but at the same time would have brought before his eyes the constraint and the liberty of the child of God. This legalism is to blame for the lack of imagination of average Christianity, which ever and again sacrifices the spontaneity of love to legalistic rule-of-thumb and leaves in practice hardly any room for the embodiment of the creative, intuitive and unpharisaic freedom of God's children. It is this Pharisaism which is just as much a mark of Christianity as it is of Judaism and therefore in practice denies justification by faith alone, although lip service is paid to the latter. People have not dared really to live in the Spirit, and consequently, in everything that relates to the management of their life, have relapsed into Judaism. The word of Paul "But if ye be led of the Spirit, ye are not under the law" (Gal. 5: 18) has not been taken seriously, but, entirely against its true sense, has been taken to apply merely to guilt, and not to the way in which men organize their life. The law has its place in the organization of the order of society, but not in our relationship to God. The Spirit who puts us immediately in touch with God knows nothing of law, and conversely the man who does not understand himself in the light of God's self-bestowing love knows of no higher authority than the law. In Christ God's claim on us is "Act in harmony with the love that you have received."[2] The neighbour whom I am to love in Christ is my Thou, as God Himself is my Thou.

The second misunderstanding is the contrary one; a conception of sanctification which remembers the gift bestowed and forgets the task, and which, through sheer fear of understanding Christ as a mere example, loses sight of the *imitatio Christi* in the New Testament sense. The quietistic misunderstanding is the opposite of the moralistic misunderstanding. Quietism is just as unscriptural as moralism. The summons to obedience is necessarily bound up with the gift of grace. True, sanctification is God's work alone, but He does not do this work

[1] See on this point my Appendix II, "On the Dialectic of the Law", in *Man in Revolt*, pp. 516–26

[2] See n. 2 on Ch. 22, p. 306

without claiming us for it. The demand for sanctification is unmistakable in the New Testament witness to Christ.[1] This is quite remarkably clear in the Gospel of John. Only he who "dwells in Him, can bear fruit" (John 15: 1–8) by actively confessing his Lord and doing His will. It is a false conception of grace which pays attention only to the gift, and not to the claim of the Lord bound up with the gift, the assurance of God. But this is not a law, it is a personal commandment—it is not an "It" —as the law is—but the personal imperative which can be heard only by one who is bound to the Lord Himself. This claim leads us along the way of Christ, and thus into the world. As a false individualism is bound up with quietism, so on the other side there is always bound up with the commandment of Christ the will to assert God's Lordship in the world. True faith is always related to our neighbour in his concrete situation, and this is always the neighbour in his concrete *relationships*. To assert the love of Christ in the world means to show it to our neighbour in his involvement in structures of the world which operate according to their own laws. And just because the world is bound by law in this manner, this will never be directly but always only more or less indirectly possible.

Christian love accepts the task thus given of reshaping itself[2] and does not let the alien character of the world deter it from realizing this indirect manifestation of love in the world, even when the world repeatedly misunderstands this manifestation because of the reshaping it has undergone. Only in relation to the person of my neighbour, in immediate personal relation to him, can love assert itself directly, as it were without concealment. But this must not be a reason for limiting neighbourly love merely to the field of "personal relationships"; quite the contrary. The energy with which Christian interest penetrates into the world and expands in social and even political activity is the measure of the power and purity of the love, that is, of its dependence on Christ.

There has therefore been much debate on the question whether the results of this sanctification, which the New Testament describes as "fruits of the Spirit", are observable and visible or invisible and purely interior. Here also we meet with the same misunderstandings on the right hand and on the left. On the one side it is said that the Christian never scrutinizes

[1] An extreme form of the denial of this demand for sanctification is Kohlbrügge's doctrine of sanctification, which also exerted an influence on the Barthian theology in its early stages

[2] Cf. Ch. 23, "The Christian in the World", esp. p. 319

himself or indeed the fruits of faith, not even to test himself by this standard, but that he looks only to Christ. The other side maintains that our standing in faith can actually be assessed, as it were "proved", by the fruits. The New Testament can be adduced to support either view. "For your life is hidden with Christ in God" (Col. 3: 3). Justifying faith means in fact that we should place our sole confidence in the Word of Christ, living entirely on the gift of grace, and making it the sole foundation of our life. On the other side it is just as clear that when scripture speaks of the fruits of the Spirit it means visible manifestations of the Spirit. There are no "invisible fruits" for it, any more than there are for the botanist. Thus it is expressly said, "Let your light so shine before men that they may see your good works and praise your Father which is in heaven" (Matt. 5: 16).

Obviously we have here come to a point where the truth of the gospel can find expression only in paradox. And yet we are on dangerous ground when the Reformed doctrine of the *syllogismus practicus* which is mentioned in the Heidelberg Catechism maintains that we must "be assured of our *faith* by the fruits thereof". Yet statements of a quite similar tenor are to be found in Luther also. It is clear that faith must bear visible fruit, it must prove itself in action. But, on the other side, this verification can never be the *basis* of faith and faith's certainty. We must teach both things: the necessity of practical verification in love and the continually humbling fact that such love comes short of God's claim upon us. "For all our deeds are nothing worth, even in the best of lives." Both things must be said: the believer looks not on himself at all, but on Christ, and inasmuch as he looks on Christ he sees in Him One who summons him to discipleship.

But true discipleship consists above all in this, that we should dwell in Him, in being rather than in doing. It is not quietism to lay the accent on this new being, for what the world needs beyond anything else is not action, but new men. From this new being there arises ever and again a new action. The world, that is the unbelieving world, has no understanding of the new being. Its only standard of ethical measurement is action. Therefore Christ's command is "Let your light shine", the light that Christ alone can give, the light that shines forth only from those who *are* in Him.

This is what we Protestants have to learn from the saints. The saints prove themselves as such, not so much by their doing as by their being, as men who live from the love of Christ and in His love. What makes us true saints is not our action. It is equally the case that what the world needs is not action, and this is quite specially true of our so pragmatic modern technical world. What we are able to achieve—even the holiest of us—can be a manifestation only, a demonstration which does not heal the world. The new being, indeed, like our action, is something which comes far short of what is meant by that sonship of God which is identical with true humanity. But it can at least be a pointer thereto. True humanity, however, is never solitariness, but always a being-with. To be a true fellow man to men; that is the authentic meaning of sanctification.

Therefore all our teaching on sanctification stands under the sign of eschatological reserve. Incompleteness is an essential mark of all earthly existence. What is complete is that which transcends history, that which we never realize in time, which we can only hope for and in faith hope for with assurance. "Not as though I had already attained, either were already perfect, but I follow after, if that I may apprehend that for which also I am apprehended of Jesus Christ . . . and I press toward the mark . . . of the high calling of God in Christ Jesus" (Phil. 3: 12–14). But this goal is the consummation of the Kingdom of God, in which not only is the shape of this world transformed, but in which there will be neither sin nor death, nor law, nor satanic powers any longer. Therefore a further part of sanctification is the steady consciousness of conflict against powers with whom all human action is incommensurable, powers which cannot be expelled from the world by any human effort. They are indeed conquered by Christ (Col. 2: 15) but this victory is not yet visible. Rather is the manifestation of this victory identical with the appearing of Christ in glory, the revelation of His Resurrection and our own divine sonship.

What does it mean to fight against this anti-Christian, anti-human demonic and satanic power? A direct struggle is impossible, for we can fight only against its visible manifestations. The only fight against the power itself is to watch and pray, to keep constantly in mind that these powers are there, and to pray for their annihilation. Therefore we pray for the coming of the Kingdom. But we cannot bring it about ourselves.

We must neither underestimate the power of God's enemy nor be afraid of it. To believe that man himself, namely man in the power of the Holy Spirit, could overcome it, that he himself would be able in course of time to create the perfection which God wills—this would be to underestimate the power of evil. This utopian optimism can only be the fruit of an arrogance contrary to the nature of faith. But fear of this power would be simply a lack of faith, a failure of confidence in its final defeat by Christ. "See, I have overcome the world" (John 16: 33). "This is the victory that overcometh the world, even our faith" (1 John 5: 4). This watchfulness in prayer is the true criterion of the saint. In its double nature as confidence in victory and consciousness of one's own weakness, it is the result of justifying faith; complete humility partnered by the certainty that Christ is conqueror.

CHAPTER 22

THE COMMANDMENT OF LOVE AND THE LAW

As one who belongs to God, the believer stands under the commandment of God. But for him this commandment is no longer a law. Rather is it the imperative which follows from the bestowal of God's love. It is a sense of obligation that continually reawakens in him, giving expression to a spontaneous union of his will with the Will of God. It still remains, as before, the claim of the Holy God, who lays claim to man as His own, but this claim results—and that is the new thing—from the assurance, the new life in the love of God.

The question of the relation of the commandment of love and law to each other is an important aspect of the great problem "Law and Gospel" with which Lutheran theology has especially concerned itself. Even the concept "law" is exceedingly ambiguous. What a variety of shades of meaning "law" can have in Biblical usage![1] "Law" is the general description of the Old Testament as the original document of revelation. At first it was used for the orally imparted detailed instruction of the priest in cultic, legal and moral questions, but was then expanded to describe the whole revelation of the Will of God to His people. It is in a special way identical with the Decalogue. "Law" is used to describe the summing up of all the commandments in the twofold commandment to love God and our neighbour. We Christians think above all of the interpretation of the Decalogue by Jesus in His Sermon on the Mount. And finally Karl Barth has called "law" what we called the claim of God, in its indissoluble conjunction with His assurance in Christ.[2] When it has such a variety of meanings, how can this concept still be of use in giving an answer to the question, "What does God enjoin upon those who are 'in Christ' as their right behaviour in the world?"

One thing is beyond doubt. The Christian has received, along with God's love, the imperative to let himself be guided solely and in all things by this love of Christ. The message of the grace of God lays claim as such to our obedience. Even when I am living in the grace and in the self-bestowing love of God, God

[1] See on this point my discussion in *Dogmatics* II, Ch. 8, "The Law"

[2] Karl Barth, "Evangelium und Gesetz", *Theologische Existenz heute*, 1935 (E. T. *Theological Existence To-day*, Hodder and Stoughton, London)

remains the Lord who commands, and I remain the one who is commanded. May we call this divine Commandment of love, law?

I

We will examine first the question: How are the Old Testament law and the New Testament commandment of love related to one another? The Decalogue is not an absolute moral code of ethics. The people of God accepts along with it the sovereignty of its God, and in this acceptance the election of Israel becomes a reality. The fulfilment of the commandments is not an act of merit, but the obedience which the covenant people owes to its God. The law is a divine gift, it is a salvation-event as a revelation of God.

It is not until the days of post-exilic Judaism that the law changes from an ordinance of salvation to an independent entity, to an abstract law which requires literal obedience. Its importance for the relationship of man to God now acquires an ever more dominating position. Now it creates the relationship to God. Only through the fulfilment of the law can man attain to fellowship with God. The law becomes the way of salvation. And with its achievement of independence is also conjoined the disastrous tendency to casuistry.

In the New Testament the law is indeed affirmed as the will of God, but it loses its position of mediator. It is not the law that determines our relation to God, but faith in Jesus as Lord and Christ. He alone is the Mediator. Our relation to Him determines our relation to God. He alone, not the law, is the way of salvation.

The law only reveals the sin of man in the sight of God. It accuses man as a sinner in God's sight, it condemns and "slays" him, but it has not the power to free him from sin. It can only forbid sin. But it has not the power to deliver man from the power of sin. Only through the justification of the sinner, of which man receives assurance in the Cross of Jesus Christ, is man set free from the power of sin, brought into a new relation to God, and receives the love of God. Only by being incorporated into the death and resurrection of Jesus Christ does man become free from the law. The man who is declared righteous in Jesus Christ no longer obeys a law, but obeys his living Lord and His immediate guidance, which is imparted to him through the Holy Spirit. The life of the Christian stands under the leading of the Spirit, not of the law.

In the Second Epistle to the Corinthians Paul contrasts the law as *gramma*, as letter, as something prescribed, as the precepts of the law, with the living life-creating spirit (2 Cor. 3: 6). Not the law, but only the renewal of the heart through the Spirit accomplishes the fulfilment of the Will of God. Therefore this contrast between law and Spirit culminates in the glorious words about freedom, "But where the Spirit of the Lord is, there is liberty" (2 Cor. 3: 17). But this liberty is not lack of constraint. Rather are we bound by the Spirit to Jesus Christ, without any intermediary; no longer bound by the interposition of an impersonal authority, but directly and immediately bound to the very God who addresses us in Christ, the God who is love. The love which in Him has not only been revealed, but communicates itself to us, cannot be identified with any law or with anything that has been decided in advance. It stands just as much outside and above the law as God's I-Thou revelation stands outside and above all the laws of thought; that is, above our reason. The tersest expression of this truth is to be found in the Prologue to St. John. "For the law was given by Moses; but grace and truth came by Jesus Christ" (John 1: 17).

But this love has in it the quality of direction. It is no rigid juridical instruction, but it is the guidance of the Spirit, which with its concrete interest in the individual is always only to be known at the contemporary moment in the encounter with the "Thou" of our neighbour. But in every case its meaning is that we should be there to help the other man, that we should be open for him, that we should meet him without prejudice, that we should accept him as a "Thou". This love can be confined by no law. To meet our neighbour as "Thou" is to meet him in freedom, without prejudice, without principles of action. But it cannot really be enjoined, at least not on everyone. It is intelligible only to the man who himself "has been loved first" (1 John 4: 19), who himself has received the love of God through faith. Love, *agape*, is "shed abroad in our hearts through the Holy Ghost" (Rom. 5: 5), into the heart of every man who is "in Christ" through justifying faith.

Agape is known only to the man who believes "in Christ". It is the unfathomable self-bestowing kindness of God, which is to be confused with no duty or virtue. Of this love the Sermon on the Mount speaks as of something which is by no means intelligible or accessible to every one. The Sermon is addressed to the disciples who as such are already dwelling in this love—however imperfectly, however much its self-manifestation in them may be broken by the old nature. These words are thus definitely not what Kant makes them out to be: the law of love, the universally known Categorical Imperative. While the Categorical Imperative is rational, the universally known law of reason, *agape* is non-rational. First, in respect of its origin, because it is bound to a historical event, to God's self-communication in Jesus Christ. But it is also non-rational in its nature, because it is not universal, does not generalize, but individualizes. And lastly, it is non-rational because it is ec-static just as faith, being in Christ, is ec-static. The "Thou shalt" of love results from the "Thou art" of faith. For this reason faith is called the obedience of faith. The content of the Commandment of love is this: "Do to man what God has done to you." Love is identification of the "I" with the "Thou". As "overflowing love" it is intelligible only as the creation of God's unfathomable love. It is the identification with the "Thou" which results from justification with its twofold identification.[1]

Love possesses the character of "overflowing", of "irrationality", of "superabundance", of "immensity". It is not concerned with reciprocity. Law, on the other hand, must be concerned with reciprocity in order that it may adapt itself to the promulgation of general laws. In this respect Law is rational and general, both with regard to the man for whom it is intended and with regard also to its subject matter. Law is not personal, it is not interested in the "Thou". Kant's conception of the law, the moral law, is clearly analogous to that of the laws of nature.

Agape, which by the nature of things is entirely incapable of formulation in a law, has at any rate a rational analogy, the Categorical Imperative which we have just mentioned. *Agape* and the ethic of reason are at the same time similar to and different from each other. Kant formulates the ethic of reason in his *Metaphysic of Ethics* as the claim that we should acknowledge and reverence the same personal dignity in every man. This principle is immanent in the reason of man. It is that law, on the strength of which every man can be addressed as a man; that law, which because of its formal character is fitted to be the foundation of a universal moral legislation. It is the principle on which the stoic rational ethic is founded, that I should "love" the man in man as one akin to myself by reason of the same faculty of reason, as "one like myself".

This moral law of reason is at the first glance similar to love of our neighbour, and has consequently also been confused with it

[1] The twofold identification of which Luther says: "God took upon Him that which was ours so that He might give us that which was His."

by many teachers of the Church, even by Calvin.[1] Zwingli, too, considered that *agape* and this rational love of man were the same thing. Among the Reformers it was Luther alone who—for example in his great *Sermon on Good Works*,[2] one of the most splendid writings of the Reformer (indeed of all Christendom)—clearly recognized the spontaneously individualizing nature of *agape*, its origin, its oneness with faith and its antagonism to all law.

On account of its individualizing spontaneous ec-static character, *agape*, as we have seen it springing from justifying faith, self-bestowing—or as Luther says, "overflowing"—love, is not fitted to form the foundation of a moral order, since the principle of reciprocity is not contained in it. The man who loves with *agape* goes also "the second mile", he requites evil with good, he "turns the other cheek", he loves his enemy (Matt. 5: 39–45). From these examples of *agape* given by the Sermon on the Mount there can be deduced no universally obligatory ethic. Unlike the rational ethic we spoke of, *agape* cannot be formulated in general laws. One cannot speak of it as a "principle". It is, on the contrary, something without principle, hostile to principles, just because it loves its neighbour in his uniqueness, in the individuality of his particular and given character, which cannot be grasped in general terms. The essential law of *agape* is just this, that it cannot be grasped in legal terms. It is directed not to the human race but to the "Thou" who encounters us.

II

Human society, however, requires a universally valid ethical foundation as principle of its orders. For this purpose the universal ethical law of reason is alone of use, which has in it the element of mutuality, of reciprocity. Society needs the ethical law. But where *agape*, the Sermon on the Mount, is understood in a legalistic manner, as it was for example by Tolstoy, and earlier by certain "enthusiasts" of Reformation times, confusion and anarchy result. Not only the institution of the State but the institution of property and also marriage and the family are shattered, a fate of which the tragedy of the end of Tolstoy's life is a moving but, at the same time, warning example.

That this was not the intention of Christ's commandment of

[1] Cf. Karl Barth, *Kirchliche Dogmatik* I, 2, p. 463, E.T. *Church Dogmatics* I, 2, pp. 419–20: "This is more a Stoic than a New Testament doctrine. It is not supported either by the text or by any other part of Holy Scripture." The reasons which K.B. gives, however, seem contestable

[2] *W.A.* VI, pp. 196 ff.

love the Apostle Paul is once more the great witness. He who wrote the great hymn to *agape* (1 Cor. 13) knew truly what the meaning of this word is. And it was he whose idea of the Ekklesia grew out of his apprehension of the connection between faith and love. This same Apostle Paul has also given a piece of instruction about the significance of *agape* for the world which must remain fundamental for Christendom. In the 12th to the 14th chapters of the Epistle to the Romans, he treats of *agape* as the sole norm of the Christian. From it follows what is so astonishing for the world in the disciples of Jesus—the refusal to take vengeance, the feeding of the hungry enemy, the overcoming of evil with good (Rom. 12: 19–21). This *agape* is that disposition of man which results from faith in the Christ who at the same time calls us to follow Him. *Agape* is the end of the law.

Then, in the midst of his discussion about *agape*, Paul turns to the question of how the Christian should relate himself to the world institution which today we call the State. And now follows Romans 13: 1–7, the astonishing and at first glance extraordinary discussion, which culminates in the statement that this power, the (Roman) State, is the ordinance of God and that its officials are the servants of God. Now the State does precisely what the Christians, the members of the Ekklesia, are not permitted to do; it avenges evil, it punishes. For this power which is so opposed to the nature of *agape* is "God's ordinance" "to thee for good". For the Ekklesia, too, like all human life, needs this ordinance, for otherwise there would be chaos. Now this has nothing at all to do with *agape*-teaching, this is simply the world—the world in which even the Christian lives. But he must not oppose this secular ordinance or even despise it. Rather must he regard it as God's ordinance, to which he owes obedience, and whose officials he should honour as "God's servants".

Has Paul, in saying this, suddenly forgotten his theme of *agape*? By no means. The following verses bear witness to this, for they resume the theme of *agape* and develop it to its climax. But at the same time he now establishes a connection between the theme of ordinance and the theme of *agape*, by referring to the fact that this ordinance which is so strange to Christians none the less serves for their good, and that Christians should therefore fulfil their obligations to it.

In Paul's utterances about the State there is no mention of Christ and *agape*. "The State knows nothing of love" (Karl Barth). How should it, seeing that it is the very epitome of everything that is secular, which as such stands over against Christ, and is different from the Church and stands in antagonism to it! This antagonism is most clearly seen in the fact that force is a characteristic of the ordinance of the State, the hard brutal power of compulsion and retribution—the sword. There has never been a State that was able to dispense with the sword, to do without the power of weapons, whether of the police or the military forces. Without this it would cease to be a State. And yet this State is "the minister of God to thee for good". Paul neither says anything about the kind of order which should hold in the State, nor does he say what has been falsely read out of this passage, that the Christian must give it unconditional obedience. Thus he neither calls for the obedience of blind submission, nor advocates a democratic conception of the State. All these ideas were not yet at that time a matter of practical politics. Paul limits himself to one thing: "By this example you Christians see that you are in fact in the world, and I say to you that in the first place you should respect the powers of this world and adapt yourselves to them. Although by doing so you enter into an entirely different sphere—you emerge from your Ekklesia-brotherhood into the world—you do not thereby cease to be under the sole Lordship of Jesus Christ and His *agape*. And in this way you must understand the commandment of love, that it has validity even in the world and the realm of its laws, but as the motive power of your action and not as itself a law." What is given here, then, is not a Christological justification of the State but the clear contrast between *agape* and world order.

This is made clear by yet another example which is brought before the eyes of the community in the shortest Epistle of Paul, the Epistle to Philemon. What should be the attitude of a Christian to the social institution of slavery, which at that time was completely taken for granted? Not a word is said about slavery as such being something unworthy of a human being, so that the Christian should fight against it. On the other hand the Epistle makes it unmistakably clear to us that a Christian master must treat every slave that belongs to him, whom he did indeed lawfully purchase, not as a slave, but as a brother. The institution of slavery is, as it were, undermined from within and transcended, although there is no polemic against the institution as such. This does not imply that this is still the right attitude for us today. For in the interval the tiny band of Christians has become a power in the community which carries a responsibility corresponding to its size.

Similar teaching is given us by the "house lists", those statements about the relation of parents and children, of man and wife, of master and servant (e.g. Col. 3: 18–22 and Eph. 6: 1–9) where by "servant" we must always understand "slave". Here we are shown that *agape* never has the effect of opposing or disregarding given institutions, but results in their ennoblement or sublimation. In the case of the State this was impossible. The sword, force, cannot be sublimated, but marriage can, and so can the relationships between parents and children, and the relationship between slave and master. But always these institutions are in the first place recognized and taken for granted as something given. Of Christian marriage alone it is expressly said that in the last resort it is to be understood as an analogy of the relationship between Christ and the Christian community.

Thus it became clear in what sense the institutions of this world or their rational ethical foundation and the task of *agape* which flows from the gift of Christ are to be linked together. There is in the New Testament no trace of any attempt to derive this natural order from *agape*; no suggestion of a "Christologically based social ethic" appears at any point in the New Testament. The only Christological thing is the summons to *agape*, that is, the claim which follows from the assurance. The institutions in which the Christian who lives in the world participates can certainly not be Christologically derived, for the good reason that the world as such confronts the Ekklesia as something alien. The attempt to understand the world Christologically would mean not to understand it as world, to misunderstand its nature as world, to regard it as not-world; that is to say, as a world already united to God's will. In short, it would be to speak of it in another sense than the New Testament does.

The commandment of love remains in force as our sole guidance. The Christian stands under the sole Lordship of his Lord, but he must give expression to the love which is required of him by this Lord in the institutions of the world. Only then can he think of giving these institutions a more humane form. But there can be no question of the Commandment of love itself serving as norm in this fashioning of institutions. This function is reserved for its rational analogy. *Agape* is only the motive power for the improvement and humanization of secular institutions according to the law of the acknowledgment of the equal dignity of persons, a law immanent in reason itself. The improvement of the secular order can at the best be only a pointer to the coming Kingdom of Love, never its realization.

CHAPTER 23

THE CHRISTIAN IN THE WORLD

I

In what sense does the New Testament speak of "the world"? Not in the sense in which we today mostly use this word. When we say "world" we mean the totality of all existence, the cosmos, the universe, the earth among the millions of heavenly bodies. The New Testament—in the Old the world is barely mentioned,[1] the expression "heaven and earth" being used instead—does not speak of the world in this, so to say, neutral and impersonal manner. It means by "world" humanity in its (negative) relation to God; created indeed by God but fallen away from Him. This word can certainly on occasion describe the totality of all created things. But the meaning which relates the word to sacred history, to creation and to sin, is the predominant one.

It is therefore not easy to bring our word of today into line with the meaning that the New Testament gives to it. In the changing significance of precisely this word we find a reflection of the intellectual history of the West, especially in the last centuries. And yet this is a common element in the Biblical and the contemporary meanings of the word: man is born into the world and is thereby subordinated to its laws. Through birth and death he also is subjected to the law of growth and decay. In the New Testament indeed this man is always the man whose origin and Creator is God, just as everything else that exists, the universe, is of course God's creation and possession from the beginning.

John and Paul are the writers who use the word "world" most frequently. Both do this in a predominantly negative sense. The world is for them humanity estranged by sin from God. Therefore there is a clear contrast between being "in Christ" and being "in the world". The man who through faith is "in Christ" has been taken out of the world, Christ has "chosen him out of the world" (John 15: 19). To have been chosen out means just this: to have been released from the godlessness of the rest of mankind, and its enmity to God. Paul

[1] Cf. *ThWb*, article "Cosmos" III, pp. 867–96. "Thus 'cosmos' in the sense of 'world' is first found in the last writings of the Septuagint, whose way of thought is fundamentally Greek" (881)

says the same thing in still sharper terms: "He delivered us from the power of darkness and translated us into the Kingdom of His dear Son" (Col. 1: 13). Faith is participation in the Christ who "has overcome the world" (John 16: 33). Therefore faith is "the victory that overcometh the world" (1 John 5: 4).

But now, as before, believers have still to live in this world. Even the Apostles acknowledge this fact, and they are only able to combine it with the thought of the victory of Christ over the world because they are certain that "the fashion of this world passeth away" (1 Cor. 7: 31). Even Christians, like all other men, must die. Even they, as far as their empirical reality is concerned, are subject to the laws of this world, which they have not the power to annul. Obviously this is the boundary which separates ethics from eschatology.

This means that we have already reached one important conclusion, albeit of a negative character: Christians cannot "sanctify" the world, that is, humanity, in such a manner as they should sanctify themselves. In spite of this, the Lord sends them expressly into this hostile world. "I send you forth as sheep in the midst of wolves" (Matt. 10: 16). They are to be the "light" of the world, and they are to be this by so acting "that men may see your good *works* and glorify your Father which is in heaven" (Matt. 5: 16). On the other hand, the warning is clearly expressed: "Love not the world, neither the things that are in the world" (1 John 2: 15). "Be not conformed to this world" (Rom. 12: 2). There is reason for this warning, for "the whole world lieth in wickedness" (1 John 5: 19). It is ruled by the prince of this world. True, this prince, the whole satanic demonic power, is conquered in the Cross. When through Christ's death God had "spoiled principalities and powers, he made a show of them openly, triumphing over them in it" (Col. 2: 15). But this is clearly an event which has taken place, not in the empirical world but in an invisible world, accessible only to faith; a world that will not be revealed until the Parousia. For in the visible empirical world these powers are still, as formerly, at work in full power and just for this reason the world is a hostile and dangerous world of which we must beware.

Our question now is: "How should, and how can faith actively vindicate itself in this world, which is governed by its own laws?" It is a question of quite special importance for non-theologians, since it deals with Christian practice, with the vindication and manifestation of Christian life in this world. It has already in principle received its answer in the sense that the believer, the Ekklesia, now (again) belongs to Him who created man, and who has won him back again as His property through the Christ event and through faith. This faith consists simply in the reception of the love of God, and to belong to God means, now, to exist and to live in this love which we have received. Therefore the Lord's commandment of love is not a "law" but the task of the Christian, which results from the gift of Christ. This love is the *telos* of the law in the double sense; end, and at the same time, fulfilment. "By this shall all men know that ye are my disciples, if ye have love one to another" (John 13: 35). For only that faith is vital and real "which worketh by love" (Gal. 5: 6). This is the only commandment that is given to the disciples. For them the law is done away. "But if ye are led by the Spirit, ye are not under the law." This is the way we must understand the word about love as "the end of the law". But what does this mean in the concrete affairs of the world?

II

To this fundamental question Christendom has in the past given different answers. We shall make special reference to three very widely divergent ways which have been followed, with the intention of conforming to this fundamental commandment: the way of world-renunciation or flight from the world, the way of world domination, and the way which has been indicated by the catchword of "the two Kingdoms".

(*a*) The way of world-renunciation is that of the mediaeval monastic movement. The underlying belief here is that life in the world is too dangerous, since the disciple of Jesus is quite unable to avoid surrendering to its special laws and thereby falling a victim to the world and becoming untrue to his Lord. Even as Protestants we cannot avoid acknowledging the great and exemplary achievements in Christian living that have been attained by this way of world-renunciation. We must indeed draw attention to the fact that genuine Protestants too have in their own manner also decided for this way of life, even if they did not utterly renounce the world but only in such a manner as, for example, the Quakers of early times, who would have nothing to do with the State, or certain pietists who withdrew from public life into quietism. But however radical the attempted path of renunciation, it has always become evident that this was not the only and universally valid way of Christian discipleship.

Contemporary Catholicism has placed monastic life in an entirely different perspective: that of concentration on the one thing needful, and that of liberation for the service of one's fellow men through submission to the strict rule of a spiritual brotherhood. In this form the "cloister" indicates to the world an impression of what it means to live solely for the service of God and man, and to renounce everything which does not immediately conduce to this twofold purpose.

The Reformers, in repudiating this way in principle, were motivated chiefly by the belief that it led to the danger of a false consciousness of belonging to an *élite* minority, of self-righteousness and work-righteousness, and that full service to man was thereby hampered. Further, a way which can in principle be taken only by some few persons, not by all, cannot be *the* way of true service of one's fellow men. The motive of world-renunciation is indeed partly justified; without some form of asceticism no man can be a Christian; but *the* answer to the question: "How is the disciple of Christ to live in the world?" is not world-renunciation, however necessary at certain times such an active protest against worldliness may be.

(*b*) The second way goes, so to speak, in the opposite direction. An attempt is made to bring the world into obedience to God and to dominate it in the name of Christ and by His authorization, to set up the Kingdom of God that is not of this world, but is in it. This is the programme of theocracy. This word theo-cracy comes from the political realm and means the subjection of the State to the will of God. But so long as the world remains world, and has not been transformed into a brotherhood in Christian faith, this domination is only possible through a twofold *quid pro quo*; through the identification of the will of God with law, and through the confusion of the rule of God with the ruler of the Church. This way also was taken in the Middle Ages. But we must remember that this was the way, not only of the Papacy, but also of certain Calvinist and other reformed groups. Today, however, it is no longer a real possibility, because the majority of those who have power in the State are not willing to subject themselves to the rule of the Church. The peoples of modern times have emancipated themselves from the Church's tutelage. But even apart from its practical impossibility this way is today forbidden to us for reasons of faith. We have recognized that only in freedom, and never under compulsion, can faith be true faith.

(*c*) The third solution is the one which immediately resulted from Luther's knowledge of justifying faith: the "Doctrine of the two Kingdoms". In faith the Christian is wholly and solely bound to his Lord Christ. But through the commandment of love he is instructed to serve his neighbour, by subjecting himself to the law of the world. Lutheranism has been stamped by this doctrine. In his struggle against the theocratic Papacy, Luther himself emphasized the independence of the State and all secular institutions over against the Church, and regarded this same liberation as one of the most important consequences of the rediscovery of Biblical faith.

From this, in very recent times, Luther has been misconstrued as having ceded to the State, thus emancipated, complete liberty to follow its own laws. There can be no question of this, since even for Luther the State stands under the law of God. On the other hand it is certainly correct that he did not clearly formulate as a critical principle the law which should be normative for the State, so that after all the substantial result was an uncritical acceptance of the State and secular institutions. Even the latest very numerous publications about the law[1] move in such a field of abstractions and generalities that no clear guidance has been given to the Christian as to how he is to behave in the world, especially as to what norms are also valid for secular associations. Luther's Doctrine of the two Kingdoms was not fitted to bridge the gap between the life of faith and life in the world. The tendency to leave secular institutions to themselves was still more accentuated by the repudiation of natural law in the romantic doctrine of the State and of law, and by the consequent legal positivism. The contrary tendency which has asserted itself since Karl Barth, to understand the State Christologically and measure it by the norm of faith, has inevitably resulted in a complete uncertainty and in an oscillation between a merely postulatory and declamatory and therefore ineffectual theocratism, and an attitude of political indifference based on the *sola gratia* principle.[2]

III

If we now turn to the problem of "The Christian in the World" with the new knowledge of the Ekklesia in mind, we

[1] By this I do not indeed mean the special systems of ethics such as Thielicke's in particular, but the dogmatic discussions about law and gospel. Cf. on this point "Erwägungen zur Lehre vom Gesetz" by G. Ebeling in *Zeitschrift für Theologie und Kirche*, 1958, pp. 270 ff.

[2] The first is the case where, ostensibly as a consequence of faith, it is postulated that Christ must be also Lord over the State, and where Luther's Doctrine of the two Kingdoms is expressly repudiated. The second, however, makes itself conspicuous in the most recent phase of development of the Barthian theology, especially in the "Letter to a Pastor in the German Democratic Republic", 1958 (*How to Serve God in a Marxist Land*, Association Press, New York)

may try by some examples to make clear to ourselves what is meant by these words. In concrete terms "The Christian in the World" means: the Christian as working man or working woman, as employer, as trade union leader, as judge, as welfare worker or educator, as husband or wife, as father or mother —in short, the Christian in his secular calling. Everyone who has such a calling knows how hard it is to obey Jesus' command of love in this social "niche" of his. It is particularly hard for the man who has a strong and pure determination to serve Christ. For the autonomy of the world is always and everywhere a frightful reality which, when it first confronts him, impresses the individual with a sense of his own impotence.

To this we must add the fact that the various autonomous areas, of business, of the State, of school and education, and so on, intersect in the individual human being. One is at the same time a husband or a wife, a citizen, a worker and member of a trade union organization, or an employer, and in addition a Church member. In none of these fields, even when each is taken by itself, is it possible quite simply to act according to the commandment of love of the Sermon on the Mount. The policeman or the judge cannot obey the word about turning the other cheek or about not judging without neglecting his duty as a policeman or a judge. His office, his professional duty, requires from him a quite definite action that cannot be brought into harmony with this rule of love. Business must be carried on by the employer in such a manner that it continues to be solvent —indeed that it more than pays its way. Only such practical instances make it clear beyond question that the legalistic interpretation of the words of the Sermon on the Mount is an impossibility. We must hold to Luther's insight: the law of the world as such cannot be transformed by the *agape* of Christian faith. But this does not mean that this law of the world is not accessible to influences exercised by the Ekklesia; that the State, for example, must be accepted just as it is and that there is no critical principle by which all secular institutions can be measured, and by which, even if they cannot themselves become Christian, they can at least be improved, made more humane, more serviceable to mankind.

We owe especially to Zwingli the first practical application, if not the theoretic development, of this thought. He was the first man to reform secular law and secular institutions on the basis of the faith[1] of the Reformation. But the chief influence

[1] Zwingli abolished the institution of serfdom and "small tithes", and was the first man to organize a State system of welfare for the poor

upon world history has been exercised by those Churches which did not so much think of themselves as institutions but were governed rather by the thought of a brotherhood based on faith, and regarded[1] the secular associations, for example, the State, the "civic community", as analogous to the "Christian Community", the Church.

IV

From the "Christian community", especially from the English and American Free Churches, that is, the Churches which pictured themselves and organized themselves as corporate bodies rather than as legal bodies, an impulse has gone out into the world that we may describe, in a wider sense than the purely political, as the tendency to create democratic forms of life. In the believing fellowship of these Free Churches it was easier than in the continental European State Churches to discover the analogy between the "Christian community" and the "civic community"; the principle of the recognition of every man as a person of equal dignity, the "democratic principle" (in the widest sense). Only by means of this principle was it at all possible to give an ethical basis and norm to secular associations.

Historians of law pointed out long ago[2] that the modern democracy of the U.S.A. has one of its essential roots in certain of these Free Churches. But this is not the only way in which the pattern of the Ekklesia has influenced the forms of human society. The same impulse has also led to the introduction of democratic ideas into business and the securing of equal rights and social privileges for women as for men, and thus has made "democracy as a way of life"[3] if not a dominant, then a real creative component factor in the whole life of man in every field. One of the most splendid products of this ethic of the equal dignity of man is the Constitution of the United States of America, which, as every historian knows, has had a decisive influence upon the evolution of political democracy in Europe.

[1] Karl Barth's book *Christengemeinde und Bürgergemeinde*, 1946 (E.T. *Community, State and Church*, Doubleday and Co., New York; "The Christian Community and the Civil Community", in *Against the Stream*, S.C.M. Press, London) represents a new approach of Barth's in the field of ethics, which differs considerably from that represented in *Rechtfertigung und Recht*. (E.T. *Church and State*, S.C.M. Press, London.) Fundamental to it is the concept of analogy which is also represented in our work. The only Biblical basis for this is what Paul says in Ephesians 5: 22–23, about the analogy between the relationship of Christ to the Christian community and that between husband and wife

[2] Cf. G. Jellinek, "*Die Erklärung der Menschen- und Bürgerrechte*", 1895

[3] Thus Ernst Wolf: *Die Königsherrschaft Christi*, 1958, p. 59 which adopts a terminology formerly current in Political Science

Here the significance of the Ekklesia as a pattern for secular fellowship is particularly evident.

V

It is not, however, the most urgent task of the Christian to give expression to the spirit of the Ekklesia in the State and in the institutions of human society in general. Much more important than all the institutional effects of faith is the daily life of the Christian in his environment. This would deserve treatment in concrete detail, but that is the task of ethics.[1] Like all other men, the Christian is placed in relationships which he can neither shape nor alter. It is here, however, in spite of all the autonomy of the professions, that faith, life with Christ and in His strength, must and can manifest itself. Certainly, the more that public considerations dominate the life of the individual man—business, professional duties, the autonomy of politics, of business and technological civilization—the narrower is the scope for the faith-ethic of *agape*. And yet every living member of the Ekklesia will perceive every day the summons and the guidance of his Lord, and bestir himself to prove that he belongs to Christ.

In this quite narrow personal circle the difference between a life in the spirit of love and a life with a purely secular orientation is most manifest. But here also it will be a matter of daily experience that the practically necessary and possible decisions cannot and should not be anticipated by a moral law, but that here especially the Christian is dependent on, and must seek for, the leadings of the Spirit, which are never predictable. But this means a life of prayer. A part of prayer is that we should be quiet before God and hear His voice, which has something new, original and, for the unbeliever, perhaps strange to say about every concrete problem of life. This it is which, next to a daily listening to the Word of scripture, truly marks the Christian as such, although this same activity can happen only "in secret".

VI

But the Spirit and the Word of Christ do not, however, mean guidance only, but also (as we saw) creativity, a new creation, a transformation. The history of the Church gives convincing evidence of this. The Christian is a changed man, that is, a man who is different from what he would be without faith, without the link that binds him to his Lord. This change must

[1] Cf. on this point H. Thielicke's great work *Theologische Ethik*, 1951 ff., 3 volumes (E.T. in preparation, *Theological Ethics*, S.C.M. Press, London) and his *Zeitschrift für evangelische Ethik*, Bethel Bielefeld

show itself in his daily life much more than in his political and social views. Both things are important and both things really happen: that through faith political, social, and cultural views are changed, but above all that another practical life issues from the changed heart. We must not let ourselves be misled by the superficial assertion that Christianity has changed nothing and improved nothing in the world. This opinion which we hear so often is certainly false, when stated in these general terms, though unfortunately there is only too much truth in it. The power of transformation that goes forth from the Ekklesia is, so to speak, proportionate to the degree of the effectiveness of the Holy Spirit within it. These life changes are the standard by which to measure the vitality of faith.

This is true both of the Ekklesia as a fellowship of faith, and of the individual Christian as such. Christians and the Church have not taken nearly enough to heart the question: "How much life-changing power flows from you?" But when, as a result of this connection between faith and life-changing, the belief arises that it might be possible to change the *whole* human race and transform it into the Ekklesia, that is fanaticism. The example of Jesus Himself, who had a Judas among His nearest and most trusted friends, disproves this. We must not indeed set limits in advance to the transforming power of the Holy Spirit. Rather must we acknowledge that through the changing of individual lives far-reaching consequences and whole sequences of changes have occurred. But to infer from the fact that such changes (perhaps of a wholly improbable kind) have actually been experienced, that the whole world can be changed, is an illusion that must end in bitter disappointment.

Yet, even so, that great transformations in world history resulted when men were apprehended by Christ, anyone who comes from the "Christian West" to the Far East will at once be aware. Men there are indeed neither worse nor better than the men in our hemisphere. But one notices that there decisive things are wanting which have taken shape in the Christian West in the course of a long history: the implicit acceptance of social responsibility, the idea of personality and its social and cultural consequences, the belief that things ought to be—and can be—otherwise, and additional differences. On the other hand we must also acknowledge that many things that were first known to Western man have today through the most diverse channels come to influence the whole world, not only where for long there has been genuine Foreign Mission work of vital spiritual power, but even in lands where the name of

Jesus Christ has hardly yet been heard. It would be much more effective than it is if the connection of Christianity with State compulsion and the power of money had not repeatedly obscured its illuminating power. We have no reason to be proud of our "Christian culture" or to paint for ourselves a romantically coloured picture of the "Christian world" of the Middle Ages. The history of the Christian Church provides inspiring pictures as well as those pictures which disgust and fill us with deep shame. The New Testament witness to Christ gives us reason for hope, and at the same time warns us against exaggerated hopes. The *great* hope, the hope of the Kingdom of God, is not a hope for this earthly world but the hope that "the fashion of this world passeth away" (1 Cor. 7: 31), and that one day this earthly historical world will be swallowed up in the victory of Christ. The life of the Christian in the world is therefore above all the life of a man who hopes for "that day"

CHAPTER 24

THE THEOLOGY OF PRAYER

It is significant that the chapter on prayer should form the conclusion of the doctrine of the new life through faith and the threshold to the last part of our *Dogmatics*, which deals with Eschatology. As we have repeatedly seen, and particularly in the chapter "The Christian in the World", the new life in faith is always "in part", infected with the questionable character of earthly existence. The Kingdom of God is something that we cannot ourselves create, certain though it may be that through faith we have a share in it by anticipation. We can only pray for its coming. But prayer is not only a *part* of sanctification, it is its very heart.

I

The new life, life in Christ through faith, has a periphery and a centre. The periphery is the life of the Christian in the world. This life is one broken by the nature of the world, a life which can only give indirect expression to its character as life in Christ, since the "fabric of the world" is determined by its own special laws, and therefore only allows the light and life of Christ to shine through it and express itself in it indistinctly. The life of the Christian in the world, and particularly in the State, as appears especially in Romans 13, does not admit of a direct but only of an indirect expression of the love of Christ. It is life in that realm which is furthest from the personal centre. This was our theme in the preceding chapter on the life of the Ekklesia and Christ's disciples in the world order. This is why we call it the periphery of the new life.

But the new life has also a centre, the "little point" in the world of which we spoke, the new being of the self, of the person, the love which is immediately bound up with faith. The sanctification of this centre is accomplished through the act of faith or when a man is apprehended by the Word of Christ. In prayer faith becomes event. Prayer is faith in action, "acting one's faith"; faith is a definite action in the life of the Ekklesia or of the believer. Through prayer we turn to the God who has communicated Himself to us, and thereby we withdraw from the world. Prayer is, philosophically expressed, "transcendence as event" on the part of man, corresponding to the "immanence of the Transcendent" in God's self-communication. The task of this chapter is not to give practical instruction in the right method of prayer—that is rather the task of preaching and Church "practice in Christianity", which unfortunately is cultivated much less by the Protestant Church than by the Catholic Church—but the working-out of the theological problems which reflection on prayer brings to our consciousness; in short, the project of a theology of prayer.

II

Prayer means conversation with God, calling upon God. The theological problem is exclusively connected with the true character of prayer, that it aims at conversation with God, that its true and decisive intention is that God should hear and that man should be heard. The person who has grown up in the traditions of the Church takes this for granted. He is not conscious of the astonishing character, the boldness and "irrationality" of this act. To make him aware of this is the first theological task.

There is, of course, a form of prayer which has in it nothing offensive to reason, namely meditation, quietism and contemplative absorption. To lose oneself in the divine mystery, to give oneself up to the feeling of reverence in the presence of the Inscrutable, the truth above all truths, the Being above all beings, the Ground and Abyss of all being, is an act which seems reasonable to thought. For this reason the "withdrawal of the intention to the One which never comes to our natural sight but must be conjured up with effort" appears as "recollection of the Spirit and turning inward of the same upon itself".[1] We need such moments of studied detachment from the distraction of sensuous life, in order to bring home the eternal truth to ourselves and to recollect ourselves.

Yet the invocation of God in the belief that He hears and attends to our call, that He hears and answers our prayer, and with the intention that He should do so, can be regarded only as a presumption of the insignificant creature in face of the infinite God. Indeed, is it not faith itself, is it not the knowledge of the Almighty, the Creator of heaven and earth, which must protest against this and condemn it as a ridiculous and at the same time overweening disregard for what is fitting, as a disregard of all true reverence? How can an infinitely small and insignificant creature harbour the thought that the Lord of the

[1] J. G. Fichte, *Die Anweisung zum seligen Leben*, 1806, p. 413 (Collected Works, ed. Fritz Medicus, Vol. III)

world will condescend to listen to its voice? He who rules the infinite universe, who thinks in terms of infinite space-time, who takes thought for and guides equally all the destinies of the millions of millions of His creatures, how should He "have time" to give Himself to you, this individual, and to listen to what you have to tell Him? If you believe that, you are looking on Him as your equal and by so doing are breaking the first commandment of reverence for God; you are doing something which is at the same time an absurdity and a blasphemy against God. There is therefore—so this reasoning concludes—more true reverence in the attitude of those who become speechless and silent in the presence of God. "To reverence the Ineffable in silence" (Goethe)—that seems the only form of prayer which is appropriate and can stand before the bar of reason.

III

"Silent reverence before the Ineffable", even though it has its place in prayer as prayer's environment, so to speak, is not what the Apostles and Jesus Himself have taught us about prayer. For God, who has communicated Himself to us in Jesus Christ, is not "the Ineffable". Indeed, even he who reveres the Ineffable does so because somehow he knows it as that which is exalted above all finite being. What is wholly unknown cannot and should not be the object of reverence. But more than that: we have a different God from Faust, who says: "Who can name Him, and who can confess 'I know Him'? The name is an echo, resounding amid clouds of fragrant incense, concealing a heavenly glow." Reason tells us that there is an Absolute which is behind all existence, the truth in all truths, a Transcendent in all things to which we give the name of "world". But this *ontōs on*, this true Existent, as reason tells us, has no name, for every name implies limitation. It never confronts us, least of all is it a subject confronting us. It is not a Thou to whom we could appeal, with whom we could hold converse. It can be described only by abstract concepts—"Being", "The Ground and Abyss", "the Infinite", best of all by the most abstract of all concepts, "The Absolute". But one cannot pray to the Absolute and no one has ever done so. That is the verdict of reason. Every trespass over this boundary of silent reverence is irrational, idolatrous. Yet precisely this is given to faith. "I have declared unto them Thy *name*" (John 17: 26).

While the reason of the solitary self forbids every trespass over this boundary as contrary to reason, as an illegitimate limitation of God, the self-communication of this absolute God has created a new situation. In Jesus Christ God has revealed to us His name as One on whom we must call. This is what the New Testament asserts, and this is the foundation on which the Ekklesia stands. The logos, the Eternal Word of God, has manifested His eternal Personal Being in a historical Person; He has indeed become man, and by revealing Himself to us He has communicated His own Personal Being to us to be our own. It is this event which is the concern of Christian faith. A man of history, Jesus, stands before us with His summons; indeed, His history, His life, His death and Resurrection *are* this summons. But the faith which has been the theme of the whole of this second section is simply the answer to this summons, the answer which consists in repeating the summons like an echo that is called forth in the heart of man by the call of God. Because, and only because, God has named His name we have the right and the power to make the incredible venture of calling upon Him by His name.[1]

In His high-priestly prayer (John 17) we find that He, who is the Son of the Father's eternal love, stands in our place and intercedes for us. Because of this we also are permitted to pray "in the name of Jesus". It is He, Jesus Christ, who is the sole legitimation and foundation of our prayers. He who knows this name as the name of God cannot but pray as Jesus has prayed. It is very significant that here in the high-priestly prayer, for the first and last time in the Gospel of John, God is called "Holy Father". Obviously what is meant by this is that here, at the conclusion of Jesus' revealing work, the holiness of God—that aspect of the divine Nature which describes God's distance from the world, His total otherness, His transcendence of the world—no longer implies a dividing barrier, but that His holiness has been revealed as one with His self-revealing love.

Jesus' invocation "Holy Father" is the high-priestly act by which the way is opened up for us to call upon the Father. At the same time we are given the sole ground for the legitimacy of our prayer. "Holy Father, keep through thine own name those whom thou hast given me." This is also the tenor of the first petition in the Lord's Prayer: "Hallowed be thy *name*". As we have said, prayer is the very centre of sanctification; but just at this point it is acknowledged in truth that God alone can sanctify. In the petition "Hallowed be thy name" it is confessed that we ourselves are not able to do this, since we do not know how to call truly upon the name of God "in spirit and in truth" (John 4: 23). Only God Himself can sanctify this

[1] Cf. *Dogmatics* I, Ch. 12, "The Name of God"

centre, this act of prayer, because He Himself is the only source of holiness. No prayer can, in fact, be addressed to the "God of the philosophers", that is, to the God who can be reached by our thought, the Absolute, the nameless One. But the God of faith is not the God of rational thought, but the God of historical revelation. He is the God who in His self-communication not only reveals to us His name, but bestows Himself upon us and thus not merely enables and permits us to call upon Him, but makes us glad and bold to do so.

IV

For this reason prayer is the touchstone of faith, and the theology of prayer is the touchstone of all theology. The Christianity of our theology is decided by whether we understand by "God" an I-Thou God or a nameless Absolute.[1] We have not a God, like the Absolute of the thinkers, alone in His absolute Being, uncommunicating and non-communicative, who "broods" in that silence which is described by the mystics of the Absolute, but a God who emerges from this silence and solitude by creating us as His counterparts and communicating Himself to us. And His will is that this creature should make use of this communication and call upon Him. To answer to the creative loving call of God with responsive love; this is the destiny for which man was created, and this call is the foundation of his being. It is the inconceivable tragedy of sin and its consequences that the creature, instead of giving this answer, answers with self-love and disobedience. In faith we understand it as the profoundest of these consequences that the spirit of man in its self-inflicted solitude should be compelled to form as a substitute the idea of an abstract impersonal Absolute, to which no prayer is possible, but at the most a "silent reverence" which is at the same time a contemplative absorption in one's own being. Where there is no longer a summons but merely an idea, no answer is possible either.

V

It is this loveless, solitary, prayerless creature on whom the loving Creator took pity by calling it back into the fellowship which had been lost. This is the meaning of the mission of the Son, Jesus Christ, who broke down the dividing wall of sin and by the word of reconciliation called the creature back to Himself. The call reaches us as the assurance which bestows upon

[1] It is acknowledged that Schleiermacher's work on the Christian faith will not stand up to judgment by this criterion. We wait eagerly to see what Tillich will have to say on the subject of prayer

us fellowship with God, and as the claim which calls us as God's possession to obedience. The answer to this summons is possible only in faith in Him who gives us access to the Father. The words "in the name of Jesus" are therefore no mere formula. They are, on the contrary, the recapitulation of the whole of saving history. In this "formula" we remind ourselves ever and again of the foundation on which we stand, and of the justification or legitimation of our praying.

Only in God's self-communication in Jesus Christ has the Creator and Lord of the world come so near to us as to be accessible to our call. For in Jesus He has become a Person, or rather in the human Person of Jesus he has revealed His eternal Personal Being. "I have manifested thy name unto men" (John 17: 6). This word was spoken on the eve of the Crucifixion. On the Cross was completed God's self-communication, the revelation of His name, which began in the Old Covenant. And only thereby is the completely personal relation to God realized in those "who believe on His name" (John 1: 12). The Word of the Cross is the personal call of God which is answered by the call of the child of God—"Abba" (Rom. 8: 15), which is at the same time the call of the Holy Spirit and the answer of the believer.

Here then too it becomes perfectly clear why for reason, which with its abstract idea of God remains alone, solitary and without counterpart, prayer is impossible. Prayer presupposes the personal God, and the personal God is the God who speaks to me, saying to me, "You are my child". Only the God who is revealed as love, makes a completely trustful and fearless prayer possible, in which at the same time there is reverence for the *honour* of God, the Lord.' The conversation between God and man, "The Communion of the Christian with God" (Wilhelm Herrmann), was begun by God when He took the initiative by "revealing His name". This conversation has already begun in Old Testament religion, in the Psalms, which presuppose the prophetic revelation, and it there received an incomparably personal expression. But only in communion with the God who has *wholly* revealed to us in Jesus Christ His Personal Being, does prayer attain to its full heartfelt confidence; a confidence which yet never allows us to forget the holiness of Him whom we meet in prayer, or to forget in mystical enthusiasm to keep that distance from Him which reverence demands.

This line of theological reflection seems to contradict the fact that prayer is by no means a specifically Christian phenomenon, but one that belongs to the history of religion in general.

In all religions prayer is offered in some manner, and we must not make light of this fact or relegate the prayers of the "heathen" merely to the field of psychology. When we face the wealth of evidence provided by Heiler's classic work on prayer, we must take this as fully established. Every prayer, even the most primitive prayer of a non-Christian, should be regarded by us with no other feelings than those of the deepest respect, as a sign that "God has not left Himself without witness" (Acts 14: 17).

Even the consciousness of solemn moral responsibility, which we can deny neither to heathen nor to atheists, is a sign of such a witness borne by God to Himself. How much more is this true of calling upon God! Both are fundamental manifestations of our humanity which is based on the Divine.[1] But this is only one side of the truth. The other is no less clearly seen from Heiler's book. Where God is not known in His special, historical revelation, both prayer and the underlying conception of God are full of "primitive" anthropomorphisms. And where it is spiritualized it turns into mere meditation or mystical absorption, as Heiler's other work *Buddhistic Mysticism* clearly enough shows. At least in its original and pure form which has survived in certain places till the present day, Buddhism neither knows of prayer nor practises it.[2]

In the different forms of "spiritualized" religion in Hinduism the situation is similar to that in the "spiritualization" of Buddhism. The more spiritual they become, the more they approximate to a thinking about divine things which leaves no room for "communion with God", but which practises in its place a contemplative absorption in the ground of the soul such as is familiar to us from Western mysticism. The true mystic does not pray, he meditates and seeks to reach a condition in which he knows and feels his unity with the Infinite. The prayer of Jesus is that prayer in which spiritualization is complete, but here it moves not in the direction of dissipating the personal character of God, but in the direction of conceiving His will as the will to realize the Kingdom of God. Therefore it does not lead to the annulment of the distance separating man from the God who confronts him, but combines in a perfect manner personal trust with reverence and a sense of distance. It is just for this reason that prayer can function as the criterion

[1] See above, pp. 147 ff.

[2] A Buddhist hermit philosopher in Northern Thailand declared to the author very proudly, "We Buddhists do not pray. We have the command of the Master to save ourselves"

of faith, and the doctrine of prayer as the touchstone of all theology.

VI

But with this knowledge we have at the same time come in sight of the decisive theological problem: the problem of the answering of prayer. This is the great stumbling-block for reason. For it makes the incredible assertion that the Almighty not only hears us, but that, *because* we ask Him, He does something that without this He would not do; that consequently our request is not in vain, but that it takes effect in an action of God. Here the sharpest protest is made, not only by unbelievers, but also by many thinking believers. In fact, this is the point where primitive anthropomorphism, which pictures God as a Father similar to man, and the highest conception of God are in the closest proximity. Is it not all-too-naïve and childish, or even the utmost arrogance, to believe that by our prayers we can and must come to the help of divine Providence? Did not the Lord Jesus Himself warn us "your Heavenly Father knoweth what things ye have need of, before ye ask Him"? (Matt. 6: 8.) And does not Jesus' own prayer in Gethsemane, which ends with "Nevertheless, not my will, but Thine be done", teach us that every trespass over this boundary, such as the belief that because of our prayer something happens that would not otherwise happen, is impermissible? On grounds of reverence for God's supreme wisdom and goodness, must we not renounce all petition, since it is an encroachment upon the sovereignty of God?

And yet the believing witness of the Bible and also that of the whole Christian community goes counter to this thought. When we think of the host of weighty witnesses such as Augustine, Luther, Calvin, Pascal, Hamann, Kierkegaard and many others, it becomes hardly possible to assert that the conception of the answering of prayer is the expression of a naïvely anthropomorphic conception of God. The truth is rather that here the rational speculative conception of God and that of faith come as it were into head-on collision as incompatible opposites. But we owe a theologically thought-out answer to this plausible objection of reason. This answer is as follows:

Prayer in the name of Jesus which is confident that it will be answered is the final proof of genuinely Christian faith in God, because it takes seriously two fundamental Biblical thoughts: that of the personal self-communication of God and that of correspondence on the personal plane. The God who calls us in Jesus Christ into fellowship with Himself desires that this will of His to fellowship should be taken seriously. Fellowship is possible only in freedom. It implies just as much the independence of the human subject as it primarily implies that of the Absolute Subject, that is, God. It is the miracle of the divine self-communication—a miracle never to be understood by logic—that it regards and treats the man to whom it communicates itself in Jesus Christ as a person; that is, as a counterpart whom God takes into account. The supreme act of faith is "reckoning" with the God who listens to the request of His child and grants it. God hears man. This means that He condescends to receive as a gift what the believer says to Him. This is the uttermost condescension of God: that He accepts the trust and obedience bestowed upon Him as something that He would not otherwise know about, and that creates a new state of affairs for Him.

This, when all is said, is simply that the God who bestows love on us allows Himself to be loved in return. The always inconceivable self-communication of God presupposes the equally inconceivable (yet to faith, certain) self-limitation of the absolute ineffable God to the personal and "communicating" God. And this self-limitation is the foundation of what we know in simple faith: that God answers our prayer which we say, calling upon the name of Jesus, that is, upon the miracle of His self-communication.

This is the completest antithesis to the absolute Divinity of reason. God, who in Jesus Christ declares Himself to be our Father, declares thereby that we are His children on whom He bestows the filial right of supplication. What corresponds on the side of man to this inconceivable condescension is the equally inconceivable confidence of faith, which takes His Fatherhood seriously and exercises our right of sonship. Of course God, as the Almighty and Omniscient One, knows what we reveal to Him, even without our saying it. But He does not know of it in such a way as is alone possible for Him to know it through our prayer, which is made in childlike trust. For this reason, as John 14–16 says, there is a strict and necessary connection between prayer in the name of Jesus and the answering of prayer.

In faith, that is, in real correspondence on the personal plane, God's self-communication becomes communication in the literal sense. God lets us say something to Him on the ground of His self-communication to us. Through His self-limitation God makes room for the freedom of the creature.[1] Through His

[1] Cf. *Dogmatics* I, Ch. 18, "God, the Almighty"

self-communication He creates a real relationship of confrontation, which is both the identity with Him posited through the Holy Spirit in faith and at the same time the non-identity which receives its greatest emphasis in faith in Him as the Lord and Creator. God, as it were, rescinds His omnipotence in order to make room for our freedom, and in like measure He renounces at this place His independence of the creature. Of His own free choice He makes Himself dependent on what His child says to Him. He not only hears, but He answers.

This self-limitation, identical with His condescension, is the utmost expression of His self-communication. As God has limited Himself in the Incarnation of His Son, without ceasing to be the Infinite, so He limits Himself when He graciously condescends to hear and to answer prayers. This is why Jesus says in John that *that* prayer is answered which is made in His name. The one self-limitation is based on the other and at the same time limited by it.

These thoughts reach the uttermost limit of human comprehension, but must be followed out by theological reflection if this is not to be overwhelmed by the impersonality of the idea of the Absolute. They are legitimated and justified by their Christological rigour as well as by their truth to the apostolic witness of faith. Briefly and simply expressed: The God who communicates Himself in Jesus Christ is a God who hears and answers prayer. The thought of the divine self-limitation is the only thought which necessitates a decisive renunciation of the impersonal conception of the Absolute. This thought is simply the conceptual reflection of the *kerygma* that Jesus is the Christ. That we should pray in the confidence that our prayer will be answered is an expression of our faith in Jesus the Christ. It is just in relation to this problem of the answering of prayer that we show, by our readiness and ability to maintain our belief in God's self-limitation, whether we are taking seriously the thought of God's self-communication in our theological reflection.

That God answers prayer does not, of course, mean that He answers every prayer in the way that the supplicant intends. The reason for the answering of prayer is at the same time the norm by which we judge what expectations about the answering of our prayers are legitimate, and what are illegitimate. This has been from early times the theme of practical Church instruction in prayer. God often answers in a quite different way from what we intend, when we pray. But He answers every prayer genuinely spoken in the name of Jesus. Therefore in the genuine prayer of faith there is always conjoined with the certainty of an answer the thought "nevertheless not what I will, but what Thou wilt".

Through God's self-communication man becomes a "labourer together with God" (1 Cor. 3: 9)—a thought of such audacity, that a man whose heart is rooted and grounded in the sovereignty of God as the foundation of all his faith scarcely dares to give it expression. And indeed he does not really do so, but cancels it again by the qualification "in the name of Jesus". It is only the Christ in him, the Holy Spirit, that can say this. What he hears in faith in Christ is not primarily Christ's claim. Rather is he placed "at the side of God" by the assurance of adoption as a child of God or son of God, and precisely this is the astonishing privilege of being a labourer together with God. He is not only a labourer together with God, as a witness to Jesus Christ in the visible world, but also in what happens through prayer in the invisible realm. But he is this solely and wholly "in the name of Jesus".

VII

Can man then through his prayer influence the will of God? This way of speaking betrays that it comes from another dimension than that of faith. There can be no talk of "influencing" the will of God, for such talk would be to turn God into an object and prayer into a cause. Not only the *expression* of faith, as it is authoritatively to be found in the New Testament, but also its *intention* lies in a quite different dimension from that in which cause and effect are to be found. But God's gracious and appreciative reckoning with the prayer of faith is totally different. It is, as we said, the expression of the complete fellowship between Him and man "in Christ".

To the objections made by the advocates of the abstract conception of God, that God is thereby limited in an unseemly manner and thus turned into an idol, we answer: "Quite the contrary!" God is so great that He is even able and willing to hear the prayers of His children. But this greatness can certainly only be recognized by the man who knows that the living God of Biblical revelation, the Lord of the world and the God of love, is infinitely greater than the "Absolute" of rational speculation, which—with Spinoza—is only willing and able to conceive of a God that is loved, not of a God who Himself loves. As we believe in the God who is so great that He knows and loves every individual, so we believe in the God whose omnipotence permits Him to answer prayer. Indeed, the belief in the answering of prayer is victory over the abstract impersonal concept of God, even within Christian theology.

VIII

For Christian faith, however, prayer is not in the first instance supplication, but praise, worship and thanksgiving. A prayer is a prayer that springs from faith, only when it is praise and thanksgiving in the presence of Him from whom the believer has received everything that he is and that he has. In thankful praise that end is achieved, for whose sake God created man. For in thankful praise and in worship God receives due honours from His creatures; He finds that counterpart which answers Him in the same way as He in love calls it into being, in such a way that it reflects back the glory of God. It was to glorify God that we were created.

This is simply to take seriously the thought of God as the Lord whom no impersonal concept, no concept of the Absolute can reach, but who is exalted as the Creator above all the world and all impersonal abstractions, who stands as the merciful One above all ethical legalism, the God who is holy, and who is Love. When we thank and praise God, we remember that we are able to do so only because He has manifested His name to us, has revealed in Jesus Christ His nature and His will as the origin of our being, and has implanted and given life to this knowledge in us through His Spirit, sustaining it from day to day. The highest possible privilege on earth is that of praising God in the name of Jesus through the Holy Spirit. This is the nearest approximation to the final goal, to eternal life in the Kingdom of God. In this act of praise, faith as a life-act is "actually present". In this praise we have an anticipation of that which is ultimate and eternal.

PART 4

THE CONSUMMATION IN ETERNITY OF THE DIVINE SELF-COMMUNICATION

CHAPTER I

FAITH AS HOPE

We can describe human existence, created through Jesus Christ as new being, by the three words which are also given prominence in the New Testament as words of primary importance; faith, love, and hope. The first and fundamental word is faith, for through faith we are apprehended by Christ and apprehend Him. Faith is therefore the principal word in the proclamation of the gospel. Through faith God communicates to us His own life, His love. For this reason faith is concerned with *agape*, God's love. At the same time this love is the criterion by which we recognize whether our faith is genuine faith. In Christ, only that faith avails "which proves itself effectual through love" (Gal. 5: 6). For faith is not mere knowledge; it is the self-communication of the divine life, the love which manifests itself as the principle of the new life.

And yet every sincere disciple of Jesus must bewail the fact that this necessary fruit of faith has developed so little in him, that this fruit is rather a bud than a ripened fruit. Therefore he looks for the perfected form of this self-communication of God, in which the work that now has only begun in us will be completed. And this expectation of a future event, which is necessarily bound up with faith and love, is hope. For this reason faith is hardly distinguishable from hope. For we believe in the same Christ "whose glory we beheld" (John 1: 14) although it is concealed under its seeming contradiction (*contraria species*) in the Cross. Therefore there can be no faith which does not at once turn into hope. For this reason the life of the Christian in its totality can be equally well described by this word, as the First Epistle of Peter describes it. "Blessed be the God and Father of our Lord Jesus Christ, who according to His abundant mercy hath begotten us again to a lively hope by the resurrection of Jesus Christ from the dead" (1 Peter 1: 3).

But in treating of hope, we must now deal with it not as an act of human consciousness but considering its ground and content, that is, the consummation towards which hope reaches forward, the "objective" ground of hope by which it is begotten and sustained, and by which it is distinguished from mere human hopes.

Therefore this concluding part of our *Dogmatics* is not in the nature of an appendix which, in Schleiermacher's words, "is useful only as a pattern to which we should approximate",[1] whose justification is "the impulse to form a conception of the state that succeeds death"[2] and which therefore cannot have "the same value as the doctrines already handled".[3] On the contrary, if this concept is at all legitimate it is a "fundamental doctrine" of Christian teaching. For according as a man has or has not this hope, he is, or is not, a Christian.

I

The unconditional necessity of this bond between hope and faith and love is the first point into which we must attain a more exact insight, and this accordingly is also the theme of this first chapter. A discussion with an uneschatological theology which teaches otherwise, or which understands by Eschatology something different from this, will follow in the proper place.[4]

The ground of Christian hope is none other than the ground of Christian faith, namely and exclusively God's self-communication as it creates faith through the witness of Jesus Christ. This is also the clear declaration of the authoritative Apostles, particularly of Paul and John. But this hope is not based on the witness of the Apostles, but on Jesus Christ Himself as we apprehend Him and He apprehends us in their witness. Just as He is our righteousness and our life, so is He our future, our hope. He is the consummation, the fulfilment of the prophetic promise. On Him alone Christian hope is based; not on any apocalyptic or eschatological statements of scripture. For He Himself is the self-communication of God, He Himself is "Immanuel", God with us. Through Him we possess God as the One who is coming to us.

Our God, the "living God" of faith, distinguishes Himself from all thoughts that man entertains in his mind about God, and also from all the conceptions of God current in the religions, by this one thing above all else: that He is the God with a goal, the God of the Kingdom of God, that is, the God who not only enters into history but directs history towards a goal. This we have already made clear when we spoke of the nature of God[5] and emphasized God's will to self-communication and the affirmation of His own glory as the essential characteristics of

[1] Schleiermacher, *Der christliche Glaube*, Vol. II, Ch. 157, p. 391 (E.T. *The Christian Faith*, Edinburgh, 1928, p. 696)

[2] *Ibid.*, p. 393, Ch. 158 (E.T. p. 698) [3] *Ibid.*, p. 399, Ch. 159 (E.T. p. 703)

[4] See Appendix "On the 'Demythologized Eschatology' of Bultmann" following this chapter

[5] Cf. on this point *Dogmatics*, Part I, section 1, "The Nature of God and His Attributes", esp. chapters 14 and 15

the God of Biblical revelation. But this nature and will of God we can know only in history, in the Act and Word of His self-communication, and in this believing knowledge we are, so to speak, drawn into His own movement towards the world. To believe in this God means then simply to be apprehended by His coming to us.[1] Faith is in its very essence a being directed towards the goal of God, a sharing in His will to self-communication and the affirmation of His own glory. Faith is the "impulse" towards the goal which comes from the goal. Faith is therefore equally a being moved by Him and a being moved towards Him.

It is therefore necessarily bound up with a twofold consciousness, a consciousness of Him who has already come and of Him whom we are still to expect, who has not yet come. The God who is apprehended in Christ through faith can therefore never be apprehended apart from His *telos*. This *telos*, this goal of the movement of self-communication, may be described by different words, such as "eternal life" or "the Lordship of God" or "the Kingdom of God"—but this one thing alone is decisive, that this God of faith can never be recognized or known or believed in apart from His goal. The same thing is true on the human side. Believing existence is always at the same time hoping existence, existence in expectation of this goal.

Therefore, when we spoke of God's nature, we did not speak of Him in the concepts of any philosophy but under the two attributes of His nature which themselves point to this movement towards the goal: His holiness, which means His will to glorify Himself, and His love, His self-communicating life. God wills to reveal perfectly His majesty and glory, and He wills to communicate Himself perfectly in His love. In faith in Christ we apprehend this and at the same time are apprehended thereby. But at the same time we are aware in faith that this having apprehended and having been apprehended is something that has not yet reached its goal, is incomplete, that the perfect revealing and the perfect realization of this will is yet to come, and that therefore we are still "absent from the Lord on our journey" (2 Cor. 5: 6), but that this goal, as God's goal, *must* be reached.

II

This goal has indeed been reached in Jesus the Christ, though not yet manifestly, but only in a concealed manner; not yet in the form of glory, but only in the form of a servant in the Cross.

[1] Here there is a play on words untranslatable into the English "coming to us": a play on *Zu-kommen* and *das zu-kommende, die Zukunft*. (TR.)

Therefore, the "Kingdom of God is in your midst" (Luke 17: 21) —namely there, where Christ who speaks to us is present—but not yet in the manner that corresponds to the true will of God. It is there already and it is not there yet. But in this "not-yet", because it is comprehended in a "now-already", there is implicit the *certainty* of the future consummation. It is Christ Himself and His rule of God that is the goal.

But this Christ and His kingly rule is still concealed, so that the eye of the natural man sees nothing of this glory of His. Above all, as the Crucified, He is there only in the form of His Incognito, in the "form of a servant" and thus in contradiction to what He already and in His own nature is. This concealment was excellently described by Luther as "seeming contradiction" (*contraria species*). It is in contradiction to the glory which belongs to Christ by nature. The existence of the believer is therefore in reality "eschatological existence" (Bultmann),[1] but that means an existence that points beyond itself, an existence conscious of its own incompleteness. It is impossible to *stand* in the faith, without *moving* towards the goal. As an expectant mother carries within her the child that is to be born, and awaits with certainty the event of its birth, so faith carries the future within it. This future the believer expects wholly and solely from the coming of Jesus Christ. Like faith itself, it must come to him.

The hope of the believer has its basis in the transcendence which in Jesus Christ has begun to be imminent in history, but whose fulfilment must burst asunder the limits of history and of this world. It is God in His coming to us who creates faith as the first thing, but who, in faith, has not yet reached His goal. Even the working out of faith in love is not the perfect form of God's coming to us. For so long as we live in the world, this love is still bound to "the form of this world" and hidden by it, even though through all these concealments it is recognizable as truly human and truly divine. This form must pass away, the body of death must be done away in order that love can appear in its true and perfected form. Faith must become sight. For it is the paradox of seeing and not-seeing, of knowing and not-knowing, of having and not having, of love that is always present at the same time as its opposite. But it does not belong to the nature of divine love to be present along with its opposite. The picture of the "treasure in earthen vessels" (2 Cor. 4: 7) does indeed correspond to our present existence but not to the nature of the treasure itself.

[1] Cf. Appendix following this chapter

It is therefore wrong to describe faith as in itself the "right", the truly human mode of man's existence. Of course, just by reason of the tension between "now already" and "not yet", faith is the most inward form of existence that we know (Kierkegaard). If, as everyone does, we take the world as it is as a given presupposition, then certainly faith is the authentic form of human existence. But because it has to bear this tension, and possesses a Christ whom the world has compelled to bear the form of a servant, this is not the authentic and finally valid will of God. Therefore faith must turn into the hope of the appearing of Christ in a form which corresponds to His divine nature. God's *final* intention is not the life destroyed in the death of the Cross, not the divinity concealed under the disgrace of the gallows, but the divine life in its form of glory.

Faith stretches out as hope to the transcendence of the contradiction between Christ's form as a servant and His glory. The form of a servant taken by the Crucified was thrust upon Christ by the sinful world, by what was alien to Him, by the revolt of the world against God, by the wickedness, by the injustice and the lovelessness that constitute the nature of this "wicked" world. But the life that thus surrendered itself to death, because it is the life of God, is eternal life. In order to set the world free and restore it to the glory of its creation, the life of God surrendered itself to this conflict-burdened paradoxical form. The broken light is not the true form of light; life overwhelmed by death is not the life of God which wills to become manifest. Life without dissension, without conflict—that is the meaning and the goal of the revelation in Christ.

"Eschatological existence" is existence certain of its future liberation from this contradiction. "He who hath begun a good work in you will perform it until the day of Jesus Christ" (Phil. I: 6). He who is concealed under the form of a servant must be revealed in the form of glory. As He who has here already made a beginning Jesus is called the Risen One. The Resurrection is the beginning of the Last Things, of the Consummation, limited to Him in His historical manifestation. But Christ does not will that He alone should be the Risen One. He wills that all those for whose sake He died and for whom He surrendered Himself to death should rise from the dead. It is only His Resurrection that makes clear to us the deadly seriousness of His movement downwards towards us and the full significance of our redemption through His death on the Cross, and it does so by giving us the certainty that we too shall rise with Him.

Faith is like a seedling. It is its nature to "sprout", and this "sprouting" we call faith. The faith that has no hope of its perfecting in something more than faith, in sight, has lost that seminal power and is thus not genuine faith at all but dead faith. But this seminal power lies in the movement of God which we apprehend in Christ and by which we are apprehended. Therefore faith can never be contented just to believe. It longs to be transformed, itself, from faith to that which it believes in, and to be transformed in such a manner that the contrast between the form of a servant and glory will finally be transcended. Only then is God's goal reached: His glorification of Himself and His self-communication.

When God in Christ says to man: "I love you", He says to him: "I have loved you from eternity and will love you to eternity." A love that does not long to be boundless is not love at all. Every laying down of limits is a denial of love, the proof of its lack of seriousness. The whole of Eschatology is contained in this one saying of Paul: "For I am persuaded that neither death, nor life, nor angels, nor principalities, nor powers, nor things present, nor things to come, nor height, nor depth, nor any other creature, shall be able to separate us from the love of God, which is in Christ Jesus our Lord" (Rom. 8: 38, 39). To believe is to be apprehended by this love. Hope is the certainty that this love lasts for ever and that it will not rest until it possesses us wholly. It does not possess us wholly so long as we are imprisoned in the "body of death" and determined by the "form of this world". God's glorifying of Himself which is identical with His self-communication in love only reaches its goal by dissolving *this* form of the world and transforming the world into the form of glory.

III

Thus there is no need of an apocalyptic mythology on which to establish an Eschatology. It *is* established in Jesus, the Christ. Jesus bears the name of Christ as the One in whom the Lordship of God begins to find its realization. There is no need of special promises of eternal life. Jesus Christ is Himself in His Person the promise of eternal life. Or rather in Him it is already present (John 11: 25, 26). Therefore, the hope of the perfect reign of God is not dependent on the conceptions to be found in the Biblical witness. The apocalyptic utterances of the New Testament may stem from an alien mythology and may themselves be of a mythological nature, but they in no way compromise the hope of the eternal future which is based on faith itself. The question about Jewish apocalyptic and its validity for us is only a question of decisive importance for us so long as faith is based on the word of the Bible instead of on Christ Himself. In Eschatology once again we see that the decisive question is whether faith is faith in Jesus Christ or faith in the word of the Bible. Jesus Christ Himself is not dependent on results of critical scholarship. He Himself stands above all the discussions of scholars about time-bound apocalyptic. He Himself, not any doctrine about Him, is the ground of faith, as He is also the ground of hope.

This brings also an elucidation of the meaning of the word "hope" as it is used and should be used by the community of believers in Christ. In our everyday experience to "hope for" means the expectation of a wished-for event in the future. There is therefore always implied in it the element of complete uncertainty. But the Christian hope is of another kind. It is no uncertain expectation based on a wish, but the expectation of the future that has its basis in the known will of God, and therefore shares in the certainty of this knowledge. This knowledge—the knowledge of faith—is indeed profoundly different from the knowledge of an object.[1] It is of the nature of knowledge of the Thou, which comes into existence only through self-communication. The certainty of this knowledge which we call faith determines also the character of the certainty of hope. The same God who in Christ assures me of His love, assures me also in Him of its eternal fulfilment.

What He promises me in Christ is simply the destiny for which I was created, a destiny which can already be known from my creation—though admittedly only by faith. For this I was created, for this man and humanity was created, in order to live in His Word of love. Faith in Christ is at the same time the beginning of true self-knowledge, namely the knowledge of what I am "in God's sight", according to God's plan for me. The identity or coincidence of God's self-communication and man's self-knowledge is the witness of the Holy Spirit in me, and in this witness there is at the same time contained the certainty of the hope. It is therefore anything but subjective and uncertain, just as it is anything but wish-fulfilment. It is indeed in the highest degree subjective, inasmuch as it can be reached only through the participation of the whole man. And certainly it is wish-fulfilment inasmuch as in it the highest longings of human nature are fulfilled. But the certainty of faith and hope is based not on any subjective thoughts, but in God's Word of address, which as the witness of the Holy Spirit is His speaking

[1] See above, pp. 251 ff.

in me. And it is not as a fulfilment of my wishes that the Kingdom of God comes, but as the consummation of the self-glorifying of the divine Will and the self-communication of His life in love.

Therefore, if we may use the word, this hope has a strictly "objective" and well-founded character. It is based on the historical event of Jesus Christ and has the will of God the Creator and Redeemer as its foundation. As we have already seen that justification by faith is a subordinate part of the central revelation of God's righteousness—in it God comes to His rights over me—so the hope which is based on our faith has the honour of God and His inconceivable love as its ground and goal. What is at stake is primarily the glorifying of God and not man's happiness and salvation. That this will of God—to glorify Himself—includes also in itself man's salvation is not primary but secondary. Therefore no wish-psychology can assail the Christian hope, any more than an epistemology which talks of "emotional thinking". The hope of faith stands unshaken by both, upon its own foundation, so long as faith is based really on Christ and not on human authorities.

The Christian hope is not only the last chapter of theological doctrine; it is itself the goal to which the Christian faith reaches forward. It is what faith intends, what is at stake in faith. But this is nothing else than the full revelation of what is already given to us in faith in Jesus as the true Word of God: that the love of God is the first and last thing, through which we and the world were created. That this love will be manifest without concealment by the world and that God "will be all in all": this is the meaning of the gospel.

APPENDIX

ON THE "DEMYTHOLOGIZED" ESCHATOLOGY OF BULTMANN

IN his newest work *Geschichte und Eschatologie* (Tübingen, 1958)[1] Bultmann is concerned to indicate the eschatological character of man's existence in faith, disclosing it at the same time as the "radically historic self-understanding" of man. With his wonted ability and profundity, he shows how the Western understanding of history, which at first was determined by the Christian faith, gradually changed, and, under the influence of the rationalism of the Enlightenment and of modern natural science, fell a victim to a complete secularization, so that its course seems set, as if by destiny, for nihilism. "The end, it seems, is nihilism."[2] "Is it possible to surrender our insight into man's character as a historical being, that is to say, to demonstrate its invalidity? Or must we say that man's historical character is not yet fully understood, and must be thought through to its final consequences, in order to transcend the nihilistic interpretation?"[3] "Such questions can be answered only when we recognize clearly the *idea* of history. It seems to me that the real problem is concealed when we one-sidedly direct our inquiry to the *meaning* in history."[4]

Thus in this book it is not eschatology but history, that is, not a theological theme but one belonging to the philosophy of history, which we have before us. Yet it is clear beyond any doubt what Bultmann's own interpretation of Christian Eschatology is. He places it primarily in the context of the apocalyptic of late Judaism, which, as he tells us in more detail in another context, consists of mythical conceptions which "are no longer possible" for men in the scientific age (cf. on this point his *Kerygma und Mythos* edited by H. W. Bartsch, 1^2, 1951, pp. 16 and 21).[5] Thus one and all they are subjected to the demythologizing process, which is indeed Bultmann's general theological programme. Here naturally his great knowledge of the history of religion, to which as an exegete he has all his life applied himself, proves useful to him.

Of special interest for us is what Bultmann has to say about the "Historicizing and neutralizing of Eschatology in primitive Christianity." Paul does not regard the eschatological consummation as "the completion of the history of the Jewish nation, not even in the

[1] English original *History and Eschatology*, The Gifford Lectures, Edinburgh, 1957 (Nelson and Sons, London). As Brunner quotes from the German version, whose meaning deviates from the original English owing to a revision by the author, I have translated this German text, and supplied in the notes also the pagination of parallel passages in the English version. (TR.)

[2] p. 11, English Version p. 11 [3] p. 12, E.V. p. 11 [4] *Ibid.*

[5] E.T. *Kerygma and Myth*, London, 1953, pp. 3 and 9

extended form depicted in deutero-Isaiah and some later Jewish versions of the eschatological hope, namely, that the welfare of Israel is at the same time the welfare of all peoples which achieve a certain unity with Israel." On the contrary, his "eschatology is decisively modified" by the fact that "his conception of the eschatological salvation is determined by his anthropology."[1] "Thereby the conception of salvation is centred upon the individual. The reign of God is righteousness, and with it, freedom," and "this salvation is already present". Here Bultmann appeals to a quotation from Isaiah in the second letter to the Corinthians: "Behold, now is the acceptable time, behold, now is the day of salvation."[2] "The eschatological gift of the Spirit, expected by Jewish aspirations, has already been bestowed upon believers, so that they are now already 'sons of God' and free men instead of slaves."[3]

Certainly Bultmann concedes that faith is "something provisional in so far as the life of faith leads to the life of sight".[4] "But, firstly, this hope is centred on the individual, and Paul is no longer looking at the history of peoples and the world . . . secondly . . . the decisive event has already happened. Neither life nor death . . . shall be able to separate us from the love of God in Christ."[5] "The history of the world has disappeared from Paul's gaze, and instead of it something else has been discovered, the historical character of human life, i.e. the history which everyone experiences or can experience for himself, and in which alone he gains his real essence."[6] In this connection it becomes evident that Bultmann unquestioningly adopts the categories of Heidegger to interpret the Pauline message. "The call which comes to man from each situation is the call of God."[7] He interprets thus the battle of Paul against legalism. "The pious legalist always thinks that he is already the one he has to become. For he has anticipated all decisions by his resolution to obey the law, whose commandments relieve him from taking the particular decisions required by each situation he meets."[8]

This becomes still more evident in Bultmann's description of Christian existence. "This is the life in freedom, for which man is set free by the grace which has appeared in Christ. He is set free from his past, from his sin, from himself as the old man"—"set free for a genuine historical life, that is, free to make independent and responsible decisions in each of life's encounters".[9] In this description Bultmann uses the formulations which we also have used but with a complete change of meaning. "The true historical character of the Christian life becomes apparent also from the fact that this life is a continuous transition from the 'no longer' to the 'not yet'." "As one apprehended by Christ, Paul strives towards the goal he longs to reach. Thus the Christian life is not static but dynamic."[10] But by this Bultmann does not mean eternity beyond the grave, nor the future

[1] p. 48, E.V. p. 42 [2] *Ibid.* [3] p. 49, E.V. p. 42 [4] *Ibid.*
[5] *Ibid.* [6] p. 49, E.V. p. 43 [7] p. 50, E.V. p. 44
[8] p. 51, E.V. p. 44 [9] p. 51, E.V. p. 45 [10] p. 53, E.V. p. 46

Consummation, but a "continually new overcoming of the bonds of the flesh in the power of the Spirit". "The indicative of Christian existence is actually the basis of the imperative under which the life of the believer is lived." "And thus Paul achieved the solution of the problem of history and eschatology, as it was raised by the non-appearance of Eschatology." [*Sic*!][1] This solution was "the conception of the eschatological event as happening in the present" which was developed even more radically by John. And yet Bultmann finds himself compelled to make the observation that "For both Paul and John the present time here is a time between the coming of Christ and the Consummation."[2]

It cannot have escaped the reader who has his New Testament open before him that Bultmann has two aims. First, an existential interpretation of New Testament faith, which really does achieve what Bultmann expects from it, namely to make this faith intelligible to the thought of our times; and, secondly, a demythologization which implies an almost complete elimination of everything that does not fit his definition of faith as self-understanding. To achieve this, certain violent exegetical measures are necessary; for example, the assertion that "Paul is no longer looking at the history of peoples and the world, nor is he looking into a new history".[3] This assertion flatly contradicts what Paul actually says. If we keep in mind Romans 9–11, it is impossible to say that this faith is no longer concerned with the history of his people, and further, the contrast between Christ and Adam has clearly a significance for the history of mankind. In Christ, the curse which lay upon the previous history of mankind is taken away, and through the new life bestowed by Him a new humanity is founded, which is marked not by the curse of sin but by the power of the resurrection of Jesus.

It is, of course, entirely correct to say that the decisive event has already happened, and is thus present, but this does not change the fact that the realization of this decisive event in a form corresponding to its nature has yet to come. There can be no possible doubt that Paul *expects* an eschatological future, namely the Parousia of Christ, when what is now present only in the form of a pledge (*arrabōn*) and first fruits (*aparchē*) will be present in its true form of glory. *That* is the character of the "not-yet" and the "already", the interim condition, which marks the "eschatological existence" of the believing community as a time of expectation.

But the interpretation of the New Testament witness of faith in terms of Heidegger's existential philosophy shows itself not only in the interpretation of Paul—which is just as much elimination as interpretation—but also in that of John. Only by means of violent eliminations, above all by textual deletions, is it possible to maintain the thesis that John surrenders the (apocalyptic) outlook on the future, which Paul still retains. Certainly this outlook on the future is transformed, but it is still there, and can be just as little expunged

[1] p. 53, E.V. p. 47 [2] p. 56, E.V. p. 49 [3] p. 49, E.V. p. 43

from John's proclamation of Christ as from Paul's. Bultmann himself is forced to concede that an eschatological expectation of the future is to be found even in John, although it is altered in its character; namely, by the fact that it is no longer of the Jewish-apocalyptic type, but has an affinity with the "conceptions of gnostic eschatology".[1] In spite of the assertion that eternal life is already ours, an eternal life present through our union with Christ, John also believes that our present Christian existence is "a time between the coming of Christ and the Consummation".[2]

Bultmann's view is that the New Testament Eschatology of the future was dependent on Jewish apocalyptic, and became such an embarrassment when the Parousia did not occur, that it called for a re-interpretation. Here we must enter our protest. There are certainly in Paul and even in John vestiges of this Jewish apocalyptic. But the decisive thing is that the foundation of the eternal hope both for Paul and for John is of a quite different nature, namely the Christ who is present in faith, and this foundation is entirely independent of Jewish apocalyptic conceptions.

That the present state of the believer is itself a temporary and provisional condition which implies the expectation of a consummation, is something quite different from "apocalyptic ideas". "Believers are already taken out of the world, and their being is an eschatological being, and yet they still live in the world 'and it is not yet revealed what we shall be' "[3]—this is in fact the connection between the eschatological present (faith) and the eschatological future (hope). And this double aspect of Christian existence is based on the fact that Jesus, the Messiah Christ, is at the same time the Risen Lord and the Crucified. Here, in this fact of history, is the reason why faith must at one and the same time be hope, hope in a future that will remove this contradiction. Bultmann fails to achieve this insight just because his understanding of faith is one-sidedly anthropological and subjective and not at the same time theocentric and related to history. Faith is in fact—and here Bultmann is right—an understanding of oneself. But it is an understanding of oneself based on the self-communication of God in the historical Jesus, the Christ. If once faith is understood in this light, then the fact that the expectation of the Consummation is an integral part of it becomes just as clear as the fact that it is independent of all Jewish apocalyptic at the time of Jesus.

But what we find in Bultmann is this: he replaces Eschatology, the hope of the Christian faith, by a radical historical self-understanding which he calls eschatological existence. That in so doing he can appeal neither to Paul nor to John is clear to himself. But he believes that he owes such an "existential interpretation"—a demythologization which leads to an elimination of eschatology—to the man of today, who can no longer believe in such a consummation of history.

[1] p. 56, E.V. p. 49 [2] *Ibid.*
[3] p. 56; E.V. passage not present in text! (p. 49)

CHAPTER 2

THE OBJECTION OF UNBELIEF TO THE CHRISTIAN HOPE

I

As men argue against our faith itself, so also do they argue against our hope. This argument against our hope seems at the first glance better founded than the hope itself. The world of daily experience is of such a kind that this Christian hope must appear a completely baseless wish-fulfilment. What we hope for, as Christian believers, is in flat contradiction to the facts of mundane reality. We will not attempt to refute this contradiction by our logic and so prove the rationality of the hope in which we believe. There is in fact "no visible sign" that the future will be what the hope of the Christian expects it to be. Nothing within the world as we experience it points in this direction; everything points against it. Therefore—so argues unbelief—this hope can be explained only as the product of subjective wishes and is consequently illusory. But here it is in error, for neither faith nor hope originate in this way. On the contrary, both of them originate in a historical fact in which faith recognizes the self-communication of God. And indeed this historical fact is of such a kind as to contain within itself, with unmistakable and indubitable clarity, that contradiction between the grim actuality that lies before our eyes and what is certain to faith: the contradiction of the crucifixion of the Son of God as a criminal.

The opposition between faith and unbelief thus centres on this one point: whether, as unbelief maintains, it is really only an illusion to maintain that the historical fact of the Cross is the self-communication of God and the revelation of His love, or whether the faith that God's self-communication happened there is the truth, and that, on the contrary, unbelief is based on an illusion. But how is faith to establish this contrary thesis?

We cannot do this in any other way than by referring back to what we said earlier about faith.[1] If it is true that man's independence is an illusion, then to cling to this independence when confronted by the message of the Cross is still more an illusion. It is, as it were, illusion raised to a higher power, an illusion created by man's powerful instinct of self-assertion, above all

[1] See above, Ch. 11 of Part Three; "Faith and Unbelief"

by the instinct of moral self-assertion, and based solely upon it. In this case it is not the Christian hope, but unbelief, that is an illusion based on a wish.

Unbelief does not even admit to itself that it is unbelief. It disguises its character in the form of doubt, which claims to rest upon the perception of reality. But this doubt really stems from flight from one's own real self into an imagined knowledge of the self, based on the arrogance of the self which makes itself the measure and the lord of all things. But faith—we are, of course, speaking of genuine faith—arises from the humiliation of this autonomous self, from despair of oneself, from "repentance". The sovereignty of the autonomous self is annihilated in face of the majesty of the love of God in the Cross. And with this the doubt also disappears, which concealed itself under the pretence of perception of reality. When a man stands fast at the point where he gets a glimpse of himself as he really is, this line of retreat, the flight into "objective" perception of reality, is cut off for him.

A special form of doubt is the explanation of religion offered by Feuerbach and Freud. According to this, religion—and it means in the first place Christian faith—is a wish-fulfilment. The life we long for (so runs the objector's argument) since it is not to be found in reality, is projected into an imaginary transcendence. The happiness which man cannot have in life he expects "in faith" to enjoy in a transcendent future of which he dreams. Freud has summed up this theory in the title of his work *The Future of an Illusion.*[1] But this false illusion shipwrecks on the reality of faith. Far from the Christian hope—which Freud rightly equates with faith—being based on wishes and therefore itself having the character of an illusion, it grows directly out of the disillusionment of man. For that is the message of the Cross of Christ; the destruction of man's lordship over himself, the unmasking of the underlying deception of independence, the shattering of the arrogance that leads to doubt. So long as a man is a sceptic, so long as he allows himself to persist in this "spectator attitude" (*skepsis* means "looking on"), so long the message of the Cross seems to him folly and an offence. But he does not notice that this sceptical attitude itself rests upon self-deception.

This state of affairs is concealed by the supposed objectivity of knowledge. It is the scientific man who, on the basis of his observation of reality, propounds his theory. But in so doing he

[1] Sigmund Freud, *Die Zukunft einer Illusion* [2], 1928 (E.T. *The Future of an Illusion*, Hogarth Press, London)

does not notice that through this objectivity he actually distorts the truth about himself by turning a responsible agent into a spectator, and a person into a zoological species, *homo sapiens*, in order not to be compelled to see himself. Man understood in merely biological terms has no responsibility. But if once responsibility, non-independence, is acknowledged, then the possibility of describing or explaining man merely as an object of natural knowledge disappears. But with this the basis of Freud's theory also is removed. The theorist about other men's illusions acknowledges himself to be the victim of illusion.

But doubt is only possible as a point of transition. Either it becomes faith or counter-faith. The radical counter-faith is nihilism. By this we do not mean atheism, as we know it from the eighteenth and nineteenth centuries, for this was a half-way house, inasmuch as it gave up the thought of God but did not deny ethical responsibility and the claim of morality. Radical unbelief is that unbelief which repudiates not only faith in God but also ethical responsibility, which does away with the ethical norm by explaining it as a mere product of social convention, and, by so doing, emancipates itself from it. The scientific explanation of man, his religion, his ethic and his culture, is the device by means of which man gets rid of his responsibility. The price which he pays for this is the total annihilation of his existence as a human being; the result is nihilism as the antithesis of Christian hope. This is the philosophy of antichrist. It is indeed itself anti-faith, the antichrist.

Nihilism cannot be refuted by arguments. The only thing that one can do in opposition to it is to unmask its lying character by unmasking its origin in arrogance, the delusion of absolute freedom. Absolute freedom from restraint is the motive and the philosophical basis of nihilism. The nihilist can adduce no justification for his view other than that he *wills* not to be restrained, that he simply denies all restraint.[1] But by so doing he comes into contradiction with the reality of his existence, for in fact he is never free from restraint. Nihilism can be set up only as a postulate; it can never be justified, for it postulates a freedom of man which is not possible. This postulate is a senseless gesture, man's revolt against the fact that he is a created being, that he has a Creator. In faith we say "This is the rebellion of the creature against the Creator." Here all reasons are unmasked as fictitious, as a manœuvre. Nihilism is an

[1] Cf. J.-P. Sartre, *L'existentialisme est un humanisme*, 1946 (E.T. *Existentialism and Humanism*, Methuen, London)

unreasoning existential protest based on nothing but the will to autonomy.

But does not the real world justify it? Is life not, *in fact,* meaningless and nothing but a refutation of faith in a loving Creator? After all, the nihilists have not invented these facts with the description of which they fill their novels and dramas, all that is cruel, loathsome, disgusting, senseless and evil. No, they have not invented all this, but in the panic that overtook them when confronted by the grim reality they saw *only* this sinister side of the world, and, sèeing it, denied their own responsibility. In horror at the bestial and demonic things that are revealed in human nature, they represent man as an offspring of nothingness and ignore the image of God which is present in him, though concealed.

Man is always both God's creation *and* a sinner. His life and his history always show this double character, even if in the most varied forms: that he is destined for the highest, and that he denies his destiny. "Man is neither an angel nor a beast" (Pascal) but always "Man in Revolt". Christian teaching is therefore infinitely more realistic than the existentialism of a Sartre or the teaching of any of the "realist" philosophers—not to mention idealism. But where man owns up to his sin and admits it, then his arrogance, his delusion of absolute freedom collapses, and with it his resistance to the message of the Cross. Then he is again able to believe in his eternal destiny in whose negation sin consists.

In the message of the Cross there is disclosed to man along with his own nature, full of contradictions as it is, the truth wherein there is no contradiction—the truth of the divine Love as the foundation and goal of his being—the truth to which we hold fast in the hope of the final revelation of the love of Christ. In the Cross of Christ the negation which the nihilist adduces as the reason for his despair is acknowledged as a fact. But only there, where he recognizes and acknowledges the Cross as the unmasking of his own revolt against God, is the origin of all this negation disclosed as lying in himself and in the sin and godlessness of men. And therewith his existential protest, his nihilistic counter-thesis to faith, his anti-faith, is revealed as a lie. The negation in the world is then seen as a consequence of the Fall, the original evil in humanity, which manifests itself as the fundamental sin precisely in rebellion, in the existential protest and in the nihilistic assertion of the absolute freedom of man and in the denial that he was created by God.

On the Cross the protest of existence against this world in its present state is heard as the verdict and judgment of God, and is thereby affirmed; but at the same time the world, as God meant it to be, there becomes visible. In the justification of the sinner the world that has become a stumbling-block to faith for unbelieving man is also justified. In spite of all the cruelty and senselessness of the world, faith sees it as the creation transfigured in the fulfilment of the divine purpose, restored and approaching its consummation. The Cross as the eschatological turning point is the only theodicy possible and permitted for the Christian—the hope of the Consummation which the Creator and Redeemer God will Himself accomplish.

II

But instead of the polemical form of the "illusion thesis" the denial of the Christian hope can take another form which is less easy to recognize as a counter-thesis: namely, the form of substitute hopes which stem from a secularization of the Christian hope. It follows from what we have said that these substitute hopes originated in the lands of the Christian West and are understandable only as post-Christian phenomena. We are thinking above all of the bourgeois concept of progress and of the "eschatology" of Marxism. We describe them both as "illusory hopes". The ancient world and the non-Christian world are unacquainted with any hope relating to the whole of mankind. This is because they have no consciousness of the unity of human history and no reason for looking into the future with joyful expectation. The ancient world, including the great Eastern religions, have indeed a certain historical consciousness which manifests itself in their history, but their understanding of man is not essentially historical in character. History plays no part in the self-understanding of ancient man, and for this reason there is no ancient or Indian philosophy of history. But their mythology is absolutely dominated by the cyclic idea, the eternal recurrence of the same thing; a thought of a radically anti-eschatological character.[1]

On the other hand history—namely as sacred history—is fundamental to the Christian faith. The Christian understands himself in his faith in the light of history, in the light of the event of Jesus as the Christ, that is, the One who fulfils the preceding sacred history. By reason of his faith in Christ, his

[1] The eschatological religion of Zoroaster is the great exception in the religious world of the East. But this original form, as we find it in the Gathas, was very soon overgrown by mythology and remained without historical influence. It is nevertheless worthy of note that the Second Isaiah acknowledges the (Zoroastrian) Cyrus as the servant of the Lord (*ebed Yahweh*)

gaze is directed with eager expectation to a future perfection. In Jesus Christ alone is to be found the reason why men look into the future with joyful expectation.

(*a*) In the time of rationalism the place of the Christian hope for the future was taken by the forward-looking optimism of the idea of progress. This is indeed unthinkable without the Christian eschatology which preceded it, but is in itself the replacement of the former by a rational principle. The Christian hope is the expectation of the future Consummation from the hand of God: but the concept of progress is the self-confidence of the human spirit projected into the future. This expectation is based on the unlimited "perfectibility of reason" (Rousseau). Just as the Christian hope is hope on the basis of man's assurance of God, so the belief in progress is hope on the basis of the self-assurance of man. This idea was formulated for the first time by Abbé St. Pierre in his work *Observations sur le progrès de la raison universelle.*[1] His main thesis is this: that it belongs to the nature of reason, first, that it is universal; that means that it is the same for all men at every time; and second, that it expands; that is, that in the course of time it overcomes the obstacles which at first oppose it. It rests, as Rousseau later emphasizes, on "the capacity for self-perfection".

In the nineteenth century this concept of progress received both new depth of content and a wider application, and finally became the subject of an impressive practical demonstration. The new depth of content was given to it by the idealist philosophy of history, which interpreted reason theologically as the Divine Reason, which unfolds itself in human history, becomes aware of its divine origin, and thus approximates more and more, if only in an asymptotic manner, to the absolute goal. This goal is the identity of human and Divine Reason on the one hand, and, on the other, the identity of objective forms of culture and subjective awareness in the self-knowledge of philosophy. This idealistic and teleological concept of evolution was then in the age of the magnificent upsurge of biological science expanded into an evolutionism of a universal cosmic kind, whose basis and nature were of a completely different character. This evolutionism, which found in Darwin its most gifted interpreter, embraced the whole world of living organisms. Evolution is regarded here no longer as the unfolding of possibilities latent in the human spirit from the first, but as a causal process, which is set in motion and kept in motion by natural selection. Man in particular appears in this picture as a

[1] John Baillie, *The Belief in Progress*, 1950

latecomer, who has passed through a long series of previous stages until he has become what he now is, and correspondingly has an unpredictable higher evolution before him. The most important point here is that this idea was translated by Darwin out of the realm of philosophical speculation into that of the exact knowledge of natural science.

But it was above all as a result of the impressive demonstration in the field of modern technology that the concept of progress achieved universal dissemination and the status of a rational dogma. In view of the undeniable numerous advances of (scientific) technology, who could have doubts about it? And yet today in Europe no one any longer believes in progress. Doubts about it began to set in as long ago as the end of the nineteenth century, and with every further decade of the new century the field of its authority grew narrower and its power of conviction weaker. Two world wars, but above all the rise of the totalitarian State with its sinister organization of power and the invention of the atom bomb, which threatens mankind with the madness of a suicidal war, have destroyed faith in it.

Where then was the error in the concept of progress? For one thing there was a confusion at the root of the idea of the unlimited perfectibility of reason. It was correct that no limits can be set to the increase of the knowledge of mankind and to the corresponding "capacity for education". But this idea of reason is a purely formal one, and limited to objective knowledge. Mankind's ascent higher and higher upon this ladder does not in the least imply its advance in humanity. On the contrary, for some time it has been evident that the fundamental evil of modern history is that there is no improvement of man to correspond to the evolution of technology and science, and that there is no sign of any rational possibility of overcoming this tragic one-sidedness. On the other hand, the idea of progress in the sense of hope of an ever higher evolution of mankind does not reckon with the irrational and demonic elements in human nature, which remain ungovernable in spite of all rational methods of increasing knowledge, and which for this reason have become even more sinister and destructive in their efforts.

(*b*) The second form of secularized Christian hope is the Marxist "eschatology". This is acknowledged to be a descendant of the German idealist philosophy of history. No one who has any knowledge of the early writings of Karl Marx can have any doubt on this question. And yet it has to be conceded that he is a child who expressly repudiates his own father. For from the absolute idealism of Hegel, Marx created the absolute materialism when he made a decisive change in fundamental principles. It is not spirit that is the dynamic and dominating element in history, but matter. In the process of human history it is not God who comes to Himself in the self-consciousness of man. On the contrary, according to Marx, the result of a realist philosophy of history is the unmasking of the idea of God as an illusion. There is no Creator, no creation, man owes his existence to himself—this is the thesis of Marxism. The Marxist system can be grasped only when it is understood as a Christian dogmatic with a minus sign affixed. The whole system can be deduced from the thesis that God is an illusion.

But with this philosophical system Karl Marx has combined important insights in the field of political economy, which give to the whole a scientific aura. From the communist system here projected there follows with necessity the total State. The step from Marx to Lenin is just as inevitable as the step from Lenin to Stalin. The nationalization of all the means of production—and this is, in a word, the content of the Marxist programme—leads necessarily to the nationalization of the whole of life and so to the nationalization of man, that is to his total functionalization and consequently to his dehumanization.

The astonishing thing is that Karl Marx, and many of his "idealistic" fellow-travellers with him, were not conscious of this consequence of his system. He would doubtless have been profoundly shocked by it, for this result was in direct conflict with his own expectation, the hope of an earthly paradise. This eschatology still today haunts the minds of idealistic communists. It is nothing but the idea of the Kingdom of God which promises justice, freedom, peace and humanity—but all without God. It can be shown point for point how this eschatological idea is in irreconcilable contradiction with the system of Marxism realized in the communist totalitarian State. This State brings neither justice nor freedom. The peace it creates could at best be described as the repose of the graveyard. And lastly human values are excluded from the outset by the functionalization of the human person. Marxism in its realized form is the proof that the Marxist eschatology of a kingdom of justice, freedom and humanity is in contradiction with its atheistic materialistic basis and therefore illusory. The ideas of freedom, of justice, of humanity and peace certainly remain what mankind has always longed for, they remain the universal wish of mankind. But the theory which claims to be scientifically proved, that through the realization of the

Marxist system these wishes and dreams of man can and must be realized, is an illusion.

Why is this so? First because the denial of God is the basis of the whole system, and second because the materialistic conception of man is from the outset in contradiction with the ideals of freedom and humanity. It is clear enough what has happened. As a legacy of the idealist philosophy of history and the Enlightenment Karl Marx took those ideas which stemmed from stoic philosophy and the Christian understanding of man and conjoined them capriciously with his economic and metaphysical materialism. He then fitted together his great and admittedly scientific knowledge of economics with his materialistic metaphysics into a pseudo-scientific system and so gave the impression that his prognosis of the future was scientifically demonstrable. The mixture of economic science, materialistic Enlightenment philosophy and Christian and humanist ideas satisfied on the one side the hopes and longings of men, and on the other side the resentment and hatred of the dispossessed, and thus made Marxism the greatest revolutionary force of the present, especially among the socially and politically backward peoples.

The disappointment which nearly everywhere follows close behind the Marxist Revolution is unmistakable, but is forced to remain ineffectual in the totalitarian State which holds a monopoly of power. By its terroristic methods, by the monstrous machine for propaganda and indoctrination which is absolutely at its command, by means of its monopoly of the Press, and schools at all levels, by all its methods of creating public opinion (theatre, film, television, etc.), above all, by means of the "iron curtain", that is, the absolute exclusion of all information from outside, but also through the actual progress in industrialization and the State's encouragement of school and public health, in a word through the "progress" of the Welfare State, it is able for a while to deceive its subject peoples and those who as a result of bad living conditions are susceptible to its propaganda, and to maintain itself. But in the long run even it cannot escape the nemesis to which at the last all lying and tyranny falls a victim.

But a last word must be directed to us, the Christian Church. Marxism must be regarded as a judgment of God upon empirical Christianity. It is, so to speak, a deficiency disease, which can be explained only in terms of an actual deficiency. And for this deficiency a great part of the blame is borne by the Christian Church—more or less in all its forms. Both the exploitation of the peasants under the feudal system and of the industrial workers by *laissez-faire* capitalism as it prevailed in Europe until after the middle of the nineteenth century and in colonial countries until a very short time ago, and as it in part still today prevails, were tolerated by the "Christian nations" without being essentially disturbed by the protest of the Christian conscience. It was taken for granted that Europe and America should become rich and achieve world power through the sweat and the labour of the unprivileged under conditions unworthy of human beings. It would certainly be in the highest degree unjust to make Christianity responsible for all this. But it would be blindness to deny that the Christian Church bears here a heavy share of guilt. And this consists principally in the fact that through its institutionalism and its lust for power the Church has denied that spirit of brotherhood which was the life-principle of the primitive Christian Ekklesia, and by so doing has blurred its witness to Jesus Christ and the meaning of the true *communio sanctorum*. The answer to communism is not Christian preaching alone, but the Ekklesia whose foundation is in the love of God.

From the standpoint of the Christian knowledge of God the exposure of systematic atheism and materialism means also the unmasking of the illusory character of the Marxist eschatology. But like nihilism—with which Marxism is at heart identical, although differing from it in programme—communism cannot be refuted by arguments, because its roots are irrational and of a demonic character. History itself—to be more correct, God Himself—will do this by perfecting the Ekklesia. But it is our task to clarify our minds both as to the divine judgment which is being passed upon us in this sinister phenomenon of our times, and as to its truly devilish character. Without the Christian hope, which is founded wholly upon what God Himself will do to conquer these powers and to reveal His sole and final Lordship, we are left with nothing but the vision of Nietzsche as an outlook on the future:

> The greatest event of modern times—that God is dead—that faith in the Christian God has become incredible—begins already to cast its first shadow over Europe. For those few at least, whose eyes or the suspicion in whose eyes is strong and sensitive enough for the drama, it is as if some sun had set, some old deep trust had turned into doubt: to them our old world must daily appear more twilit, less trustworthy, stranger, "older". Generally speaking, however, one may say that the event itself is far too great, too distant, too far beyond the intellectual grasp of many, for even

> the news of it to be considered as having *arrived*; let alone that many people should already know what it really implies—and all the things that, once this faith is buried, must collapse because they are built up on it, have supported themselves on it, and have grown together with it: for example, our whole European ethic. This long profusion and train of damage, destruction, collapse and downfall which is now impending: who could today guess enough of it in order to be impelled to act as the teacher and foreteller of this monstrous logic of horror, the prophet of a darkness and solar eclipse whose like has probably never yet happened on the earth?[1]

There is no third way out; either complete hopelessness or the certainty of faith, the Christian hope, whose sole foundation is in the living God. Christian faith sees history as a struggle between Christ and His adversary, but as a struggle that is already decided. It recognizes in the Cross and Resurrection of Jesus Christ the victory of God, which has once for all been achieved. Therefore faith means victory over despair and is not merely the basis of joyful expectation of what is to come, but also an incentive for our own struggles. Precisely in those who cherish this hope most intensely it reveals itself as an ever new motive for action, for sacrificial service of this Lord, and will continue to do so, provided only that it remains faith in Christ.

[1] F. Nietzsche, *Fröhliche Wissenschaft*, pp. 343 ff., Leipzig 1900 (E.T. *Joyful Wisdom*, Allen and Unwin, London)

CHAPTER 3

THE KINGDOM OF GOD AND ETERNAL LIFE

I

GOD wills to have His people, His mankind, His Kingdom. For this reason the final realization of His will is the coming of His Kingdom, the coming of that which brings humanity and history to their consummation. This is the basic content of the word *basileia tou theou*—God's kingly rule. This fundamental New Testament concept means not only God's sovereignty in itself, but His sovereignty in a humanity united and bound together by His will, in His Kingdom.

The sovereignty of God is present in the Person of Jesus Christ. The realm where Christ's sovereignty is immediately exercised is the Ekklesia, meaning the fellowship of those who have their new life in Christ. It is filled by the consciousness that it is the Messianic People on whom the salvation promised by the prophets has been bestowed, in whose midst the Messiah-Kyrios, the King of the Last Times, is present. He rules as the Lord in the hearts of men. He leads the community through His Spirit and fills it with His powers. He is the life which makes it—in contrast with all that preceded it—a reality of an incomparable kind.

Faith is the new life, the ultimate life, life in its fullness and its purity, for it is life in the love of God. This love of God is not only something believed in, but (in and through faith) something real, a reality—no, not *a* reality, but *the* reality. When the Apostles think of this in its dynamic, they speak of the "Holy Spirit". The Holy Spirit is what they have experienced and continue to experience overwhelmingly as the new reality. What then should the Holy Spirit be but God Himself, and indeed God as the One who speaks in us, who acts in us and through us? For this reason the event of Pentecost is in very truth the event by which the Ekklesia was established. Peter's speech at Pentecost also makes it clear that the outpouring of the Holy Spirit is the decisive *eschatological* event, as the prophet Joel had promised it would be (cf. Joel 2: 28-32). Life in the Holy Spirit is in fact "*eschatological existence*".

Life in the Spirit is above all life in *agape*—life in a love that is not merely enjoined upon us and of which we are conscious only that it is obligatory, but a present life in the love which through faith in Christ has become a reality in the life of the Ekklesia brotherhood. For through this faith man is changed from one who lives for himself into one who lives for God and his brother. Certainly the essence of faith is the knowledge of the *agape* of God, and nothing else. But such is the nature of God's self-communication, that He not only gives Himself to be known, but in this revelation and knowledge He communicates His own nature and life, so that *agape* is now itself also the characteristic of these men who know Him. They do not merely live *on* the *agape* of God, but *in* it, and have thereby recovered the destiny for which they were created, life in the image of God.

But the Ekklesia experiences the working of the Spirit not merely as love, but also in the form of other powers and the ministries corresponding to them. Love is indeed the highest gift of the Spirit. "God is love, and he that dwelleth in love, dwelleth in God, and God in him" (1 John 4: 16)—but God is not only love, but also creative Power transcending all human understanding. Therefore love is not the only manifestation of the Holy Spirit and of the final salvation that is present with us. On the contrary it was a manifold variety of powers, and indeed of such powers as are not to be found in our usual experience, that the Ekklesia at first experienced as the effects of this supernatural dynamic, even before it rightly understood their relationship to the love of God in Christ. In the mighty experience of the presence of Jesus Christ in the Holy Spirit the Ekklesia recognizes itself as the new humanity in and through Christ.

And yet it was also conscious of something else; the Last Things are not yet here, we are only at their beginning, we are the vanguard of the coming Kingdom, we have only the *aparchē*, the first fruits (Rom. 8: 23),[1] not yet the whole harvest. The Ekklesia knew itself always as the community of those expecting the Consummation, as the fellowship of those who hope. For only in the strength of hope could it bear the tension which was implicit in the fact that it, the little flock, saw itself as the new humanity.

The tension between now-already and not-yet was the paradox of its existence. It pervades all the writings of the New Testament even though it is not expressed with equal precision or equal emphasis in all the witnesses. This tension lies in the nature of faith itself, which in the New Testament as in the Old is one with hope and yet not identical with it. Faith is

[1] Cf. also 2 Corinthians 1: 22 and Ephesians 1: 12–14, where the Holy Spirit is described by the words *arrabōn* (pledge) and *sphragis* (seal)

the future as present, it is the anticipation of the future. "We are *now* the children of God, and it doth *not yet* appear what we shall be" (1 John 3: 2). "We walk by faith, not by sight" (2 Cor. 5: 7). When we said above that in faith the self-communication of God attained its goal, this sentence was correct only up to a point, for even in faith the self-communication of God has attained only its provisional goal; the final goal still lies in the future. It is not faith that Christ really wishes to bring us, but the perfection and completeness of the divine Presence. We do indeed have salvation in faith in Christ, but we have it only in the form of hope.

II

Is this hope the salvation of the individual or of mankind? In the New Testament there are found two eschatological concepts, which seem to mean rather different things: eternal life and the Kingdom of God; individual salvation and the universal hope of mankind. The second concept is akin to Jewish apocalyptic, but the first has more affinity with gnostic ideas. And yet it would be wrong to say that the eschatology of the primitive Christian community was Jewish apocalyptic or Hellenistic gnosis. The present experience of final salvation in Jesus Christ distinguishes the New Testament from Jewish apocalyptic. In Him the decisive thing has already happened, since in Him the love of God *has been* revealed.

To this fact appeal is made, in this present love the Ekklesia lives. Not only has the decisive event already happened, but the Victor is already here and in Him believers have a share in the final victory. Jewish apocalyptic looks only forward, but New Testament faith principally looks back in the form of recollection to what has happened in Jesus Christ, while it looks forward in the form of hope. Christ Himself is the salvation of mankind. In Him the fellowship of His disciples is rooted both now and here, and also in the future Consummation. This constitutes a clear difference between the New Testament's expectation of the Kingdom of God and that of Jewish apocalyptic.

But the contrast with gnosticism is also clearly recognizable, even where the resemblance to it is greatest, in John. In John the knowledge, which in gnosticism is identical with eternal life, is aware of its own incompleteness. The mark of this incompleteness is the imperative which is always conjoined with the indicative, the task of sanctification which is all the more laid upon us when the gift of grace has been received. For this reason, the so-called mysticism of the New Testament—if we may speak of it at all—is always at the same time an ethic; the gift is never separated from the task. There is not even a trace to be found in the New Testament of that ethical indifference which is characteristic of genuine gnosticism. The second and equally significant mark of difference is that of fellowship. Gnosticism is merely an affair of the individual, but the eternal life which according to John is indeed given to man along with faith in Jesus Christ, but nevertheless is conceived of as a life whose perfect form has not yet been manifested, is always at the same time a life in the Ekklesia. These are the differences between the Johannine and the gnostic conceptions of eternal life.

Thus neither Hellenistic gnosticism nor Jewish apocalyptic is to be found in the New Testament. Christian faith is distinguished from both by the same characteristic, by its relation to Jesus Christ Himself. He is the salvation bestowed on the individual, and both the fellowship and the task of the Ekklesia, the faithful, are rooted in Him.

III

But what is the relationship between the Kingdom of God and eternal life? Both expressions describe the future aspect of salvation, both refer forward, to the goal, only each of them does it from a different viewpoint; the one from that of the individual and the other from that of humanity. Jesus Christ is inevitably the One who fulfils hope both in the most personal and the most universal sense. In Him the *dikaiosynē theou*, the righteousness of God, God's will and God's plan, is revealed not only for the individual but for the whole of humanity. To believe on Him or "to believe in Him" means thus that not only individual but universal "integration" is the object of our confident expectation. The coming Kingdom of God brings with it the consummation of human history as well as the consummation of the personal destiny of each single individual human being. Redemption through Christ is on the one side the most personal decision of the individual, and on the other the indivisible redemption of mankind. Hence the parallels between Adam and Christ (Rom. 5: 12).

How is this related to the fact that Paul and John speak so little of the sovereignty of God or of the Kingdom of God? This does not mean that for them the outlook for universal humanity has been displaced by an individualist outlook. Bultmann is wrong when he claims that in Paul eschatology is looked at from an anthropological viewpoint and thus has taken on an individualistic character which distinguishes it from Jewish apocalyptic. It would be just as true to assert the contrary; in Paul everything is thought of in universal terms and related to humanity because his thought starts with God as the acting Subject, just as his central concept, the righteousness of God, is the decisive "theocratic" concept. It is only Luther's mistranslation which has turned this into the anthropocentric "Righteousness that counts in God's sight".[1] Because Jesus is the salvation of men, He is the salvation of mankind, and because He is this, He is the embodiment of God's sovereignty.

We find the clearest witness to this twofold expectation in the Epistle to the Philippians: the expectation of eternal life for the individual in life with Christ and the expectation of the coming Kingdom, the first finding unmistakable expression in the first chapter (Phil. 1: 23 ff.) and the second in the third chapter (Phil. 3: 20, 21). If in John the Kingdom of God seems to be neglected in comparison with eternal life, it is in fact only apparently so. Even John never speaks of eternal life except as a life in fellowship, and it is always the circle of disciples to which Christ speaks of eternal life, with express emphasis on the word "Ye". New Testament scholarship has hitherto brought out clearly the difference between the two aspects, but not their equally important unity.

To ask whether the New Testament thinks of salvation in individual or universal terms is to pose an entirely false alternative. It must accordingly be answered: "Salvation is both, it is both individual and universal." The false separation between individual hope of eternal life and universal hope of the Kingdom of God is caused by forgetfulness of the fact that Christian faith is faith in Jesus Christ and nothing else.

Jesus Christ is He who makes God's sovereignty and the Kingdom of God a reality, and He it is in whom I have eternal life through faith. He is "God's Word for the world" (Chr. Blumhardt). He who in faith knows Him to be this hopes in Him for the coming of the world of the Resurrection, the Consummation of God's creation. He who believes in Him lives already in the love of God from which he knows nothing can separate him.

[1] Cf. Ch. 14 of Part Three, "The Justification of the Sinner by Faith Alone"

CHAPTER 4

THE KINGDOM OF GOD AS THE MEANING AND GOAL OF HISTORY

I

HISTORY is not a Biblical concept. The Bible does not speak of history. And yet it is the most historical of books. Christian faith, Biblical faith in general, is historical existence in the highest sense of the word.

In order to understand this thesis, we must enter for a little into the field of the philosophy of history. We must first and foremost abandon the neutral concept of history, according to which history embraces everything that ever happened. This neutral concept of history reminds us that from the very start the word "history" is an ambiguous one; history as what has happened and history as knowledge or information about what has happened. In the concept of *historia*, knowledge of history, there has been implicit from its origin (in Herodotus) a double qualification of the events that have happened. *Historia* is the record of *human* events, and further, of the *memorabilia* of human history. This means that a distinction has been made between human events worth remembering and those not worth remembering. From its beginnings "history" means events worth remembering, and human events, in distinction from all other events.

In this human history there have been two decisive events: the birth of Greek humanism and the Israelitic history and conception of history. Greek humanism is significant because in it for the first time man contrasts himself as man with nature, as something independent of it. One could say that this is the discovery of man. Man understands himself as a being who has reason and is in this respect superior to nature. By this discovery man lifted himself out of the cycle of natural events. By so doing he discovered the subject of history. The break between history and nature was made. But at the same time man also withdrew from history by defining his essential nature, his true humanity as something supra-historical, as participation in the eternal Logos. Thus Greek humanism on the one side discovered the realm of history, namely the essence of humanity, and yet at the same time denied the essential importance of history by its supra-historical conception of man.

The second event was the history of Israel and the Jews and with it the rise of the Biblical understanding of history. Here no separation can be made between events and thinking about events. For the Israelite, everything that happens is God's activity. Thus all action is seen as a unity. God is the true Subject of history, of the history of the nations and of mankind. And this outlook itself is based on a historical event, namely on the revelation on Sinai, and on all the revelations of God which followed it. Here too man and his history is given a significance above that of other beings and events. Unlike everything else man is not only God's creature but God's creature *par excellence*. He is created in the image of God. This thought seems akin to that of Greek humanism. But while the Greeks saw man's distinctively human character in his human endowment of reason, in the thought of Israel the whole accent lies on man's ethical and practical relationship to the will of God. God wills to have a people obedient to Him. The disobedience of man is seen as an impediment to the divine will. God's call through the prophets not only makes man responsible but threatens him with divine judgment. Thus history becomes the drama of the divine will and the human will opposed to it.

In the New Testament this struggle between God's sovereignty and human rebellion becomes acute. In the one Christ event the rebellion of man reaches its climax, and discloses its truly demonic character in the Crucifixion. But this same event of the Crucifixion is, for faith, God's act of reconciliation and the revelation of His forgiving love. Man is given the assurance of divine sonship and a share in the everlasting Kingdom.

II

Just for this reason Christian faith is historical existence in an unconditional sense. This shows itself in three ways.

(*a*) Historical events, in contrast with natural events, have the character of uniqueness. But this uniqueness applies only in a relative and conditioned sense to historical events. The Jesus of whom the Gospels tell us is a unique event in history, not to be confused with other personalities in history. His uniqueness in this general historical sense is an essential part of the fundamental confession of Christian faith. It is implied in the cardinal apostolic affirmation "The Word became flesh" (John 1: 14).

But the uniqueness which in the New Testament is expressly predicated of Christ goes far beyond this general historical sense of the word. This consciousness of uniqueness as faith understands it relates especially to His death upon the Cross. Faith understands the death of the Cross as the decisive event of the atonement. The atonement and redemption which was achieved through the death of Jesus Christ on the Cross is an event which does not lie in the dimension of the historian. It is for that reason not something which the historian as such can recognize, but which is apprehended only by faith. It is an action of God, an act of the self-disclosure and self-communication of God, and thus is something which cannot be perceived as a historical occurrence. While the uniqueness which the historian apprehends in the Person and history of Jesus is only something relatively unique, that which faith apprehends in this historical fact as God's deed and God's Word of atonement and redemption is something absolutely unique, it is something that by its very nature either has happened once and for all, for all times and for every man, or else has not happened. For the atonement of which the New Testament speaks is an act of God, which, if it is really the atonement, is unrepeatable. But the faith of the Christian community and the faith of every individual Christian consists in the appropriation of this event that happened once for all on the Cross of Jesus.

Here then and here alone we find this circumstance, that an event which is unique in the relative sense known to world history is apprehended by faith as an event which in its nature is absolutely or unconditionally unique. The historic event of Golgotha, which is in principle within the range of everyone's knowledge, is the visible shell of the invisible kernel, the absolutely unique event which is apprehended only by faith. This is precisely the meaning of the assertion from the Gospel of St. John which we quoted above, in which faith sees the significance of the story of Jesus in the Incarnation of the Word. That which lies outside of all history and above it, as its origin and goal, has become historical; the Eternal has become temporal.

The category of uniqueness, in contrast to the perpetual recurrence of natural events, constitutes the nature of the historical as such. For this reason Christian faith is the faith which possesses an unconditional historical character through its twofold relationship to the unique—namely to the historically and relatively unique, and to the absolutely unique as faith understands it. There is in the history of religion no second instance of faith being so unconditionally bound to an absolutely unique event, as is the Christian faith to what has happened in Christ. It is a symbolically significant expression of this fact that the time of world history is reckoned backwards and forwards from this event as its central point—namely from the birth of Jesus Christ, and that the years are numbered B.C. and A.D. This means that the conception of history implicit in Christian faith has passed over into secular chronology.

(*b*) But there are two further important concepts which demonstrate the historical character of the Christian faith in a special and pregnant sense of the word. The first of these concepts is that of personality and the second that of universal humanity. Christian faith is unconditionally personal and it is unconditionally concerned with all humanity.

It is *unconditionally personal* in several senses. First, and fundamentally in the sense that it is related to a Person, and indeed to a historical Person, and related to Him in an unconditional manner. In Jesus Christ Christian faith recognizes the divine Person, the mystery of the personal character of God Himself. The Word of God, that wherein God reveals Himself, is now no longer a prophetic Word, but a Person in history. The prophets of Israel support their claim by saying "Thus saith the Lord". Thus they refer beyond themselves to Him who gave them this Word. But Jesus no longer refers beyond Himself like a prophet to the One who has commissioned Him, to Him who spoke and gave the Word. On the contrary, He utters in His own name the divine authoritative "I am" just as in the Old Testament God utters the words "I am". While the prophet is only the "postman" of the divine message, and his person is of no importance, in the New Testament Jesus Christ as Person is identical with the content of this message. The message has itself become a Person, the Person has become a message.

As this is the peculiarity of faith in Christ, without analogy in any other religion, so in Christian dogma this, its special character, is impressed on us by the Doctrine of the Trinity which gives expression to the unity of Him who is revealed (the Father), the Revealer (the Son), and the Revelation as event (Spirit). This claim to personal revelation is made only by Trinitarian Christian faith, and this is what offends both Jews and Muslims, just as the claim to exclusiveness implied in it is an offence to Hindus and Buddhists.

But the gospel of Jesus Christ is personal in yet another sense. It is not only asserted of a man named Jesus that He is in His Person the revealer of the divine mystery and the author of the divine atonement, but we are told how this act of revelation and this redemption or atonement was achieved in a personal manner as a personal struggle of the man Jesus with the power of temptation and the powers of darkness. Jesus did not merely suffer the Cross passively but "took it upon Himself", He "became obedient unto death, even the death of the Cross. *Wherefore* God also hath highly exalted Him, and given Him a name which is above every name" (Phil. 2: 6 ff.). We have here not merely the metaphysical event of a physical incarnation of God—man—as it might often appear from the subsequent developments of the history of dogma—but a personal historical act, with voluntary suffering, and self-surrender.

To this objective historical element there corresponds on the subjective human side of "appropriation" a faith which once more is not belief in a doctrine, but a faith which can be described by the formula "obedience of faith". Thus, as Christians understand it, faith is not primarily the acceptance of a dogma, but an "existential" personal happening which Paul describes in the words "dying with Christ", "being crucified with Him". It is the self-surrender of our own person and its claims, its selfish will, to the God who encounters it in Christ. Faith is the most personal act conceivable, the surrender of self to the Redeemer who surrenders Himself. Faith in Jesus Christ is a total transformation of existence.

(*c*) But in it the element of universality is radicalized at the same time as the factor of personality. Here it is no longer possible to restrict the personal to signify what is merely individual and private. On the contrary, the significance of the Christ event concerns mankind as a whole. For before Him, the Christ, we as sinners are bound together in one single mass of sinful humanity, and in the same way through faith we are in Him bound together in one mass of redeemed humanity. This is the meaning of the contrast between Adam and Christ, the first and the second Adam (Rom. 5: 12 ff.; 1 Cor. 15: 45 ff.). As sin is on the one hand guilt of the most personal character and on the other side the indivisible sin of humanity, so is redemption through Christ the most personal decision and on the other hand the indivisible salvation of mankind. In contrast to all mysticism, the Christian faith is bound up with the history of the world, the history of mankind. To be a Christian believer is to think in terms of universal humanity.

The delimitation of an area of religious inwardness in contrast with the realm of public and social questions is here in the nature of the case impossible. For to believe in Jesus Christ is to hope for redemption and fulfilment for all men and for all human things. The goal disclosed in Jesus Christ is not a private blessedness of souls in the Beyond, but the coming Kingdom of God and the consummation both of the history of mankind and of the personal destiny of each separate individual human being. Personality and society, the individual and fellowship, the person and humanity, are seen as an absolute unity. Here we find the most absolute and radical manifestation of the character of history, first in its aspect of decision and responsibility, and second because here world history is seen as a unity.

But what in these three respects constitutes the essential character of history is inaccessible to the historian as such. It is *sacred* history, *revelation* history, not world history, although it can only be grasped as sacred *history* within world history (Jesus crucified under Pontius Pilate). As an external fact, of course, it belongs to world history; in its true quality, which can be seen only in faith, it is revelation history. The Cross on Golgotha is, of course, in the first place a unique event of history in the sense of the historian, but when it is apprehended in faith as God's act of atonement it becomes the absolute historical event. Christian faith is historical existence in the radical sense of the word. Inasmuch as faith knows that in the Cross of Jesus Christ God acts and speaks in a revelation unparalleled elsewhere, that in this event He communicates Himself and glorifies Himself, faith perceives in Jesus Christ the basic and fundamental meaning of all history, that is, of all human life; the meaning of my life history and yours, the meaning of all life histories and national histories.

III

The history of philosophy speaks of the meaning of history as of something demonstrable, which shows itself in the historical facts. Hegel's philosophy of history—the most imposing, and, if the possibility of such a philosophy of history be affirmed, the most perfect—regards the course of history as an evolution to its immanent and transcendent goal, the self-realization of reason ("World history is the representation of the divine absolute process of reason in its highest forms"), and supports this by a rich variety of illustrative material from the whole field of history then known. Hegel sees the *telos* of history in this unfolding, but at the same time he sees it as a never-reached goal.

Faith cannot look on the process of history in the same light as Hegel. His picture is an idealization of real history, reached by passing over all the negative, irrational, accidental and meaningless characteristics of history, especially the evil and demonic things in it. Thus a continuity in the humanization of man is asserted which is recognized as an ideal only, not as a reality. The background of demonic evil is a necessary part of the Christian picture of history. For what is the Crucifixion but the manifestation of the demonic opposition to the Son of God? Thus also as early as the Apostles' Creed we find this dark side of human history expressed and characterized in the words "suffered under Pontius Pilate" (*passus sub Pontio Pilato*).

This means that it is futile to seek to demonstrate a meaning *in* history. The Kingdom of God does indeed grow continuously. But it is hidden among the "tares" of world history, as Jesus has clearly said in His parable (Matt. 13: 24 ff.). The two crops grow up side by side so intermingled until the ripeness of Judgment Day that man cannot separate them. In the Cross the nature of this world and the Kingdom of God meet in conflict. The Crucifixion of Jesus Christ is simply the protest of world history against its invisible Lord who in Jesus Christ has entered into history, the protest against the Kingdom of God that has broken into it, though under concealment as yet. In the Easter event this incognito of the history of the Kingdom of God is as it were for a moment lifted. But there is no visible continuum of such lightning flashes, no demonstrable continuity in the humanization of man, such as Hegel would indicate. The Christian picture of world history bears clearly the marks of a theology of the Cross (*theologia crucis*).

And yet faith in Jesus Christ the Crucified contains also an element of the fulfilment of an immanent meaning of history. All history means the humanization of man, even when it is not aware of this. The Greeks were the first on whom this truth dawned when they recognized man's difference from nature. This truth it is, again, that has been grasped by the German idealist philosophers of history since Herder. But both they and the Greeks regard reason as the distinctively human characteristic, and this makes a fundamental difference between them and faith. Yet reason is not the self of man, only the necessary presupposition of the self. The achievements of reason are therefore not in themselves the essentially human thing. It is not the gift of reason that makes man human. Even a genius can be inhuman. What is it then that constitutes true humanity? Simply love. A man who lives in love is a truly human man. In Christ we have learnt that the truly human thing is what flows from the nature of God, love. The Incarnation of God Himself in Jesus Christ is the establishment of true humanity. In Him both true divinity and true humanity are revealed.

But at the same time it has become clear to us that this true life is not in us, but must come to us, although we were created for it. For we have lost our origin, and can recover it only if it comes to us. And that is what has happened in Jesus Christ. Therefore our hope is based on Him. He restores our true original nature. The divine humanity revealed in Him is nothing but the true humanity.

The meaning of world history does not lie in world history itself. This meaning comes from beyond history to history in Jesus Christ, the One who comes, the consummator and bringer of the Kingdom of God. Not only the Cross and Resurrection of Jesus Christ, but far more the Coming of the Lord in glory will give to history a meaning that is concealed in all apparent meaninglessness. God has set a goal for it and as a movement towards this goal it has gained a direction and a meaning, an unconditional God-given meaning. In this goal God wills to let it find its end and at the same time its consummation. In the prospect of the consummation of the Kingdom of God an eternal future is opened for it. The eternal glory of Jesus Christ will be manifested as our glory. If the Cross of Jesus Christ says to us: "God so loved the world", the Coming of the Lord in glory says to us, "Thus God brings to its consummation the world that He loves."

CHAPTER 5

THE CHRISTIAN UNDERSTANDING OF ETERNITY

I

CHRISTIAN faith is not alone in speaking of the contrast between eternity and transience. On the contrary, the eternal was from the earliest times the theme of philosophy and religious thought. The philosophy of the Vedanta may well be called the oldest philosophy known to world history, although it lacks that systematic character which is one of the essential marks of philosophy, and therefore is not acknowledged by many as philosophy[1] but only as religious thought. And it is founded on the contrast between the eternal and unchangeable and the world of transience, as is Greek philosophy since Parmenides and Plato. The eternal is the *ontōs on,* that which truly is; that which is temporal and transient is a mixture of being and non-being. Man participates in the eternal, either through knowledge of that which truly is, or through mystical experience which transcends all antitheses. The fact that through reason he can know this eternal being in its contrast with non-being and transience is to him the proof that in the deepest roots of his being he himself is eternal. This, in a word, is the thesis both of the Upanishads of the Vedanta and of the idealistic philosophy of the Greeks.

But this is not the Christian concept of eternity. The Bible does not speak of an eternity which man essentially possesses in himself and which he can recognize as his own true being. It speaks rather of the eternity that comes *to* man,[2] which lays hold of him, which is bestowed upon him. This seems at first to be a self-contradictory thought. What does it mean to describe eternity as that which comes to us? This expression points to the same paradox as does the saying of John about truth as having come through Jesus Christ (John 1: 17).[3] To understand this we must not start with the concept of eternity as human

[1] Cf. *Allgemeine Geschichte der Philosophie,* Vol. 16, by P. Deussen: *Die Philosophie der Upanishads.* (E.T. *The Philosophy of the Upanishads,* T. and T. Clark, Edinburgh)

[2] Here is the same untranslatable word-play on the word *Zukunft* (future) and *Zu-kommen* (to come to) which we have noted before and which occurs in the title of Brunner's book on Eschatology, *Das Ewige als Zukunft und Gegenwart* (E.T. *Eternal Hope*). (TR.)

[3] Cf. my *Wahrheit als Begegnung,* 1938 (E.T. *The Divine-Human Encounter*)

thought itself naturally construes it, understanding eternity as timelessness or as infinite duration. We must start with the Biblical conception of God. God alone is eternal because He is the Lord of time, which He has created. But this eternal God wills to communicate Himself to His creatures and glorify Himself in them. The God of the Bible is the God who moves towards the world, lays claim to it, and gives Himself to it. And this God is only to be known in this movement of His towards the world and in His self-communication.

Faith is *not* interested in knowing an eternal divine being of man behind the deceptive appearances of the world of the senses, or in achieving a mystical union with it, but it is interested in being apprehended and grasped by the Eternal Being of the Personal God. And therefore this concept of eternity is from the outset bound up with history. For it is in history that this self-communication and apprehension takes place. God's coming to us is the theme of revelation history and saving history. Only within this history can the eternity be known which God communicates. And it is, of course, a real history which everyone can acknowledge to have happened, even though only faith can apprehend God's self-communication in this history. *This* is why it is so important that this history should have a history preceding it and should have a climax. For that which has not a history preceding it is not really historical. It is of no importance whether we regard the Biblical prophets or Moses or Abraham as the bearers of this preceding history. It is just this indeterminate character, this lack of clear demarcations which is characteristic of "preceding history" as such. The "dispensation of the fulness of times" (*oikonomia tou pleromatos tōn kairōn*, Eph. 1: 10) is a necessary mark of Christ as the fulfiller. Only as the fulfiller of this preceding history is He the Christ. From it He gets His name of Messiah, and it is itself the historical commentary on the name of Christ. Only when He is seen in relation to the history which precedes Him and prepares for Him is He Himself truly historical, truly the Christ. And conversely this character of sacred history as a dispensation makes clear to us the meaning of His coming to us.

It is, however, the perfected form of God's coming to us, the story of Christ, which shows that we have the new life as a historical existence in the authentic sense of the word. Only in the decision to accept Him, the God who has come to us, do we possess faith. Faith is created by this history, and finds therein its content. And this content is that in Christ the eternal God

Himself, the Lord of time, the Eternal comes to us as "Eternity within time" (H. H. Farmer). Christian faith knows nothing of any other eternity than this, but in this it has "enough and to spare" (Luke 15: 17).

II

This concept of eternity differs from the philosophical concept in not having a formal, empty and purely negative character as negation of time. It is full of positive content. Eternity as we apprehend it in faith is the presence of the self-communicating love of God. To philosophy this concept of eternity seems to have nothing to do with eternity. For philosophy knows the latter only in the form of an abstraction, as a negation of temporality or transience. Natural, unreflective thought has at least a certain inkling of the fact that what endures for ever is the true present. But the thought that the presence of the living God is not only the true present, but at the same time the true eternity, eternal life—this is known only where men perceive in faith this presence in God's self-communication in Jesus Christ and live in this faith. Neither the negation of time, nor infinite duration as such,[1] are the factors which determine this understanding, but only the Spirit of God who is present and effectual in faith.

So in Biblical faith the presence of love and the confident hope of the perfected presence of God which accompanies that love, this concept of eternity which is full of positive content takes the place of the empty negation of time and the equally empty endless duration. And further, here the present is no longer conceived of as a mathematical point without extension (*punctum mathematicum*), where the future passes over into the past, a concept which is the most pregnant expression of transience. Rather is it the concept of the present as the presence of the God of love, a concept filled with content, and eternity is understood as the eternity of God which becomes our present in the Parousia (presence) of Christ the Kyrios.

Therefore it is said that he who believes in the Son *has* eternal life. Faith is the form, admittedly still imperfect, of the eternity for which we are destined. The presence of Christ through the Holy Spirit is in fact eternity, for it is the presence of God who alone in Himself is eternal, because He is the Lord and Creator of time. This "having" which is characteristic of faith, this

[1] O. Cullmann (*Christ and Time*, 1946) in his opposition to the philosophical and Platonic conception of eternity advocates this popular conception of it as endless duration which is by no means that of the Bible

presence of Christ in faith (*in ipsa fide Christus adest*) is admittedly at the same time a "not yet having" inasmuch as the full presence of Christ is not promised us until His future Advent. But what faith in Christ already possesses is—in substance, so to speak—the same as what it merely hopes for.

It is implicit in the nature of *agape*, that as it is unconditional so also it has no limits. "For I am persuaded that neither death nor life . . . shall be able to separate us from the love of God which is in Christ Jesus our Lord" (Rom. 8: 38, 39). In this one sentence, as we have already shown,[1] is contained the whole of Eschatology, and in it there is contained also the completely transformed concept of the present and of eternity. As it is said of Zion "God is in the midst of her" (Psalm 46: 5), so it is said of faith and the Ekklesia "God is in it, in the midst of it." And through this indwelling of God, eternity itself is "brought within time". That from this there results also as a complementary doctrine a new understanding of time, is more the concern of a Christian philosophy than of Dogmatics.[2]

This new understanding of eternity is not unconnected with philosophy, inasmuch as the latter is fundamentally determined by the Socratic "Know thyself" (*gnothi seauton*), and is primarily concerned to attain knowledge of man. For this Christ who creates new life through His presence is also He who calls us back to that destiny for which we were created, and which we have lost. Therefore only knowledge of Christ is at the same time true knowledge of self, and to come to Christ through faith is to come to oneself. Rebirth through faith is at the same time the restoration of the image (*restitutio imaginis*).[3] In Christ we recognize our true selves. But it is not merely a matter of *knowledge*; on the contrary, through the self-communication of God, who is life, it is also a new *life*. For this knowledge which faith gives is not just "knowledge" in the usual objective intellectualistic sense of the word, but a knowledge that transforms our existence at its heart.[4] And this is why it contains the presence of the Holy Spirit and at the same time the certainty of eternal life. It is *eternal* life because it is participation in the life of Christ and through Him the presence of the Eternal God. It is eternal *life* because as the love of God it is at the same time His eternal life.

[1] See above, pp. 339 ff.

[2] Cf. on this point the indications of this new understanding of time in my book *Das Ewige als Zukunft und Gegenwart*, pp. 46 ff. (E.T. *Eternal Hope*, Lutterworth Press, London, 1954; Westminster Press, Philadelphia)

[3] See above, Ch. 19 of Part Three, "Regeneration", pp. 269 ff.

[4] See above, Ch. 17 of Part Three, "Faith and Knowledge", pp. 251 ff.

As even natural love aims at unlimited duration—without the will to last for ever, as love for a limited period, temporary love, it is not real love at all—so much more does the *agape* of God have this aim. It aims at, and guarantees, unlimited duration. So in this understanding of eternity there is indeed included the negation of time in so far as it means transience. But this negation is not the primary thing, as it is in the philosophical concept of eternity as timelessness, but rather what results from the primary datum, the love of God. Eternity is thus not merely *negation* of time, but in so far as the element of duration is contained in our natural reflection on the experience of time, it is *fulfilment* of time, the fulfilment of that element of duration as eternal life. Faith is the reception of that which by its nature can have no ending, and it originates through the self-communication of the God who is above time, of Him who is Himself immutable.

The Ekklesia as the fellowship of faith is the vanguard of the coming of the Kingdom of God, of that life in fellowship with God which is at the same time fellowship with man and brotherhood. Existence in the Spirit is at the same time the presence and expectation of the fullness of presence of the Last Things, of the Parousia which gives to existence its eschatological character.

In the historical character of faith there is at the same time implicit our continuing involvement in time, and our already achieved transcendence of it. Therefore a part of faith is the knowledge that faith itself is not the true goal meant for us. What we have in faith, the eternal life that through the presence of Christ has begun in those who believe in Him, is not yet the consummation of life. Faith is at the same time a having and a not-yet-having. But this not-having is the certain expectation of the Consummation.

Thus faith embraces at once[1] the past—our election before all ages; the future—the Advent of the Lord; and the present in which sonship of God has already been bestowed upon us, a sonship which is already the presence of the Holy Spirit, who as the Spirit of love makes us belong to the present—for in our lovelessness we do not belong to the present, but are entangled in our past and tormented with cares about the future. This unity of the modalities of time is what makes faith time filled with content. Thus the Biblical concept of eternity includes these three modalities of time within itself, without dissolving

[1] Cf. my Earl Lectures *Faith, Hope and Love* already quoted (p. 17 above), whose theme is the threefold character of the modalities of time

them. But the dominating modality is the presence of the God whose nature is love.

But this certainty of eternal things is by no means "anthropologically based".[1] On the contrary, it is based on the salvation history which culminated in Jesus Christ in the event of the Cross. In the certainty of the Resurrection as something already accomplished, this history by anticipation takes the form of glory to come, and in all these events reveals the righteousness of God; God's will to reveal Himself and to save. If justification by faith is really the truth communicated by God's Spirit Himself, the truth of the self-bestowing love of God, how then, in spite of all appearances to the contrary, shall not that life in the eternal love of God be realized in which faith's hope is set?

[1] Cf. R. Bultmann, *History and Eschatology* (Gifford Lectures, Edinburgh, 1957), pp. 41 ff.

CHAPTER 6

THE MYSTERY OF DEATH

I

Is death a mystery? For the man who regards himself essentially as the product of natural events this question seems one easily answered: No, death is a universal law of nature, to which even man is subject. Man must die, just as all living things must die. Death is no mystery, but something only too familiar. Everyone knows what it is—the doctor and the biologist know it only more accurately than the rest; it is the disintegration of the organic unity into its component parts brought about by natural causes. It is decomposition, dissolution. With the disintegration of the organic unity there cease also the manifestations which we meet with only in our experience of it: life, activity and consciousness. All that is left is the material substratum. The scientific rationalist sees here no mystery, but a fact of nature. He describes all talk about a mystery of death as a flight from reality. In the fear of death he sees simply an instinctive shrinking from destruction, and in the conception of a "life after death" nothing but conscious expressions of resistance to death. That is all there is in the so-called "mystery of death". For the scientifically trained man there *is* no mystery of death. This is on the contrary an invention of theologians and philosophers, and is surrounded by an aura of higher knowledge which is nothing but a self-deceptive projection of the desire for life.

And yet, why is the man who speaks thus not free from the feeling that death is something mysterious, a boundary phenomenon? One of its sides which is turned to him he, of course, knows, but the other side, which is turned away from him, disturbs him profoundly. Whence comes this unrest, this feeling that there is a mystery in death?

The man who merely understands himself as one living creature among others does not notice that by so doing he misrepresents his own real nature. It is thoughtlessness to say that man dies like all other living creatures, since he demonstrably does not live like them. Human nature is without parallel in the world of living things. Something of this otherness is known to every one. Philosophy only makes us conscious of this knowledge when it refers to the fact that man alone has intellect, pursues intellectual aims, recognizes and realizes intellectual values; that he alone creates culture, that he alone knows of the truth, strives for the good, struggles for justice. It is our knowledge about this peculiar character of our being which refutes the assertion that man lives as do all other living creatures. But his death is no more like theirs than his life is. His death is something quite different from that of the brutes. For just this is the particular thing about man, that his life—and only his—is a "life unto death". He anticipates death by his knowledge of its approach.

This certain knowledge of his inevitable fate of death lies like a shadow over his whole life. Only man goes consciously towards his death, and to his death. He alone knows what he loses in death. And just in proportion as man reflects upon his otherness, in proportion as he recognizes that he—and he alone—is a person, his death becomes to him an impenetrable mystery. He can observe and still understand the death of an organism, the dissolution of the living unity into its constituent parts—although even here there is a residue that he cannot explain, since no one knows what happens to that which bound the individual component parts into a whole. But he can form no exact concept of the "death of the self" or of the words "I am dying". For this event is something we cannot exchange with each other, just as we cannot exchange our own selves. What it means to say "The self disintegrates" passes man's power of comprehension, for the self does not consist of component parts which can disintegrate. What "I am dying" means I shall not know until I experience it.

The belief that science, biology, physiology, neurology, have given us a knowledge of what death is, so that talk of the mystery of death merely rests upon ignorance, is itself the product of a superstition. Materialism is not science, but metaphysics, and indeed the most ill-founded and most frequently and irrefutably disproved of all metaphysical systems.[1] So long as we do not know how from something objective (the movement of a body in space), something subjective (a feeling or a thought) originates, we do not know either what a person or the death of a person is. Therefore the last word here is Dubois-Reymond's, "We do not know, and we shall not know" (*Ignoramus et ignorabimus*). But men have never been able to satisfy themselves with this. The impenetrable mystery of death has driven them to seek for a

[1] Cf. esp. F. A. Lange's classical work *Geschichte des Materialismus* (E.T. *The History of Materialism*, London, 1925). See further P. Apel, *Die Ueberwindung des Materialismus*, 1909, and C. F. v. Weizsäcker, *Zum Weltbild der Physik*, 1943 (E.T. *World View of Physics*, London, 1952)

disclosure which can no more lie within the realm of objective knowledge than can our knowledge about personal being.

II

Beliefs of a survival of the soul after death have been widespread among all peoples of the earth and in all ages. These beliefs imply the view that death is "the separation of the soul from the body". This view finds expression in a great many forms[1] varying from primitive animism to the philosophical doctrine of immortality. But it takes also the form of the Indian doctrine of *karma*, that is, the doctrine of the reincarnation of the soul in a subsequent existence in a manner corresponding to its moral deserts. And it finds expression, too, in the thought occurring first in ancient Egypt, of a transcendent Judgment in which some souls are allotted a bright, sunny and happy existence in the world beyond the grave, while others are condemned to a dark and joyless or miserable existence. In such conceptions of a mythical kind we find traces of the knowledge that man's personal being is not identical with that of nature.

But a special significance for the spiritual history of the West must be ascribed to the Platonic doctrine of the immortality of the soul. The principal reason why it made such a deep impression on the thinking of Western man was its adoption—admittedly with certain modifications—by Christian theology and Church doctrine, even to the point of being declared a Dogma by the Lateran Council of 1512. Since Calvin's day it has counted in post-Reformation Protestantism as an accepted Christian doctrine. Only in most recent times has a deeper understanding of the New Testament led to the expression of serious doubts as to its compatibility with the Christian conception of personality, and attention has been increasingly drawn to its essentially pre-Christian origin in idealistic philosophy.[2]

We shall treat here of this doctrine only in the context of our question "What is death?" For if the soul is immortal in the sense that Plato and his successors teach, and for the reasons

[1] Cf. N. Söderblom, *La vie future d'après le mazdéisme à la lumière des croyances parallèles dans les autres religions*, 1901. (The Future Life According to Mazdaism in the Light of Parallel Beliefs in Other Religions)

[2] Cf. the controversy between C. Stange and P. Althaus on the Doctrine of Immortality in Luther. C. Stange, *Zur Auslegung der Aussagen Luthers über die Unsterblichkeit der Seele, Luther und das fünfte Laterankonzil* (1928); P. Althaus, *Luther und das fünfte Laterankonzil* (1928), *Unsterblichkeit und ewiges Leben bei Luther* (1930). Also. C. Stange, *Das Ende aller Dinge* (1930), P. Althaus, *Die Letzten Dinge* [5] (1949)

that they adduce, then the problem of death is solved in such a way that death does not intimately touch man as a person. We know in that case that we are so "constructed" that in death "nothing can happen to us" in our essential part. The immortal soul can no more be assailed by death than the lighthouse by the raging seas that encircle it. Thus in death the soul remains as it is. It is only liberated from its dark partner the body. But this means that there is no essential bond between man and time; the truly human and noble part of man is timeless, only his common, lower part, his bodily and sensuous nature, falls a prey to death. The body is mortal, the soul immortal. The mortal shell conceals this noble and eternal kernel which in death is set free from its shell.

But this conception of death which results from the dualistic self-understanding of man as a composite being consisting of a (mortal) body and an (immortal) soul is incompatible with the Christian view of man, which sees him always as a unity before God. The Platonic dualism leads not only to an unconvincing idealization of death, regarding death as the liberation of the immortal soul from the prison-house of the mortal body. It leads also to a conception of man's personal being which fails to do justice to the core of his person, man's responsibility and his knowledge of his responsibility. Who then is in this case really responsible for moral evil? The soul which as divine knows nothing of moral evil, or the body which can know nothing of it?

The answer of Plato—and of all the idealists after him including Kant—is that only our animal nature, "the dark horse of the pair" (Phaedrus), our sensuous or bodily nature, is responsible for moral evil. Moral evil is consequently not an act of man's spirit but merely an expression of the instincts which have not yet been tamed by the spirit. In a word, moral evil is a retardation of the spirit, an absence of the spirit, ignorance—but it is not sin. Moral evil is not contradiction, but merely sluggishness of the spirit. It has no relation to the will of God; it is merely an imperfection or disharmony between the rational and the irrational nature. The higher, spiritual self, on the other hand, plays no part in it. For the spiritual self is of divine nature, a spark of the divine fire, a part of the divine reason, substantially divine. It is not I who do what is morally wrong, but the animal in me. This means that the self and responsibility are torn asunder; the person is not apprehended as a unity. This idealization of the self proves the unrealistic character of the idealistic view of man.

Among all the philosophers from Plato to Schopenhauer and Nietzsche who have expressly concerned themselves with the problem of death, Heidegger holds a privileged place, if only for the reason that he and he alone not only regards death as the end of life, but looks on the whole life of man as marked by a consciousness of coming death, as a "being unto death". No philosopher before him perceived or acknowledged this. For they all followed the tendency to protect man as a human being from this horribly senseless fact of nature which threatens the significance and splendour of his humanity, by this very division of it into an essential and a non-essential part. But in Heidegger we find no trace either of an idealistic bisection of man or of a crass materialistic view. Man is seen as a totality which is not distinguished from his "being in time", but actually identified with it. And just for this reason man's being is a "being unto death".

That is the *first* important point. But just as important is the other point, that Heidegger brings death into the closest relation to personal being. For it is his thesis that precisely through his knowledge of death man attains to his personal being, his "authenticity". By a conscious acknowledgment of his being unto death, by resolutely looking death in the face, he is lifted out of an impersonal collective mass-existence and, as we understand Heidegger, becomes a self.

This view is not only something new in philosophy, but it comes, as we shall see, remarkably near to the Christian conception of death,[1] admittedly without reaching it. It is unsatisfactory in one respect: that it does not understand personal being, authenticity, as responsibility and does not bring it into a definite relation to obligation, thus leaving this authenticity void of content. And therefore this conception is open to a nihilistic interpretation; and indeed followers of Heidegger, for example Jean-Paul Sartre, are exponents of a barely disguised nihilism.

III

And what is the *Christian* conception of death? The Old Testament seems to have no original view on this matter. Like all other living things, man dies, and accepts this fate as a fact of the Creator's ordering. On the subject of his survival of death the Old Testament shares the widespread views of a shadowy existence in Sheol, the underworld. The religious man humbly

[1] Cf. my essay "Christlicher Glaube und Philosophie der Existenz" in *Festschrift für Heinrich Barth* (1960)

accepts the fate of death as an ordinance of God, without penetrating deeper into its mystery. But in some passages another view breaks through. Psalm 90 says "For we are consumed by thine anger, and by thy wrath are we troubled. Thou hast set our iniquities before thee, our secret sins in the light of thy countenance. For all our days are passed away in thy wrath. . . . Who knoweth the power of thine anger? Even according to thy fear, so is thy wrath. So teach us to number our days, that we may apply our hearts unto wisdom". It is thus the thought of death that makes man "wise". But beyond this, death is understood as an effect of the divine anger. Sin and death are related to each other. Death is seen in connection with responsibility before God. It is a judgment decreed by God. Man no longer sees death as a natural consequence of his bodily nature as a created being, but as God's reaction to his sin.

If this connection begins to be seen already in the Old Testament—even if only hinted at and imperfectly grasped—it is radically acknowledged in the New Testament: death is the consequence of sin, and punishment for it. "Death is the wages of sin" (Rom. 6: 23), death entered into the world through sin (Rom. 5: 12). Since man is no longer confronted merely by the prophetic Word as was the Psalmist, but by the Word Incarnate in Jesus Christ, the New Testament no longer speaks, as does the Old, merely about sins, but about *sin* as a negative entity comprising the totality of existence.[1] In the New Testament sin and death are seen as a unity; where sin rules, there death also rules.

Why is there an inseparable connection between sin and death, so that death follows from sin? Sin is not merely moral evil, but the rebellion of the creature against the Creator. When man as a sinner denies his dependence on God and turns it into independence, he is severed from God the original source of all life; his guilt stands between the living God and himself as he actually is. Thus the creature destroys the root of its own life, its fellowship with God. But man is unable utterly to destroy the relation to God which was established by God the Creator. He remains bound to God, but now instead of living in the love of God, he is under God's wrath. The life-giving relationship has become a disastrous relationship. His destiny of life in fellowship with God has become a life in exile from God, and in an exile which has been ordained by God Himself. To

[1] Cf. *Dogmatics* II, Ch. 3, "Man as Sinner", and Ch. 4, "The Consequences of Sin"

use a figure, man is driven out of paradise, the cherub with the flaming sword stands before the entrance, there is no way back, man is held responsible for his sin, it is "reckoned to him" as guilt. It is this which separates him from God. The shadow of judgment lies upon his whole life and makes it a life in darkness, in exile. This life in its totality is in fact a "being unto death" Bodily physical death is only the final full revelation of this character inherent in the life of sin, that it is forfeited to death, that it hurries towards the goal of annihilation and bears in itself the traces of futility because it has lost its roots in Him who is the source of all life and who Himself is life. Just as the body is the instrument and the outward manifestation of the true life of the person, so bodily death is but the outward manifestation of the person perverted by sin.

But this death is certainly not simply physical death; it is not mere mortality, the creaturely end of our bodily nature. It is the death of the person, it is corruption, *thanatos*. This *thanatos*, as the New Testament sees it, is thus a decree of God but it is not a primal decree. Its foundation is not God's order; it has arisen from disorder. It is the reaction of the divine wrath to human rebellion. It is thus an interposed decree of God, which is contrary to God's true will, to His love; an order of God's wrath conditioned only by the sin of man, by the disturbance of the original order. But the God who created man in love and for love does not will this interposition. In order to assert His true will, in order to reveal the righteousness of God, He has restored in Jesus Christ His original and unconditional order, the life-order of love. There is no possibility for man in his own strength to break the bonds of sin and to return to his union with God. This can happen only through Him in whom "the Word that was in the beginning" is bestowed again and bestowed in such a way that, as the Word of life, it restores his original personal being.

Nevertheless, we do not yet live in the Consummation, but only in faith in the reconciliation accomplished in Jesus Christ. Redemption from this body of death, the full realization of fellowship with God—eternal life—is promised to us in Christ; we have a share in it in faith, but it has not yet become visible tangible reality. Therefore we live indeed as men in principle set free from sin, but visibly and empirically marked by it; as men indeed reconciled, united with God's will through the love of God in us, but as actually ever and again enemies and rebels against God. This residue is not yet destroyed. We are still in "the body of death", therefore some part of death is still our lot. This residue is physical, bodily death. For the unbeliever this something is *the* reality, but for the believer it is the still existent unreality. Therefore for the believer in Christ to die is merely "to depart and be with Christ", and therefore an easy death in spite of all death's terrors. For he knows that it is only a transition to eternal life, not final, only provisional.

This is the Christian view of death. In it the mystery of death is disclosed, certainly in such a manner that this too, like all the knowledge of faith, is and remains knowledge "in part" until we know "face to face".

CHAPTER 7

TO DEPART AND BE WITH CHRIST

I

THE result of our inquiry into the mystery of death is that for faith death is no longer the conclusion of life but the point of transition to eternal life. "I have a desire to depart and to be with Christ" (Phil. 1: 23). This is the clearest expression of the way the knowledge of approaching death is transformed by the fact that the believer now stands in the light of Christ. Death is no more the dark door that shuts forever behind man, but the opened door through which he enters into true life.

This outlook into the future beyond death is based on the fact that the man who believes in Christ already *has* eternal life (John 6: 47). To believe in Christ is to lay hold of the divine love revealed in Him, from which even death cannot separate us. For love is the nature of the eternal God, and to participate in that love—in faith—is to have a share in eternal life which can indeed still be shadowed but cannot be annulled by death and its consort, the "life unto death". Thus death is, from the standpoint of faith, an episode, which has merely the character of something that no longer counts, is no longer tragic. It is in fact now merely this point of transition, however terrible in other respects its aspect to us here may be. Death does not *rule* any longer, any more than sin rules over those who are united to Christ by faith. The Word of justification has broken its power, and thereby taken away also the power of death. From this side also can be seen the solidarity of sin and death in the positive sense, whereas we saw its negative sense in the last chapter. If sin is removed—and that is what justification means—then death also is done away. We are to understand in this sense the utterances of the Johannine Christ. They are in full agreement with those of Paul, only they give even more decisive expression to the motif of life.

This means that the believer stands already on the side of eternal life. We saw that the New Testament concept of eternity is qualitative, and draws from this its eschatological power. The believer is united with the love of God, and through it with eternal life, from which no earthly power can ever separate him again. The episode of earthly death has thus no longer any serious significance.

But this New Testament thought seems to be akin to the

Platonic idea of immortality which we have rejected, for both say the same thing, that through death man is set free for his true life. At this point we must be very alert and watchful that after all faith is not confused with idealism, nor the meaning of the Christian message confused with the Platonic idea.

In fact there is an approximation between idealism and faith to which earlier we had to make reference,[1] namely that man is meant for a higher destiny. In the gospel this destiny is called man's creation for fellowship with God. Man is destined, not for a short life, but for eternity. This is implied by his creation "in God's image", by the Christian idea of the *imago dei*. He is created in the eternal Word of God, and for eternal life in fellowship with his Creator. This destiny of man has another character and another origin than those adduced by idealism. Man does not partake of the divine Being by virtue of his reason, but he has a share in God's life through the divine Word of Creation, through God's act and bestowal. This he has not in virtue of his own reason, but in virtue of God's self-communication.

This destiny he has lost by turning away from God—that is the deepest difference between the two viewpoints. He has lost it by his own fault. If he is to recover it, it must be restored by a new creative act of God. It was based wholly and solely on God's Word and His grace. It is not within man's power to retrieve this loss through some act of memory, to restore it from latency to actuality. Access to salvation is barred for ever for man; precisely this is the fact of *guilt*. That is how it looks from the side of man, but not from the side of God. On God's side the connection is not simply destroyed. Man cannot annihilate the Creator's will. It has indeed become invisible and inaccessible to him, but he could not erase it. In Jesus Christ the lost Word comes back again to man. When it is bestowed upon him again, he recognizes it as what was destined for him from God's creation. "The Word that was in the beginning", when it comes to humanity, does not come to what is alien to it, but "to its own".

No one has expressed this in so Biblical and theocentric a fashion as Luther.

> Wherever or with whomsoever God speaks, whether in anger or in grace, the same is certainly immortal. The Person of God who speaks there, and the Word, indicate that we are such creatures with whom God wishes to speak to eternity and immortally.[2]

[1] See above, pp. 140 ff.

[2] *W.A.* XLIII, 481. My attention was drawn to this passage by P. Althaus

Here we find expressed a genuinely Christian Biblical and Christological concept of immortality which is entirely different from the Platonic concept, even if it touches it. We have immortality not in the qualities of our soul, not in ourselves, but only in God's creative Word that "calls us into existence". This Word that we have lost—and lost irrevocably—comes to us again through the sending of Christ, through a historical act of God, and communicates itself to us, restoring us in this way to the destiny for which we were created.

This Word that addresses us in the justifying verdict of God is what faith allows to be said to it, and it is this faith in Christ which brings with it eternal life. In this faith death is not indeed overcome (this last conquest has yet to be made) but radically changed. It is no longer final but has become merely provisional, and thus, for all its grimness, is not a frightful death but even an easy one. For how should the transition from the world of the transitory into the world of eternal love not be something joyful, something longed for? "I have a desire to depart and be with Christ". How should we not rejoice that the divine Master restores our image, which is our true nature, and frees it from the deception and bondage of enmity to God? Thus death becomes the transition to eternal life and the beginning of perfect fellowship with God.

II

But can this idea be combined with the Biblical concept of the Kingdom of God, with the idea of the coming universal event of the consummation of God's sovereignty? This question has for long given a great deal of trouble to the theologians. For are not the thoughts which are here brought together entirely diverse, in fact, incompatible? The Church has always retained both these Christian concepts, setting side by side the thought of an individual Eschatology and that of a universal Eschatology. It has linked together "going to heaven" with the coming of the Last Day and the Resurrection of the dead, and has done so in the strangest manner.

Some theologians, obviously laying the chief emphasis on the universal human event, have taught that the soul at death passes into a state of sleep until "at the Last Day" it is raised together with the body to eternal life. But others have sought to do justice to both the trends of Biblical thought, that of the individual's eternal life and that of a general Resurrection, by teaching that at death the soul at once receives life in Christ—that is the meaning of the words "to be with Christ"—, but that it is still "unclothed", not clothed with the resurrection body, and must await the day of the general Resurrection. But, apart from the obviously mythical character of this idea, its dualism indicates its unbiblical character, while the first conception clearly contradicts what Paul and John say. Neither view agrees with what the New Testament says. It teaches rather—and most clearly in the Epistle to the Philippians[1]—that death is at once followed by life with Christ, and at the same time in the third chapter of the same Epistle it teaches that Christ will come in glory in His Kingdom, that Kingdom whose citizenship we already possess through faith.

The theological explanations just mentioned, that is, the sleep of the soul until the general Resurrection, and the life of the soul alone, without its body, in fellowship with Christ, are obviously attempts to solve the embarrassing problem created by the paradoxical statements of Paul. The more recent exegetes have sought another solution by assuming a change in the Apostle's views near the end of his life, or by regarding the view expressed in Philippians 1: 23 as accidental and "completely without emphasis". But neither explanation does justice to Pauline or Johannine thought. On the contrary, we must assume that Paul was quite unconscious of any contradiction between what he says in Philippians 1: 23 and what he says in Philippians 3: 20 ff., but that he regarded "departing and being with Christ" and "the coming of the Lord 'in glory' " as one and the same thing.

But how *could* Paul regard these two very different conceptions as one and the same thing, and not find them contradictory? The apparent conflict in conceiving of two movements in different directions, a conflict between going to Christ and the coming of the Kingdom of God, turns out to be a reflection of the one event which transcends human reason, a reflection which Paul's faith knows to be inadequate. He is therefore not disturbed by the change of images. In the same way faith regards as one thing the twofold event of apprehending Christ and being apprehended by Him, though this also transcends our power of conception.

The same thing is true of the difficulty contained in the fact that the time of our departure to be with Christ does not coincide with the coming of the world of the Resurrection. It is impossible for us to picture both these events as one and the same happening, because for our time-bound thinking they are separated from each other—perhaps by thousands of years. But

[1] Cf. on this point what was said in chapter 3 of this Part, pp. 365 f.

we have no *obligation* to picture it. On the contrary, we must be content to know that both things are true. For here we stand on the frontier of the temporal world. Human reason cannot overcome this contradiction either. Only the eternal God can transcend it. Clearly the insight of Paul's faith has enabled him to disregard with an ease that at first appears incomprehensible to us these thoughts of the "distance" which for our thinking must separate the two events. But this is in accord with the character of the Biblical conception of eternity, which differentiates it from temporal thinking in distance. Perhaps events which lie at a distance from each other in time are not separated from the standpoint of eternity, but simultaneous in the eternal Now.

The New Testament bears witness both to "departing and being with Christ" and to the appearing of the glory of Christ and His world of the Resurrection as one and the same hope. He who believes in Jesus as the Christ knows that both things are true: I go to Him and He comes to the world. We shall be with Christ, thanks to the love of Christ which has already apprehended us in faith, and we wait for the Resurrection and the return of Christ because Christ first came to us in the form of a servant, and the full revelation has not yet been made. As now the glory of Christ is still concealed, so also our divine sonship is still concealed. But both will become manifest in the same act of revelation to which faith looks forward in hope.

CHAPTER 8

THE COMING OF THE LORD IN GLORY: THE PAROUSIA

I

THE word "Parousia" which in the New Testament frequently describes Christ's future Coming and the coming of the Consummation, has literally the simple meaning of "Presence".[1] This simple word of everyday speech means the revealed presence of that which is already present in concealment, the unveiling of what we already see now *sub contraria specie* in the form of a servant, as "His glory, the glory as of the only begotten of the Father, full of grace and truth" (John 1: 14).

If we inquire how far this thought of coming to us and the self-representation[2] of God which fulfils itself in His coming to us belongs to the essence of the Biblical message, *the Bible as a whole* gives a clear answer. This is the theme from the very beginning of salvation history, that God comes, that salvation comes, that a movement from above downwards is in progress. The theme is the coming of that which is lacking, and which alone can give life its full meaning, its wholeness, its salvation; that through this coming God becomes present and "dwells among us", that God is "here" with His people. This is not one theme of the Bible among others; it is *the one* theme that dominates everything else. Especially do we hear even in the Old Testament the promise of the "coming" of the Messiah in whom God's sovereignty becomes present and real. The day of the Lord "comes" and with it, through His judgments, His glory. "Behold, the days come, saith the Lord, that I will make a new covenant with the house of Israel, and with the house of Judah . . . I will be their God, and they shall be my people" (Jer. 31: 31, 33).

The witness of the New Testament is: He *has* come. The formula "I am come", too little noticed in its simplicity, is met with often on the lips of Jesus. In His Person the "coming" has now become reality. In this "come" is contained the whole message of the Messiah and of the presence of salvation. And this is why the Baptist asks only one question: "Art thou

[1] Cf. also on the sacred and profane use of the word Parousia, *Griechisch-deutsches Wörterbuch zum Neuen Testament*, W. Bauer, pp. 1049–1050

[2] See Translator's Note, p. 4

he *that should come*, or do we look for another" (who is really he that should come)? (Matt. 11: 3.) Between the Old Testament and the New, there is this difference: that in the Old Testament the coming is only the object of hope and expectation, while in the New it is object of faith as something that has already happened. But this "having already come" and this "presence already" is of such a kind that it is not yet consummated; it has only begun and therefore has yet to await its consummation.

The coming of God, the theme of the Old Testament, is thus unfolded in the New Testament into three dimensions of time: He has come, He is here, He will come. In faith we are brought into relation to the *past*, to the Cross of Christ, we are incorporated into His death and thus have a share in what then happened. Life in the *presence* of God in Jesus Christ is life in the love of God and as such a true life in the present. Inasmuch as we participate in the Resurrection of Jesus Christ, which is the beginning of the Parousia, we go to meet the Lord who comes to us in the future. In this hope our present is already full of His *future*, His coming to us. In the unity of faith, love and hope[1] consists the existence of the Ekklesia, the Body of Christ. In all three dimensions of time it is the one Christ Jesus to whom we open our hearts in faith, in hope and in love. Each of these acts is directed to Immanuel, God with us, the personally present God. To take away one of these dimensions would be to destroy the whole. Faith is nothing, unless it is effectual in love; faith and love are nothing, if they are not permitted fulfilment in what we hope for.

If the Crucified is really the Son of God and His death on the Cross of Golgotha is not a tragedy, but *victory*, if there the decisive thing happened through which God is present to us and we are present to Him, then this concealment and hiddenness cannot be the last word. It belongs to the essence of faith, that it knows its own provisional nature, which one day will be transcended by the final perfection of sight. Faith without hope is just as nugatory as faith without love. But the Resurrection of Christ through faith has become our new life, and must, in His coming to us, be our Resurrection.

Therefore even hope can have no other object than this, that He who *came* in the form of a servant *will come* in glory. Here our hope is directed not to "something" but to Him. We look for the future Coming[2] of the Lord in His glory, without

[1] Cf. above, p. 379, n. 1

[2] *Translator's Note*. Here we have the customary word play on *Zu-kunft* which in German means both a "coming towards" and "future"

concealment, in His true nature, which is no longer under the law of the appearance of the opposite (*contraria species*). And therefore the second authoritative expression used to describe this event of the future is the *apocalypsis*, the unveiling, the revelation. "Beloved, now are we the sons of God, and *it is not yet revealed* what we shall be; but we know that when *it is revealed*, we shall be like Him" (1 John 3: 2). Here, too, we have to do with the revelation of what is now present under concealment.

As the pangs of childbirth "mean" birth, so faith "means" the revealing of His true form and ours, emergence from concealment and His unquestionable presence where we see no longer "through a glass darkly" but "face to face". Just as the beginning of a speech has no meaning unless it comes to an end, so faith has no meaning unless it comes to its goal in the fullness of revelation, in the unveiling (*apocalypsis*) which is called the Parousia, and in the Parousia which is called the *apocalypsis*.

From all this it is clear that this thought of the future is anything but superfluous mythology. Whatever the form of this event may be, everything depends on it, the future Coming itself, on its happening. To call it in question would be to undermine the foundations of faith, to tear out the keystone that holds everything together, and without which everything falls apart. Faith in Jesus without the expectation of His Parousia is a cheque that is never cashed, a promise that is not made in earnest. A faith in Christ without the expectation of a Parousia is like a flight of stairs that leads nowhere, but ends in the void. As Paul says of the Resurrection: "If Christ be not raised, your faith is vain, ye are yet in your sins" (1 Cor. 15: 17), so we must say similarly of the Parousia: without the Coming of the Lord in glory, the new life remains in concealment; there is no consummation for the unredeemed world.

II

But if now we ask, what will the event of the Parousia be *like*? then we come upon statements of the New Testament that are mythical in the sense that they are in fact "impossible for us to follow" (Bultmann) since we no longer have the world picture of the ancient world and the Apostles. "For the Lord Himself shall descend from heaven with a shout, with the voice of the archangel, and with the trump of God: and the dead in Christ shall rise first: Then we which are alive and remain shall be caught up together with them in the clouds, to meet the Lord in the air" (1 Thess. 4: 16, 17). To the question whether the Apostle meant all this literally we cannot answer with a confident "Yes" or with a confident "No". He can hardly have pictured God as blowing a trumpet. But for the rest we must not postulate too clear a consciousness of the symbolic and inadequate character of these expressions in Paul the writer or in the contemporary readers of this Epistle. The reader of today "demythologizes" willy-nilly, whether he is aware of doing so or not, even if he is a fundamentalist. What is in question is only the amount of this demythologizing. We find, in a word, that here the world picture of the Bible conflicts with our world picture.[1] But at the same time everyone who has understood the central importance of the Parousia-expectation sees that here there is no other possibility of expression than the symbolic.

It belongs to the character of the Final Event that its character as event is unimaginable. We shall then do best to stick to the New Testament symbols, knowing that they are symbols, and knowing, at the same time, that we need symbols. In our theological reflection we shall repeatedly risk the attempt of expressing abstractly the same truths that we utter symbolically in prayer and in divine worship. But we shall not deceive ourselves as to the fact that even this language of abstraction is symbolic—for what is the concept of transcendence if not a symbol? And further we shall remain aware of the danger of this advance from naïve symbols to the symbols of reflection, and not think that the measure of abstraction is a measure of approximation to the truth. Let the man who wishes to go further in the demythologizing project see to it that he does not end up with a philosophy of timelessness and the impersonal absolute; in other words, that the change of the *form* of expression does not lead to a radical transformation of *substance*. For this would mean that the divine "Thou" who Himself speaks to man would become an "It", a mere object of human thought, and the God who acts would become timeless Being; and thus the theme of the whole Biblical preaching, God's action and His coming as the Lord of the world, would be transformed into a monologue of man's self-achieved self-understanding.

We know that our knowledge is "in part" and we say this with express reference to our eschatological conceptions. But we know also that faith in the Coming of the Revealer and Redeemer which brings all things to their end and Consummation is a necessary part of faith in the Crucified and Risen Lord, who is made unto us righteousness and life, even if we can

[1] See our Appendix, "The Problem of Demythologization", at the end of this chapter

formulate this Final Coming and revelation only in the stammering language of apocalyptic symbolism. How would it be otherwise since it will indeed be the "wholly other" and only as the "wholly other" can it be the Redemption and Consummation? We are protected from capricious fantasy by the fact that this "wholly other" is related to what we already have in Christ, and to the newness of life already bestowed upon us, as the birth is related to the child already begotten in the concealment of the womb. The Final Event is not wholly other in relation to the new being already begotten. It is not wholly other in relation to the Christ who through the Holy Spirit is already "in us". Rather is He "The same yesterday, today, and forever". He is the same "who was and is and is to come". But it is wholly other in the sense that what is still concealed will be publicly revealed, that what is now still concealed in flesh will receive its Consummation in a fully spiritual bodily form.

III

In conclusion we have still to deal with the question of the expectation of the Parousia in the near future, which has always been of great importance for Christendom. The school of "consistent eschatology"[1] has certainly the merit of having attracted attention to the fact that Jesus and primitive Christianity expected the appearing of the Messianic glory and the consequent end of this world in the immediate future. We may judge this fact as we will, but to doubt it is hardly possible today for anyone who knows and takes seriously the text of the New Testament. But since this so immediately expected event has not yet occurred, the conclusion was drawn that the whole primitive Christian eschatological and apocalyptic view of salvation, which culminates in that end of history, and should have been confirmed by it, has been refuted and rendered untenable as a result of the non-fulfilment of that expectation, namely, by the course of history itself. And it is held that the Christology developed by the Church in the course of the first centuries is to be understood as a substitute for this vainly awaited event, and bears in all its artificiality the traces of this embarrassment upon it.

What are we to make of this theory? In the first place it is remarkable that in the New Testament the non-occurrence or delay of the Parousia, as was inevitable, was very clearly noted; that the Apostle Paul, who in the earliest Epistles hoped

[1] This was the way in which the school of Johannes Weiss and Albert Schweitzer described itself

himself to live to see the coming of the final revelation, later faced seriously the possibility that he would not live to see it, but was thereby in no way disturbed in his faith in salvation as based on Jesus Christ alone. This undeniable fact can be explained only on the assumption that the question of the date of the Return had not such central importance as is claimed. Next we must say that besides the expectation of the nearness of the end of the world two other equally well-attested sayings of Jesus have been handed down, which at least relativize the validity and importance of His sayings about His speedy return. "But of that day and that hour knoweth no man . . . neither the Son, but the Father" (Mark 13: 32). "And this gospel of the kingdom shall be preached in all the world for a witness unto all nations; and then shall the end come" (Matt. 24: 14).

The reason why faith is comparatively independent of the chronological element of immediate expectation is that primitive Christianity, unlike Jewish apocalyptic, believes that the decisive event of saving history has already happened (Cullmann). One looks back to it as something in the perfect tense. It is the Christ-Cross-Resurrection-Event which has happened "once for all". With Jesus Christ salvation has come; in faith in Him, in faith's fellowship with Him, He is Himself present. He Himself, the Crucified and Risen Kyrios, is salvation. But what still remains the object of expectation is that the still concealed living fellowship with Christ, the salvation still concealed under the flesh should emerge from its concealment, and that then faith should become sight and the provisional and imperfect enjoyment of salvation should receive its definitive consummation. This faith in Christ as the salvation bestowed by God, the presence of God given—even if only in a veiled manner—in His Person, now serves as a starting point and basis for the later dogmatic development. The theory of Christology as a substitute for the disappointment of Parousia-expectations is entirely superfluous as an explanation of the rise of this doctrine and therefore completely capricious.

All Jesus' words about His return are veiled in the mystery of the humanity of the Son of God, the servant form of the Suffering Servant of God, who made as little claim to omniscience as He did to omnipotence. The conception of "realized eschatology"[1] is right inasmuch as it correctly apprehends where the centre of gravity of primitive Christian faith lies, in the events which have already happened in Jesus, in the grace of God's

[1] C. H. Dodd, *The Parables of the Kingdom*, 1936

presence in the Holy Spirit already bestowed upon the Ekklesia. But it is wrong in not doing sufficient justice to the Messianic character of the existence of the believing Ekklesia, which is shown also in its sense of expectation of the fullness of revelation in the coming of the Lord in glory. In the primitive Christian community the certainty and power of the expectation of that which was to come were so great that they took shape in an expectation of its immediacy which no longer reckoned with the possibility of a history spanning hundreds or even thousands of years, and therefore were bound to be disappointed by the actual course of history. But who will exclude the possibility that the postponement of the end of history is the expression of a divine concern for the unreadiness of mankind?[1] On the other hand we can trace in the history of Christendom something like a law, that the more vitally hope is present in the Ekklesia, that is, the more powerfully life in the Spirit of God is present in it, the more urgent is its expectation of the Coming of Jesus Christ; so that the fullness of the possession of the Spirit and the urgency of expectation are always found together, as they were in the primitive community.

[1] This thought plays a very large part in the thinking of both Blumhardts, especially Johann Christoph

APPENDIX

THE PROBLEM OF DEMYTHOLOGIZATION

THE idea of an end of history, which we find in the New Testament witness and subsequently in Christian doctrine, undoubtedly contains an admixture of mythical elements whose origin is to be found in late Judaism and in the heathen Hellenistic world. But there are today many who as theologians feel bound to respect not only the Biblical revelation but also the claims of science, and who are convinced that the thought of an end of history has no other foundation than these mythological ideas. The historical question of the origins of these ideas need not concern us here. But on the other hand we are confronted with special urgency in this connection by the general problem of myth and the demand of these theologians for "demythologization", a problem which is relevant to every theme in dogmatics.

The character of certain conceptions in the New Testament which today we feel to be mythical, quite irrespective of their origin in non-Biblical mythology, seems to be based on the fact that men of that age lived in a world, had a picture of the world, that differed from our picture, bearing as it does the imprint of science. For this reason these conceptions are strange and unintelligible to us. The pre-scientific element in them is not indeed the most important aspect of the problem of myth, but it looms large for our generation, whose understanding of truth is predominantly determined by science. We shall therefore deal first with this problem, even though it is of secondary importance, before we advance to the more fundamental problem which remains of equal urgency whatever one's world picture may be.

I

Every person who has received some measure of education is aware of the fact that our modern world picture is fundamentally different from that of earlier times, whether it be the world picture of the Middle Ages or that of the ancient world. Thus it is different from the world picture of the Reformers, the scholastic philosophers, or the Apostles and prophets of the Bible. This change is as it were a matter of our common destiny and no one is able by an effort of will or by means of his "faith" to exempt himself from it. Granted that this pressure does not lie with equal weight upon all, but only in proportion as a man has received a scientific education. But even in the case of a man who believes for reasons of faith that he must remain true to the Biblical world picture, this inevitable change results in the fact that, without noticing it, he lives in two worlds at the same time, and dovetails the one into the other in the strangest fashion. This attitude of mind has done much to bring faith into disrepute with those who are primarily interested in science. The task of demythologizing is therefore a pressing, even an urgent requirement, even if it is not also a problem of the first importance.

The change in our world picture effected by modern science can be illustrated principally at three points: in relation to our conception of space, our conception of time, and our causal thinking.

(*a*) We live today in a world of *space* which is a billion times greater than that of ancient Biblical and mediaeval thought. The world of the prophets and Apostles, which of course also seemed tremendous to them, the world in whose centre the earth stands and round which the stars revolve, was a world whose limits could be seen. The world of contemporary science—and that means the world of every thoughtful man of today—is one which can no longer be measured by visible yard-sticks. Its unit of measurement is the inconceivable magnitude of the "light year" which corresponds to a distance of 5·8 million, million miles. At the beginning of this new age man was attacked by cosmic vertigo. There was no longer an "above" or a "below", he had lost every spatial orientation in unfathomable space. All earthly things seemed to have been reduced to nothing. The latest developments of science have indeed brought a certain reaction, since today it is not customary any longer to speak of infinite space as Kant did, but rather of a finite but unlimited space. But this has made not the slightest difference to that terrifying expansion. The world of the Bible has vanished and has been replaced by this paradoxical reality that can be apprehended only by abstraction. In this world both man and the whole of humanity seem to have been reduced to an insignificance that stultifies the Kantian "Copernican revolution", which is based on the reflection that it is man himself who knows this paradoxically finite yet unlimited world.

(*b*) But even more disturbing is the change in our conception of *time*. For the four or six thousand years of the ancient Biblical world picture there was substituted a period of time that embraces no longer thousands but millions of years or even thousands of millions of years, and in which not only the life of the individual man but also the time of human history was contracted to a mere second in the cosmic year. Here also, it is true, science has most recently introduced a certain reaction, since the concept of infinite time also—which Kant unquestioningly took for granted—has had to give way to the knowledge that the universe is by no means infinitely old, but must have had a definite beginning, whose date can with more or less accuracy be estimated. But this refutation of the "scientific myth" of infinite time, that is, time without a beginning, is also without immediate significance. For the fact remains that the limits which the Bible set to world time have once and for all disappeared, with the result that human history seems to have become a mere bagatelle—and if this has happened to human history, then surely a similar fate has overtaken the Biblical picture of man based upon it.

(*c*) The third great change took place as a result of the demonstration of unbroken *causality*. We are the first people to live in a coherent calculable causal world, while Christians of earlier ages lived in a world which acknowledged non-causal as well as causal events, and was therefore in part a magical world. But where within a strictly causal world is there room for the freedom and responsibility of man—in a world which is determined by its own peculiar law of cause and effect?

The reaction which proved that the thought of a causally closed universe was itself a "scientific myth" seems, however, to have immediate significance at this point. At the least it makes us realize that the causality which is apprehended by the thought of man has a limit which does not allow the picture of man to be submerged in that causal world.

Of course we must not draw premature conclusions from this critical reflection, but we see again more clearly the problem which has its roots in the thinking of man himself, and perhaps—seen from the standpoint of science—leaves also room for a view of man which regards him as standing at the same time outside and inside the causal world. Perhaps it is the case (this is how we would have to describe the situation from the viewpoint of science) that in faith, and in the realm of responsibility in general, there is present a view of man and of human history which is indeed compatible with the scientific picture, but is of a quite different kind. In that case we understand the language of the Bible as an expression of this human history understood in non-causal categories, but must remain conscious of the fact that this outlook is still expressed in the language of images drawn from the world, that is, as we put it today, in symbols taken from the realm of objects.

And this brings us to a problem concerning the mythical, which is not merely conditioned by the alteration of our world picture by science, but which preoccupied the philosophy and theology of ancient times. It is only on this plane that the most important decisions have to be made.

II

Since the beginning of Christian history the Biblical concept of God and all talk of a personal God, of an action of God in time, has been regarded as mythical, as something that cannot be expected of mature philosophical thinking. If there is indeed truth contained in Christian faith, yet it is truth in a completely inadequate form, which if it is to stand the test of critical reflection must be translated from its symbolic and mythical form into an unmythical one. This is the criticism which Christian faith had to face from the beginning at the hands of the philosophers, from the days when the philosopher Celsus was the first to attempt to pour ridicule on the Christian message. This reformulation has been going on through all the centuries of history, partly outside the Christian Church and partly inside it, partly in frank repudiation of the Christian message, partly by means of an adoption of philosophical criteria of truth for the evaluation of concepts of faith which are the product of theological reflection. *This* is the real core of the problem of myth and demythologizing.

We must be clear about one thing from the outset; that not only certain conceptions in the New Testament but the Biblical *kerygma* as such, not only the conception of an approaching end of history but the thought of a God who reveals Himself in history, who forgives sin, who intervenes in the life of history, is regarded by rationalist thought as mythology—today exactly as in the time of Celsus. The postulate of demythologizing without limits thus demands not only the surrender of those conceptions of a "pre-scientific" character which were conditioned by the world picture of earlier times. It demands in addition "de-kerygmatization", that is, a fundamentally unhistorical interpretation of human existence. It rejects the dependence of faith on a saving history, on a historical revelation, by describing the latter as mythical, meaning not wholly in accord with reason.

To the thinking which seeks to obtain final truth purely from man's reflection about himself and his world, and consequently repudiates dependence on a historical fact—revelation or saving history—the very thought of a personal God, a divine Thou who addresses us, is mythical. This thinking is opposed by the faith which knows its dependence on such a historical happening, because in that happening it recognizes the revelation and self-communication of God. This means the acceptance of what we wish to name the "fundamental myth" of the Christian faith, which is identical with the content of this *kerygma*. The God of faith is the God who makes Himself known, who as such can never be reached by thought, who graciously gives Himself for us and thereby glorifies Himself. Faith points to a moment in history, a happening, in which this self-communication took place and through which faith itself is begotten.

Faith cannot give up this "fundamental myth" without giving itself up. In other words: what would be surrendered through the demythologizing of this fundamental myth would be nothing less than faith itself. Its place would be taken by a philosophy of the self-understanding of man, non-historical and non-revelational. This is the alternative, this is the boundary at which demythologizing must halt, if faith in the self-revealing God who acts in history is not to be replaced by the rational idea of Absolute Being or Absolute Truth, a philosophical "theology" of the non-historical self-interpretation of the thinking subject. In such a "theology" the thinking subject is not addressed from beyond itself, but merely carries on a conversation with itself. It is therefore not really responsible, but only reverences its own ("deepest") nature, and redeems itself through self-recollection, knowing nothing of the forgiveness of guilt but only of self-purification. What is denied by all this is "truth as encounter", the truth that is identical with grace (John 1: 17); what is affirmed in its place is truth as monologue, a philosophy of the solitary self, of the "I" without the "Thou", of the self that does not receive but draws from its own resources, that has neither been created nor received the gift of grace, that does not stand over against God, but in the last resort is identical with Him.

It is, then, this antithesis that underlies the postulate of unlimited demythologizing. But if a limit is to be set to demythologizing, then it has become clear that the criterion of this necessary limitation is just this "fundamental myth" of which we have spoken.

We agree with philosophy in this point, that we call the decisive *kerygma* of God's self-communication in Jesus Christ "mythical" inasmuch as we concede that in faith we are aware of the inadequacy of all our speaking about God. The language of the Bible—of the New Testament as well as the Old—is symbolic and mythical in a manner that is inadequate for the abstract thought of philosophy and therefore seems unacceptable. What the philosopher calls inadequate and "primitive" is marked by two characteristics: by the symbolism of God's Personal Being (anthropomorphism) and by His intervention in history (miracle). The symbolism of Personal Being is to be found in expressions such as God, the Father, the King, the Lord, the Judge, etc.; that is, in gross anthropomorphisms. The symbolism of divine action is obvious in the conceptions: God comes, God speaks, He creates, He hears, He saves, He forgives sins.

It is obvious that the prophets and Jesus Himself do not hesitate to use these symbols in the plainest and most daring manner, because obviously their whole concern is to assert God's personal character, His speaking to us, in contrast with every kind of abstraction. And this is how the Bible speaks—and it does so in its sublimest passages, not only in the so-called primitive magical parts—with the plainest of visual images, for the second reason; namely to emphasize at all costs the "living" character of God, His action, His self-revelation in history. In this context a third point must not be overlooked; in both cases the misunderstanding of these symbols through conceiving of God as finite or as belonging to this world is obviated by the use of a third type of symbols, which express—to use again the language taken from the world of objects—God's "transcendence" of this world, His in-finity, His in-comprehensibility, His in-dependence of our purposes. God is "over" all the world, He is the Creator-Lord, He is incomparable, and therefore may not be depicted by any image, and His action within time is founded in His thought and will "before all time".

If now it is asked why we do not apply ourselves with greater assiduity to the task of replacing these symbols and mythical expressions by others more adequate, we must answer that the alternative would be to use the concepts of a philosophy which would replace the "living God" by the Absolute, replace the faith in a God who speaks to us, by timeless and eternally divine Being. In a word, it would mean substituting a philosophical self-interpretation for faith, a philosophy of the Solitary "I" for the revelation of the "Thou", a philosophy which finally sets on one side even the love of God as a mythical concept, as Spinoza did. Thus it becomes manifest that here we are faced by an ultimate Either-Or.

But when in rejoinder we inquire for the concepts by which this philosophy seeks to replace the Biblical symbolism and mythology in the interests of spiritualization, we discover that they lie in the direction of abstraction. The assumption apparently is that the more abstract the concept, the more spiritual it is. This is in fact characteristic of this way of philosophical thinking, which behind the concrete existent seeks for neutral "Being" itself, behind all mere appearances the one "ground", behind all truths "the truth". But here it is not noticed that when the utterances of the Bible are "interpreted" in this fashion, by abstraction, their meaning is totally changed. The world of God of which the Bible speaks is transformed into Plato's world of ideas, into the ontology of timeless Being, into the Absolute of the Advaita doctrine, the Absolute which has nothing confronting it but which is at once the eternal ground of everything and its negation.

It also becomes evident that this abstract system of concepts is not, as was intended, unsymbolical and adequate, but that all that has happened is the replacement of the symbolism of time and personality by the symbolism of space and of things. There is no philosophy, however abstract, which can evade the necessity of speaking of ultimates symbolically even if the abstractions of impersonal being and timelessness are used as such symbols. This is the quintessence of the spiritualization which is aimed at: the symbolism of personalism and of happenings in time is replaced by that of the impersonal, of the "It" and of timelessness. When we have once realized this fact, our zeal for "demythologizing" will have cooled remarkably. Our efforts will be confined to the relatively unimportant task of eliminating the conceptions which are determined by the ancient world picture, or at least making clearly recognizable their purely symbolic character. Even today men continue to say "The sun rises, the moon sets", although they know that this is "actually" not the case. But what they are to put in the place of these expressions taken from this world of our perceptions, no one today, not even the most learned astro-physicist, can honestly tell.

Thus the result of our previous reflections is as follows: while on the one side we entirely agree that the decisive *kerygma* of God's self-communication in Jesus Christ is mythical, we reject most emphatically the conclusion that from this inadequacy there follows the inference that the specifically Biblical mythical form of thought can be dispensed with. For in it we see the only possibility of giving expression to the one thing that is essential to faith, and that distinguishes faith from the philosophy of the solitary self. The mythical form of expression is simply the necessary consequence of the incommensurability of the Creator and the creature, whose transcendence we can hope for only when that final revelation occurs which is the object of our faith. "For we know in part. . . . But when that which is perfect is come, then that which is in part shall be done away" (1 Cor. 13: 9, 10).

But to admit this inadequacy, this symbolic character of all the thoughts of our faith about God, is thus something fundamentally different from what is meant by the demand for unlimited demythologizing. We know that our knowledge is in part, a limitation that will not be removed until that which is perfect is come. But we are not ashamed of the symbolism that lies in the name of God as the Lord, the Creator, the Father and Redeemer; we are proud of a truth which as bestowed upon us is identical with grace and is to be gained only by the surrender of that usurped autonomy of reason which results from the monologue of the rational self.

We acknowledge that the truth of faith comes to us in the self-communication of God, which culminates in Jesus Christ. How could the man who recognizes his true being in the Word of God have concepts that are other than inadequate? How could he be able to express this truth, that transcends all reason, except inadequately, in mythical symbols? Anyone who as a dogmatic theologian reflects upon that which is given in faith, may well see his task to consist in purifying this symbolism from all that is accidental and capricious; but he is not at liberty to surrender the symbolism itself. For by so doing he would surrender faith, and exchange it for a philosophy which neither knows nor wishes to know anything of the truth which comes to us, remaining instead the captive of its own thinking. He who already has the truth in himself, needs no justification. But he is also incapable of faith in a Thou who encounters us. But we confess that *we* only possess the truth that we have in faith as a result of the encounter with the God who reveals Himself in history, as a result of the salvation-history and revelation-history which culminate in Jesus Christ. This decision of faith is simply the acknowledgment of the justifying assurance and claim of God in Jesus Christ.

CHAPTER 9

THE RESURRECTION

I

It can hardly be denied that the conception of a resurrection of the dead came from Parseeism into Judaism and thence into the New Testament. There are indeed hints of it already in the Old Testament, but they all belong to the exilic or post-exilic strands of the Old Testament documents of our faith. We must therefore concede that the Old Testament, even the prophetic preaching, does not concern itself with the fate of the individual after death and also knows nothing of a consummation of the Kingdom of God beyond the limits of historical existence. But in the New Testament the idea of the Resurrection is already assumed to be familiar to everyone, though not accepted by all circles of the Jewish religious fellowship. Jesus Himself gives His support to this teaching, and at the same time links his belief with the Old Testament: "But as touching the resurrection of the dead, have ye not read that which was spoken unto you by God, saying 'I am the God of Abraham, and the God of Isaac, and the God of Jacob'? God is not the God of the dead, but of the living". With Jesus too, as in the Old Testament, the accent is laid not on the individual Resurrection of the dead, but on the coming of the Kingdom which now certainly is no longer thought of as an event within history, but as one breaking in "from beyond".

The preaching of the Apostles has another point of departure, and, at least on the surface, another content. Everywhere and without any question the point of departure is the fact of the Resurrection of Jesus. But this perfect tense never stands in isolation. It is inseparably bound up with the present tense—that this Jesus Christ is present, that His presence through faith and through the Holy Spirit is a present experience. It is precisely as "community theology", as witness of the experience of the believing Ekklesia, that the words ascribed to Jesus receive special significance: "Lo, I am with you alway, even unto the end of the world" (Matt. 28: 20), and "Where two or three are gathered together in my name, there am I in the midst of them" (Matt. 18: 20). The Pauline theology—here Albert Schweitzer is right—is "Christ mysticism" but this Christ mysticism is at the same time and primarily faith in

Christ, faith in what has happened once for all in His Cross. And the farewell discourses of Jesus in the Fourth Gospel similarly are "Christ mysticism" based on faith in Christ.

But it is to turn things upside down to assert that faith in the Resurrection is "simply faith in the Cross as a saving event".[1] The events of Good Friday left the disciples in an indescribable state of sorrow and disillusionment. If nothing further had happened, no Ekklesia would have come into being, and the message of Jesus would not have come to us. The Jesus-event would have vanished in the shadows of world history as an insignificant episode in the history of a Jewish sect. That this did not come to pass, but that, on the contrary, the tiny band of disciples filled and conquered the world with their message about Christ, happened wholly and solely because Jesus attested Himself to them as the Risen One, and as the living and present Lord created a new existence in them.

The New Testament witnesses to the Resurrection of Jesus do not speak with one voice. There are a number of widely divergent statements about it. We may regard the variety of the Easter narratives as a sign that the fact which they report is in the strict sense of the word an "eschatological fact", that is, the beginning of the coming of the eternal Consummation, of the new world, which cannot be apprehended by the categories of this spatio-temporal world.[2]

As for the interpretation of the Resurrection narratives, two mutually conflicting conceptions may be referred to. The first is depicted by Bultmann who describes the Resurrection in the following words: "that a dead man was raised again to physical life".[3] If Paul, who was not only the greatest missionary but also the first and greatest theologian of primitive Christianity, represented himself to the Christian community as standing on a level with the original Apostles as a witness to Christ's Resurrection, and not only claimed equal authority and originality for himself as a first witness, but had his claim fully acknowledged by the primitive community, that surely means that at least the primitive community's resurrection witness does not agree with the view described above. The second of the two conceptions terms the "appearances" of the Risen Lord, of which Paul speaks and which he mentions in one breath with his Damascus experience, mere visions and therewith discounts

[1] Bultmann, *Kerygma und Mythos* I, p. 46. (E.T. *Kerygma and Myth*, S.P.C.K., London, 1954, p. 41)
[2] Cf. K. Heim, *Weltschöpfung und Weltende*, 1952
[3] See *op. cit.*, I, p. 20

them as mere subjective experiences. But thereby the existence of the Ekklesia and the whole history of Christendom and the Church is regarded as based on a subjective delusion.

The Resurrection of Jesus, as the beginning of the Parousia, is the absolutely inconceivable and incomprehensible event, whose characteristic—one might say, whose natural characteristic—is incomprehensibility, its "inco-ordinable"[1] character, the impossibility of grasping or expressing it in categories of our thought and our imagination. The Resurrection is an incomprehensible event because it is the invasion of our temporal world by the eternal world of God. It is something that no one can conceive or describe, because it transcends spatio-temporal existence. On the other hand, it is unmistakably the self-authentication of Jesus Christ the Crucified as the Living One. The New Testament narratives emphasize in different degree and in different ways this twofold aspect:

The Risen One is recognizable as the same Jesus whom we knew in His earthly life, and He is at the same time wholly other than He was in His earthly existence. The story of Thomas, who puts his finger in the print of the wounds of the Risen Saviour and so assures himself of the identity of the Risen One with the Crucified,[2] is the strongest expression of the first tendency. The voice and the light from heaven which turned Saul the persecutor into Paul the Apostle of Jesus, or the story that tells how the disciples on the way to Emmaus at first did not recognize Jesus, and only became aware in the breaking of bread of the identity of their mysterious companion who vanished from their sight as suddenly as he had drawn near to them—such traits and others like them indicate the element of the "wholly other" in the mode of His existence and of His presence.[3]

In any case this is the common element in all the Resurrection narratives, that He who died on the Cross has revealed Himself to the faithful as the Living One. Therefore with Easter Day the New Age has dawned. But this new age manifests itself not only through the Resurrection of Jesus but just as much through the new life, life in the Holy Spirit, life in the presence of the Risen Lord,[4] and in the fellowship with Him which distinguishes believers from unbelievers, from those who are "in

[1] Cf. G. Spörri, *Das Inkoordinable*, 1929 [2] John 20: 24–29
[3] Acts 9: 3 ff.; Luke 24: 13 ff.
[4] Cf. E. Ellwein, *Vomneuen Leben*, 1932. The Lutheran hesitation to do justice to the full New Testament emphasis on the newness of life appears also in A. Nygren's commentary on the Epistle to the Romans (1951), especially in his exegesis of Romans 7

the world", and makes them members of the Body of Christ, makes them the Ekklesia. The existence of the Ekklesia, life in the Holy Spirit and in His gifts—these are signs and results of the world of the Resurrection which is already invading the present. That which is future and eternal has become present. The existence of the Christ-community is "messianic" or "eschatological" existence, life in the presence of God in the midst of the stream of time, God's Kingdom in the midst of the world of sin and death.

II

Of course—and on this point the witness of the Ekklesia's own experience leaves us in no doubt—the life of believers, the life of the Ekklesia is Resurrection life in its hiddenness, and therefore only a preliminary stage of the newness of life which the full revelation of the Resurrection will bring in the Parousia of Jesus Christ. The new life, eternal life, life in the likeness of Christ can only manifest itself brokenly through the medium of this "old existence", whose characteristic is the "life unto death". But this makes no difference to the fact that this new thing already exists. Christians do not live "between the ages" but wholly in the new aeon—even if for the time being only in the first stage of this coming world.

This can be seen above all from the fact that the Risen Lord is called "the first born of many brethren" (Rom. 8: 29). We are brothers not only of the earthly Jesus, but also of the Risen Lord. He who believes in Him shares with Him in the Resurrection, and is an heir of the eternal world even in this life. The call of God gives us the goal of being conformed to the image of His Son. It is our destiny to become the image of God. But only through the Resurrection, which gives us a share in God's glory, will this image be perfected. "We know that when it is revealed, we shall be like Him" (1 John 3: 2). Only in the full revelation of His glory, when we stand fully in His presence, shall we also be perfectly changed into His image.

This last change, which will happen through the coming of the Lord in glory, will one day happen radically without any co-operation or imitation on our part; solely through God's act of new creation. Yet it already is true of the provisional mode of the Resurrection life that it consists in a progressive transformation. It begins already here in those who reflect back, in faith, the *doxa*, the glory of God in Jesus Christ (2 Cor. 3: 18). *This* transformation is thus in its essence not something sudden or immediate. Neither is it something that excludes our own participation, but on the contrary includes it, for we are bidden "Be ye transformed by the renewing of your mind" (Rom. 12: 2). If it also is only a reality in faith, not yet in sight, yet it is an *experience* of faith "that we have passed from death unto life, because we love the brethren" (1 John 3: 14).

Thus the existence of the believer, that is, the life in Christ the Risen One, is itself Resurrection and yet at the same time only expectation of the Resurrection. "But if the Spirit of Him that raised up Jesus from the dead dwell in you, He that raised up Christ from the dead shall also quicken your mortal bodies by His spirit that dwelleth in you" (Rom. 8: 11). The change from the "being unto death" into a "being unto life" takes place in concealment, just as death is at work in a hidden manner in human existence. But this "being unto life" is only a being-unto, not yet a being-in. It still "appears" as a "being unto death" although it is this no longer. Paradoxically it is precisely the word "I die daily" that is the law of the new life (1 Cor. 15: 31). For it is just in this active dying that the new element resides, as *agape*, as true presence. It is no accident but a result of this paradoxical law of life that *agape*, the love bestowed by Christ, is depicted in the New Testament hymn to love just as much in negative as in positive terms; "love envieth not, vaunteth not itself, is not puffed up, seeketh not her own, is not easily provoked, thinketh no evil. . . ." The self-assertive self is disappearing, for "I live, yet not I, but Christ liveth in me" (Gal. 2: 20).

One of the most manifest results of the new life is the certainty of the Resurrection. "He that believeth in me, though he were dead, yet shall he live" (John 11: 25).[1] Of course every one of us will have to pass through physical death, but he does not die into nothingness but into Christ. Therefore it is said "to die is gain" (Phil. 1: 21) for it means "to be with Christ" (Phil. 1: 23). Therefore the Apostle can even say "I have a desire to depart". Death has indeed lost its "sting" (1 Cor. 15: 55, 56). If then it is true that the love which we have in Christ is God's love, and thus God's presence, God's life, then eternal life begins with faith in Christ.

But how shall we be raised? Of the "Resurrection of the flesh"—as the Apostles' Creed expresses it—the New Testament knows nothing. On the contrary, this concept is in sharp contradiction to the Christian witness, especially that of Paul. "Flesh and blood cannot inherit the Kingdom of God" (1 Cor. 15: 50). This body of flesh is not destined for eternity, it is

[1] Cf. also John 3: 36 and John 6: 47

destined to be annihilated, as sin was annihilated on the Cross of Christ. But we shall indeed be given a spiritual body (*soma pneumatikon*). What can we make of this paradoxical self-contradictory concept? What necessity of faith underlies this expression? We believe, a very important one, even a central one. The body is on the one hand the principle of distinction between Creator and creature, and on the other hand the principle of the individuality of man.

God alone is pure Spirit. He has no corporeality, although He has the glory (*doxa*) in which he manifests Himself as the Creator and Lord. But He wishes to distinguish us, His creatures, from Himself even in eternity, and to have us in His presence as His creatures, to whom He communicates Himself and whom He allows to reflect his glory. He remains what He is to eternity, and that means, He remains to eternity the Giver, the One who communicates Himself, and glorifies Himself in His creature. —On the other hand, the concept of the spiritual body (*soma pneumatikon*) expresses the wholeness of the person as an individuality created by God. I, this man here, am called by God. I, this particular man, who am not to be confused with anyone else, am to rise again. "I have called thee by thy name; thou art mine" (Isaiah 43: 1). That which stamped upon us even in this earthly body our individual character is not to be annihilated but on the contrary to be perfected. "It is not another self than mine that is created, but in 'raising' me God *preserves* my self, in order to perfect it" (Althaus).[1] The spiritual body is what is to belong to us in eternity as individual persons to whom God in eternity says "Thou".

And yet we can make no picture for ourselves of the Resurrection to eternal life. We only know that we shall not be submerged, melted and dissolved in a universal spirit. As God's confrontation of us is preserved intact, so is our confrontation of God. This confrontation is the presupposition of fellowship. Where it is lacking, the place of fellowship is taken by the unity which corresponds to monologue-thinking, the interfusion of elements that were—essentially—one from the beginning. And here there is no "Thou" to speak and no "I" to answer.

There is one last truth contained in the paradoxical concept of the spiritual body. The body is the instrument of service and of communication, both of service of God, and of service among the many who are our equals. That which is given prominence as essential mark of the Ekklesia, the praise and worship of God

[1] *Die Religion in Geschichte und Gegenwart*,[3] "Auferstehung" (Resurrection), VI, 696

and the brotherhood of mutual service, is also to be preserved in the Consummation. Thus the Pauline concept of the spiritual body becomes an expression of the decisively and specifically Biblical emphasis; fellowship instead of unity, answer and worship instead of monologue, love instead of the solitude of the self.

We await our Resurrection in the Parousia, the coming of the Lord, when the hidden sovereignty of Jesus Christ will be revealed in the fullness of His glory, when God will be Lord over a humanity united through His will and bound to Him. If the coming of the Lord for the individual human being, as Paul expects in his own case, happens in an experience which seen from this side is a "departing", the extinction of earthly life, why should not a final experience of mankind and analogous to death be the aspect seen from this side of the Parousia, the Coming of the Lord in glory? To this coming the word of the Psalmist might be applied: "We shall be like them that dream" (Psalm 126: 1)—like men who awaken from an earthly dream to a heavenly reality.

CHAPTER 10

UNIVERSALISM AND WORLD JUDGMENT

I

THE gospel is the message of the coming of God to His creatures who have fallen into sin and under the dominion of death. In the Word of reconciliation which has been spoken in Jesus Christ, God summons us to accept this reconciliation as His self-communication, and to believe that we are His beloved sons and the heirs of His glory, of eternal life. This Word, the true Word of God, as the "Thou" Word of Him who "calleth to those things which are not, that they may be" (Rom. 4: 17) has absolutely personal character. It creates me as a person and gives me true humanity at the same time. Inasmuch as this word of reconciliation wipes out the curse which lies upon my past, it makes me a member of the new humanity, the humanity that is liberated from its past. This humanity has its origin in the unfathomable and therefore truly unconditional love of God. But just as God loves me, this sinner, without a cause and promises to me—even me—His eternal love, so He also loves all other men. There is no reason why He should show a preference for me. For my faith is not the cause of His love; quite the contrary. God overlooks my enmity, and declares to me that in spite of my enmity He still loves me. If thus His will is fulfilled in me in spite of me, why should it not just as well be fulfilled in everyone? Thus then the message of unconditional grace includes in itself the knowledge of God's decree of universal salvation.

Just as surely as God's Word of love in justification through Christ is received as something un-fathomable, so surely is it in itself un-conditional and un-limited. The will of God, as it has been revealed in Jesus Christ, is indeed His will to communicate Himself to all, and to glorify Himself in every creature. Thus it is expressly said in the New Testament witness, that it is the will of God in Jesus Christ "by Him to reconcile all things unto Himself" (Col. 1: 20), "to gather together all things in Christ, both which are in heaven and which are on earth" (Eph. 1: 10). The faith that God wills to give salvation to all men thus corresponds to the message of the gospel. The will of God that has become manifest in Jesus Christ has absolutely no limits. The message about this will is the gospel.

God "will have all men to be saved, and to come unto the knowledge of the truth" (1 Tim. 2: 4). Through Jesus Christ who "gave Himself a ransom for all" (1 Tim. 2: 6), He has proclaimed that this will of His is one which encompasses all men. As God's will revealed once for all in Jesus Christ, it is the content of our faith. The realization of this will in the future is our certain hope. To believe *this* and to hope *this*, is to be a Christian.

Whether a man believes this gospel or not, is on the other hand clearly a second question, whose answer cannot invalidate this gospel. Just because we have become certain of the revealed will of God as an unconditional will, we are not at liberty subsequently to declare that it is a conditional or limited will, as a result, perhaps, of our experience that many are unable or unwilling to believe, but refuse to trust God's promise and to obey His claim. This can make no difference to the revealed will of God. There are in our experience believers and unbelievers—we must say unbelievers *as yet*—for how should we forget that everyone who believes has passed from unbelief to belief? But everyone who understands this empirical state of affairs to imply that there is also a double will in God, one will that some men should be saved and another will that others should be damned, misunderstands the gospel and "supplements" what Christ reveals to us by adding secondary considerations of his own construction, that is, a speculative causal inference to the effect that the unbelief of the others must have its origin in the will of God just as the belief of the first group. This causal inference from experience is simply "natural theology".

The doctrine of the "double decree", according to which "all men are not created on equal terms, but some are preordained to eternal life, others to eternal damnation" (Calvin)[1] is a shocking caricature of the Christian message which can be explained only as the result of a retrospective inference from the supposedly clear scriptural doctrine of a twofold issue of world history to a twofold will of God as the cause of this twofold result. But by this the meaning of the whole message of Christ was obscured. The good news (*eu-angelion*) became bad news (*dys-angelion*). The gospel of the unconditional love of God, who acquits the sinner, became the doctrine of the particular love of God, which extends only to one part of humanity and has at its side that which is not love—a will to the damnation of men.

[1] Calvin, *Institutes* III, 21, 5: "*Non pari conditione creati sunt homines sed aliis vita aeterna, aliis damnatio aeterna praeordinatur*"

The Biblical word "election" played a leading part in the rise of this misunderstanding, because it was understood as a matter of course that it referred to the final Judgment. But this is certainly not its meaning. Throughout the entire Bible "election" means in the first place that it is God alone who destines man for salvation, and that He has done so from eternity. ("According as He hath chosen us in Him before the foundation of the world", Eph. 1: 4.) In the second place, it means that it is God alone who calls man from his condition of lostness into fellowship with Himself. And this implies the creation of a new relationship between man and God, a new creation, namely the creation of the man who is united with God. Thus Israel is elect; thus in Christ the Church is elect. It has its new being in the Word of the loving God—in spite of its own empirical form.

A falsely objective interpretation of the New Testament words about judgment has also favoured belief in a double decree. Instead of asking, "If we start from the centre of faith, from the unconditional love of God known in Jesus Christ, how are we to understand what is said about judgment?", judgment itself was made the starting point, and consequently the knowledge of the bestowal of grace in Christ was modified and grace was degraded to the status of a cause of the double conclusion of history. At the decisive point Christocentric thinking was abandoned, and was replaced partly by a false exegesis of the Bible, partly by natural theology. The place of Christ-centred thinking was taken by the speculative concept of omnipotence, and the result was the monstrous doctrine of the "double decree".

In opposition to this we say that whatever the significance of the teaching about the Last Judgment may be it can never limit or modify what we have known as God's will in Jesus Christ. Judgment is never the goal of the divine Will. If it is objected that the Will of God is not merely the will to communicate Himself (love) but also to glorify Himself (holiness), that is indeed correct, but must at once be supplemented by the addendum that in the revelation of Christ the decisive thing is the unity, the coincidence of love and holiness. If now we pass on to interpret the Biblical concept of judgment, then we must follow the universal rule of interpretation and explain what is obscure by what is clear. What has already come to our knowledge is clear, namely the revelation of the un-conditional and therefore un-limited love of God in Jesus Christ. The teaching about judgment is at first sight obscure.

II

The Word of judgment belongs to the fundamental *kerygma* of the entire Bible. Every Bible reader knows that most of the utterances of the Old Testament prophets are utterances of judgment, utterances in which the judgment of God's anger against sinful Israel and against the godless nations is set forth. But it would be an utter mistake to imagine that this thought of judgment belongs merely to the Old Testament while in the New Testament only grace is proclaimed. It is the case here as with all the themes of the Bible; they are the same in the Old Testament as in the New, but in the New Testament they are all made absolute, "radicalized". To take responsibility with absolute seriousness means to believe in Him who judges us in the Last Judgment, where not only the whole of our past is revealed before Him, but the guilt of the whole of humanity along with mine as a solidarity of guilt. In Old Testament days this thought was not yet known.

But in yet another respect the New Testament takes a more radical view of judgment and human sin. The Old Testament divides men into righteous and unrighteous, the first of whom can stand in the sight of God, while the others cannot. It is, of course, also said, "For in thy sight shall no man living be justified" (Psalm 143: 2); but this insight is found only very sporadically. The Old Testament as yet knows nothing of a last Judgment, which will reveal us all as sinners. It knows as yet nothing of a revelation of God still to come, but certainly expected, which concerns the whole of humanity; a manifestation of God and of man at the same time most personal and absolutely universal. It is only Jesus who brings this radicalization and universalization. Only in Him does God's "Thou", God's absolute claim, become concrete. Only here is there mention of a final Judgment, of the absolute, definitive separation of the righteous from the godless, of eternal death as the alternative to eternal life, of perdition as the alternative to salvation in God (Matt. 25: 46).

What is the theological foundation of the thought of judgment? It is a necessary inference from the knowledge of the holiness of God. God is the One who takes His Will in deadly earnest. "God is not mocked, for whatsoever a man soweth, that shall he also reap. For he that soweth to his flesh shall of the flesh reap corruption; but he that soweth to the Spirit shall of the Spirit reap life everlasting" (Gal. 6: 7, 8). The holy God tolerates no opposition to Himself. He sets His face against all opposition to Himself and asserts His absolute authority. God counters man's self-assertion in God's despite with His own self-assertion in man's despite.

The God who makes Himself known to us in the revelation of the scriptures is not light *and* darkness, life *and* death. The thought of judgment brings to light the original God-given connection between obedience and life. To be with God is life, to be against God is death. As unity with the divine will is salvation, so resistance to it is perdition. Jesus Christ is the revelation of the Holy God who will bring with the final realization of His will an end to all indecisive intermingling of obedience and resistance. All evil must be judged and cast down and removed in order that the sovereignty of the Holy God may be fully revealed.

In the same way the foundation of our responsibility comes to light in the thought of judgment. When man really recognizes his responsibility, he knows that it is not merely a human responsibility. Responsibility means to be summoned to give an account, to be reckoned responsible. What could this authority be, which calls us to account, if not God? and for what should we be reckoned responsible if not for our whole life? To take our responsibility seriously means nothing else than to stand before the face of the divine Judge. To have to answer for oneself before God is the highest expression of moral responsibility. Only this thought of judgment gives ultimate depth to the concept of responsibility and therefore makes clear the relationship between God and man. Without the prospect of judgment man can always misunderstand his freedom as irresponsible freedom, as absolute independence, and this self-misunderstanding is at the same time real sin and real death. But it is only through judgment that this is revealed as its true nature. If we remove the thought of judgment, then the way is open for the misunderstanding which stems from the arrogant belief that only absolute freedom is real freedom. But this conception of freedom is the denial of responsibility.

Only if we understand responsibility literally as the necessity of giving an account to the Judge who judges impartially and knows everything—only then do we understand ourselves as really responsible. The idealistic philosophy has attempted to circumvent this "theological" interpretation of responsibility by making man responsible to a moral law. This is the monological and consequently unmythical interpretation of responsibility. But it is possible only if man is split into two halves. The one half, the better self, is identical with the legislating authority. The moral law is the law of autonomy. The other half is the empirical man, who in fact contradicts the law, the "lower" self. But by so splitting himself, man at the same time exalts himself above the judgment which is passed upon him by the law. He identifies the better self with the "true" man. Moral evil is then something for which he is not really responsible. The self appears as the immaculate self of the "good man" which is identical with the law. He has cast away the burden of guilt and is "really" in his heart of hearts free from it. But here man deceives himself. He deceives himself with this illusion that he is really one with the good, but not with the evil. And thereby at the same time he makes his responsibility unreal. If he has not to answer for the moral evil he has committed, wherein can his responsibility possibly consist?

This intermingling of seriousness and trifling is brought to an end only when the "Thou shalt" is detached from the self; when I really understand it as the call "*Thou* shalt", when for the abstract law is substituted the claim of God who "summons" man and calls to him. In the light of God I am revealed as I really am, and my guilt is given the weight that it really deserves. To stand before God and to know oneself really responsible is one and the same thing. The God who addresses me by the word "Thou" is the God who not only holds me responsible, but who proclaims me guilty. God's word "Thou" and my answer "I am a sinner" are simultaneous. When I come to see God as "Thou" I recognize myself as burdened with the weight of sin, and what I previously conceived to be the law of my autonomous reason I now hear as the commandment of God.

But in this judgment which is passed on us—and whose eschatological verdict we still await—God's claim is transformed into His gracious promise, because the place of our missing righteousness is taken by the righteousness of Christ. In Him, the Crucified and Risen One, the Holy God acquits us as "righteous" by reckoning to us the righteousness of His Son; the God who does not let Himself be mocked, who unconditionally asserts His will, the God who, because He Himself is holy, wills that we also should be holy. Therefore when we let this righteousness of Christ be given to us, the judgment lies already behind us, although we have still to wait for its final manifestation—the Coming of Christ to judgment. Inasmuch as we understand that Jesus Christ is "our righteousness" we are saved from the wrath of judgment. But this also holds true only in faith, not yet in sight. We shall have once more finally to pass through the fire of judgment. We shall all have "to become manifest", for to God's full manifestation in glory there corresponds full manifestation of man, of the depth of his sin hitherto graciously concealed from him. But we know now that we shall come forth from judgment to salvation for the sake of Christ who is our righteousness and who abides even the least and the most exacting judgment. We can have confidence that we shall be brought safely through the judgment by the grace of God.

This is the miracle in the absolute sense, namely, that which it was quite impossible for man to know or even to guess beforehand, and which contradicts all the laws of thought; the bestowal of righteousness, which is identical with love. We can indeed say retrospectively: how could it be otherwise than that God's holiness is identical with His love, how could His self-communication be different from His self-glorification? What is His righteousness but His will to fulfil His purpose? But God does not reach His goal, as we men imagine, through our own achievement of righteousness, but by bestowing upon us what we strive after all our life long and yet do not attain, and only through this gift revealing fully that we receive all things from His hand and are dependent upon Him alone. The Christ who will save us through judgment is present in faith as One who already calls us His future brothers and thus places us at the side of God. Christ is Himself present in faith, and only in faith.

Thus in faith itself there is no contradiction between the thought of judgment and the thought of universal grace. On the contrary, the latter cannot be understood without the former. What the New Testament says about judgment is the final and radical expression of what is already implicit in the words "I am a sinner". We cannot understand the gospel of the grace of God in Christ without the thought of judgment, true though it is that the gospel of God's universal loving purpose remains the end and goal towards which the thoughts of the believer move. And yet we do not believe it is right to say that Christ has closed the gates of Hell for ever.[1] In the objectivity of its affirmation this statement—like the other one which asserts that there is a Judgment which involves the damnation of some and the admission of others to eternal life—is "natural theology", since it expresses in the general form of a doctrine something which has validity only in the most intimate relationship to the words "I believe".

We teach both; the Last Judgment, the double *dénouement*

[1] Karl Barth, *Kirchliche Dogmatik* II 2, p. 182 (E.T. *Church Dogmatics* 167). On this point see my *Dogmatics* I, "Karl Barth's Doctrine of Election", Appendix to Ch. 23

of history, and universal salvation. For we cannot understand the grace of God without keeping in mind also the thought of judgment. It would be wrong to think that through faith one had been exempted once for all from this judgment. Faith must not be separated from works. It is just this separation that creates the "cheap grace" which has so much weakened and corrupted the Lutheran faith. But neither have we to maintain a "dialectical see-saw" between fear of judgment and certainty of salvation. On the contrary, faith is the decisive movement from the one to the other which we must repeatedly make by passing through judgment to faith, to the justifying grace of the Cross of Jesus Christ.

It is of course inevitable that the question will be asked, as it were, with angry impatience. "How do things stand then? Is there such a thing as final loss or is the doctrine of universalism true?" The Church, as everyone knows, has answered the first question very bluntly: "Yes, there is such a thing as final loss", and therefore it has condemned the doctrine of universal salvation as a grave heresy. It seemed at first sight to have the authority of Christ's words on its side, above all the narrative of the judgment of the world (Matt: 25). Against these obvious arguments the few passages in the Bible which speak of universal salvation failed to make an impact.

The greatest mistake of this doctrine was that it gave an answer at all to the question: "*Is there* such a thing as final loss or *is there* a universal salvation?" No answer should be given to this question, any more than to the question "*Is there* a God?" Just as this last question is best answered paradoxically by saying "No, *there is* not a God", so we should answer the question "Is there damnation or is there universal salvation?" by "No, *there is* neither of these things, for both are false questions." The world of faith is not the world of empirical objects, of objective knowledge, the world of "there is". God's love does not *exist* in the same sense as continents and the Milky Way exist. God and all divine things are not to be found on this plane which we can, as it were, pace out with our question "Is there?" and about which we can make similar observations. God does not belong to the realm of perceptible objects, but to that of speaking and being spoken to.

In order to see God one must be "summoned", and this "summoning" He Himself brings about by speaking to us in His Word of claim and assurance. This speaking of God, this Word of address is heard only in the dimension of responsibility, not in that of objective fact-finding. This dimension is marked by the conviction "This concerns *me*." This is the dimension of Biblical discourse. The words of Jesus too are always words that "concern" us, words of "confrontation". They are meant for the man who hears them as one vitally concerned, not for the spectator who looks on from a position of superior neutrality. This is the reason why, measured by purely logical standards, they are so often illogical and contradictory. Logically intelligible discourse lacks this character of confrontation, of address, of speech intended for one who is vitally concerned. Purely logical discourse is intelligible in itself without *my* being existentially concerned. The logical contradictions of the discourse which "summons me to encounter" are the means whereby I am compelled to pay attention and to participate. Logical contradiction is, so to speak, the place for existential participation. I can understand what is said, only when I am involved and when I cease to be a spectator; when the discourse is directed at *me*. But then the contradiction ceases to be a contradiction.

So it is with the two doctrines of damnation and universal salvation. They are not logically compatible. It is wrong to affirm one or other of them as one does a logically intelligible proposition, a doctrine. They are true only when taken together, and this togetherness is understood only if we are participants, if we cease to be spectators who ask "Is there this, or is there that?" I can only really hear the apostolic *kerygma* of justification and the word of universal salvation that belongs to it, when I hear along with it the Word of judgment. These two conflicting doctrines are related to each other as one "law and gospel". Only when I have understood and taken seriously the law and its absolutely unconditional claims upon me, do I rightly understand the gospel of forgiveness.

The Word of the law culminates in the Word of judgment. Therefore, when judgment is spoken of, it is always judgment according to works that is meant. "Inasmuch as ye have *done* it unto one of the least of these my brethren" (Matt. 25: 40); "For we must all appear before the judgment seat of Christ, that everyone may receive the things *done* in his body, according to that he hath done, whether it be good or bad" (2 Cor. 5: 10). Only when I "hear" the final and utterly radical judgment of my sin that is implied in the *kerygma* about Him who was crucified because of me, am I in the position to understand the gospel of grace which reaches me in the message about Him who was crucified for me. Taken as objective representations of reality, as discourse about visible facts (*theoria*), rather than as discourse addressed to the hearer, understood as doctrine rather than as *kerygma*, the two doctrines present a contradiction incapable of logical solution, whose solution accordingly has been repeatedly attempted by weakening one or other of the two positions. But it is precisely the logically insoluble antithesis of damnation and universal reconciliation which compels me to leave the objective attitude, the dimension of "there is", and to become a hearer, a participant. The judgment must "find" *me*, just as *I* am the man reconciled through Christ.

In these two concepts of final judgment and universal reconciliation the self-communication of the Holy God and the self-glorification of the loving God finds its perfect expression. Therefore we must hearken to the voice that speaks of world judgment as God's voice, that we may fear Him, and we must hearken to the voice that speaks of the reconciliation of all as God's voice, that we may love Him. Only in this irreducible co-ordination do we apprehend the two aspects of God's nature, His holiness and His love. All "symmetrical" logically satisfying knowledge of God is fatal. Therefore the criterion of all true theology is this, that it should conclude with the words "God be merciful to me a sinner" (Luke 18: 13) and over and above that with this other word: "But thanks be to God which giveth us the victory through our Lord Jesus Christ" (1 Cor. 15: 57).

CHAPTER II

THE CONSUMMATION

I

THE New Testament witness of faith speaks unambiguously about the Consummation of the world as the final goal of God's self-communication and self-glorification. It does this in concepts which belong to various contexts and whose imagery is indeed also drawn from different sources. The opinion has thus gained currency that in this witness we have to do with cosmological statements, which do not belong to Christian faith itself but stem from apocalyptic or gnostic mythology and speculation. Although this thesis is praised as the newest exegetical discovery, it is basically only a new variation on an old theme which we can still clearly remember as originating in the school of Ritschl and Schleiermacher: faith is concerned not with judgments of existence but only with value-judgments or—as we find it in Schleiermacher—only reflections about pious feeling have a place in systems of dogmatics. But since the Christian community has experienced what an impoverishment resulted from this thesis, it ought not to let itself be led a second time into this cul-de-sac.

The thesis of a cosmology alien to faith has particularly in view the two passages which have always been cited as the chief evidence for the New Testament doctrine of the cosmic significance of faith in Christ, and in particular for the doctrine of the Consummation of the world: the two "deutero-Pauline" utterances of Colossians 1: 15–23 and Ephesians 1: 9–23. It is asserted that they are based on a gnostic hymn which has later been revised by a Christian hand. But this reasoning is irrelevant to the main point at issue, the cosmic significance of the Christ event; for our question is, as always, directed not to the Biblical witness but to Jesus Christ Himself, and it is formulated thus: "Does our faith in Jesus Christ as the decisive self-communication of God imply something also about the origin and destiny of the world?"

For us this question was in principle answered a long time ago by the confession that God the Creator is revealed in Jesus Christ and that the creation of the world is the basic self-communication of God. The gospel of Jesus Christ would collapse into meaningless disconnected fragments, if the warp of faith in God the Creator were pulled out of the fabric. The God revealed in Jesus Christ is none other than the Creator of the world, "The Creator of heaven and earth." What distinguishes the Christian faith in the Creator from the Old Testament Jewish faith is merely the fact that it recognizes in Jesus Christ the Logos in both senses, as the One "through whom" and the One "for whom" the world was created. In Jesus Christ we know the origin and the goal of Creation in one: the God who is my beginning and my end.[1]

This is not only the teaching of the "deutero-Pauline" Epistles to the Colossians and the Ephesians. On the contrary it is already unmistakably present in the unquestionably Pauline First Epistle to the Corinthians. "But to us there is but one God, the Father, of whom are all things and we in Him: and one Lord Jesus Christ, by whom are all things and we by Him" (1 Cor. 8: 6). The entire Bible knows nothing of a revelation of God the Redeemer that is not at the same time revelation of God the Creator. The two passages just mentioned —of supposedly gnostic origin—are thus only especially explicit in their development of the implications which are already contained in the confession of Christ as Lord.

The new man, who is created in faith as a "new creature" by the verdict of justification, is in fact the man made new in Christ (Col. 3: 10) who has been chosen from eternity. Even if we had not the express statement of the Epistles to the Ephesians and the Colossians, we would know equally well that in Jesus Christ "the mystery of His Will is made known to us, according to His good pleasure—to gather together in one all things in Christ, both which are in heaven and which are on earth" (Eph. 1: 9, 10). What the Prologue to the Gospel of John says is the really essential expression of faith in Christ: the will of God which is revealed to us in Jesus Christ as the cause of the world, is also revealed in Him as the world's goal, its purpose (*telos*). The "Word that was in the beginning", "by which all things were made", is the same as the Word in which God in the Person of Jesus Christ makes us children of God and bestows upon us eternal life.

It may at the first glance appear strange that in both the passages named the confession of Him who reconciles us with God is so boldly expanded to a confession of Him as the cause and goal of the world. One asks at first: What then has this personal happening, the forgiveness of sins, to do with the origin of the universe, with the goal of history and the cosmic Con-

[1] Cf. *Dogmatics* I, section 2, "The Will of God", pp. 303–53 (E.T.)

summation? This "cosmic expansion" makes us feel something of the offence which the man who has not yet been touched by the Word of Christ feels in general in relation to the message of the gospel. It is by no means only the modern man, the man who feels himself obliged to accept scientific thinking and the scientific world picture, who feels the New Testament message like a blow in the face. And it is not principally the "cosmological" element in the utterances of faith which seem strange to him. His "offence" is of a far more elementary kind. The "mythical" element begins for him, not at the point where statements of faith receive their "cosmic expansion", but at the earlier point where the believer speaks of the Lord of the world as a "Thou" who speaks to him, calls him by his name, and gives him the right in his turn to name Him also by His name and to call upon Him. In other words, even the "forgiveness of sin"—the centre of the gospel—is for him mythology. If we reflect upon this, then the attempt to delay demythologizing until the point where the "cosmic expansion" of the *kerygma* comes in question will strike us as somewhat naïve. And, on the other hand, the man who has heard the address of the divine Thou and believes in the forgiveness of sin, cannot take offence at the "cosmic expansion" which occurs in the Epistles to the Colossians and the Ephesians; the less so, because in believing in Jesus as the Christ he believes in Him in whom the Creator speaks and acts.

It is, however, a meaningful question to ask what the forgiveness of sins has to do with the creation and consummation of the world. For this is to ask what is the connection—and indeed the intrinsic and necessary connection—between belief in God's forgiveness and belief in the creation and the divine goal of the world. There is in fact such a connection. Sin is not only that which has come between us and God and which separates us from Him; it is at the same time what obstructs our vision of our origin and goal. Thus what we have here is by no means a matter of cosmology or *Weltanschauung*, but the understanding of my own existence. I cannot understand my existence as dependent on God unless I understand my being as created by God and destined for God. It is just this which distinguishes God's personal call from a merely moral imperative as Kant understood it. For in the latter the relationship to my being is lacking. A categorical imperative has nothing to do with my being. The "ought" and the "is" fall apart. In belief in the God who speaks to me as one dependent on Him and belonging to Him, this wall which separates the "ought" from the "is" is abolished. "Justification of the sinner" restores my vision of my origin in God's creation and of my destiny of eternal fellowship with God.

When I hear God's word "Thou art mine", I know at the same time that I was created by Him and am destined for His eternal life. This was why we said that the justification of the sinner was at the same time the restoration of the Creation, the restoration of the image of God. Through it I know my origin and destiny. Sin resulted in my being able to understand God's will only in the form of law. This is why the connection between law and sin is so intimate, as Paul long ago perceived, when he became a believer in Christ.[1] Sin makes God's will a naked imperative; justification by faith restores me again to the being of God.

But what is true of my being is true of the being of the world in general. For my being as creaturely being is not thinkable without a being which embraces it. By acknowledging God as my Creator I acknowledge Him as the Creator of the world. It is not the case, as is commonly held, that I infer that God created me from the fact that He created the world. Things may be understood thus in a cosmology, in a theistic and philosophical *Weltanschauung*. But in faith the order is the reverse of this. This is illustrated by the fact that Israel knew God first as *its own* Lord, and only later knew Him as the Creator of the world. And similarly this explains why it was only gradually that the "cosmic expansion" of the knowledge of Christ became explicit. This expansion was already present in embryo in the confession "Christ is Lord" and is then clearly, if only briefly, expressed in the First Epistle to the Corinthians.

II

The second question is of a preliminary character. How are the relations between the cosmos and history understood outside the Christian faith? The man who thinks in terms of myth regards himself and his history—in so far as he has any consciousness of it—as a particle fitting within the cosmic cycle. Something similar happens in the thought of modern times, which is estranged from the Christian faith. It too regards man and his history as a tiny and insignificant part of the cosmic process. The myth of the ever-recurring cycle, which in a certain respect was able to give significance to existence, has been outmoded by the Biblical faith in the

[1] Cf. on this point my book *Der Mensch im Widerspruch*, pp. 150 ff. (E.T. *Man in Revolt*, pp. 155 ff.)

Creator. For modern man the world has been demythologized. To Nietzsche indeed the doctrine of eternal recurrence came as an illumination, and he thought that by means of this idea he could reawaken this myth to life. For him personally this idea was a salvation from nihilism. But this post-Christian attempt to resuscitate a myth was unavailing. The secularized thought of modern man which is at the same time estranged from the Christian faith is therefore clearly moving towards nihilism. For a cosmic process in which man and his history are swallowed up is the negation of meaning.

Idealism, on the other hand, was the attempt to escape this negation of meaning through a philosophy of timelessness by means of the idea of an "eternal self". By dividing man into an essential and timeless part and an inessential and mortal part this attempt achieved a semblance of success. But this essential part was at the same time "a-historical"—and this meant the surrender of history. History can have no meaning since it is compounded with what is temporal and inessential, and thus void of eternal meaning. For a short time the idea of universal progress was able to conceal the eschatological vacuum in idealism, but today—as we have already shown—it has lost its credibility. Nothing remains but the old thought of the Vedanta philosophy: happenings in time—consequently history as my personal life-history as well as the history of mankind—belong to the world of appearance, of futility. We must rise above it in the knowledge of what is eternal and timeless and in such transcendence find our consolation.[1]

These are the two world-outlooks which are alternatives to the Christian faith; the submergence of history in meaningless cosmic process and the salvation of the timeless and eternal self by means of the idea of timeless and eternal essence. With these is contrasted the Christian faith, which *relates the cosmos to history* by its faith in the event of God's revelation in history and the message of the reconciliation of mankind through Jesus Christ. The advocates of the "existential interpretation of the New Testament" will have in the end to decide whether they are finally to side with nihilism or ostensibly save themselves from it by the idealism of timeless or a-historical eternity, or whether they are willing to take the Christian faith seriously by

[1] Fichte's *Anweisung zum seligen Leben* (E.T. *The Way towards the Blessed Life*, London, 1849). In the Western world of today idealism has lost nearly all its intellectual prestige. The contrary is true of the East. Cf. Radhakrishnan's important book *The Fellowship of the Spirit* (1952) which with conscious pride seeks to prove that the ancient philosophy of the Vedanta is the truth underlying all religion and philosophy

once for all giving up the attempt to discredit the "cosmic expansion" of Christian faith as mythology. Faith in the reconciliation in Jesus Christ is the encounter with the God who has made heaven and earth and whose will is revealed to me as the coming Consummation of the Creation in Jesus Christ. The Christian faith is either this or it is an illusion. There is no third possibility.

III

The question, however, whether this faith is "tenable" for a man of the twentieth century confronts us once again with the decisive question whether we can still, in the Christian sense of the word, believe. Here once more it is a case of all or nothing: not of a postscript to Christian doctrine, possibly worth preserving but possibly inessential. Thus here the question becomes all the more crucial: Does the scientific world picture of modern times demand or not demand that the decisive "No" should be spoken at this point?

It is in fact true that if we are speaking of man as the "inhabitant" of this cosmos with its astronomical immensities, if that man is meant who is a mote of dust upon this mote of dust, the earth, then he can have no significance. In the objective world picture of cosmology man is *une quantité négligeable et invisible*. This means accordingly that within a system of thought for which the objective world—the universe known by natural science—is the final reality, man together with his faith in God is lost. Within this world, too, the encounter with a God who forgives sins has the significance only of a beautiful illusion.

The situation of the idealist is different. For him the continual and incredible expansion of the universe since the days of Copernicus has no terrors. He feels himself in no way threatened by the fact that as a result of this expansion man is being more and more reduced to a vanishing point. For he is familiar with what Kant called the "second Copernican revolution". He knows that for man as subject the vast universe is a mere phenomenon—if not a mere appearance. The spirit-subject is not impressed, not threatened, by the size of the object-world, for it is just this spirit that measures and weighs the world. The subject is *superior* to the object, even if the object is the immeasurable universe. This "second Copernican revolution" which Kant claimed to have set in motion—but which the philosophy of the Vedanta had accomplished as long as three thousand years before him, and which has until today remained in unbroken continuity the philosophy of Hinduism—this philosophy of timelessness and the immortal spirit of man achieves its metaphysical salvation of man at the price of flight into timelessness and the surrender of history.

In contrast with these two serious possibilities of thought we must admit that Jewish apocalyptic, even as it is interwoven with the New Testament witness of Christ, is not a serious third possibility. The man who shares in the scientific movement of our times, who thus, when he thinks of the universe, sees himself confronted by a world of inconceivable dimensions, cannot any longer entertain the conception of a final cosmic catastrophe in which "the sun shall be darkened, and the moon shall not give her light, and the stars of heaven shall fall" (Mark 13: 24, 25). It can at the best be for him a symbol of an inconceivable event; in which case the question must be asked what content of reality underlies this symbol.

But what we called the "cosmic expansion" of faith in Christ points us to a quite different solution, which is clearly distinct from both materialistic objectivism and idealistic subjectivism, and which is not bound to these apocalyptic symbols. This solution, which we find in the New Testament witness to Christ, we call the "theanthropocentric" (God-man centred) solution. According to this the world is not a self-sufficient entity, nor is it merely an entity that is "there for me", but it exists through and "for" the Logos of the Creator and Redeemer God. This faith speaks of the beginning of the world as its origin in God's Word. "For He spoke, and it was done; He commanded, and it stood fast" (Psalm 33: 9). And thus too it speaks of the world's end: God speaks, and it stands there no longer. He commands, and a new world appears. The existence and the form of the universe is—to use an expression of the mathematician—a function of the Word, the Logos. By this we do not mean the rational logos accessible to human thought, but the revealed divine Word of the Creator and Redeemer. By it the Creation and the whole universe is "theanthropocentrically" orientated. The goal of the whole vast universe is not man, but humanity redeemed in the God-man Jesus.

From the standpoint of materialistic objectivism this assertion appears madness, an absurd over-estimation by man of his own importance. From the standpoint of idealistic subjectivism it seems a half-truth, since it fails to do adequate justice to the unconditional priority of spirit over matter. But it is what follows with necessity from the revelation in Christ, the "God-man centred" faith in the eternal decree of creation and salvation revealed in the man Jesus Christ.

What is to be said to the "God-man centred" faith of New Testament Christianity from the standpoint of the world picture (*Weltbild*) of modern scientific man? We must answer: Nothing at all. So far as science remains within its limits, that is, remains critical and does not turn into a pseudo-scientific *Weltanschauung*, it will leave uncriticized the statement of faith—that the world was created by God through the Son and for the Son, in order that in Him all temporal being should come to its end and its fulfilment—as an assertion which lies entirely beyond its competence, and which it can neither prove nor contest. For as a critical scientist, man knows that his objective world picture does not impinge upon the mystery of personality. How could he in this realm know anything of the fate of the world of persons, or of history? In the objective world picture there is no object called "history" any more than there is an object called "the person". If the critical scientist remembers that he himself is not merely a possessor of scientific knowledge, but also a responsible man passionately seeking for the meaning of his existence, he too will be able to give his attention to this witness of faith, which expressly emphasizes his origins in a realm that lies beyond human knowledge. For it is directed to him simply as a man, and not as representative of a scientific world picture.

But the critical philosopher, who is conscious of living in the dangerous zone where the standpoint of the thinker tends to take absolute form in systems of metaphysics, will see in this confession of the Logos revealed in the God-man Jesus Christ something essentially different from a philosophy. He will see something that can only satisfy the inexorable requirement *logon didonai*, to give one's reasons, by referring to a Logos which has been received and which speaks for Itself, but which Itself calls all human reasonings and philosophies to account. Perhaps when a doubt about the final validity of his thinking has been awakened in him, when he begins to suspect that the reason with which he thinks *is* not the master, but that it *has* a master, he will even begin to acknowledge a necessary connection between faith in the Creator God and the Eschatology of world consummation.

IV

The expectation of the end of the world which so moves and agitates apocalyptic is not an independent theme of Christian preaching, but it is implied in the *kerygma* of the Parousia. The end of the world as an event is comparable only with creation from nothing. It is not however the negative aspect of it, the end, which is the true Biblical theme, but the Consummation which cannot come save through the ending of the present form of the world: "for the form of the world passeth away" (1 Cor. 7: 31). There is only one point where the negation receives an independent emphasis: as the end, the annihilation of the hostile "powers". By these the New Testament witness means the law, sin, Satan and death. These four powers form a unity; they are one entity, although manifesting more forms than one. Of course the description of them as "powers" is a mythical form of expression. But we shall do well provisionally to leave this, since it would be difficult to describe what is meant in an unmythical form.

(*a*) The Pauline concept of "the law" is the one where the mythical element causes least trouble. We are at first absolutely astonished to discover that Paul should even think of the law as one of the hostile "powers" because it appears elsewhere as given by God Himself. Further, it is Paul alone who regards the law in this negative light, just as he also is the only writer who explicitly speaks of justification by faith. "Moreover the law entered" (Rom. 5: 20). It is only something provisional, leading to Christ, a "schoolmaster unto Christ". These are, of course, not yet really negative statements. But then he goes on to call it "the sting of sin", even "the law of sin". How does this entity which not only in the Old Testament but often even in the New Testament, and even in Paul's own writings, stands so near to God and like God Himself is called holy and good, come to be mentioned in such a context?

The answer is to be found only in the Pauline view of justification. So long as man sees his relation to God as determined by the law, this relation is inevitably marked by self-righteousness. We can now express ourselves more clearly about it: the law binds man to *something*, not to God Himself. It is of course God's law, but in so far as it is law it is not the true will of God, but God's will in a strange, neutral, impersonal form. The law is an "It", not a "Thou". Therefore it makes man a slave. Only the "Thou" of self-bestowing love can set him free. This love is revealed only in the Cross of Jesus Christ *choris tou nomou*, "apart from the law".

The law is an abstract impersonal entity. It makes the relation between God and man abstract and sets a distance between them. But the loving will of God leading us and laying claim to us through the Holy Spirit is present with us, free from all rigidity and all statutory character. It binds us immediately to

God Himself, to the Person of God who Himself is absolutely free, neither bound nor rigid, the living One. The law is "the letter" that "killeth", but the Spirit "giveth life" (2 Cor. 3: 6). The law "entered in". It has broken the immediate relationship between God and man. And just for this reason it is "the law of sin" and belongs together with sin. But the revelation in Christ creates first of all the freedom which remains bound to God Himself. "But now the righteousness of God without the law is manifested . . . which is by faith of Jesus Christ unto all . . . that believe" (Rom. 3: 21 and 22). God's will can be apprehended only as a gracious will, as free, self-bestowing, unfathomable love.

But the law, the principle of all morality—and as such most necessary for sinful man—is done away through Christ. Of course, it has still its work to do in the service of order, as the principle of all social order. But in the expectation of the full appearing of Christ the disappearance of this provisional entity is included. Not till then shall we be wholly free, free for the divine Thou, and for our fellow man.

(*b*) Sin, the second of the four powers, is a mythical concept only in so far as it is personified by Paul as an active agent and a power enslaving man. But this power of sin is something which we daily experience. It compels us to do what we do not wish to do (Rom. 7: 15–17). Even in the true believer it remains powerful as that entity which Church doctrine describes by the somewhat erroneous expression "inherited sin",[1] for the negative relation to God is no more biological or juristic than is its positive counterpart. This description is correct in so far as sin has on the one side a connection with the body, and on the other side has guilt as its profound effect. What separates us most profoundly from God is the *guilt* of sin. In Jesus Christ this guilt is blotted out. In spite of justification man remains a sinner. This empirical reality contradicts what is assured to him in Christ. Both in its individual and in its social and historical character it is identical with the "body of death". Until this is done away, that is, until transitory things are swallowed up by eternity, man remains unredeemed, though he is reconciled. Until then the experience of the faithful will continually be that which causes the Apostle to cry out: "O wretched man that I am! Who will deliver me from the body of this death?" (Rom. 7: 24.) This redemption will come with the Resurrection, with our release from this body of death, with the perfect presence of God when we "see face to face" (1 Cor. 13: 12).

[1] Cf. *Dogmatics* II, pp. 119–25 (E.T. pp. 103–7) of Ch. 3, "Man as Sinner"

The disappearance of sin in all its forms of moral evil, cruelty and injustice was from the beginning the content of the prophetic promises. Isaiah's hope of the kingdom of peace is —as our Christian pacifists repeatedly forget—bound up for the prophet with the condition that "the knowledge of the Lord" shall fill men and nations "as the waters cover the sea" (Isaiah 11: 9). This peace is of course already present in faith in Jesus, the Christ. "He is our peace" (Eph. 2: 14). But we, even the most loyal disciples, repeatedly lose this peace. Paul once gave most dramatic expression to the ending of the discord between God and man. Through Christ, God has "blotted out the handwriting of ordinances that was against us, which was contrary to us" (i.e. the law, and that in its statutory, rigid character); "and took it out of the way, nailing it to His cross. And having spoiled principalities and powers, He made a show of them openly, triumphing over them in it" (Col. 2: 14, 15)—like a victorious Roman general over captive kings. It is faith that speaks thus, and, as hope, anticipates this last future event. But this will one day be no longer anticipation. What is anticipated must become present reality.

It is decisive for the understanding of the Biblical concept of sin that it is conceived as an active reality, as a determined negation, and not (as in ancient philosophy) a mere absence of good, or error. It is just this that is meant by the description of sin as a "power". This is the first thing that must be said about sin. And yet a second thing must be added, which, if it were given the first place, would destroy the Biblical concept of sin. Sin is *also* unreality. If God alone is life and if sin is a turning away from God, then to sin is necessarily to fall a victim to unreality. In all sin this grasping at emptiness, this slavery to something that is nothing, is a characteristic trait. Above all, conscious self-emancipation from God, the revolt of the creature against the Creator, the assertion that God is nothing in order that man's freedom may be absolute, is a grasping at emptiness. For this usurped absolute freedom results in nihilism.[1] It results in the opposite of freedom, the vacuum of nothingness which enslaves man.

(*c*) But the emptiness, the nothingness which takes shape as a power is the manifestation of the demonic and satanic. Satan is the father of lies. Nothingness holds sway by pretending to be something, as if only freedom from God were true freedom. In this delusion there is contained nothing less than the transgression of the boundary of our creaturehood, the usurpation of

[1] Cf. what was said in chapter 20 of Part Three, p. 286, about J.-P. Sartre

absolute freedom which belongs to God alone. This is the way that Satan rules, by the exercise through such deception of his enslaving power. But the nature of his being is unknown to us.[1] He lives by the negation of God and therefore has no independent existence over against God. Anyone who concedes only psychological existence to God finds it easy to set the devil beside God by teaching that there is not a Trinity but a Quaternity (C. G. Jung). The *empirical* reality of the satanic can be doubted by no one who has obtained some insight into the depths of human nature. After rationalism had mocked at the belief in the devil, the latter—as he has always done when his existence has been denied—manifested himself all the more powerfully, above all in the satanic structures of the totalitarian State. Contemporary theology is therefore once again more inclined to acknowledge the overthrow of this power as a specially important aspect of the final Christian hope.

(*d*) Death, the fourth of these powers, is expressly described in the Bible as "the last enemy" (1 Cor. 15: 26). We have already spoken of it at length.[2] Death is indeed overcome "in Christ" through faith. "He that believeth in me, though he were dead, yet shall he live" (John 11: 25); but this conquest, like the creation of the new personality, covers at first only the "little point without extension" of which we have spoken.[3] It is not yet visible in the "periphery" of the physical. Death still rules in the visible world. It cannot be overcome as physical death until the other powers are overcome: the law, sin, and Satan. Death is called "the last enemy" because it impinges on the outermost periphery, our physical existence. Its elimination by the Parousia of the Lord in His form of glory is the negation of negation. Eternal life will then come into force in its own full glory.

From the viewpoint of an objectivistic outlook on reality this is an absurd conception. But this objectivity was questionable from the very beginning; for man as a responsible subject, as a person, could not be included in this objective picture. As we saw, man in his dependence on God cannot simply be made subject to the natural law of death. This is the true kernel of the doctrine of immortality—in its Christian, not its Platonic form. The true Biblical word is indeed not immortality, but Resurrection. This word expresses the truth that the eternal life for which man was destined from his creation, but which he has

[1] *Dogmatics* II, Ch. 5, "Angels, Spirits and the Devil"
[2] Cf. chapter 6 of this Part, "The Mystery of Death"
[3] See above, pp. 273 f

forfeited through his revolt from God, will be bestowed again upon him and at the same time consummated through God's act, His perfect self-communication.

When this happening is described by Paul as the overcoming of the last *enemy*, the reason is that death forms a unity with the law, with sin, and with Satan. Only thus does the full meaning of the word "death" in the writings of Paul become intelligible. Between death and moral evil there is from the standpoint of experience a scarcely comprehensible, but none the less real, relation. Moral evil, in so far as it is not pure defiance but also weakness, is rooted in anxiety, and this anxiety is in the last resort always the fear of death. All insatiable hunger for power, all the cruelty of tyrants, all the timidity of the narrow-minded—what are they but attempts to find security from an unknown threat? Our wickedness—human wickedness—is not so much (at any rate is never solely) a defiant "No" to the Creator's will as the expression of a latent panic in the face of coming death. Fear of death is the secret cause of moral evil, as death itself is moral evil's manifest result: "the wages of sin".

Thus death is called the *last* enemy in a double sense. It is the last in the sequence, since the victory moves from the centre out towards the periphery, and the last as the real focus of all evil in the world, identical with alienation from life in God. The "victory" over death—the expression is of course taken from the dramatic and mythical character of Pauline thought—means in fact simply that the darkness disappears when the sun rises. Death and all the other hostile powers with it disappear when the light and life of God are disclosed in the perfection of their power. It is the death of death, the negation of the negative by the positive, the affirmation of the most positive thing of all, of the life of God as omnipotent holy love. Thus the victory over the powers is simply the full appearing of that which Jesus Christ already, in a hidden manner, is. "When Christ, who is our life, shall appear, then shall ye also appear with Him in glory" (Col. 3: 4). Or, as John puts it, "And it doth not yet appear . . . but we know that, when it doth appear, we shall be like Him, for we shall see Him as He is" (1 John 3: 2).

The Last Event is on its negative side the removal of that which does not yet allow the divine sonship promised us in Christ to take its full effect. The expression "victory over the hostile powers" has proved to be the mythical and symbolic description for a future happening, which, so long as we are confined to the conceptions of the spatio-temporal world, we cannot express in any other way than by symbols. But that this mythical expression at the same time points beyond itself and is also an expression relating to persons and to time, is entirely in line with the "fundamental myth" of the Bible, which is identical with faith.[1]

V

God's coming to us is an event which above all concerns man and his history. As such it is called eternal life and the Kingdom of God. What is at stake is God's self-communication and glorification in that creature which answers Him in faith. What is at stake is the realization of the sonship which in Jesus Christ is already a certainty for faith, but which still awaits its consummation. Theanthropocentrism, God-man centredness, leaves behind both the objectivism of a nature philosophy, which conceives of man as a piece of nature, and also idealistic subjectivism. Neither the "It"—the natural world—nor the "I" stands in the central point, but the "Thou" of God, who speaks to us in His Word. Our hope is directed both to the perfect revelation of this divine Thou as the true life of men, and to the revelation of man, who finds in God's Word of love his true personal character, his divine sonship.

The "world" is, however, as we have said, a "function of the divine Word". In the Consummation "a new heaven and a new earth" are promised to us: for "heaven and earth shall pass away" (Matt. 24: 35), and "the fashion of this world passeth away" (1 Cor. 7: 31). "The end of the ways of God is corporeality." In this famous dictum of Oetinger[2] an important thought is expressed which is entirely in keeping with the Biblical *kerygma*, namely that the Consummation will not remove the creaturely character of the creature, the contrast between the Creator and His creature. It will, on the contrary, bring about its perfect expression. Oetinger's assertion is directed against the philosophy of abstraction, which is at the same time a philosophy of timelessness; it is directed against the rationalism of the age of Leibnitz. For the aim of this philosophy is precisely to transcend the contrast between Creator and creature in unity. It sees in our creatureliness as such, in our finitude, and thus in our non-divinity, the cause of all evil and wickedness. The philosophy of timelessness aims not at fellowship but at unity. It is monistic, even if it does not express this monism so

[1] Cf. on this point the Appendix to chapter 8 of this Part, "The Problem of Demythologization", esp. pp. 404 ff.

[2] F. C. Oetinger, *Theologia ex idea vitae deducta*, 1765

openly as, for example, the philosophy of Fichte does or that of the Vedanta, which expressly describes its fundamental concept as *advaita*, non-duality.[1] Its "eschatology" can therefore result in nothing but the transcendence of the duality, of the confrontation of Creator and creature.

Oetinger's sentence about corporeality as the end of the ways of God expresses the contrast between genuine Biblical faith and this whole philosophical doctrine of the unity of Spirit, which, as everyone knows, has penetrated also into Christian thinking. That alongside of God there exists a world of creatures —this is no error that must disappear at the Consummation. But what kind of a "world" this will be—on this point even the revelation in Christ does not authorize us to make any definite statement. We must at least describe as questionable the pictures of a perfect world very like the earthly world.[2] For we can know nothing of another self-communication of God to which at the same time a self-understanding of man does not correspond. There remains, as a limiting concept, this: that there belongs inalienably to human existence an environment without which the creature as such is not thinkable. In this sense the words about "a new heaven and a new earth" may have validity, even if we cannot have the slightest conception of their form. What can be said with certainty, on the basis of faith in Jesus Christ the Risen One, is that "the whole creation groaneth" and "waiteth for the manifestation of the sons of God" (Rom. 8: 22, 19) which has become a certain hope to us through the Word of justification.

The Consummation is not only Kingdom of God but eternal life. If we call it "eternal life", the accent is laid on the fact that the Consummation will be the perfecting of the presence of the love of God with man and the presence of man with God, and that, further, no empty eternity or timelessness is meant, but "fulfilled time". The abstract concept of eternity belongs to speculative thought, not to faith. Eternal life means fundamentally the same thing as the Pauline spiritual body, that is, an individual existence that will not be swamped by eternity. The absorption of the human spirit in the Divine is an idea of mysticism, not of faith. It belongs to thought originating from man and not to a faith based on the Word of God. The "thou"

[1] The title of Radhakrishnan's book mentioned earlier should in fact not be "The Fellowship of the Spirit" but the Unity or All-oneness of the Spirit

[2] The same is true of E. Thurneysen's statements about Christ and the future, *Zwischen den Zeiten*, 1931, p. 209. "These forests, these fields . . . will be the scene of redemption"

whom God calls "my son" in the Word of justification will be addressed by Him as "thou" to all eternity. For it is the "thou" of love.

If for "Consummation" we substitute the term "Kingdom of God", then the accent is laid on the fact that in eternity not merely the particular human being, the individual, but at the same time the history of mankind finds its consummation. For seen in the light of Christ man is always at the same time the individual and the human race. For this reason the symbols of the Consummation always refer simultaneously to the consummation of the individual in eternal life and to the consummation of the fellowship which we know in a provisional manner as the Ekklesia. For how could love express itself as love if there were not present a multitude of persons who are bound together by the bond of mutual love? The Consummation as eternal life is the relationship to God in which we see Him "face to face"; the Consummation as the Kingdom of God signifies the perfection of the relationships between men.

We shall see God face to face. Our present will be filled by the presence of God. The "qualitative concept of eternity"[1] finds its expression in the fact that here the determining factor is not the negation of time but the positive presence of the love of God. The phrase "see face to face" gives expression on the one hand to the immediacy of the bond, and on the other hand to the fact that there is no fusion into a unity. This thought is expressed by Paul in connection with that of the consummation of our fragmentary knowledge. "Now I know in part: but then shall I know even as also I am known" (1 Cor. 13: 12). Seeing face to face is set alongside of knowing as we are known. Both bring the hymn to *agape* to a conclusion. The problem of knowledge and the problem of fellowship find here their final elucidation. Eternal life is the realization of what we know through faith and receive in justification. It differs only in that the place of faith will be taken by sight, the place of the fragmentary by the perfect. But what we receive in faith in the Word of justification is life in the presence of the loving God, a life rooted in the love of God, but not as yet perfected.

In the teaching tradition of the Church the foremost place in the description of the Consummation is given to the concept of blessedness. But this reflects rather the natural human longing for happiness than the New Testament witness. There is not even a word in New Testament Greek which could be translated

[1] See above, p. 377

by "blessedness".[1] Seen in the light of Christ, the Consummation is centred not in the happiness of man but in the realization of the will of God, His intention as Creator, His self-communication and self-glorification. The end of the ways of God is the glory of God, not the blessedness of man.[2] But because this God-centredness is a God-man centredness, it is at the same time the realization of human destiny and the satisfaction of the human desire for life and happiness. For this reason its message is called *eu-angelion*, a joyful message. The achievement of the Consummation is represented under the figure of a marriage, a feast, or a banquet. This joy consists not only in the negation of negations, in redemption from death and from suffering, but it is determined by the element of fulfilment: "I am come that they might have life, and that they might have it more abundantly" (John 10: 10). For joy is the natural accompaniment of the fulfilment of one's destiny. The man who has reached the goal cannot but be happy.[3]

It is worthy of notice that, where the Bible speaks of the Consummation, it speaks not of blessedness but of knowledge. True, this knowledge is wholly different from our present knowledge. It is identical with life in the love of God. But it is still seen under the aspect of knowledge. Man is the being whose distinctive characteristic is knowledge. So also the final and eternal thing which faith discloses to our sight is "knowing even as I am known". We could render this by "becoming transparent to oneself", understanding that this transparency is effected by the light of God.

So long as we live in "this body of death" we are "opaque" to ourselves and to others. There is a darkness in us that conceals us from ourselves. We said indeed that faith was a *self-understanding* in the light of God's self-communication. But this understanding of ourselves, like everything in faith, is only coming to be, only in its first beginnings. Just as one cannot see from a seedling what it will turn into, so, even in faith, that

[1] The "blessed" of the Beatitudes does not refer to the state of heavenly blessedness. Cf. Schniewind, *Das Evangelium nach Matthäus*, p. 40

[2] From this it becomes clear how impossible is Sigmund Freud's derivation of the Christian religion from the unsatisfied desire for happiness. Cf. his *Die Zukunft einer Illusion* (E.T. *The Future of an Illusion*). Cf. also chapter 2 of this Part, p. 352

[3] It is significant that it was only possible to find a scriptural basis for the mediaeval erotic-mystical description of the achievement of the Consummation through the allegorical interpretation of the Old Testament Song of Songs. But the Song of Songs is in reality not meant to be interpreted mystically and allegorically, but as a quite natural love-lyric. The most famous example of the mediaeval interpretation is provided by Bernard of Clairvaux's sermons on the Song of Songs

which we shall be is still hidden. We only know that "then" everything will be different.

For this reason knowledge is identical with fellowship. For the self-communication of God, in which we know ourselves, is the love of God, which then will be perfected in us. Only as those who are "known by God" shall we be wholly ourselves. Being known by God is the same thing as His love. From this standpoint we get a new grasp of our present problem of knowledge. Knowledge through fellowship is another kind of knowing than what we are accustomed to describe as knowledge. And in the same way it is not until we know, in the sense of understanding ourselves, in the sense of becoming transparent to ourselves and to others, that we shall fully become ourselves. The self is the great mystery of self-knowledge. This mystery is understood in the light of the gospel as self-knowledge in the love of God. This fulfilment, and not blessedness, is the theme of the gospel.

This theocentrism, God-centredness, of the gospel is not theocratic in the sense of oriental despotism. The decisive thing about the Biblical message is that God's will brings man to honour by asserting itself. Its final concern is for man, for God is the God who comes towards man. Man must become perfectly human. The humanization of man is the goal of God. *This* is what the Kingdom of God means. It is one with the Kingdom of perfect humanity. Man must attain in God the destiny for which he was created.

VI

The continuation of the mythological passage which deals with the overcoming of the last enemy gives us occasion for a final consideration. "The last enemy that shall be destroyed is death. For He hath put all things under His feet. But when He saith all things are put under Him, it is manifest that He is excepted, which did put all things under Him. And when all things shall be subdued unto Him, then shall the Son also Himself be subject unto Him that put all things under Him, that God may be all in all" (1 Cor. 15: 26–28). This subordinationism characteristic of salvation history can only with difficulty be reconciled with orthodox Trinitarian doctrine, which speaks of the identical nature of the Father and the Son. This formula is incompatible with Paul's statement. We must not, however, forget what we said above about the orthodox doctrine of the Trinity.[1] It is directed to an interest that was not at all the

[1] Cf. chapter 15 of Part Three, "Justifying Faith in Christ and the Creed of the Church", pp. 226 ff.

true interest of faith. It is speculative and therefore static, while the Bible is consistently concerned with salvation history, and is therefore dynamic.

How is this subordinationism to be understood? The whole Biblical message is concerned with God's self-glorification and self-communication. Consequently God has the last word. Both the revelation and grace have their origin in His sovereignty. He is the theme, naturally as the God who graciously communicates Himself and majestically glorifies Himself. What He gives and creates is embodied in the Son. But the Son Himself has been sent by the Father. Salvation history has its origin in God. The "substance" of salvation history is the divine Sonship. With its full realization the "function" of the Son is completed. It was His function to point to the Father, to draw upon His resources, to assert His honour over against the boasting of man. Once this has been wholly eliminated, God's honour itself can take its due place.

Only in concepts taken from salvation history, not in concepts of a static and speculative character, could this be asserted without giving rise to the misunderstanding that the nature and gift of the Son is something less and of less account than the Father Himself. This misunderstanding disappears as soon as we put our question in terms of salvation history, as the Biblical witness requires, instead of asking a speculative question—which would necessarily be followed by a static answer. But then this eschatological subordinationism which belongs to salvation history is of an entirely different character from the subordinationism which is to be found within a speculative and static Trinitarian doctrine. We are not concerned with the substance of the Son, but with His "function". But there can be no question that this consists in honouring the Father and in communicating His life. With the conclusion of this Consummation in the last things the Son retires "that God may be all in all"

Even the Christology of the New Testament is, in the last resort, theocratic. The theanthropocentrism of the gospel has its origin and its goal in God. It may be difficult for those who are accustomed to orthodox Trinitarian thinking to understand this. But in rejoinder we can only appeal to the Biblical witness, to which this way of thinking fails to do justice. In the Bible it is never the Son who elects and creates and sends, but the Father who sends the Son and creates the world and calls man *through* Him. That even the orthodox pattern of thinking left room for a final pre-eminence of the Father over the Son showed itself in the continued retention of two points that were not compatible with an absolute consubstantiality; it is the Father who sends the Son, it is the Father who, even if He does not "create" Him, yet "begets" Him, from His own nature. These thoughts remained here as alien elements. But they are quite natural within the thinking of salvation history. The origin of salvation history is in the Father. Its goal is also in Him. And beyond this we have nothing more to teach.

But this word of Paul also gives an answer to a question which oppresses and disquiets us in relation to *all* thoughts about the final Consummation—indeed in relation to the whole of Christian Eschatology: Can we really take the responsibility of expressing and giving doctrinal formulation to such thoughts, which lie beyond the capacity of our knowledge and understanding? To this the word of Pauline witness answers—if not explicitly, then implicitly: all legitimate Eschatology rests upon what has really *happened* in salvation history, above all upon what has really *happened* in Jesus Christ. Thus it bases its assertions upon a history accessible to experience; true, a history which can be apprehended in its full significance only by faith, but none the less a real history. Faith in Christ necessarily embraces both the origin of Creation and the goal of the Consummation. The source of our knowledge of both is the same, the sending of the Son, the self-communication of God. If our thought then has this legitimation; if, in spite of all the head-shakings of the sceptical scientists, it is based on the *experience* to which they also appeal, on an experience, namely, which comes to us from history, then our theological thinking even in the field of Eschatology is a responsible and consciously responsible undertaking.

But at the same time this word of Paul indicates to us the limits of such thinking. For salvation history in fact lies "beyond our thinking" in its first beginning and in its final goal. With Paul we can but refer to the glass in which for the time being we are able to read only dark and puzzling words. But one thing we know—even this, admittedly, inconceivable!—the divine sonship now already bestowed upon us in the form of a promise will be realized in the Consummation as full participation in the *doxa theou*, the glory of God. With this the Biblical goal of *soli Deo gloria*, to God alone be the glory, is attained. And with this Christian doctrine also has attained its goal and its end.

POSTSCRIPT

THE circumstances which have made my work difficult in the last years, and particularly in the last months, have impelled me, with a view to the concentration of my powers, to forgo in great measure the practice of furnishing this concluding volume with the learned apparatus and the references which are customarily supplied in such a book as an indication of independent research. Further, the onset of illness at a time when the first parts of the book were already in print prevented me from giving an intended final revision to the Fourth Part, the Eschatology. I believe that these omissions will appear the more justifiable because many of the necessary references to theolcgical literature and my discussion of it are to be found in other books of mine, and because my book *Eternal Hope* could in great measure be dovetailed into the Fourth Part. I may indeed assume that my readers will understand that only thus was it possible for me within a foreseeable time to bring to a conclusion this work on which I had set my heart.

EMIL BRUNNER

Zürich,
April 1960.

INDEX OF SUBJECTS

INDEX OF NAMES

INDEX OF SCRIPTURE REFERENCES